The First World War is history; the last survivors of that conflict are now all dead. Three generations on, public perceptions of the war are formed from books, films and photographs. In the last two decades, revisionist historians have attempted to correct the narrative left to us by the war poets and early diarists; a chronicle of sacrifice, futility and the 'loss of a generation' at the hands of the 'bunglers' and 'butchers'. In spite of the efforts of these writers, commentators find it hard to move beyond the losses of 1 July 1916 and the mud of Passchendaele. The history of the war is 'bookmarked' by a series of iconic battles, from First Ypres, through the Somme, to Passchendaele and Cambrai and the final victory of the Hundred Days.

When reading the accounts of the battles it is easy to overlook the very limited perspective of the individual soldiers. Battalions were moved in and out of the line every few days; most were involved in only a few of the battles, and then for only a short period and on a limited front. The troops who participated would have had little idea of how their unit's contribution affected the outcome of a particular operation.

The York and Lancaster Regiment had one or more battalion in all of the major battles of the war, but each saw only a small part of those operations. This book uses the war diaries of those battalions to trace the history of the conflict through the limited perspective of those whose horizon was little more than their 500 yards of trench line.

Private Patrick Dillon (the author's grandfather) served in three battalions of the regiment. Dillon and his mates all did their 'bit' in the conflict that became the First of two World Wars but, like so many, he said little of it when he got home and left almost no written record of his experience. The battalion war diaries show us how limited was the overview of the ordinary soldier and his regimental officers, there is little context to the actions in which they were involved beyond their immediate front and flanks. While this book does outline the broader operations in which the battalions were involved, it is not a 'history of the war', rather it is an account of how those units (often at short notice) were fed into the line of battle. The luxury of a bird's-eye view of its progress (as well as hindsight) was not available to the soldiers who did the fighting and we should remember that during the various centenaries that take place before November 2018.

John Dillon was born in Sheffield in 1945. After joining the RAF as an Apprentice, followed by three years as a Cranwell Cadet, he spent some years as a navigator on Vulcan bombers before leaving the service in 1976 for a thirty-year career in computers. Early retirement in 2005 was an opportunity to study for a history degree at Reading; a First was followed by an MA and a PhD. It was during those later years that he was able to research his grandfather's service in the Great War with the York and Lancaster Regiment, and take part in a number of battlefield tours with that great biographer of the British Tommy, Richard Holmes. John and his wife live in Berkshire where retirement allows time for his photography, military history and travel.

BATTALIONS AT WAR

The York and Lancaster Regiment in the First World War

John Dillon

Helion & Company Limited

Helion & Company Limited
26 Willow Road
Solihull
West Midlands
B91 1UE
England
Tel. 0121 705 3393
Fax 0121 711 4075
Email: info@helion.co.uk
Website: www.helion.co.uk
Twitter: @helionbooks
Visit our blog http://blog.helion.co.uk/

Published by Helion & Company 2018
Designed and typeset by Mach 3 Solutions Ltd (www.mach3solutions.co.uk)
Cover designed by Paul Hewitt, Battlefield Design (www.battlefield-design.co.uk)
Printed by Lightning Source Ltd, Milton Keynes, Buckinghamshire

Text © John Dillon 2017
Images © as individually credited
Maps drawn by George Anderson © Helion & Company 2017

Every reasonable effort has been made to trace copyright holders and to obtain their permission for the use of copyright material. The author and publisher apologize for any errors or omissions in this work, and would be grateful if notified of any corrections that should be incorporated in future reprints or editions of this book.

ISBN 978-1-912174-05-8

British Library Cataloguing-in-Publication Data.
A catalogue record for this book is available from the British Library.

All rights reserved. No part of this publication may be reproduced, stored in a retrieval system, or transmitted, in any form, or by any means, electronic, mechanical, photocopying, recording or otherwise, without the express written consent of Helion & Company Limited.

For details of other military history titles published by Helion & Company Limited contact the above address, or visit our website: http://www.helion.co.uk.

We always welcome receiving book proposals from prospective authors.

To Private Patrick Dillon

Contents

List of Illustrations		viii
List of Maps		ix
Acknowledgements		x
Introduction		xi
1	The Regiment goes to War	15
2	"Gas" – Second Ypres	28
3	Aubers Ridge and Hooge	43
4	Gallipoli – the 6th Battalion at Suvla Bay	58
5	Unfavourable ground – the Battle of Loos	81
6	"There was no wavering" – The Somme	100
7	"A process of trial and error" – the tanks at Flers-Courcelette	129
8	April 1917 – the Battle of Arras	140
9	"We shared in the great victory" – Messines Ridge	154
10	"The ground is like a bog in this low-lying country" – Passchendaele and Third Ypres	166
11	"Steel monsters" – the tanks at Cambrai	185
12	*Kaiserschlacht* – the German Offensive, 21 March 1918	195
13	Kicking away the props – Salonika and Italy	220
14	The Hundred Days	246
Appendices		
I	Finding Private Dillon (apologies to Private Ryan)	262
II	Private Stanley Butwright	265
Bibliography		267
Index		272

List of Illustrations

Menin Gate memorial. (Photo J. Dillon)	41
Private Patrick Dillon. (Photo J. Dillon)	61
"A" Beach. Suvla Bay. August 1915. (IWM Q 57866)	69
Loos. Looking towards Cite St. Auguste. (IWM Q 41998)	86
Dud Corner cemetery, Loos. (Photo J. Dillon)	98
Memorial to Private James Dillon, Dud Corner cemetery, Loos. (Photo J. Dillon)	98
Mark II (Female) Tank. (IWM Q 64483)	130
6 pounder gun on 'Male' tank. (Photo J. Dillon)	130
Mounting for Hotchkiss machine gun behind the 6 pounder. Photo also shows exit door for the gunner. (Photo J. Dillon)	135
British troops eating their Christmas dinner in a shell hole, Beaumont Hamel, 25th December 1916. (IWM Q 1630)	141
Canadian war memorial, Vimy Ridge. (Photo J. Dillon)	145
Spanbroekmolen Crater – Pool of Peace. Left after the detonation of the largest mine at Messines Ridge. (Photo J. Dillon)	161
Men of the 2/4th York and Lancaster Regiment in their trench cookhouse, January 1918. (IWM Q 8443)	170
The sunken road, Map 16. Taken from point 'X'; the bushes are at point 'Y'. (Photo J. Dillon)	202
Soldiers of 1/York and Lancaster manning trenches on the 'Birdcage Line' defences outside Salonika in 1916. (IWM Q 31608)	228
Granezza cemetery on the Asiago plateau, Italy. (Photo J. Dillon)	241
Memorial to the storming of the walls at Le Quesnoy by the men of New Zealand. (Photo J. Dillon)	250
Professor Richard Holmes on the ground defended by 2/York and Lancaster on 21 March 1918. (Photo J. Dillon)	263
Private Stanley Butwright, killed in action 27 August 1917. (Photo Andrew Wegg)	265

List of Maps

1	British line, October 1914.	20
2	Hooge Chateau, October 1914.	24
3	BEF line, November 1914 and April 1915.	26
4	Second Ypres, April 1915.	30
5	2/York & Lancaster at Hooge, August 1915.	53
6	Suvla Bay, August 1915.	67
7	Loos, September 1915.	84
8	Battle of the Somme shows British front on 1 July 1916. Inset relates to Flers/Courcelette, 15 September 1916.	102
9	Battle of Arras, April 1917.	143
10	Messines Ridge, June 1917.	157
11	Third Battle of Ypres: 31 July 1917 objectives.	168
12	Third Battle of Ypres: Progress to 17 November 1917.	172
13	Lancaster, Third Battle of Ypres, September 1917.	181
14	Battle of Cambrai, November 1917.	187
15	Kaiserschlacht: British line, 21 and 27 March 1918.	197
16	Position of 2/York & Lancaster, 21 March 1918.	203
17	Successive positions of 13/York & Lancaster, 23-30 March 1918.	211
18	Macedonia – Salonika and Lake Doiran.	227
19	Italian theatre showing lines of advance during battle of Vittorio Veneto, October 1918.	234
20	British position on Asiago Plateau, June 1918.	239

Acknowledgements

Thirty years ago, my father gave me what remained of the pencil notes his father had made while in Egypt in 1916. He asked me to find out what I could of my grandfather's war; sadly, my father died before I had been able to learn very much but his request planted the seed of this book. I must also thank Richard Holmes who, in 2005, helped me to locate the field in which 2nd Battalion York and Lancaster Regiment occupied trenches on the morning of 21 March 1918. That was the day that Private Patrick Dillon became a Prisoner of War. Richard, biographer of the British Tommy, died in April 2011.

Andrew Wegg was good enough to send me a photograph of his relative, Stanley Butwright, as well as an account of his time with the Royal Warwicks. Duncan Rogers at Helion deserves my thanks for agreeing to publish my take on the war as experienced by the men of the York and Lancaster Regiment. Also at Helion, Michael LoCicero acted as editor, while George Anderson did an excellent job of producing readable maps from my poor sketches.

Lastly, I must thank my wife Susi for her patience, forbearance and encouragement over the last two years. How often have I put off jobs that needed doing while I retreated to my keyboard.

Introduction

For the last twenty years, I have been fascinated by the Great War. Born at the end of the Second World War (the Great War had now become the *First* World War), I remember my grandfather as a sick, old man, largely chair-bound with a dreadful catarrhal cough, the result of having been gassed. As I grew up, I knew nothing of his war service. Like so many of the soldiers of that conflict, he said little of his experience to his only son, my father. Four decades after my grandfather died my father asked me to try to research his war, but the family held precious little in the way of written records. The war never featured in my history education; Caesar's Roman Legions and the marital exploits of Henry VIII were 'history' while the Great War seemed too recent to fall into that category. Like many of my generation, what views I had of that conflict were gained through the war poets, R. C. Sherriff's play *Journey's End* and John Mill's portrayal of Sir Douglas Haig in the 1969 film version of *Oh! What a Lovely War*.

My grandfather, Private Patrick Dillon, worked as a labourer for Sheffield Corporation when he returned from the war. With only a basic education, he left no diaries, letters or private accounts of what must have been the most formative event of his life. There were three pieces of evidence which led me to discover a little more of Patrick's service and his time with the York and Lancaster Regiment. Many of the soldiers kept small notebooks in which they recorded events for inclusion in letters home, unfortunately these were usually written in pencil (the ubiquitous biro had yet to be invented), and 80 years later the entries are very difficult to read. Only a few pages remained from my grandfather's 'diary', giving a few details of his routine in Egypt. The two most useful documents were each just a single page. The first was to inform my grandmother, two months after the event, that Patrick Dillon was posted as 'missing' on 21 March 1918 but this did not necessarily mean he had been killed, or was a prisoner of war. The second recorded his medals and the 'Theatre of War first served in'. With these two documents, I was able to fix some details of his service: his regimental number was 20003; the first theatre of the war in which he served was 'Egypt' (Gallipoli) from 5 September 1915; he had served with the 2nd, 6th and 10th battalions of the York and Lancaster Regiment; he was with 2/York and Lancaster when he was captured. Sadly, Patrick's service record was among those destroyed in the 8 September 1940 fire at the War Office records repository in Arnside Street – the 'Burnt Records'.

With so little of my grandfather's war record available, it was difficult to build up a picture of his personal war. Although his service with three of the regiment's battalions is known, the dates of his move between them are not. He was with the 6th in Gallipoli in September 1915; with the 10th when it disbanded (late 1917) and with the 2nd when he became a POW in the spring of 1918. It would have been enlightening to see his enlistment details and have some knowledge of his training prior to arriving in Egypt. In addition, did he have a good or bad conduct sheet, and when exactly was he gassed – all these details were lost in the German bombing of 1940. In the absence of any such detail, my attention turned to the regiment in which he served, the York and Lancaster. My first foray into the addictive field of military history research was the building of a web site (no longer available) that concentrated on my grandfather and his time with the three battalions in which he served. It was at this point (2002) that my wife and I felt that we should try a First World War battlefield tour and signed up to travel with Professor Richard Holmes in July of that year. From then until he died in 2011, we were 'regulars' on his First World War tours. Richard's knowledge and enthusiasm for the British Tommy were infectious; he was indirectly responsible for my decision to become a mature student and eventually complete a PhD. After the publication of my first book,[1] I decided to write an account of the war experienced by the soldiers of my grandfather's regiment – many of whom lay in those Flanders cemeteries I had visited – but it should not be a strict 'regimental history'.

Military historians have written at length and in detail on the First World War, individual battles have whole books devoted to them, is there space in the historiography for yet another volume? My approach was to try to get a little closer to the soldier and his battalion. For the men who fought in that war the battalion was their 'family', these were their mates who shared their food parcels, played football with and frequently saw them killed. The brigades, divisions and corps that constituted the order of battle in many histories were too large and impersonal for the ordinary soldier to relate to; the company NCOs and subaltern's were the ones he looked to for support, example and leadership. When we look back at the conflict, especially during these centenary years, it is easy to overlook the fact that the soldiers' lives were not all about the trenches and fighting, far more time was spent playing football than most histories acknowledge. This account is not a comprehensive history of the war, still less is it a detailed record of all the actions in which the regiment took part.

The war years are punctuated by major battles and I have also used these way-points to trace the progress of the conflict. However, those battles are not covered in detail. My approach has been to introduce the battles and their context and then to limit the description to the part played by the individual York and Lancaster battalions. In some of the battles only one of the regiment's battalions participated, in others (such as the Somme) there were more. Many of the iconic battles – like the Somme and Third

---

1   Dillon, J., *'Allies are a Tiresome Lot': The British Army in Italy in the First World War* (Solihull, Helion, 2015).

Ypres – lasted for months, but individual battalions were moved in and out of the line during that period. As a result, the men who had fought in any particular battle – let us say the Somme – would have had only a limited time at the front, and not necessarily always in the same sector of the line. For the soldiers, their view of any of the actions they were involved in would have been limited to their own few hundred yards of trench. Additionally, because they were continually rotating between the front and the rear areas, their appreciation of the whole battle (let alone its strategic or tactical significance) would have been minimal. This 'soldier's view' was well summarised by Charles Carrington after the Battle of the Somme.

> How do you know when you have lost a battle? No one in front can tell you what is happening a mile to right or left. In the rear the general waits for messages that fail to come, since wires are cut and runners killed. Those who have advanced send back optimistic reports and those who have retreated don't advertise the fact. [...] The best troops have vanished into enemy country, so that no one can tell whether they are still holding out in forward positions where reinforcements might reach them. [...] in my central position I did not learn that the counter-attack had been successful until 7.30 in the evening.[2]

Accordingly, I have restricted the descriptions of the major battles to the limited view of the battalion war diaries.

It is appropriate here to say a few words about my methodology. Those who have read any of the battalion war diaries in the National Archives at Kew will understand that some are written in great detail, some are quite sketchy (it all depended on the individual making the daily entry), but all record every action that occurred, whether that was a major battle or the daily round of front-line exchange of fire. For those soldiers who died (and their families) the result was no less final whether it occurred during a 'quiet' period or a major offensive. This narrative is a distillation of those entries in the battalion war diaries. 'There is something unutterably poignant about a diary entry written by somebody who didn't know whether he would be alive to eat his supper that day';[3] Holmes was writing about personal accounts, but the comment is equally relevant to those Army Form C.2118[4] records in the boxes at Kew. My approach may lead the reader to feel 'cheated' of a full appreciation of each of the battles but I am attempting to convey something of the limited perspective experienced by the soldier in the line. Anyone who reads the 10th battalion's diary for the battle of Loos will gain little insight into what had gone on prior to or after their insertion into the line, but they will have some understanding of the total confusion

---

2   Carrington, C., *Soldier From The Wars Returning* (Barnsley, Pen & Sword, 2006), p.118.
3   Holmes, R., *Tommy. The British Soldier on the Western Front 1914-1918* (London, HarperCollins, 2004), p.xxiv.
4   The forms used in the battalion war diaries.

felt by the battalion officers, their limited appreciation of what was happening around them, and why the action went so badly for them.

This book is not a history of my grandfather's war experience; I have titled it *Battalions at War* because it limits the account to the narrow viewpoint of the battalions of the York and Lancaster Regiment as written down – often very briefly – in their war diaries. In the decades since the war, it is the 'futility' literature of 1918-1928, which has coloured our impression of the conflict, reinforced later by Alan Clark's *The Donkeys* and Paul Fussell's *The Great War and Modern Memory*. Too rarely do commentators mention the football matches, sports and divisional concert groups, which did so much to fill the soldiers' time and hold morale together. Those who are organizing the centenary events will have to face the problem of 1918: how to commemorate the victory of the Hundred Days, because in the end, the Allies 'won'. It was not the fault of the soldiers that the eventual terms of Versailles were to become a 'cause' of the Second World War:

> And so *we* remember the war not as we might, through the eyes of 1918, as a remarkable victory so very dearly won, but through the eyes of 1928 as a sham which had wasted men's lives and squandered their courage.[5]

Private Patrick Dillon volunteered to serve in the war and so, presumably, believed that Britain's involvement was necessary. As he spoke so little of his experience to my father, I do not know if he later came to see it as 'futile'. However, I do believe that if he had answered the "What did you do in the war, Daddy?" question, his son would have come away with a piecemeal, disjointed and incomplete picture of an event that absorbed four years of my grandfather's life, and contributed to the ill-health of his later years.

Lastly, a few notes on the war diary extracts which have been used in this book. It will soon become apparent to the reader that those who wrote the daily entries did not conform to an agreed convention on the forms of abbreviation. Battalion will frequently appear as 'Battalion', 'Battn.', 'Batn' or 'Bn.' Other examples are Headquarters, Company and time abbreviations (a.m., am etc.). In most cases I have cited them as they were originally written. Place and trench names were usually written in capitals. Except in the cases where I have indicated that italics or emphasis are my own – the use of [My italics] – then they are as written in the original. Map references have been omitted, as they are meaningless without the original maps to which they refer. When soldiers are named in the diaries as having been killed, I have attempted to give details of the cemetery they are buried in, or the memorial to the missing on which they are named. The least I can do is acknowledge their sacrifice.

---

5   Holmes, *Tommy*, p.xxiv.

1

The Regiment goes to War

On 4 August 1914, Britain declared war on Germany. The whole of Europe was about to be plunged into the First World War, one in which millions would die and where the subsequent peace treaty would arguably be one of the causes of the even more devastating conflict of 1939-45. When Gavrilo Princip, a Bosnian Serb activist, murdered the Austrian Archduke Franz Ferdinand in an assassination plot with all the hallmarks of a Whitehall farce, the man on the Sheffield tram would have been forgiven for thinking that it had nothing to do with him. Britain's preoccupation was not with the Balkans. Ireland, and the divisive issue of Home Rule, had the potential to cause a real split between politicians and the military, as the Curragh incident had already demonstrated. Additionally, Britain had an empire to look after and the jewel in the crown was India. The North-West Frontier and the 'Great Game' were a constant worry for politicians in London; the frontier had to be guarded against possible expansionist moves towards Afghanistan by Russia, and the upstart Kaiser's overtures towards the Ottoman Sultan might unsettle Britain's Muslim subjects in the Indian sub-continent. When war came and the British Army had to be mobilized, these two trouble spots were the home base for two battalions of the York and Lancaster Regiment.

In 1881, the Regiment was formed by the amalgamation of the 65th and 84th Regiment of Foot and was originally given the title of the Hallamshire Regiment. "Where's Hallamshire?" I hear you ask. That was also the sentiment of many of the officers at the time who felt that 'Yorkshire' should be in the title. As the 84th had been raised in York in 1793, with a second battalion from Lancashire, the new formation became the York and Lancaster Regiment. Prior to the amalgamation both the 65th and 84th served in the Seven Years' War, the American War of Independence, the wars against Revolutionary France, the Anglo-Mahratta war in India and the suppression of the slave revolts in Jamaica. Following the formation of the new regiment in 1881, these men of the industrial midlands found themselves serving the Empire in Egypt, the Sudan, and the Boer War of 1899-1902 where they took part in the Relief of Ladysmith.

On the evening that the British Foreign Secretary was commenting that 'the lights are going out all over Europe', the men of the 1st Battalion of the York and Lancaster Regiment were waking to the cool of the early morning in Jubbulpore (Jabalpur as it is today) in the state of Madhya Pradesh in the middle of the Indian subcontinent. By mid-November, the battalion had moved to Bombay for embarkation to England. Arriving in Southampton on 23 December, they disembarked and joined 83 Brigade, 28 Division, at Hursley Park in Hampshire. The regiment's second battalion was based in Limerick, on the west coast of Ireland. The remaining two battalions of 16 Infantry Brigade (one of the three that made up 6 Division) were based at Tipperary and Fermoy, while divisional headquarters were in the port city of Cork. At 5.30 p.m. on 4 August, the mobilization order was received by the battalion, arrangements were immediately put in place to recall men from leave and bring the unit up to strength. The procedures that had been put in place by the War Office for mobilization worked well and by 6 p.m. on 9 August the battalion war diary recorded 'mobilization completed'.[1] As might be expected, not everything went completely to plan; 'In many cases the boots issued to Reservists at the Depot were very badly fitted & had to be replaced'. With route marches on the program for the following three days, it is highly likely that the new boots caused many of the men to suffer with sore feet. Blisters were something the troops could get used to but, with an intended move to France, (the war diary termed it 'destination unknown') the men had to be inoculated against the possibility of typhoid breaking out in the close confines of the trenches.

Following the declaration of war, the call went out for volunteers to join the ranks: the response was overwhelming. Looking back with the vantage of hindsight those young men might be thought of as naïve, in their eagerness to join the fight; 'all ranks [were] trying to overcome their growing impatience to get to the front, and their increasing fear lest the 6th Division should arrive too late'.[2] Most of the soldiers had not yet seen wounded men returning from France, it was still one big adventure for them. In preparation for the move to France, the division relocated to the Cambridge area for further training. The men were based at Grantchester Camp, where their time was spent in the usual round of drill and route marches. The war was new to the officers and men, and nobody quite knew what to expect, but being 'buggered about' was already becoming a regular part of the soldiers' routine. These few weeks in the neighbourhood of the University City also demonstrated the privileges of rank; while canteens and recreation rooms were set up for the men, the officers were treated to the hospitality of the university colleges.[3] On 8 September, they sailed for St Nazaire on the *S.S. Minneapolis*.

1 TNA WO 95/1610, war diary, 2/York and Lancs.
2 Wylly, H.C., *The History of the York and Lancaster Regiment, Volume 1* (London, 1930), p.340.
3 Marden, T.O., *A Short History of the 6th Division, August 1914-March 1919* (Uckfield, 1920, reprint by Naval and Military Press), p.1.

As well as the two regular battalions stationed in Ireland and India, the regiment was large enough to also have two Territorial units based in England, the 1/4th and 1/5th. For the Territorials the timing of the declaration of war was fortuitous, they were just coming to the end of their annual training camps and had not yet dispersed, making their mobilization much quicker and easier than it might otherwise have been. By 11 August the 1/4th 'found themselves at Doncaster on a war footing [...] and in those exciting days quite prepared for immediate orders to proceed overseas'.[4] In August 1914, the 1/4th and 1/5th battalions of the York and Lancaster Regiment were stationed at Sheffield and Rotherham, as part of the 3rd West Riding Brigade of the West Riding Division. In the subsequent six months, they would both be moved to Doncaster then Gainsborough and York. The 1/5th battalion received their notification to mobilize at 6 p.m. on 4 August and immediately sent out 896 notices to the officers and men informing them that they had been 'called up'.[5] By 10 August, the unit strength was 28 officers, 876 other ranks (ORs), and 47 horses and by 4 September, the number of ORs had risen to 966.

At this stage of the war the army was manned by volunteers, conscription was not introduced until 1916. Under the terms of their enlistment, those in the Territorial battalions were not obliged to serve overseas and in September 1914, 87 NCOs and men of 1/5 York and Lancaster exercised their right to remain in Britain by not signing the Imperial Service Obligation.[6] The country-wide response to Kitchener's "Your Country needs You" posters was tremendous, especially in the early months of the conflict, and it is easy to believe that *all* men were eager to be 'at the Hun', but that was not the case. Understandably, there were many who would have had family or work obligations that made Foreign Service problematic, and some would just not have wanted to go. Before war broke out, the Territorials were as much a social group as a military formation. Once hostilities were declared there would have been some who did not want to make the leap from weekend soldiering to real combat. Additionally, those under 19 years of age were not allowed to serve overseas – although we know that many lied about their age so that they could go. On 5 December 4 officers and 148 NCOs and men remained behind either because they elected not to go abroad or because they were under the age of 19; these men were sent to the Reserve Battalion.[7]

As keen as some of the men were to join the war (it would be over by Christmas!), those who signed on for Foreign Service would have to wait until April of the following year before sailing for France. During the nine months between mobilization and embarkation, the battalion occupied itself with training and coastal defence duties. This routine was acknowledged as having allowed the men and their officers to

---

4   Grant, D.P., *The 1/4th (Hallamshire) Battn., York and Lancaster Regiment, 1914-1919* (London, Arden Press) Reprint by Naval and Military Press, p.11.
5   TNA WO 95/2805, war diary, 1/5 York & Lancs.
6   WO 95/2805, war diary, 1/5 York & Lancs.
7   WO 95/2805, war diary, 1/5 York & Lancs.

get to know each other 'in a way that had never been possible in the ordinary course of peace training' but while the preparation had been considered appropriate at the time, it was 'in the light of subsequent war experience, inappropriate'.[8] These early months could easily have been a precursor for the television comedy, *Dad's Army*, where Captain Mainwaring's unit of the Home Guard were tasked with defending the fictitious coastal town of Walmington-on-Sea. The men of the 1/4th had to do the same for the coast near Mablethorpe. Unfortunately, trenches dug in sand could not withstand the spring tides. In spite of this, there was no invasion to repel and 'all was well, while ample and strenuous daily occupation was found in repairing the assaults of wind and tide'.

Once it became apparent that the war would not be over in a matter of months, the raising of new units became a War Office priority – at the height of the conflict the York and Lancaster Regiment had 22 battalions. As the new units were formed, they became part of the First, Second or Third Kitchener Armies: 6/York and Lancaster was a K1 unit; 7th battalion was K2; 8th, 9th and 10th were all designated as K3. All of these were constituted in late 1914. Perhaps the best known in popular history were the 'Pals' battalions, formed of men from similar occupations, or from the same local area. Egging each other on to join together in a great adventure, these units had great *esprit de corps* but their heavy casualties (especially at the Somme) could devastate those same districts when the lists of the dead were posted. Our regiment had three of these locally recruited units; 12th battalion (Sheffield City Pals), 13th (1st Barnsley Pals) and 14th (2nd Barnsley Pals).

In August 1914, the British Army was miniscule in European terms. The British Expeditionary Force (BEF), which crossed the Channel to take its place alongside the French, had only two corps, each of two divisions. As part of the folklore of the war, the histories remind us that the Kaiser is reported as having referred to Sir John French's BEF as a 'contemptible little army'. Robin Neillands argues that the German Warlord's choice of adjective may well have referred more to the size of the BEF, rather than the quality of the soldiers, based on the translation of the Kaiser's original order.[9] Although the size of the British Army in France did grow during the latter part of 1915, and the early months of the following year, it was still small and those units raised by Kitchener would all need training. Consequently, only one battalion of the York and Lancaster Regiment saw action in 1914, the 2nd, with 1/York and Lancaster joining the front in January 1915 after their move from India. The arrival of 2/York and Lancs in France in early September was too late for them to take part in the action at Mons, the subsequent retreat and the 'Miracle of the Marne', but they were to take some part in the stabilization of the front on the River Aisne.

---

8   Grant, *Hallamshires*, p.11.
9   Neillands, R., *The Old Contemptibles. The British Expeditionary Force, 1914* (London, John Murray, 2004), p.2.

The battalion, together with the rest of 6 Division, disembarked at St Nazaire on the evening of 9 September to begin some ten days of movement to the front. With the rapid advance of the German army in the first months of the war, the British base for units arriving in France had been moved from Le Havre to St Nazaire; consequently, the division was some way in the rear of the BEF's III Corps. On their way to the front, the men saw their first Germans on 14 September; they were prisoners being brought in by men from the outpost line. By this point, the divisions who had formed the spearhead of the BEF were tired and in need of relief and to that end on 16 September, 6 Division was broken up. The 17th and 18th Brigades were temporarily attached to I Corps, while 16 Brigade (and 2/York and Lancs) went to II Corps. After further moves, our battalion was in trenches at Vailly, about 9 miles to the east of Soissons, on the north bank of the Aisne. On 21 September, they had their first fatalities; three men were killed after the enemy shelled their trenches with shrapnel. By the end of the York and Lancaster Regiment's first month in action their casualties were; 6 ORs dead, 1 officer and 29 ORs wounded, 3 ORs missing. During the course of the war a further 8,808 members of the regiment would be killed. The troops quickly learnt that sticking their heads above the parapet would draw sniper fire, so a tool was necessary to allow them to observe the enemy line without attracting the attention of the snipers. The battalion war diary for 30 September noted that 'The use of small mirrors on the end of a stick was found very useful for observing the enemy without being seen'.[10]

By October, the men of 2/York and Lancs were becoming used to taking their turn in the line, and being constantly moved from one village to another, sometimes by route-march, at other times by train. One such took them to the vicinity of Radinghem en Weppes (hereafter, Radinghem), about 5 miles south-east of Armentières where, on 18 October, the battalion was ordered to 'advance and take village of RADINGHEM and having done this to push on and take high ground running SE from CHATEAU DE FLANDRES'. The battalion was part of General Keir's 6th Division which, with the 4th on their left and the French cavalry on their right, was ordered to 'test the strength of the Germans holding the line some three miles long from La Valleé to Pérenchies, to push them back if they were weak, but to wait for the co-operation of the 4th Division if they were strong'.[11] The assault on Radinghem was intended to 'turn the enemy's flank from the south'. Between the two towns of Lille and Armentières was the Pérenchies ridge along which the Germans were dug in. The term 'ridge' conjures up images of imposing high ground – one might think of Missionary Ridge above the rail-town of Chattanooga in the American Civil War – but in Flanders, they were not so dramatic. Here, where much of the land is close to sea-level, any small elevation gave one side the advantage. Edmonds describes

10   WO 95/1610.
11   Edmonds, J., Military Operations France and Belgium, *1914, Volume. 2* (Nashville, IWM, reprint of 1925 original), p.111.

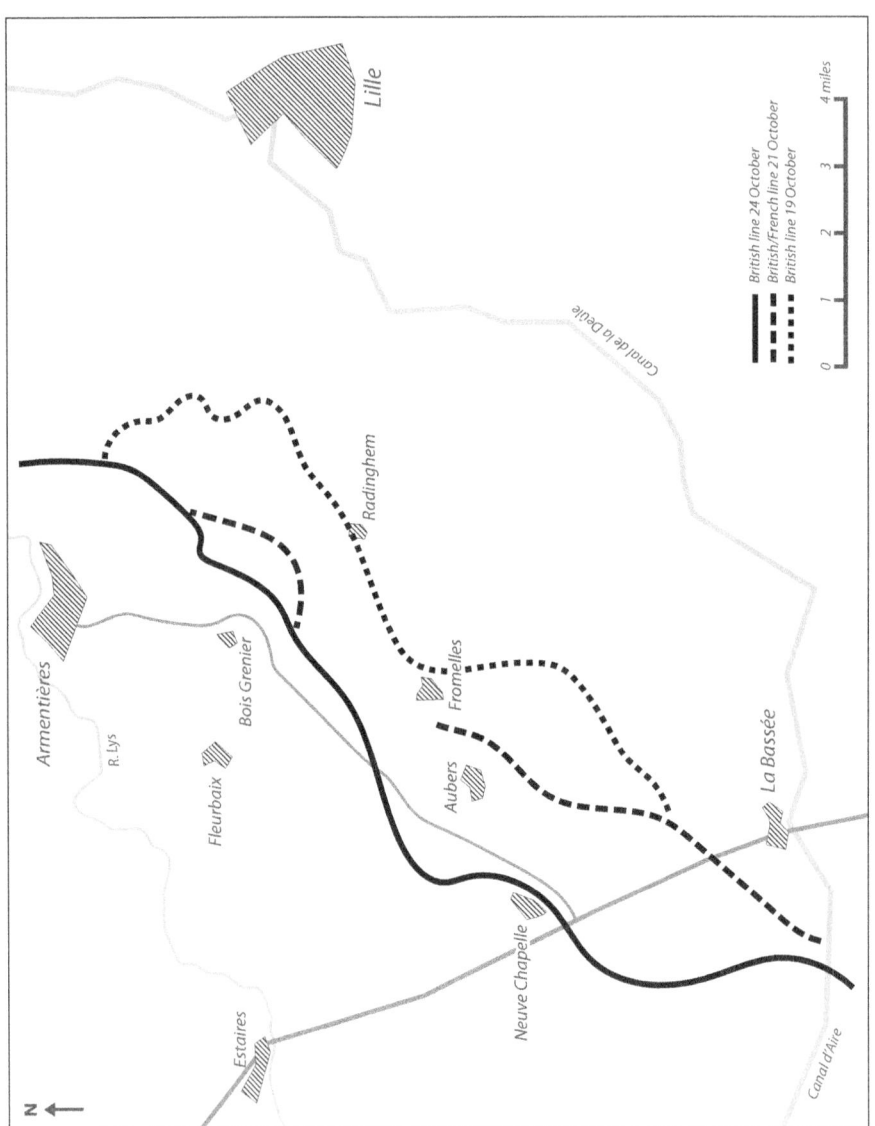

Map 1 British line, October 1914.

the ground held by the Germans at Pérenchies; 'this low clay ridge [...] apparently appeared to rise abruptly from the ground and with its command of 40 to 50 feet above the general level, crowned by rows of small houses, was a very important feature of the topography'.[12]

The village of Radinghem was taken by the battalion 'without difficulty', but while attempting to push on and take the second objective they 'came under heavy shell fire from [a] southerly direction'.[13] Although some of the men had reached the woods of the Chateau de Flandres, heavy machine gun and shrapnel fire caused them to pull back to Radinghem. Having withdrawn they entrenched and remained in position on the Radinghem-Fromelles road until 10:30 p.m. on 19 October when they were relieved by the Buffs. This short action cost the battalion 143 casualties; 13 men were dead, 93 wounded and a further 27 were recorded as missing.

Although the First World War ended nearly a century ago it is not uncommon for the remains of some of those for whom the rich soil of Flanders has become 'forever England', to be uncovered. In 2009, while digging a soak-away pit near the Chateau de Flandres, multiple human remains were uncovered. Items found with the bodies indicated that the burials were from 1914, which pointed to the possibility of the dead men having been in the 2/York and Lancaster action of 18/19 October. Further research and DNA testing resulted in the positive identification of 11 of the bodies.[14] All were from the battalion, and all now lie, side by side, in the Y Farm Military Cemetery at Bois Grenier. Sadly, gains made by the battalion were to be lost. The Germans broke through to the east of Radinghem and the 'Brigadier General therefore decided to withdraw'.[15] They pulled back a little over a mile to Le Touquet, about half-way between Radinghem and Bois Grenier, where their mates now lie buried.

In many of the old documentary films showing the BEF in training the men are shown running forward, rifle and bayonet outstretched, to be plunged into a straw figure of a man; cold steel was to be the last resort of trench fighting. As Corporal Dunn put it in *Dad's Army*, 'They don't like it up 'em'. At 6 a.m. on 23 October the battalion lines were charged by the Germans – Edmonds called it 'bold in the extreme' – but they were 'ejected by bayonet charges led by Lieutenants Ripley and Houston, the former officer being killed in this fighting'.[16] The Germans reached the battalion parapet where 'most of them were bayoneted on it, but a few actually jumped into the British trenches, and, after hand-to-hand fighting, were killed there'.[17] Although the action took place so close to the trench, Lieutenant Ripley's

---

12   Edmonds, *1914, Vol. 2*, pp.107-8.
13   WO 95/1610.
14   Further information can be found on the westernfrontassociation.com website.
15   WO 95/1610.
16   Wylly, *2nd Battalion History*, p.344.
17   Edmonds, *1914, Vol. 2*, p.227.

body was obviously not recovered as he has no known grave, but is remembered on the Ploegsteert Memorial.

The rest of the battalion's year is summed up in Wylly's battalion history.

> Active fighting now died away on this front, [...] but its place was taken by constant shelling and the deadly sniping which claimed so many victims at this time. The weather during November and December was truly appalling. All trenches were knee-deep and more in mud and water. Parapets would not stand and were so flimsy that many men were shot through them. But the weather eventually improved, material for revetment began to appear, and by the commencement of 1915 it was possible to move in the trenches in comparative safety.[18]

As 1914 drew to a close, the battalion history noted one of those events which has been much mythologised and even used as the basis for a 2014 Christmas television advertising campaign:[19] 'The Christmas Truce'. Whole books have been written about the event and it is known that the British high command deplored the idea of any such temporary rapprochement. General Smith-Dorrien (commanding II Corps) anticipated such fraternisation and issued orders against it. The 2/York and Lancaster war diary and history both refer to the event; first the diary, a contemporaneous document:

> 24 December, 'A change of the troops in the [German] front appears to be taking place. Keep a good lookout and report any signs of movement.'
> 25 December, 'Situation unchanged – advances for armistice (for Christmas only) from enemy, no notice taken – usual sniping and a few bombs thrown at our wire.'[20]

The battalion history takes a different slant. In Wylly's comment (mentioned above) on the state of the battalion trenches in December, and their improvement by the end of the year, he states that this was 'due in a measure to a truce made at Christmas between our men and the Saxons opposite, permitting of the parapets being built up and strengthened.'[21] Neither of the documents records the two sides playing football, joining together to swap cigarettes and chocolate, or singing Christmas carols.

The diary entries tell us that on most days there was the 'usual sniping' and that water in the trenches was a real problem; 'trenches very bad, knee deep in water'; 'communication trench flooded'; 'water in all parts of line rising'. Apart from inconvenience, it is quite likely that the state of the trenches was the cause of a month-on-month increase in the battalion sickness rate. In October, 37 men

---

18 Wylly, *2nd Battalion History*, p.344.
19 The supermarket chain, Sainsbury's, used it as the basis of a campaign.
20 WO 95/1610.
21 Wylly, *2nd Battalion History*, p.344.

had reported sick, in November there were 46 and this rose to 112 in December.[22] It is highly probable that this trend was caused by Trench Foot, a debilitating disease that afflicted many of the soldiers and was a result of their feet being almost permanently wet. By January 1915, the monthly figure of men reporting sick had reached 125. Also worrying was the fact that one of the men had died of pneumonia in December, a sure reflection of the wet and cold conditions. The low-lying nature of the ground, together with its high water table, made trench maintenance a nightmare and flooding was inevitable because 'ditches and watercourses near the trenches had filled and overflowed into the line'. According to Edmonds, 'The British defences around Ypres at this time were, at best, short disconnected lengths of trenches, three feet deep. Hastily constructed during the few hours that the troops had been on the ground, they were without wire, dugouts or communication trenches, and lacked anything in the nature of a second line'.[23] Richard Holmes put it succinctly; 'The war had gone to earth'.[24]

As Christmas came and went, reality began to sink in; the war was not over, trench life was no picnic and much of army life was not spent 'bashing the Hun'. The casualties in 2/York and Lancaster, excluding those recorded as sick, amounted to 368 by the end of the year; this, from the battalion's strength of approximately 1,000 men, meant a casualty rate of almost 37% in only three months – and they had not yet been involved in any 'major' battles. At the end of December, they moved to 'very indifferent trenches' in front of Armentières.[25] They remained in the vicinity of this small town for the first six months of 1915, before being moved to the Ypres Salient, so commencing 'its long tour in that unsavoury region'. Ypres' reputation as a dangerous part of the front was well earned and the battalion history records that, following their relocation to the area, 'trench casualties almost doubled immediately'.[26]

Before moving on to the next chapter – Second Ypres – it is worth making a brief reference to the action, which took place around the hamlets of Hooge and Gheluvelt (Map 2) towards the end of 1914. This ground would become very familiar to our 2nd battalion in August 1915. From the end of October and on into November the Germans made a determined attempt to break the Allied line around Ypres; Edmonds estimates their numerical superiority at the point where they attacked the 7th Division, (five miles from Ypres, south of the Menin road and close to the hamlet of Gheluvelt), at around six to one in their favour.[27] In the event, the Germans did drive back the British line by over a mile in places, south of the Menin road, allowing them to occupy the higher ground, but they did not break through. For the reader who wants to delve

---

22   WO 95/1610.
23   Edmonds, *1914, Vol. 2*, p.173.
24   Homes, R., *The Western Front* (London, BBC, 1999), p.49.
25   Wylly, *2nd Battalion History*, p.345.
26   Wylly, *2nd Battalion History*, p.346.
27   Edmonds, *1914, Vol. 2*, pp.283-4.

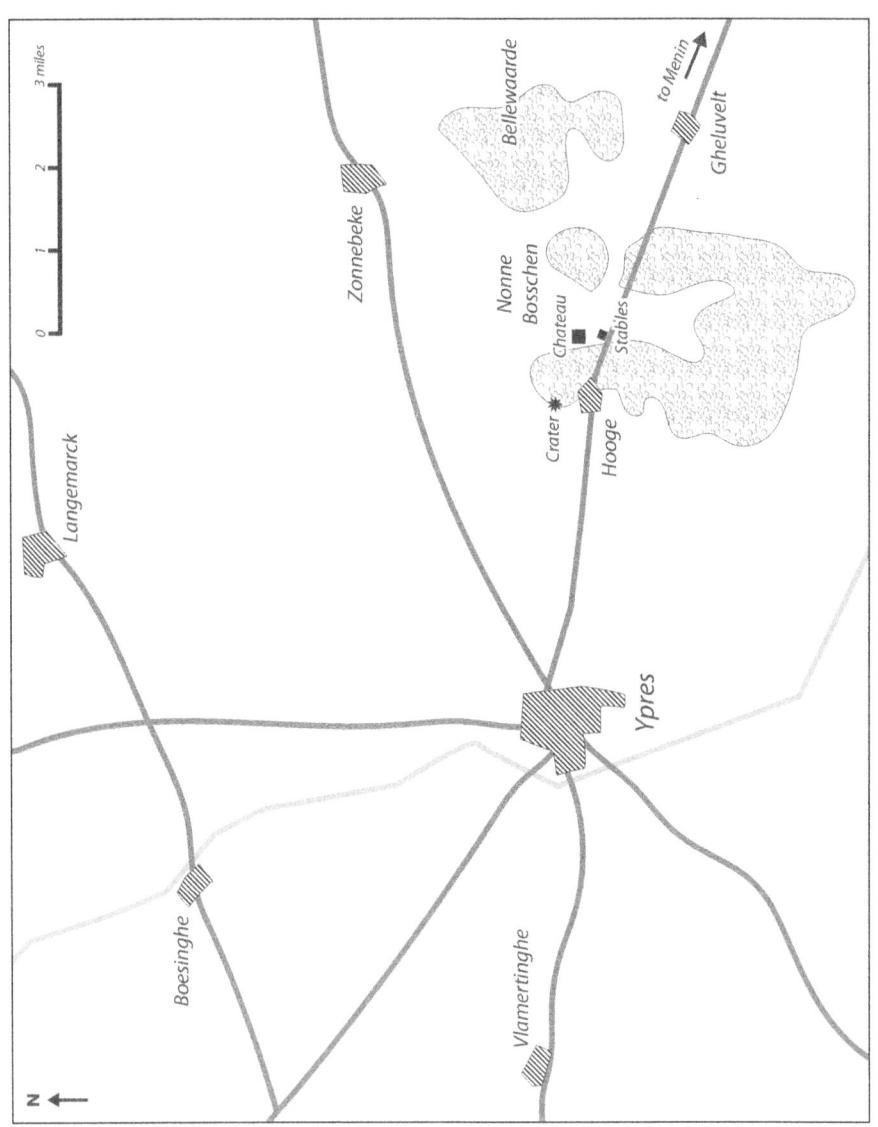

Map 2 Hooge Chateau, October 1914.

deeper into the fierce fighting that took place south-east of Ypres then Edmonds[28] and Palmer[29] make good start points. For this account, it is sufficient to review actions that took place at Gheluvelt and Hooge; sites that would be significant for the men of 2/York and Lancaster in 1915 (see Chapter 3).

Both of these small villages lay on the road between Menin and Ypres. The two are separated by a wooded area stretching from Polygon Wood, a mile to the north of the road, through Nonne Bosschen to about a mile south of the road. Both villages also featured a large country house, or chateau. As was so frequently the case, the rising ground of the Bellewaarde ridge (just to the east of Hooge) designated the area as a natural objective for both sides. On 31 October, the Germans successfully attacked Gheluvelt. The position was now serious for the British and they had little in the way of reserves with which to recover the situation. Brigadier-General FitzClarence (commanding 1st Guards Brigade, 1 Division)) informed his divisional commander, Major-General Lomax, of the need for reinforcement or counter-attack. If the line was to hold, Gheluvelt had to be retaken and Lomax told FitzClarence to use the divisional reserve from 2 Division to restore the situation; he then rode off to inform Major-General Monro (commanding 2 Division) of the decision. The only reserve available was the 2nd Worcestershire battalion whose commander, Major Hankey was ordered by FitzClarence to 'advance without delay and deliver a counter-attack with the utmost vigour against the enemy who was in possession of Gheluvelt, and to re-establish our line there'.[30] This author recalls being on a battlefield tour to the area and listening to Richard Holmes, with his characteristic enthusiasm, describe the manner in which 2/Worcester retook Gheluvelt – one of those classic single battalion actions that punctuate the history of the British Army. The battalion went forward with 11 officers and 450 ORs, their casualties were 3 officers and 189 men,[31] almost 42 per cent of their strength.

While the Worcesters were retaking Gheluvelt, the 1st and 2nd Division staffs were to suffer their own disaster at Hooge. Both divisions had their headquarters in the old chateau and as General Lomax had ridden there to inform General Monro that 2 Division reserve had been committed to the counter-attack, both divisional commanders were also in the building when it was hit by German artillery. General Monro was stunned, but able to continue in command, while Lomax later died of his wounds. Of the assembled staff officers, a further seven were killed and a number of others wounded. In spite of the heroic efforts of 2/Worcester, the Germans regained Gheluvelt in an offensive on 11 November. These early months

---

28 Edmonds, *1914, Vol. 2*.
29 Palmer, A., *The Salient. Ypres, 1914-18* (London, Constable & Robinson, 2007), pp.57-92.
30 Edmonds, *1914, Vol. 2*, p.323.
31 Edmonds, *1914, Vol. 2*, p.330.

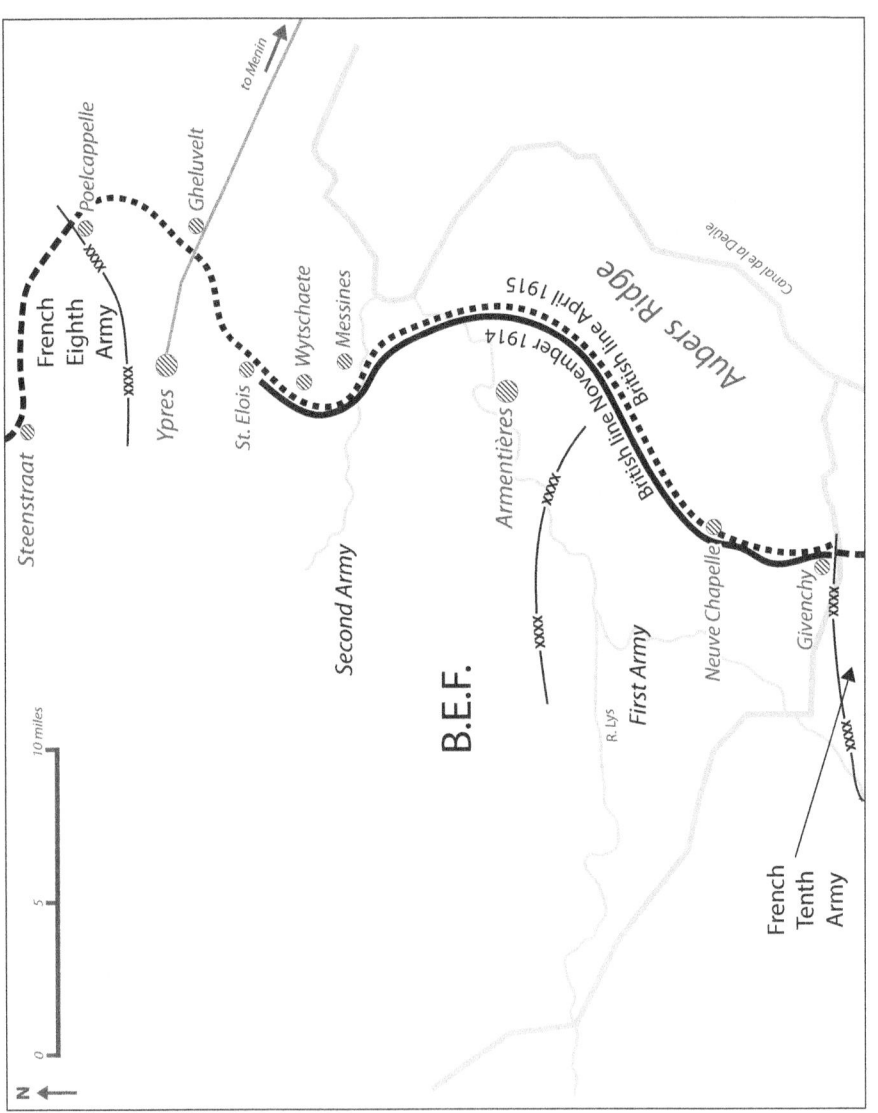

Map 3 BEF line, November 1914 and April 1915.

of the war wiped out much of what had been the cadre of old Regulars who had formed the basis of the BEF.

> In the British battalions which fought at the Marne and Ypres, there scarcely remained with the colours an average of one officer and thirty men of those who landed in August 1914. The old British Army was gone past recall, leaving but a remnant to carry on the training of the New Armies'.[32]

As the year closed, Sir John French had to rationalise the British line (Map 3). The BEF was split in two, with French Army units between the two wings. Accordingly, in the second half of November, the BEF came together to hold a compact front from Givenchy, on the La Bassée Canal, to opposite Wytschaete (about 4 miles south of Ypres). As both sides dug in and established static lines of trenches so the conflict took on the characteristics that came to define it; mud, wire and attritional frontal attacks (usually for little gain). Edmonds summed it up in his Official History, 'The battles of Ypres formed the last phase of open fighting before the belligerents settled down to undiluted trench warfare'.[33]

By early April, as more British divisions arrived in Flanders, the BEF's front was extended to form part of the perimeter around the Ypres Salient, from St Eloi to the Ypres-Poelcappelle road.[34] The remainder of the perimeter, on the British left, was held by the French and it was here that the Germans launched their gas attack on 22 April 1915, the start of the battle that is known as Second Ypres.

---

32 Edmonds, *1914, Vol. 2*, p.465.
33 Edmonds, *1914, Vol. 2*, p.460.
34 Edmonds, J., *Military Operations France and Belgium, 1915 Volume 1*(Nashville, IWM, Reprints of 1927 original), p.158.

2

"Gas" – Second Ypres

At the close of 1914, with their first Christmas of the war behind them, the 2nd battalion was the only unit of the York and Lancaster Regiment, which had sailed for France. That situation would change dramatically during 1915 as the British Army expanded rapidly to meet the needs of modern, industrial war. By the end of the first full year, the regiment had mobilized eleven battalions to different theatres; the 6th had gone to Gallipoli, while the 12th, 13th and 14th sailed for Suez in December 1915. As the armies of both sides dug in, the BEF was forced to adopt the troglodyte lifestyle that became synonymous with trench warfare. Army routine along the Western front settled into a tedious and tiring rotation between the rear areas and the front line. Discipline was hard rather than harsh; the soldiers were filthy for much of the time, constantly 'lousy', and at risk of death from German shells or snipers. Histories of the war are punctuated by large, iconic battles but it would be wrong to believe that all those at the front were constantly going 'over the top' in full-scale attacks. Men were much more likely to be part of a trench raid, or patrol in No Man's Land, than they were to charge the German trenches. One soldier from the 10th battalion wrote home in March 1916 to say that after six months in France, 'up to now I have not fired a shot, nor have I seen a German soldier'.[1] It was not all 'up and at 'em!'

After arriving in Britain from India, 1/York and Lancaster made ready for the journey to France. They left Winchester on 15 January for Southampton and embarked on SS *Lake Michigan* for the short crossing to Le Havre, where they disembarked at 10 a.m. on the 17th. After a train journey to Hazebrouk, and a nine mile night-march, they arrived at their camp in Meteren at 6 in the morning on 18 January. Sadly, the battalion suffered its first death of the war during the move; Private J Hill of 'A' Company died of a heart attack during the night march.[2] Hill is buried in Hazebrouk Communal Cemetery, along with 876 other soldiers.

1 Mortimer, J.G., Private Papers, IWM Doc. 7449.
2 TNA WO 95/2275, war diary, 1/York & Lancs.

After two weeks in camp, with a battalion strength of 27 officers and 985 ORs, the men moved in 38 motor buses to Vlamertinghe, some 2½ miles west of Ypres. From this small town the men rotated between the rest area and the front line trenches, some of which were in a bad state, with an inadequate parapet and full of water. Because of the flooding, they had to put fascines (bundles of wood) in the bottom of the trench for the men to stand on. The distance between German and British trenches in the Ypres salient was often only a hundred yards, the result was a daily list of casualties; between 8 a.m. on 2 February and 8 a.m. on the 4th the battalion lost one man killed and 8 wounded – the attrition had started. In the months of February and March, before the battle of Second Ypres opened, the battalion front-line periods were spent in the vicinity of St Elois and Verbrandenmolen, just a few miles south and south-east, respectively, of Ypres. This was a time for the officers and men to become acclimatised to trench conditions, especially the effect of wet feet. It was soon apparent to them all that flooded trenches, often with 'water above the men's knees', was not conducive to good health. Trench foot, as we saw in the previous chapter, was a real problem and was commented on in the battalion diary in February: '120 men and 1 officer were admitted to hospital with frozen feet; roughly 15% of the number of the battalion in the trenches. Every effort was made to guard against this by greasing men's feet, giving them clean socks, and washing feet as much as possible, but it is often very difficult to provide accommodation for this, except when back in billets'.[3] The constant wet feet, dirt and the steady casualty count would have been a constant drain on morale.

As well as the risk of being killed, water in the trenches was only one of the problems faced by the men in Flanders. The frequent demands for units to provide work-parties to act as labourers, particularly during 'rest' periods out of the line, meant that the troops were constantly tired and the officers could not programme adequate training:

> In this kind of warfare (i.e. trenches) the great difficulties in taking stores, ammunition, water, food etc. up to the trenches, owing to the few men available for the duty (a fatigue party of 150 to 200 men has on several occasions had to do at least 3 journeys from Battn. or Brigade headquarters to the trenches).

Although there were Pioneer battalions, whose main role was trench and engineering work (7/York and Lancaster was one such unit), trench improvements and the carrying of stores invariably fell on the front line soldier. Being 'dog tired' is a constant refrain in their letters and memoirs. Having made the negative comment on the need for working parties, the diary goes on to state that 'the men should be given plenty of work to do, the exercise does them good, and to a certain extent keeps their feet from being frostbitten' – it is safe to assume that the writer was not doing the labouring.

3   WO 95/2275.

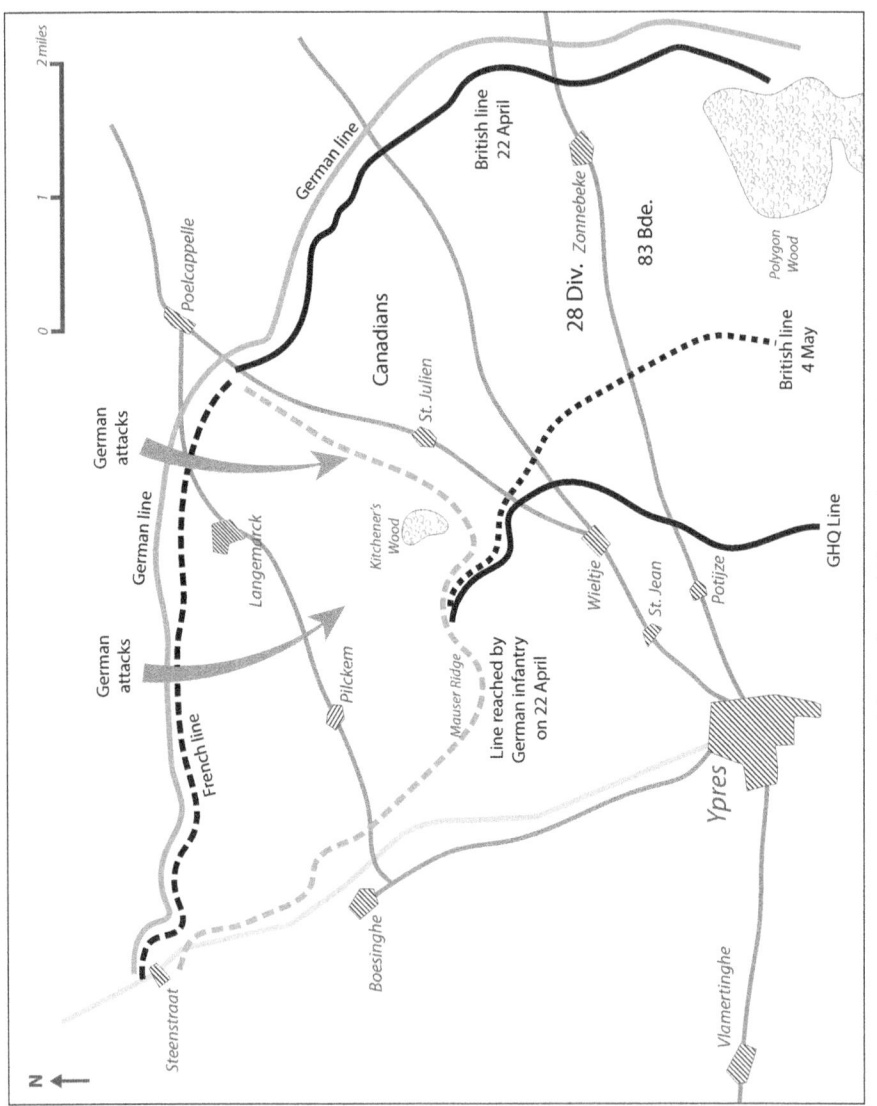

Map 4 Second Ypres, April 1915.

By the start of April 1915, with the recruitment programme in Britain allowing for the formation of many more divisions, it was necessary (as was noted at the end of Chapter 1) for the BEF to take over more of the front line. At the close of 1914, the British held only some 5 per cent of the total front. For command and control purposes, it was also obvious that there were very real advantages to national armies holding contiguous sections of the line. During the period of 1st Ypres, the British had held two sections of front separated by French divisions. On 8 April, the 1/York and Lancaster, together with the rest of 28 Division, moved to take up their part of the new British line. After the re-alignment the BEF held a continuous 30 miles (instead of the original 19); from Cuinchy in the south, swinging east and crossing the Menin road between Gheluvelt and Hooge, past Polygon Wood where it turned north past Zonnebeke and then angled west to meet the Ypres-Poelcappelle road, a little south-west of the village of Poelcappelle. The 16 divisions of the BEF now faced 11½ of the Germans.[4]

The battalion left Westoutre, a few miles south-west of Ypres, at 06:30 on 8 April to relieve the 3rd Battalion of 146 Regiment (French). It was a long march; they passed through Ypres at 8 p.m. and continued out along the Potijze-Frezenberg road, towards their section of the line near Zonnebeke. Two of the men were wounded during the relief, which was completed by 2 a.m. on 9 April.[5] After a tiring march, the mood of the men would not have improved when they saw the state of the trenches they were taking over from their French allies:

> [T]he trenches cannot be called good, in few places is the parapet bullet proof, the communication trenches being especially bad – the distance from the enemy was from 10 [yards] to 100 [yards] – the left trench is especially bad, being enfiladed from both sides, also the rear – the trenches are very poor, in fact very little repair has been done for a considerable time.[6]

The deficiencies highlighted by the battalion were not unique to their stretch of the line. The war diaries record many instances of British troops being critical of trenches they had to take over from other nationalities, especially the French and the Italians. Edmonds was critical of the whole five miles vacated by the French, while some of the line 'was good', others were 'in a deplorable condition, and dangerous both as regards safety and sanitation'.[7] Although there were 'good machine-gun posts' there were 'few traverses, no parados, and only flimsily built dug-outs which afforded little more than shelter from the weather'. However, behind the front line was a rather more substantial second line, some one and a half miles in the rear (see Map 4), which the British

4   Edmonds, *1915, Vol. 1*, p.159.
5   WO 95/2275.
6   WO 95/2275.
7   Edmonds, *1915, Vol. 1*, p.160.

would refer to as the 'GHQ Line'. After moving to Zonnebeke, the battalion spent the next two weeks (apart from two days) in the line. In spite of the German trenches being only around 100-150 yards away these days were recorded as 'quiet'. However, quiet is a relative term. A typical day was 10 April:

> Situation quiet, nothing to report. At 11 p.m. the enemy shelled our trench, with a trench mortar but did no damage, artillery informed and they shelled the enemy trenches in front of left trench with great accuracy, making two breaches in the enemy's parapet of about 25 yards each. After this the enemy did not continue to use trench mortar. The casualties during the last 24 hours were Other Ranks, killed 4, wounded 7.[8]

Both sides had fallen into a routine; the days were 'quiet' but each night the Germans would shell the British trenches, the British artillery would respond, and then the Germans would cease firing. It was almost as though, close as their lines were, each needed to remind the other that they were there – meanwhile this relatively low-level exchange resulted in a regular attrition of numbers as men were killed and wounded.

Only two weeks after their move to Zonnebeke, the men of 1/York and Lancaster were called on to play a part in the Battle of Second Ypres. The northern and leftmost sector of the British line, around Poelcappelle and Gravenstafel, was held by the Canadian Division, with the French on their left. The French line then ran west, to meet the Belgians on the Ypres Canal at Steenstraat, north of Ypres (Map 4) To the right of the Canadians was 28 Division with their three brigades, from left to right, 85, 84 and 83 (with 1/York and Lancs); to the right of 83 Brigade was 27 Division, astride the Menin road at Hooge. The junction of units from different national armies is always a potential weak spot because there is invariably no central control of those troops. The portion of the line held by the French, between the British (Canadian) and Belgian forces would prove to be the weak link on 22 April. Edmonds, albeit with the benefit of hindsight, summed up the issue:

> There were no arrangements for unity of command of the three different contingents, and the two junctions were ill-chosen: that of the French and British at a shoulder of the salient, and that of the French and Belgians at the canal, where the two forces were on opposite sides of the water. The Germans could hardly select a better sector for attack.[9]

The series of battles, which make up Second Ypres, are perhaps best known for the German introduction of poisonous gas to the battlefield. Outlawed as a weapon of war by a Hague declaration of 1899, Kitchener telegraphed Sir John French to say that its

---

8   WO 95/2275.
9   Edmonds, *1915, Vol. 1*, p.162.

use by the Germans was 'contrary to the rules and usages of war'.[10] However, as we will see in a later chapter, once the genie is out of the bottle it cannot be put back: the British opened the battle of Loos, September 1915, with the release of poisonous gas.

Thursday, 22 April, dawned bright and clear. Unfortunately, this lovely spring weather thwarted the German plan; gas needed a breeze to blow it in the direction of the enemy trenches. Still air would allow the gas to settle back into the German trenches and so affect their own troops. By the end of the afternoon, the conditions were right for the release against the French divisions on the left of the BEF. The line at that point was held by Algerian and Territorial troops, but they did not stay long in the face of the gas. Given that this was the first instance on which the weapon had been used, and the soldiers had no defence against it, their reluctance to stand their ground is perhaps understandable. Be that as it may, the consequence was a deep penetration of the Allied line, and a need for the French and British commanders to react to it. At the same time, the Canadians, immediately to the right of the French, demonstrated the resilience that these troops came to be known for in this and later battles.

Immediately the French troops realised that the 'greenish-yellow' clouds rolling towards them were gas, they began an uncontrolled retreat. The men were seen leaving their lines 'without officers'[11] and crossing the canal north of Ypres. When the Germans launched their attack, the 1/York and Lancaster was out of the line in huts near Ypres where, at 6 p.m., 'Very heavy firing [was] heard to the north'.[12] An hour later, they saw 'French troops [coming] down the road in great disorder saying the Germans had advanced overwhelming them with asphyxiating gases'. During the night of 22 April, frantic efforts were made to recover the line as the Germans had penetrated to within a few hundred yards of the Poelcappelle-St Julien road and Mouse Trap Farm. At this point, 'the Canadian line was in grave danger of envelopment'.[13] General Smith-Dorrien, commanding Second Army, was now faced with a serious threat to the town of Ypres if the line could not be steadied. Had it not been for the Canadians then the line might well have collapsed totally that night. The 10th and 16th battalions of the Canadian 3rd Brigade were ordered to retake Kitchener's Wood from the Germans and, although that did not happen, the Germans were stopped, but at great cost. The 10th could only muster five officers and 188 men the next morning, out of the 816 who had started the previous day. Their sister battalion fared little better, five officers and 263 men answering morning roll-call.[14] The French, who intended counter-attacking with their 45th Division, had requested that the Canadians launch an assault in support of this effort. At one point, the Canadians had driven the Germans out of

10   Edmonds, *1915, Vol. 1*, p.193.
11   Edmonds, *1915, Vol. 1*, p.177.
12   WO 95/2275.
13   Edmonds, *1915, Vol. 1*, p.179.
14   Dixon, J., *Magnificent But Not War. The Second Battle of Ypres 1915* (Barnsley, Pen and Sword, 2003), p.56.

Kitchener's Wood but only after suffering heavy casualties. The Canadians had 'no hope of holding unsupported such an advanced position; no news came of the French. [...] It was therefore decided to evacuate the forward position'.[15] Brave men had been let down. In some places, the original French line had been driven back two and a half miles. As dawn broke on 23 April there were 10 battalions strung out to cover the gap between the original Canadian left and the canal north of Ypres. This was not sufficient to hold the line, and, 'though some digging and wiring was done, a few [of the men] had only had time to move out to the ground, where they lay down, or occupied such rudimentary trenches as they found existing'.[16] It was to be 'all hands to the pumps' to shore up the line and 1/York and Lancaster were to be part of the bung to plug the dam.

Our battalion was part of 83 Brigade, 28 Division, but had been rotated out of the line for rest and (as we have seen above) was in huts near Ypres. Normally a battalion would go into action as part of the brigade to which it belongs but in this instance, it would operate away from the rest of the brigade. During the early hours of 23 April, Lieutenant-Colonel Geddes, (commanding 2/Buffs in 85 Brigade, 28 Division) was ordered to form a 'composite brigade', which would include 1/York and Lancaster. At 01.15 a.m., the battalion received orders to move to St Jean (mid-way between Ypres and Wieltje) where they would come under the orders of Colonel Geddes. It was only on arrival at St Jean at around 4 a.m., that they had any idea of the situation, other than having seen the retreating French troops – 'On arrival at St Jean we heard 2 kilometres of trenches had been rushed';[17] in fact, the gap was closer to 8,000 yards. At 05.30, the battalion was ordered to move forward to a position north-west of Wieltje and during that move they came under 'severe shelling' from shrapnel and high explosive shells, 'causing a few casualties'. After occupying some disused trenches, they then came under heavy shelling which lasted most of the morning.

While Geddes' force was coming together near St Jean, the senior commanders were reviewing the serious situation and what needed to be done to rectify it. During the morning, Sir John French was assured by General Foch that he intended to launch a French operation to recover the line lost by the Algerian and Territorial divisions. Sir John agreed to co-operate by launching a British attack but stipulated that if the line was not re-established within a limited time then he would be free to withdraw his troops from their 'exposed and dangerous position'.[18] At this time the Germans were believed to have 42 battalions facing a little more than 17½ British (12 of them Canadian) of which 10½ were in the front line and 7 in the second.[19] Smith-Dorrien ordered V Corps to launch a general attack between Kitchener's Wood and the canal,

15   Edmonds, *1915, Vol. 1*, p.185.
16   Edmonds, *1915, Vol. 1*, p.187.
17   WO 95/2275.
18   Edmonds, *1915, Vol. 1*, p.201.
19   Edmonds, *1915, Vol. 1*, p.198.

to start at 2.40 p.m. on 23 April; the start time then slipped until 4.15 p.m. The men of the 1/York and Lancaster were about to join their first attack:

> 4.00 p.m., near St Jean. Orders were received for Bn. To participate in an attack on the German posn.
> 4.05 p.m., Orders were issued by C.O. to Company Commanders.
> 4.10 p.m., Companies marched independently to the [Turco] farm and the attack debouched from behind it under very heavy rifle and machine gun fire.[20]

The subsequent action was very much a soldiers' battle fought by platoons, each led by a Lieutenant or Captain, moving from hedge to hedge for whatever cover they could get. According to the battalion diary the German position was on Mauser Ridge, some 1,200 yards in front, from which their guns could shell the attacking companies. The counter-attack, of which 1/York and Lancaster was to be a part, was to go in on the very left of the British line which was trying to plug the gap left by the French retreat. The left front of the attack was taken by 13 Brigade (commanded by Brigadier-General Wanless O'Gowan), the centre was formed by Geddes' Composite Brigade, while the right consisted of two battalions from 27 Division. The sheer mix of battalions demonstrates the *ad hoc* measures that had to be put in place to deal with the situation. The time pressures under which Geddes and his battalion commanders were operating is evidenced by the 'time-stamps' on the relevant signals. That from Geddes, detailing the order of battle and objectives for his brigade, was timed at 3.20 p.m., but referred to events that had started 20 minutes prior to his order. In the following transcript of Geddes' order 'AAA' was the signaller's equivalent of 'STOP' in a telegram:

> The 13th Brigade crosses by the pontoon bridge at 3 p.m. [prior to this message] and advances to the attack at 3.45 p.m. with its right on the YPRES-PILCKEM ROAD AAA First objective PILCKEM AAA O.C. East Yorks will send an officer at once to report to Gen. O'Gowan at pontoon bridge @ [sic] 19C AAA The East Yorks and York and Lancs will cooperate with this attack east of the PILCKEM-YPRES ROAD East Yorks with left [flank] on that road and maintaining touch with 13th Bde. York and Lancs will move on right of E Yorks. Two battalions 27th Divn. will cooperate in the attack on the right of York and Lancs AAA Buffs and Third Middlesex will hold their present line. 5th KORL (less 1 coy.) will follow the attack in reserve moving with its left on the PILCKEM-YPRES ROAD AAA Each Bn. will move on a front of 500 yards AAA HQ will remain for the present at WIELTJE where reports should be sent.[21]

20 WO 95/2275.
21 WO 95/2275.

One point from this message requires emphasis; the first objective was given as the village of Pilckem, approximately one mile beyond Mauser Ridge on which the battalion could see the German gun positions. According to the Official History, this attack, launched at the request of the French, 'never had any prospect of success'.[22] The message from Geddes was followed by one from the battalion adjutant to the company commanders, part of which is copied here:

> The Bn. will move in 4 lines, each company in 2 lines. Lines to be about 200 yards apart. A and C coy will both be in front line, A coy on left keeping touch with East Yorks followed by D on the left, B on the right.

The ground over which the men of the York and Lancs were expected to advance was open and sloped gently upwards for some 1200 yards towards Mauser Ridge. For infantry to be successful under these conditions they needed artillery support but, with the constantly changing situation, the short notice of the attack and little or no reconnaissance of the ground, this was not available.

The general attack finally began at 4.25 p.m.,[23] under 'very heavy and accurate shell and rifle fire' and with only 'very scanty temporary cover' from farm dung-heaps, consequently, 'losses were exceedingly heavy'.[24] During one rush of some 300 yards 'the men were in full view of the enemy and a devastating machine gun and shell fire met them'. This was unsurprising as 'in the clear light of the spring afternoon every single man was distinctly visible'.[25] Efforts were made to reorganize and although many of the officers and NCOs were disabled, a further advance was attempted. In this last rush, 'across absolutely open ground [which was] uphill for some 350 yards, the losses were again very great'.[26] By this point the battalion commander, Lieutenant-Colonel Burt, had been killed and the Adjutant, Captain Bamford, was mortally wounded. Captain Wedgwood, who had now taken command, accepted that 'with such a small number of men and exhausted as they were it would be impossible to rush the final pos[itio]n so it was decided not to push home the assault'.[27] Having cancelled any further advance the men held on where they were until dark. At 8 p.m., Captain Wedgwood could see that the battalion 'had been so weakened' that he could not hold such an advanced position and, after consulting with officers from the other battalions in the same situation, he decided to fall back and dig in. Before doing so, the bodies of the Colonel and the Adjutant were brought back to the line. Lieutenant-Colonel Burt and six other members of the battalion are buried in New Irish Farm Cemetery, about a mile to the north-east of the old town of Ypres. The Adjutant presumably died

22   Edmonds, *1915, Vol. 1*, p.203.
23   Edmonds, *1915, Vol. 1*, p.205.
24   WO 95/2275.
25   Edmonds, *1915, Vol. 1*, p.203.
26   WO 95/2275.
27   WO 95/2275.

of his wounds at a Casualty Clearing Station and is buried in Poperinghe Old Military Cemetery. One of the 'myths' of this war is that callous senior officers sent their men into battle while they stayed back out of harm's way. The deaths of Burt and Bamford are just two cases we will meet in this book where senior officers died alongside the men they led.

Although the attack was over for the men of 1/York and Lancaster, they still had a few uncomfortable days before they were able to go to the rear. Digging in was very difficult; the water table, only two feet below the surface, prevented the troops from digging trenches deep enough to provide real protection. To make it worse for men who had spent the day with the stress and strain of battle, the supply of rations was problematic; 'some food in the shape of bread and bacon was got up, but not to all'. At the end of the week's fighting, the battalion had lost its C.O. and its Adjutant as well as two other officers missing and 11 wounded. Among the men, 60 were dead, 284 were wounded, and 84 were recorded as missing. Altogether, the casualties numbered 443.[28] The losses recorded in the battalion war diary were listed within days of the action taking place; those in the Official History (a total of 425) were compiled for the 1927 publication. Casualty statistics are notoriously difficult to compile as men could get lost during a battle, some of those listed as missing would re-join their unit days later, and the wounded might be treated at different medical stations, some of them dying there, and paper records might then be lost. The reader should not be surprised to see different sources giving conflicting numbers for those who were sick or casualties of battle.

While 1/York and Lancaster tried to settle into their wet trenches, the battle to restore the original line continued, though with limited success. The map (4) shows how much ground had been lost since 22 April, but attempts were still made to try to push the current line north towards the village of Pilckem. On 27 April, the battalion, now only 280 men strong,[29] was once again ordered to become part of a composite brigade, this time under Lieutenant-Colonel Tuson of 27 Division. This brigade, 'hardly stronger than a battalion',[30] was made up of 2/Duke of Cornwall's Light Infantry (DCLI) (260 strong); 1/York and Lancs (280); 5/King's Own (400); 2/Duke of Wellington's (350). A total of 1,290 men. Tuson's brigade was to assist the Indian Sirhind Brigade, which had 'suffered a temporary check' to the right of the Ypres-Pilckem road while attacking towards Pilckem. When the war started there was a tremendous response from the Empire (as it then was) to get involved with the Mother Country, and India was no exception – around 800,000 men from the subcontinent fought for Britain in various theatres of the war. The men of the Sirhind Brigade met a withering fire from the German guns on Mauser Ridge, and the assistance of Tuson's brigade was not going to make that much difference to the situation.

28 WO 95/2275.
29 Edmonds, *1915, Vol. 1*, p.273, fn. 3.
30 Edmonds, *1915, Vol. 1*, p.273, fn. 3.

By 10 p.m. on 28 April the battalion received orders to re-join their own brigade (the 28th), 'and return to huts near Ypres', which they reached by midnight. What they would not have known was that Colonel Geddes, who had been their temporary brigade commander, was killed by a shell while visiting 13 Brigade headquarters on the morning of the 28th. He is buried in Ypres Reservoir Cemetery.

Modern industrial warfare, with its emphasis on machine guns and artillery, took a heavy toll of the soldiers in every battalion that went into action. Once back in the rest areas these units had to assimilate new drafts of men, some would be trained recruits with no previous battle experience; others might be old hands coming from other units. In addition, when units were sent into action it was normal to retain a cadre of officers and men in the 'transport lines' who would then form the nucleus of the battalion as it reformed after the battle. As they reached their huts near Ypres, 1/York and Lancaster (approximately 280 strong) would have re-joined those who had remained behind, and a new draft of 209 men who were waiting for them in the camp. As well as new men, the battalion also needed a new commanding officer following the death of Lt. Col. Burt. The new man was Lt. Col. Isherwood who arrived with brevet rank, which meant that until his promotion became substantive, Isherwood was still a Major but with the roles and responsibilities of a battalion commander. The battalion diary closes on an eventful month with a note that, although they were in huts in the rest area, at 11 p.m. on 30 April, 'shrapnel shells and high explosives burst near and over the camp for about an hour without doing any damage'.

As April turned into May, the 1/York and Lancaster would be sent out to assist in trying to hold the eastern boundary of the salient. Between 1st and 8th May, the battalion was in the trenches, moving between Verlorenhoek and Zonnebeke, facing fierce enemy resistance. Extracts from the battalion diary give a flavour of those days:

> 4 May: It is believed that the enemy are placing machine guns in these houses [in the battalion front] which will command all our trenches.
>
> 4 May 5 p.m.: Left trench reports thousand Germans with transport moving through Zonnebeke.
>
> 5 May 9 a.m.: All communication wires with my [companies] are cut by shell fire AAA.
> Report by hand says enemy have blown in trenches in many parts AAA Heavy artillery support urgently needed.
>
> 5 May 9.15 a.m.: We are suffering heavy losses & trenches are being destroyed by heavy shell fire AAA We are in urgent need of support if possible.
>
> 6 May 11 a.m.: Our artillery have kept enemy quieter today. We have opened bursts of rapid fire on parties working on trenches.
>
> 7 May 5 p.m.: Battalion relieved during the night [...] and marched back to the huts [around Ypres].
>
> Waiting for them was a fresh draft of 487 NCOs and men.

As frequently happens when an army is trying to stabilize a position in the face of concerted enemy attacks, orders come thick and fast. The men's stay in the huts was very short-lived, and the new drafts found themselves in action very quickly. At 11.35 a.m. on 8 May, the order came to 'Stand To' and within half an hour the battalion left the camp with the instruction to retake the trenches 'from which the KOYLI had had to withdraw at Zonnebeke'.[31] At 7 p.m., in the support line near Zonnebeke and with casualties which 'numbered between 30 and 40', the company commanders were receiving their orders from Colonel Isherwood for an attack to start at 8 p.m.:

> The attack was pushed almost up to the German trenches, but owing to the very heavy casualties in officers & men, it did not achieve its object. All the officers were put out of action with the exception of Lt Briscoe who was able to get together the remnants of the battalion next day.[32]

Four officers were listed as missing, including Lt. Col. Isherwood (who had only just taken command of the battalion) and Lieutenant Wylie. Isherwood's body was never found, he is recorded on the Menin Gate Memorial, where his death is given as 9 May. The situation with Lt. Wylie is more intriguing; the war diary has a margin comment for 8 May to the effect that 'Capt[ain] Copley 1st Y & L Rgt states that he, with a party, carried Lt Wylie to the dressing station at the White Chateau Potijze and handed him over to the M.O.' However, Wylie's death is recorded by the Commonwealth War Graves Commission (CWGC) as 10 May, which would indicate he died of wounds at the dressing station, but he has no known grave. Like Isherwood, his name is on the Menin Gate Memorial. If he was taken to the dressing station, as the diary states, it is unusual for his body to be 'lost', which is the implication of his name being on the memorial rather than on an individual headstone.

As well as losing their C.O. and most of their officers, the battalion strength had now been drastically reduced. At 11 p.m., Sergeant South 'brought 30 men back to the support trenches where he met Sgt. Taylor with 45 men'. Just after midnight, these two sergeants and the remnants of the battalion were met by the Brigadier-General who 'came along the trench and ordered the battalion to reform and continue the attack. The Battn. then numbered 83 men commanded by Sgt. South'.[33] The situation near Zonnebeke was obviously desperate, but the Brigade Major, on hearing that South and his men had been ordered to attack again, ordered them back to the support trenches. However, the night was not yet over. Two platoons of the Middlesex Regiment were sent as reinforcements and Lieutenant Briscoe, who re-joined with 17 men, took command of what was left of 1/York and Lancaster. They remained all day in the support trenches, under heavy shell fire. Early in the morning of 10

31   WO 95/2275.
32   WO 95/2275.
33   WO 95/2275.

May, Lieutenant Briscoe, who had been superseded in command by Captain Swales, 'was killed'. Unlike so many who died in those two days, he has a known grave in Ypres Town Cemetery. Finally, on 12 May, what was left of 1/York and Lancaster was marched to Poperinghe where they were billeted 'in sheds surrounding a farm'. After their time at Zonnebeke, it would have been a welcome respite. The battalion, by now in obvious need of additional troops, received a fresh draft of 340 men on the following day.

The battle of Second Ypres is best known for the German gas attack, the desperate struggle by the British and Canadians to regain the ground lost after the French retreat, and the eventual withdrawal to the GHQ line. Many men lost their lives and it is easy to lose sight of the individual soldier when general histories give casualty counts in the thousands. The battalion war diaries indicate how little the officers and men knew of the overall situation, or how their own short periods of conflict fitted in to that total picture. The events of 8 and 9 May were one of many occasions where the author had to step away from the keyboard and reflect a little on those individual soldiers. One of the most iconic symbols of the war is the Menin Gate Memorial to the Missing at Ypres. Of the men of 1/York and Lancaster who were killed on those two days, only one has a known grave – Lieutenant Briscoe – 130 others who fell on 8 May are remembered only by their name on the memorial. It is difficult at this remove to imagine how the bodies of 130 out of 131 men, on one day, were either never found or were so unrecognisable as to deny the soldier a name on his headstone. Although the battalion was involved in action around Sanctuary Wood (south of Hooge), at the end of the month, we will leave them as they rebuild after the heavy losses of 8 May.

The Salient was now considerably reduced in size and poisonous gas, while its use by the Germans was much deprecated, became one more weapon in the arsenal of both sides. The Canadians earned a reputation for their dogged resistance during those April days. One of the most striking of the battlefield memorials is that to the brave Canadians at Vancouver Corner near the village of Keerselare. At the top of the column of granite is the head and shoulders of a soldier, hands on the butt of his rifle in the 'reversed arms' position. He is 'mounting guard' over the graves of his fallen comrades.

Like the battle of Loos, in September 1915, Second Ypres caused a change of command at a very senior level. General Smith-Dorrien commanded Second Army under Sir John French as Commander-in-Chief. In his memoir, Smith Dorrien says almost nothing of the last battle he would command. Relations between Smith-Dorrien and French had not been good since the former took over from the latter as C-in-C Aldershot; French resented the changes introduced by Smith-Dorrien, interpreting them as a criticism of his time there.[34] Tensions between them increased over Smith-Dorrien's decision to fight at Le Cateau, during the retreat from Mons; 'a *cause*

---

34   Holmes, R., *The Little Field Marshal. A life of Sir John French* (London, Weidenfeld & Nicolson, 2004), p.132.

Menin Gate memorial. (Photo J. Dillon)

célèbre and a bone of contention' between them.³⁵ Holmes described Second Ypres as a broken-backed battle in which French had spurred Smith-Dorrien on into 'launching a series of costly counter-attacks' while confiding to Sir Douglas Haig that Second Army commander was a 'weak spot'.³⁶ Smith-Dorrien came to see that he might be the problem; 'Matters went from bad to worse, and I gradually became aware that it was the Army Commander [i.e. Smith-Dorrien], rather than the Army, who had fallen into disfavour'.³⁷ The need to consolidate the British line along a shorter front, the GHQ Line, was suggested to French by Smith-Dorrien but, coming from him, 'it was like a red rag to a bull'. On 6 May Smith-Dorrien was ordered by French to hand over command of Second Army to Lieutenant-General Sir Herbert Plumer who, recognising the difficult position in front of Ypres, recommended a withdrawal along the lines of that suggested by his predecessor. As French's biographer put it, 'Sir John himself eventually agreed that a retirement to a shorter line was desirable'.³⁸ If this had

---

35   Holmes, *The Little Field Marshal*, p.223.
36   Holmes, *The Little Field Marshal*, p.283.
37   Smith-Dorrien, H., *Memories of Forty-Eight Years' Service* (London, John Murray, 1925), p.479.
38   Holmes, *The Little Field Marshal*, p.284.

been done sooner those 130 names might not have been carved on the Menin Gate Memorial.

At Second Ypres, Sir John French had allowed his personal views of Smith-Dorrien to influence his opinion of that commander's advice; Smith-Dorrien was removed. Following the BEF's later failure at the battle of Loos in September 1915, French was removed after being undermined by Haig (amongst others). Haig became Commander-in-Chief, but his period in command was dogged by the constant criticism of him from the Prime Minister, Lloyd George. Military history is replete with examples of the personal competition between the commanders at the top of the greasy poles.

The gas attack on 22 April led to a German break-in (which they failed to fully exploit) and a dramatic collapse by French Colonial troops. From the point of view of the men of the York and Lancaster Regiment, it was a rather confused situation into which they were injected to hold the line. The Canadians performed magnificently, while to their left the British troops – many, like 1/York and Lancs, as part of hurriedly-formed, composite units – struggled valiantly to plug the gap left by the French. The men of the battalion were little affected by the gas (they came a day after this was released) and would have had little awareness of the situation on the rest of the front around the salient. They went in at short notice, did the job asked of them, and then marched back to barracks. Throughout the war, the soldier was frequently unaware of the significance or otherwise of his battalion's contribution to a particular battle.

3

Aubers Ridge and Hooge

We last met the 1/4th and 1/5th (Territorial) battalions of the York and Lancaster Regiment preparing to leave for Foreign Service. Both were warned in March of the need to be ready to move overseas and the rest of the month was taken up with re-equipping with service rifles, receiving mules and horses for transport and general preparations to leave. Foreign Service meant family separation (for many of the men this would be for the first time) and so the troops 'were now allowed to commence their 4 days leave to their homes, but this was cut down to 2 days leave';[1] travelling time would have allowed only a short stay with loved ones. After a great deal of expectation, the troops finally sailed for France on 13 April 1915. By the following day, both battalions, (with the rest of 49 West Riding Division) were disembarking in Boulogne, ahead of them was a journey that would become familiar to all British troops arriving in France. The 1/4th battalion history records that the men found it 'depressing' after a fatiguing day, which had started early, having 'to march a considerable distance up the cobbled and precipitous streets of Boulogne' to the battalion area in the camp above town – 'a steady drizzle did not improve [their] tempers'.[2] Having been issued with blankets and space in their small tents, which were 'scattered over a considerable area' necessitating 'much trudging and squelching backwards and forwards by the light of a horse lantern', they had arrived. The day did not finish for the battalion until 4 a.m. the following morning, but sleep was short; at 06:00, they were up to collect rations and were on the march by 09:00. Cosy evenings in the drill halls of Sheffield, Rotherham, and Barnsley were now behind them.

From the transit camp, the battalion moved to Doulieu:

> [It] was a pleasant little village – at that time practically untouched by war – and in the glorious weather of that early Spring, with the fruit trees bursting into blossom and the peasants doing business as usual, there was little to remind us of

---

1   WO 95/2805, war diary, 1/4 York & Lancs.
2   Grant, *Hallamshires*, p.13.

war save the occasional dull sound of a bursting shell down Neuve Chapelle way, [...] and the never-ending mutter of the guns at Ypres.[3]

It was normal practice for units arriving straight from England to be given some familiarisation with the trenches before taking over front line duties – for many of the officers, NCOs and men this was the first time they had come close to the enemy. For about a week after their arrival at Doulieu, parties of officers and NCOs from each battalion were sent forward for 24 hour periods of instruction from the 'old hands' at the front. They quickly realised that there was a world of difference between the training trenches in England and those facing the Germans in Flanders. There is a point in most of the war diaries when a battalion suffers its first death. On 21 April, the 1/4th battalion recorded that Private Saunders was killed,[4] although his death is recorded by the CWGC as having occurred on the following day. Saunders' body was found and he is buried in Sailly-Sur-La-Lys Canadian Cemetery. At the end of the month, both battalions moved to Fleurbaix, a few miles south-west of Armentières; a small town made famous by the soldiers for its 'Mademoiselle' (see Map 1).

The troops had now arrived in the 'real war' of front line trenches, No Man's Land and German machine guns. Here they 'were nursed by easy stages into a more or less distant familiarity with War'.[5] Although they were not aware of it, they had been lucky. On arrival in France, they had expected to go straight to the front, rather than spend time at Doulieu, but this 'prize' had gone to the Northumbrian Division. The Geordies 'were plunged straight from the coast [the defences in England] into the Second Battle of Ypres [...] before [they] had even had time to smell the atmosphere of the line or learnt to know, even as we knew, the immeasurable gulf which separated Training and the Real Thing'.[6] As we will see in a later chapter, 10/York and Lancaster were similarly sent directly from training in England to the Battle of Loos, where it did not go well for them.

The extent of the front allocated to the York and Lancaster men was unusually long, and not straight, leaving them to defend 'more than a mile and a half of trench line'[7] varying from 70 to 400 yards from the German line. It was a frequent complaint of British troops that the trenches they took over were in a poor state, and they then had to fix them. In this case, those allocated to the 1/4th battalion were 'bad & not bullet proof or connected up. All men not on duty working all night'.[8] By now, the men were beginning to appreciate what an infantry soldier's war was like in Flanders. After four days they were relieved by their sister battalion, the 1/5th York and Lancs,

3   Grant, *Hallamshires*, p.15.
4   TNA WO 95/2805, war diary, 1/4 York & Lancs.
5   Grant, *Hallamshires*, p.13.
6   Grant, *Hallamshires*, p.13.
7   Grant, *Hallamshires*, p.15.
8   WO 95/2805.

and the men were able to indulge in the luxury of 'hot baths'; these would become an infrequent but welcome respite from the grime of the trenches.

In March 1915, before the two York and Lancaster battalions had landed in France, the BEF launched an attack at Neuve Chapelle. The planning of this, 'the first set-piece offensive against an entrenched adversary delivered by the British army in the Great War',[9] fell to General Sir Henry Rawlinson, commander of IV Corps. Rawlinson had assembled one gun for every six yards of trench,[10] but Haig wanted him to not only take the village, he wanted the advance to get at least as far as Aubers Ridge. It was this ambitious final objective, which was to detract from the success of the first day's action. One historian wrote that 'In the long catalogue of British attempts to break the deadlock on the Western Front the Battle of Neuve Chapelle holds pride of place. [...] an attack launched with high hopes and great courage ending in disappointment and frustration'.[11] At the end of the first day (10 March 1915), the British and Indian battalions had overrun the German defences on a front of 4,000 yards, and to a depth of 1,000 yards. However, losses were heavy, 11,652 casualties in IV Corps.[12] The heavy artillery bombardment had allowed initial success but Haig's wish for the rush to continue through successive objectives (rather than Rawlinson's 'bite and hold') spoilt the day. The British learnt two main lessons at Neuve Chapelle (although they would frequently forget both in future operations). First, the weight of shells dropped on every yard of enemy trench, prior to the attack, was critical to the success of the infantry assault. Second, there was a more lasting chance of success if less ambitious advances were planned; the ground gained should be consolidated before attempting to take the second and third objectives. If the troops were required to take too much ground, they would be outside the range of the artillery barrage – a recipe for failure. For the gunners to continue providing a bombardment of extended objectives, the batteries (and ammunition) had to be moved forward and re-registered on the new targets. The relocation of the guns would take time, as it meant crossing ground that had been badly cut-up by previous shelling. This repositioning took time, but it was necessary for the successful exploitation of any infantry success. This lesson would not be quickly learnt.

In May 1915, the French were planning a 'push' in Artois and they needed the British to launch a coordinated attack to draw some of the German divisions away from the French lines. The section of the Allied front chosen for these combined assaults lay between Arras in the south and Armentières to the north. Running west to east, and almost bisecting the area of operations, was the La Basseé canal (see Map 3). The French Tenth Army occupied the front between Arras and the canal, with

---

9   Prior, R., and T. Wilson, *Command on the Western Front. The Military Career of Sir Henry Rawlinson 1914-1918* (Barnsley, Pen & Sword, 2004), p.23.
10 Holmes, *Western Front*, p.56.
11 Brown, M., *The Imperial War Museum book of The Western Front* (London, Pan, 1993), p.72.
12 Edmonds, *1915, Vol. 1*, p.151.

the British First Army positioned between the canal and Bois Grenier, a little south of Armentières. Haig had three corps in the line; the I Corps with their right on the canal; the Indian in the centre opposite Neuve Chapelle, the IV Corps in the north facing Aubers and Fromelles. On the extreme left of IV Corps, near Bois Grenier, was 148 Brigade with the 1/4th and 1/5th York and Lancaster battalions. The assault, known to the British as the Battle of Aubers Ridge, was to be the first 'blooding' of the York and Lancaster Regiment in a British offensive – First and Second Ypres had both been defensive operations to attempt to hold the line against German attacks.

Sunday, 9 May, 'broke fine and clear, with a fresh and steady breeze from the northeast'. Edmonds went on to set the scene:

> At sunrise (4.6 a.m.) the whole battle zone appeared silent and deserted except for occasional artillery ranging shots. The front trenches and breastworks in the sectors of attack were, however, already crowded with the troops of the assaulting battalions, and the reserve and communication trenches packed with those of the supporting units.[13]

At 5 a.m., the artillery opened their preliminary bombardment, which became intense at 5.30, then, at 5.40, the guns lifted 600 yards to shell La Quinque Rue (behind the German front line), 'and the infantry moved to the attack'.[14] For both of our battalions the two days, 9 and 10 May, were much less dramatic than this opening might suggest, although two of their men had been killed. Privates Cheesborough and Heppenstall are buried in Y Farm Military Cemetery at Bois Grenier. Like many of the battalions, the first of their men to be killed were named in the war diary but this practice changed quickly as the numbers became too large; soon only officers had this privilege. For the 1/4th who had gone into the line, Lieutenant Steel was killed (also buried in Y Farm Military Cemetery at Bois Grenier) and seven men wounded due to 'a good deal of shelling by the enemy most of the morning'.[15]

Although the two York and Lancaster battalions were part of the IV Corps battle at Aubers Ridge, their involvement was very different from that of the units in the centre of the line who suffered very heavy losses. Their war diaries recorded the days of the battle as 'normal':

> 9 May; Lieut. Steel was killed by a shell. A good deal of shelling by the enemy most of morning. 7 men wounded.
> 10 May; in trenches, one killed, one died of wounds, same day 4 wounded. Some shelling by the enemy.

---

13   Edmonds, J., *Military Operations France and Belgium 1915 Volume 2* (Nashville, IWM, Reprints of 1928 original), p.17.
14   Edmonds, *1915, Vol. 2*, p.19.
15   WO 95/2805, war diary, 1/4 York and Lancs.

11 May; in trenches, 1 killed & 6 wounded, were relieved by 1/5 Y & L Regt. At 9 p.m. Returned to billets at Fleurbaix.[16]

This example serves to show that the experience of all those participating in any particular battle was not the same. The 8th Division, on the immediate right of the 49th, attacked towards Fromelles and suffered 4,684 casualties; the 49th had only 94.[17] Grant went so far as to say that for 1/4 York and Lancaster the casualty figures 'of course, seem very small in the light of after events, and prove conclusively enough that the period had been little more than an apprenticeship'.[18] This was realism leavened with hindsight, but the losses would have been none the less sobering to men in their first battle.

The attack failed disastrously, primarily because Rawlinson ignored the lessons that had been learnt at Neuve Chapelle. The fundamental importance of the artillery barrage to the infantry assault was not given the priority it deserved. The five pounds weight of shell delivered on every yard of trench at Neuve Chapelle had been reduced to only two at Aubers Ridge. The support of the guns was further degraded by two more factors. First, the guns had been used extensively in the first battle; the barrels were worn, so reducing their accuracy. Second, the weather on the days prior to the attack had not been good for spotting the fall of shot, making registration of the guns difficult. The gunners' problem was compounded by the improvement of the weather to dry and clear; the difference in the humidity between the two days changed the shells' ballistics, so nullifying much of the (poor) registration that had been done. On 9 May, the bombardment 'completely failed in its primary task, the neutralization of the enemy's fire power'. For many of the gunners this was their first experience of attempting to cut wire defences, and it showed; 'Adequate lanes had not been cut in the wire and it formed a continuous obstacle'.[19] In his summation of the battle, Edmonds made a statement that the soldiers may well have agreed with:

> As a general result, the brief 40-minutes bombardment, though it raised a curtain of dust and smoke immediately above the enemy's front line, did no appreciable damage, and merely gave the enemy warning to stand-to to meet an assault which he had been expecting.[20]

The casualty figures quoted above speak of the bravery of the men who tried to go forward in the face of German machine guns that had not been neutralized by the inadequate barrage. In his memoirs Rawlinson joined the ranks of those commanders

16 WO 95/2805, war diary, 1/4 York and Lancs.
17 Edmonds, *1915, Vol. 2*, p.39.
18 Grant, *Hallamshires*, p.19.
19 Edmonds, *1915, Vol. 2*, p.21.
20 Edmonds, *1915, Vol. 2*, p.41.

who, to cover their own failings, blamed their troops: 'I fear that the E. Lancs and some Battalions of the 25 brigade got cold feet and did not advance with the dash they ought to have done [...] The E. Lancs did not gain the enemy's trenches – it is doubtful if they tried very hard'.[21] It is sad to see commanders resorting to excuses such as this after so many men had died trying to execute a flawed plan – this won't be the only example.

At this point the narrative leaves the 1/4th and 1/5th battalions and picks up the story of 2/York and Lancaster (who we last met in Chapter 1 in action around Radinghem) and revisit the chateau at Hooge.

By the middle of November 1914, 2/York and Lancaster was in billets at Fleurbaix. On this sector 'active fighting now died away', replaced by 'constant shelling and the deadly sniping which claimed so many victims at this time'.[22] The battalion had settled into the routine of periods in and out of the line, and the damage caused to the trenches by the heavy rain:

> The weather during November and December was truly appalling. All trenches were knee-deep and more in mud and water. Parapets would not stand and were so flimsy that many men were shot through them. But the weather eventually improved, material for revetment began to appear, and by the commencement of 1915 it was possible to move in the trenches in comparative safety.[23]

At the end of December, the battalion moved again to 'very indifferent trenches' in front of Armentières. Casualties were few, 'but occurred tolerably regularly'. After nine months in Flanders, the troops were becoming habituated to daily life in the trenches in that 'unsavoury region'. The war diary frequently recorded the fall of 100-200 shells a day, on the lines and the surrounding area, but considered the situation to be 'quiet'. As well as H.E. shells, gas was now a constant threat after its first use on 22 April and diary entries record whether or not the wind was 'safe' each day.

By the middle of 1915, 2/York and Lancaster was not far from Hooge. By the summer of that year, the British and German lines in the vicinity of Hooge and Bellewaarde were, in places, only 50 yards apart. Because the Germans held the high ground of Bellewaarde Ridge, they had good observation over the British lines. Hooge, not much more than a hamlet, was 'at the apex of a very acute salient'[24] and salients invariably drew the attention of attacks with the aim of 'straightening the line'. Early on the morning of 2 June, (while the 2/York and Lancs were still at Wieltje) the Germans opened a severe bombardment on Hooge. Once the shelling stopped, at around noon, they attacked the British line and captured what remained of the chateau and adjacent

---

21 Prior and Wilson, *Command on the Western Front*, p.91.
22 Wylly, *2nd Battalion History*, p.344.
23 Wylly, *2nd Battalion History*, p.344.
24 Edmonds, *1915, Vol. 2*, p.97.

stables. Given their position in relation to the road and the local woods, a British counter-attack was almost inevitable, and this took place during the night hours of 3 June. The stables were recaptured, but the chateau – by now in ruins – remained in German hands. Ruined buildings made ideal defensive positions, so the British could not allow enemy troops to remain there without some attempt to evict them.

By this stage of the war one lesson that had been learnt, though not always acted on, was that even small attacks needed careful planning if they were to succeed. The 16 June operation was intended to 'straighten out the re-entrant between Hooge and Railway Wood';[25] the wood lay 1,000 yards to the north-west of the chateau. Although it was a relatively small assault, telegraph and phone lines were laid in triplicate, and visual signalling systems (as well as pigeons) were put in place in case the lines were cut. Additionally, the RFC was to cooperate in patrolling and artillery spotting. The attack was timed for dawn on 16 June. As was so often the case, the soldiers going 'over the top' were expected to carry a great deal of equipment about their person. As well as the standard issue Lee Enfield rifle 'each infantryman carried two extra bandoliers [of ammunition], a day's rations besides the iron ration, 2 empty sandbags and a waterproof sheet; 400 hand-grenades and 150 wire cutters and breakers per battalion were distributed, and two platoons per battalion had shovels slung on their backs'.[26] In these circumstances 'rushing' against machine guns, or crawling through barbed wire, would have been difficult. Steel helmets had not yet become regular issue, so the men were going forward into battle with soft hats. On 9 August a few helmets were tried as an experiment; 'Their value was at once evident, but, as they were strange to the troops, some of the men wearing them were in the early morning mistaken for Germans and fired on by their comrades'.[27]

In the event the operation was only partially successful and by 6 p.m., by which time much of the German front line trench had been taken (but with the ridge still held by the enemy) and it was decided to consolidate the ground won. Half a mile of German trench between the Menin Road and Railway Wood were now in British hands and 'the re-entrant had been slightly reduced'. This 'win' came at the cost of 140 officers and 3,391 men in 3 Division;[28] most of them to artillery fire. However, 2/York and Lancaster had as yet played no part in the squabble over Hooge.

By 1915 the Royal Flying Corps (RFC) had added another dimension to the battlefield and aircraft, although slow and with limited carrying capacity, were extensively used by both sides for reconnaissance and artillery spotting. On 10 July the battalion recorded that there was 'aeroplane reconnaissance activity on both sides – one German aeroplane constantly flying over our lines'. There was added interest among the troops a few days later when 'at 7.30 a.m. enemy's aeroplane hit by our anti-aircraft guns

25 Edmonds, *1915, Vol. 2*, p.98.
26 Edmonds, *1915, Vol. 2*, p.100.
27 Edmonds, *1915, Vol. 2*, p.109.
28 Edmonds, *1915, Vol. 2*, p.102.

– aeroplane turned somersault and looked as if it was coming straight down – but the pilot managed to right her and flew back to Germany'. As aircraft on both sides became more successful in the reconnaissance and artillery cooperation roles, so it became necessary to find ways to hinder or destroy them and the fighter pilot was born. It was over the trenches near Hooge that a British pilot was awarded the VC for the first RFC air-combat success. On 25 July, a Bristol Scout aircraft, flown by Captain Lanoe Hawker, attacked a German aircraft at about 10,000 feet over the village. Hawker opened fire at around 100 yards, the enemy burst into flames, turned upside down and the observer fell out to his death. The aircraft crashed, killing the pilot. The German observer, Hans Roser, was seen in his death-fall by men of the Derbyshire Territorials and recorded in their war diary; 'German aeroplane shot down & observer fell in front of our trenches'.[29] Roser is buried in the British cemetery at Sanctuary Wood. Although they were still in the area of Wieltje, the incident had been seen by men of 2/York and Lancaster; 'German Taube [the aircraft type] brought down by one of our aeroplanes – fell some distance off in the lines'.[30] The young pilots of the RFC, like their subaltern counterparts in the infantry, did not live long once they had moved to France. Captain Hawker was killed by Manfred von Richtofen, 23 November 1916, who in turn was killed 21 April 1918. Ironically, Hawker's victim, Roser, has a marked grave in a British war cemetery, Hawker's body was lost, and he has no known grave.

The American Civil War General, William Tecumseh Sherman, famously said that 'War is Hell'. This sentiment was reinforced by the German introduction to the battlefield of poison gas at Second Ypres, and then by another 'frightful' weapon at Hooge; the *Flammenwerfer* (flame thrower). The new contraption was mounted on a soldier's back and spewed burning fuel from a hand-held nozzle. The British first met this weapon on 30 July, near the stables at Hooge and the experience was recorded by 2/Lieutenant Carey of the Rifle Brigade. The men of Carey's battalion were moving forward to take over a line of trenches in the grounds of Hooge Chateau:

> The silence after we got into the line became uncanny. There was something sinister about this. About half-an-hour before dawn there was a sudden hissing sound and a bright crimson glare over the crater turned the whole scene red. I saw three or four distinct jets of flame, like a line of powerful firehoses spraying fire instead of water, shoot across my fire trench. Then every noise under heaven broke out.[31]

---

29   TNA WO 95/2694, war diary 1/6th Derbyshire Territorials.
30   WO 95/1610.
31   Connerty, I., M. Gilbert, P.Hart, L. Macdonald and N. Steel, *At The Going Down Of The Sun. 365 Soldiers From The Great War* (London, Lannoo, 2001), p.198.

Carey was given the order to pull back the remnants of his platoon to the support line but 'about a dozen men were all that I could find. Those who had faced the flame attack were never seen again'. He was the only officer from his company to survive the next 24 hours. In the fear and confusion caused by the new 'terror weapon' the Germans gained ground and the British fell back. However, 2/Lieutenant Woodroffe (9/King's Royal Rifle Corps) and his platoon held their position until all their grenades had been used. Then, leading from the front as the young subalterns were expected to do, he and his men attempted a counter-attack against a hail of rifle and machine-gun fire. Woodroffe was killed and awarded a posthumous VC.[32] His body was never found and his name is recorded on the Menin Gate Memorial at Ypres.

Before we leave the action that took place on 30 July, there is one more piece of history that became well known to the British soldiers who spent time in the area around Ypres and Hooge.

Among those killed that day was Lieutenant Gilbert Talbot, 7/Rifle Brigade. Gilbert was the son of the Bishop of Winchester and brother to Reverend Neville Talbot. In 1915 a house in Poperinghe, to the west of Ypres, was given to the army and was used as a rest-home and refuge for soldiers of all ranks. It was named Talbot House in memory of the young Lieutenant by his brother Neville and the Reverend 'Tubby' Clayton. The soldiers who used the house abbreviated its name to T(albot) H(ouse) and, as 'Toc' was a signallers way of saying the letter 'T', it has come down to posterity as TocH – the name of the society set up to run the house until the present day. The author has fond memories of being one of a small number of Boy Apprentices from all three services who were invited to Poperinghe by TocH in the early 1960s for the 50th Anniversary of the organization. During the three days we met old veterans and the venerable 'Tubby'.

The flame thrower was a hideous device, death by burning is a fear many of us would recognise. However, as in the case of poisonous gas, the Allies (after suitable comments about the barbaric way in which the Germans fought) adopted a much larger variant of the new weapon. A year later, on 1 July 1916 at the Somme, the British employed their own very large Flame Projectors near Mametz. The Livens Flame Projectors were large, static structures designed to project a flame, under pressure, some few hundred feet. These were very different to the German 'back-pack' weapons used at Hooge and produced a massive flame, which must have struck fear in any German soldier in front of them. Their effect could only be temporary as the kerosene/diesel fuel reservoir for each projector was only capable of delivering three 10-second bursts of flame; death by incineration would have been the result. The remains of one of the machines was found and excavated by Channel 4 *Time Team* in 2010.[33]

---

32   Edmonds, *1915, Vol. 2*, p.105, fn.1.
33   There is a short video on YouTube which shows the effect of these machines.

Following the attempts on 30/31 July to retake the gains made by the Germans (14 Division, on the right of the 6th, had been driven back), it was clear that 'nothing but a regular attack, thoroughly prepared – as distinguished from a hasty counter-attack – would dislodge the enemy'.[34] On 30 July, 2/York and Lancaster received the order 'to be ready to move at a moment's notice to support 14th Division at Hooge – 2 sandbags per man to be carried'. On 3 August, they were told that 6 Division would be required to retake those positions lost during the action on 30 July. To that end the division (including 2/York and Lancs) during the night of 5/6 August, 'quietly and unnoticed', moved round to relieve 14 Division in their positions facing the chateau and stables.

The first few days of August – the lull between two attacks – had been relatively quiet for the York and Lancaster men, but their war diary does make a few notes, which throw a little more light on battalion life. The first demonstrates that a man could make the massive leap from the lowly rank of Private and find himself in the Officers' Mess. Private J.A. Ellor was posted to the battalion, from the Civil Service Rifles and the cadet school at St Omer, in the temporary rank of 2nd Lieutenant, effective from 24 July. The second point indicates how the make-up of the battalion had changed since leaving England: the Adjutant noted in the diary the numbers of officers and men who were still with the unit and had come out together on the first move to France; approximately 1,000 had landed in France, of which 399 were still with the battalion. Third, as we have seen before, quiet periods did not mean 'no casualties'. On 6 August, 2/Lieutenant George Munson was killed. Munson was 30 years old and had a wife, Lilla, in Beverley, Yorkshire. He was probably a Regular soldier as he had been a Staff Sergeant in the Army Gymnastic Staff before he was commissioned. On the following day, Captain Henry Rycroft, age 36, was also killed; he had been on detachment from 3/York and Lancaster battalion. Both of these officers are buried side by side in Sanctuary Wood Cemetery, about 800 yards south of Hooge.

As part of the 'thorough' planning for the operation to regain the ground lost at the end of July, some improved level of communication had to be implemented. Wireless sets, where they existed, were too large to be carried by a soldier, and very few aircraft were fitted with them. Telephone wires were notorious for being cut by artillery fire and once an attack started the commander often had to rely on his subalterns and SNCOs doing 'the right thing' – it was almost impossible for the ground commander to know where they were and even harder to talk to them. In an attempt to obviate the problem, the Operation Orders included visual signalling systems, but these would only work with line of sight and on clear days. The following is taken from the orders for 9 August; the attack was timed to start at 03:15 when it would hardly have been light:

> <u>Yellow Screens</u> will be issued, these are to be put up when advancing companies can get no further without artillery support.

---

34 Edmonds, *1915, Vol. 2*, p.106.

Aubers Ridge and Hooge 53

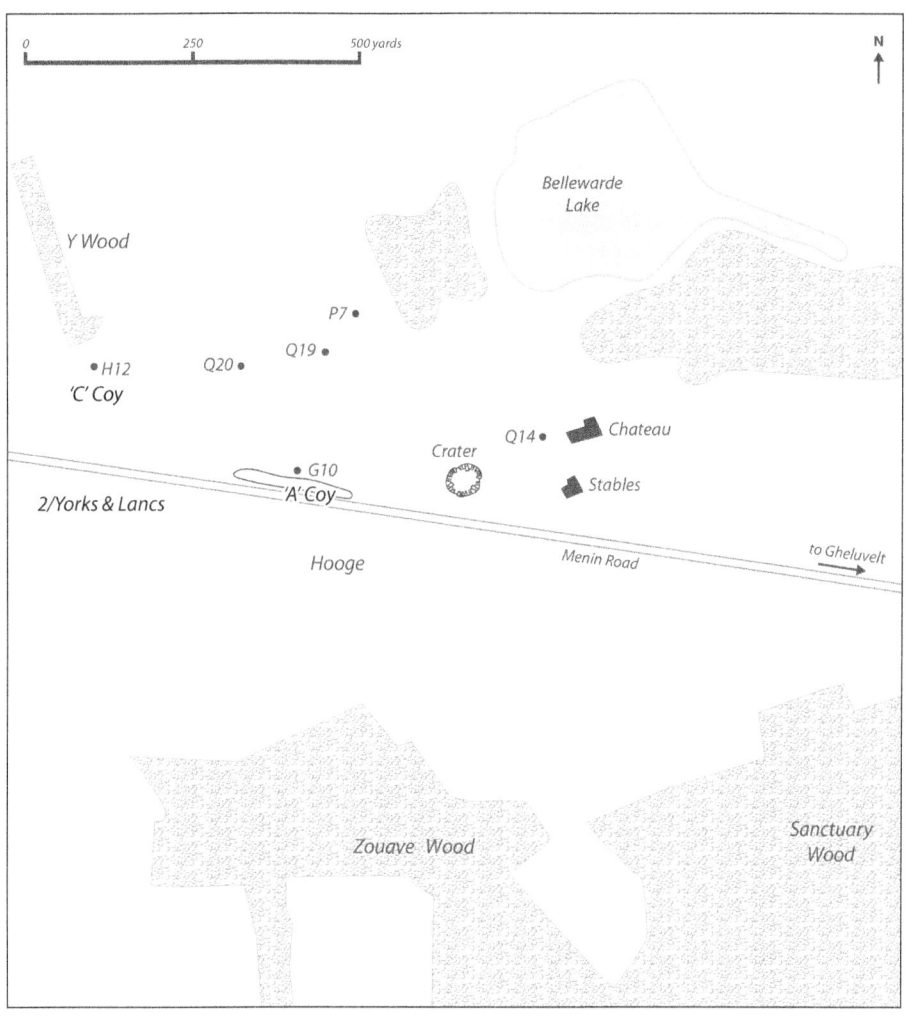

Map 5 2/York & Lancaster at Hooge, August 1915.

> Blue and Yellow flags will be issued, these are to be given to selected NCOs to wave as a signal to artillery if our shells are falling short.
> Green and Yellow flags, 2 to 'A' Company, 3 to 'C' Company, these to be given to bombers [grenade throwers] to mark their progress.[35]

35 WO 95/1610.

The written instructions for this relatively small assault were long and detailed, causing the Official Historian to remark that this was a 'complete change from the short attack orders of the first days of the war';[36] early signs, perhaps, of the 'learning curve'.[37] Additionally, 'all details were carefully explained to all taking part in the attack'.[38]

The weather in the week prior to the attack was changeable, 'but usually wet', and as a result it was postponed from 8 August to the 9th. Patrols, which had been sent out to inspect the enemy's wire, found that there was 'practically none in front of the enemy's trenches'. It was now time to put the careful preparations into play: 'Midnight of the 8th Aug. everything was in readiness for the attack and the companies started moving into their battle positions'. Two brigades of 6 Division were assigned to the assault; the 18th (on the right) and 16th (on the left). On 16 Brigade front, the leading battalions were 2/York and Lancs on the left and 1/King's Shropshire Light Infantry (KSLI) on their right. 18 Brigade were positioned along the edges of Zouave and Sanctuary Woods and would have a long advance, across open ground, before reaching the Menin Road. The start-line for 2/York and Lancs (Map 5) was in the shape of an 'L'; 'C' company was in the trench at H12, at right angles to the Menin Road, with 'A' company at G10, running along it. The front to be captured by 16 Brigade 'extended from the CRATER to Q20 – pushing on and consolidating [the line] Q14 – Q19 and just S[outh] of P7'. 'A' company, 2/York and Lancs, would have the shortest advance in the brigade. Both brigades were to converge on the crater, moving on from there to the consolidation line at Q14-Q19. While A and C companies advanced to the attack, B and D were to follow behind carrying 'ammunition, bombs, tools, sandbags etc., and had orders to start digging back communication trenches as soon as the position was gained'.[39]

The following extracts from the battalion diary give a sense of how the action progressed. The artillery bombardment began at 2.45 a.m. on 9 August and 20 minutes later A and C companies moved forward to attack. At 3.15 the barrage lifted and both companies 'dashed forward to the assault – the enemy's trench was captured with practically no resistance from enemy infantry. German artillery and Bombers [grenade throwers] were very active'. In this rush, about 20 prisoners were captured; a great many Germans, killed and wounded, were found in the trench:

> The captured position was well knocked about by our artillery but the trench was deep and well built – with a very good field of fire. The enemy were also seen to be evacuating their second line trenches and running back – these were caught by our artillery and also machine guns which had rushed up with [the] first line and were quickly in position.

36   Edmonds, *1915, Vol. 2*, p.106.
37   Sheffield, G., *The Chief: Douglas Haig and the British Army* (London, Aurum, 2011), p.372.
38   WO 95/1610.
39   WO 95/1610.

Throughout the war, when British troops captured German trenches they were invariably impressed with the depth and strength of their defensive lines and any attached dugouts.

Having captured the German trench, the next step was consolidation. At 3.17 a.m., a section from the Royal Engineers (following the attack waves) 'passed through the front line and began to wire the position. Supporting lines moved forward with ammunition, bombs, tools etc. and started to dig back communication trenches'. The initial push forward had gone well and at 3.50, (only 35 minutes after the attack had started) the situation was judged to be 'satisfactory', although the new position was now being heavily bombarded by the enemy's trench mortars and artillery. The battalion's right flank, however, was not in contact with 1/KSLI who had attacked from their start line, south of the Menin Road. This situation continued for some time and at 4.30 the 'situation on right flank [was] not quite clear. KSLI required further artillery support. This shows how confused a First World War battlefield could be as the York and Lancaster front was only 200 yards long and yet they were unaware of the state of the battalion on their right. The only method of communication between the company commanders on the two battalions' fronts was by 'runner' – a very risky job for the man chosen. At 4.45 the situation of 1/KSLI had become 'urgent' and their battalion commander had to request 2/York and Lancaster for support; one platoon (about 40-50 men) was sent forward from 'D' company which had been held in battalion reserve. The support obviously helped; by 7.55, the whole situation was deemed to be 'well in hand' and two hours later the German artillery fire was 'dying down'. This brief action, in which 2/York and Lancaster was on the attacking, rather than defending side (as they had been in their previous actions), was now effectively over:

> 105 of the enemy including 3 officers came from the direction of the CRATER & gave themselves up. Mostly Wurtemburgers of the 126th & 132nd Regts. Situation very quiet and we continued to consolidate the position and improve communications.

The operation on 9 August was a success but as 2/York and Lancaster was relieved that night by 1/Buffs, and went back to the huts near Ypres, the men would have had little appreciation of how the battle had progressed outside their own battalion front. The Official History was very positive stating that the assaults cut right through the German lines, 'the leading officers and men being in the enemy front trench immediately – some even before – the barrage lifted; *practically the only opposition came from a few bombers* [my emphasis]. The two brigades joined hands at the crater, where there was a melée of hand-to-hand fighting, and recovered the whole front of 700 yards that had been lost'.[40]

---

40   Edmonds, *1915, Vol. 2*, p.108.

The operation may have gone well but the Germans did not give ground easily and quickly launched their own counter-attack to recover what had just been re-gained by 16 and 18 Brigades; 'a very heavy enemy bombardment compelled the evacuation, during the night [10 August], of part of the trenches east of Hooge'. During their involvement, 2/York and Lancaster suffered 293 casualties. Of these, 4 officers and 197 ORs were wounded, 4 officers and 44 men were killed while a further 44 were missing, believed killed. The opposition was stiffer than Edmonds' earlier comment – *a few bombers* – implies. As ever, close inspection of the lists of names in CWGC cemeteries and on their Memorials to the Missing, make for sober reflection. It would appear that all the 'missing' were killed. In situations where No Man's Land was very narrow, it was very difficult for either side to recover all the bodies of the dead. When an attack was followed up by a heavy artillery bombardment, as in this case, then the ground between the front lines (and any bodies lying there) would be badly knocked about – the dead would be rendered unrecognisable. The Menin Gate Memorial in Ypres records 85 men of 2/York and Lancaster killed on 9 August, all with no known graves – almost every man from the battalion who was killed that day. Sanctuary Wood Cemetery, where many of the dead from the Ypres salient are buried, has a similarly sad tale to tell. Of the 1,989 First World War burials at this site, 1,353 of them are of men whose identities are not known, except 'unto God'. Lieutenant Gilbert Talbot, who we met earlier in relation to TocH, is buried in Plot 1, very close to the Great Cross. His brother, Neville, made the first list of the graves at this site; he later went on to become Bishop of Pretoria.

For all the loss, the operation had gone well and that must be put down to the planning that had been done beforehand, as well as the bravery and determination of the men. Sir John French referred to it as 'one of the best conducted of the smaller operations of the campaign'.[41]

Once out of the line, battalions quickly reverted to 'routine' and new troops started arriving to make up the losses, by 13 August three drafts, totalling 250 men, had joined and at the end of the month, 2/York and Lancaster was back up to 22 officers and 906 ORs. The constant loss and replenishment would have been a continuous reminder to the individual soldiers of the likelihood of their joining the casualty statistics. On 9 September, the adjutant made a note in the war diary:

> One year of war. Number of Officers, WOs, NCOs and men at present with Bn. who came out on 9th Sept. 1914. [...] 7 Officers, 5 WOs, 33 NCOs and 196 men.

A sobering result; just 241 out of the 928 members of the battalion had been with them since the start, 681 had gone – some were posted to other units but the majority had been casualties. In the British Army the Warrant Officers (WOs) and SNCOs were its 'backbone', these men were the most experienced, many were pre-war Regulars

---

41 WO 95/1610.

and they were the cadre to which the Other Ranks looked when the going got tough – their loss was hard to replace. A battalion had approximately 90 of these men, spread through its four companies, HQ, machine gun and other specialist sections. With only 38 remaining after a year, 2/York and Lancaster had lost almost 60% of this valuable resource.

The year came to a close with the battalion being relieved from the front line by 1/KSLI, at 10 p.m. on Christmas Day. Although 26-28 December were noted in the diary as rest days, there is no mention of any Christmas meal or other seasonal activities – let us hope they had one and it just went unrecorded. By New Year, they had moved back to the line, replacing 1/KSLI in trenches in the La Brique sector of the Salient. 1915 came to an end with battalion strength at 815 – 27 officers, and 788 ORs.

Our narrative now moves far from the trenches of France and Flanders, to the Dardanelles and the Gallipoli peninsula. For the men of 6/York and Lancaster (and the author's grandfather) their introduction to the war was to be against the Turks, in a theatre quite different from that of the Western front.

4

Gallipoli – the 6th Battalion at Suvla Bay

At the time of writing (2015) and for the next three years, Britain will commemorate many centenaries of the events of the First World War, the majority of them focusing on the battles of the Western front. However, to see that conflict only through the prism of the Somme and Passchendaele is to ignore the geographic scale of the conflict, as well as the bravery and sacrifice of those who fought on other fronts.

At the outbreak of war, the British Army was very small; the country did not maintain a large, permanent army such as those in France, Germany, and Russia. Britain had traditionally relied for its security on the power of its navy, both to protect its Empire and the trade routes that were so vital to its economy. To make up for its small army Britain, when it needed to fight on Continental soil, had paid other nations to provide additional troops. In contrast to the size of the army, Britain's navy was immensely powerful, with 24 Dreadnought battleships against Germany's 13. Additionally Britain had a further 13 under construction, while the Germans had just two.[1] In political control of the navy was Winston Churchill, First Lord of the Admiralty, and a man who (whether in the Boer War, the First or Second World War) was always able to think up new schemes for action – not all of them fully considered or likely to succeed. The operation at the Dardanelles was one such. Looking for an advantage which did not involve 'sending our armies to chew barbed wire in Flanders' was admirable, but to his question on whether the 'power of the Navy [might] be brought to bear directly upon the enemy'[2] the answer was – not in this case.

Lloyd George, Chancellor of the Exchequer, was also considering alternatives to the direct assaults, which were causing such loss of life on the Western front. At a meeting of the Committee of Imperial Defence (CID) in January 1915, he presented a paper in which he proposed that 'some alternative ought to be sought' to the current strategy. His suggestion was to attack Germany's weaker allies, so 'knocking the props

---

1   Prior, R., *Gallipoli. The End Of The Myth* (Padstow, Yale, 2009), p.1.
2   Prior, *Gallipoli*, p.10.

[from] under her'.³ In the light of what would come to pass at Gallipoli, a comment at the end of that paper was almost prophetic;

> Expeditions decided upon and organised with insufficient care and preparation generally end disastrously.

Churchill put forward various suggestions for using the Navy and the one adopted was the Dardanelles. A large fleet, mainly consisting of near obsolete vessels so that any failure of the mission would not seriously risk British naval strength, would bombard and neutralise the Turkish forts and then 'force' its way through the Straits. One historian has described the British operation as one of 'opportunity' in which the strategic goal was ambiguous.⁴ The first flaw in the plan was the assumption that naval guns, at sea-level, could destroy forts and guns on the heights above them. The plan was predicated on the success that the Germans had had against the heavy guns in the Belgian fortresses of Liège and Namur, in 1914. However, there was a major difference; the Germans had employed heavy howitzers against those cities. In its findings into the failure of the naval operation, the Dardanelles Commission⁵ made a number of comments on the comparable efficacy of howitzers and ship-mounted guns.

In the case of the howitzer:

> 1. The projectile descends at such an obtuse angle that it clears the parapet or vertical defence of the guns in the forts.
> 2. The steep angle of descent enables the projectiles to clear any hills in front of the forts and also to reach batteries in concealed positions.

In the case of guns mounted on ships:

> 1. [They] cannot be given sufficient elevation to obtain high-angle fire similar to howitzers.
> 2. Guns, owing to the small angles of descent, are not able to attack concealed forts and batteries.

In summary:

> Looking to all the facts of the case, we [the Commission] are disposed to think that undue importance was attached to the ease with which the Belgian forts

---

3   TNA WO 106/308, Lloyd George memo to Committee of Imperial Defence, 1 January 1915.
4   Erickson, E.J., *Gallipoli: Command Under Fire* (Oxford, Osprey, 2015), p.53.
5   *The World War 1 Collection. Gallipoli and the Early Battles, 1914-15. The Dardanelles Commission* (London, The Stationery Office, 2001), pp.51-2.

were destroyed, and that the extent to which there was any analogy between those forts and the forts at the Dardanelles was over-rated.[6]

The decision to prepare for a naval operation to bombard the Gallipoli peninsula was taken by the War Council on 28 January 1915. In the light of Lloyd George's comment (above) on expeditions decided upon with insufficient care, and the lives that would be lost on that sun-soaked spit of rocky ground, it is worth citing some of the points from the Commission's report. The proceedings of the War Council in making their decision were considered to have had an 'atmosphere of vagueness and want of precision'.[7] In putting forward the plan, Churchill 'was carried away by his [own] sanguine temperament and his firm belief in the success of the undertaking which he advocated'. Too much stress was laid upon the advantages of the operation and the 'disadvantages which would arise in the not improbable case of failure were insufficiently considered'.[8] In its original conception, the navy would force the Straits without the involvement of ground troops; 6/York and Lancaster found itself fighting on the peninsula because the original plan could not hold. Lord Grey (Secretary of State for Foreign Affairs) told the Commission that consent for the operation had been granted because the War Council had been 'distinctly told [...] that the troops would not be asked for; that if the Navy could not carry out the operation by itself, the operation would not be proceeded with'.[9] Although some voices advocated the plan on the basis that the navy would be successful on its own, there were others, like Admiral Sir Henry Jackson (a Staff Officer), who believed that soldiers would be necessary:

> The naval bombardment is not recommended as a sound military operation, unless a strong military force is ready to assist in the operation, or, at least, follow it up immediately the forts are silenced.[10]

On 19 February, the War Council concluded that the operation could not be conducted as a purely naval affair, there would need to be 'boots on the ground'. Kitchener decided to use Australian and New Zealand troops, at that time in Egypt; 'the slippery slope to the Gallipoli operation had begun'[11] – today we call it 'mission creep'. At the same time as the War Council was making it decision on the involvement of troops, the navy began its bombardment of the Turkish forts at the Dardanelles, the shelling would yield depressingly few results. The nadir of the naval operation came on 18 March when three battleships (*Irresistible*, *Ocean*, and the French *Bouvet*) were sunk by a combination of mines and shore-battery fire. There was now no question

6   *Dardanelles Commission*, p.53.
7   *Dardanelles Commission*, p.46.
8   *Dardanelles Commission*, p.59.
9   *Dardanelles Commission*, p.48.
10 *Dardanelles Commission*, p.61.
11 Prior, *Gallipoli*, p.34.

that, if the Dardanelles were to be forced, troops would have to be landed on the peninsula of Gallipoli.[12]

On 25 April, the soldiers of Britain, India, France, Australia, and New Zealand (the latter two nationalities being frequently referred to as 'Anzacs') began their landings on the peninsula. British troops went ashore on the southern tip at Cape Helles, the French on the Asiatic entrance to the Straits at Kum Kale, and the Anzacs on a beach some 15 miles up the west coast of the peninsula; Anzac Cove. The conditions under which the men from the southern hemisphere fought and lived for the subsequent eight months have become part of what it means to be an Australian or a New Zealander. A century later, authors are still exploring the Anzac 'myth'[13] and the operational and campaign-level decisions that led to the failure of the whole venture.[14] Although the Anzacs have co-opted Gallipoli, and (in their eyes) made it 'theirs', many French, Indian, and British soldiers similarly suffered and lost their lives. In *Hell's Foundations*[15] Geoffrey Moorhouse recounts the exploits of the Lancashire Fusiliers and their 'six VCs before breakfast'. Because Gallipoli is so closely associated with Australia (Peter Weir's film, starring Mel Gibson, is to Gallipoli what Blackadder is to the Western front) it is easy to overlook the fact that many more British soldiers were killed there than Australians, as were those from France and its African colonies. On a personal level, the conflict at the eastern end of the Mediterranean was also the point at which the author's grandfather became involved in the fighting war. Private Patrick Dillon, a council labourer from Owlerton, Sheffield, joined 6/York and Lancaster on the peninsula in early September, four weeks after 11 Division had gone ashore at Suvla Bay.

Private Patrick Dillon. (Photo J. Dillon)

12 The interested reader might want to delve further into these operations via the books of Tim Travers, Robin Prior and Alan Moorehead.
13 Macleod, J., *Gallipoli: Great Battle Series* (Oxford, OUP, 2015).
14 Erickson, *Gallipoli: Command Under Fire*.
15 Moorhouse, G., *Hell's Foundations. A Town, its Myths and Gallipoli* (London, Hodder & Stoughton, 1992).

In spite of the bravery and stoicism of the troops on the ground, no real progress was being made against the Turks but there was to be no withdrawal. In February, Kitchener had told the War Council that 'The effect of a defeat in the Orient would be very serious. There could be no going back'.[16] The effect of a defeat of British troops, by a non-European nation, on the colonies of the Empire did not bear thinking about in Whitehall.

The commander chosen for the combined operations was Sir Ian Hamilton; the chalice he was handed was poisoned. In their later report, the Dardanelles Commission posed the rhetorical question, "Was Sir Ian Hamilton the right man to command the expedition?" In their answer, they stated that he had been 'hurriedly despatched, imperfectly instructed, and inadequately provided with men, artillery and munitions'. Further, the General Staff were criticised for sending him without either 'a worked-out plan of attack or such primary requirements as verified or complete maps of the peninsula'.[17] With the whole expedition going so badly, 'Englishmen demanded a whipping boy [...] and Churchill, the ostentatious poseur, was the obvious choice'.[18] In May, he was replaced by Admiral Sir Henry Jackson. In July, General William Birdwood (commanding Anzac forces and reporting to Hamilton) had put forward a proposal for implementation in August. In its final iteration, Birdwood's plan required the Anzacs to take the heights of Sari Bair (in the middle of the peninsula) while General Sir Frederick Stopford and the newly created IX Corps landed at Suvla Bay and moved to protect Birdwood's left flank. As hard as they tried, the objective set for the Anzac forces was too difficult. The distance, the height of the ridge, and the lack of artillery support, all conspired to ensure that men, many of whom had spent months within the small perimeter of the enclave at Anzac Cove, were just not able to do all that was asked of them. No snub is intended to those brave men at Cape Helles and Anzac Cove as this narrative leaves them, to concentrate on the August landing of 6/York and Lancaster battalion.

The 6th battalion (32 Brigade) was formed on 19 August 1914 as part of the 11th (Northern) Division; its three Infantry Brigades were the 32nd, 33rd and 34th. From their formation until April 1915, the battalion was based near Grantham, after which it moved to Witley near Godalming. While there the troops were inspected by the King and although congratulated on their 'splendid appearance and steadiness' (a stock phrase following all such inspections) their equipment, largely sourced from America, was not replaced by British kit until June of that year.[19] No doubt, like others who had not yet seen war and its horrors, the men were keen to be on their way; 'at last at the end of June the order to proceed overseas was received' and as so often, it was to

---

16 *Dardanelles Commission*, p.63.
17 *Dardanelles Commission*, p.266.
18 Manchester, W., *The Last Lion. Winston Spencer Churchill. Visions of Glory 1874-1932* (Boston, Little Brown, 1983), p.562.
19 Wylly, H.C., *The History of the York and Lancaster Regiment, Volume 2* (London, 1930), pp.116-7.

'an unknown destination'.[20] During the late evening of 1 July the battalion marched, in two parties, to Milford Haven railway station where they entrained for Liverpool; a total of 29 officers and 929 men.

On 2 July, they embarked on the *Aquitania*, the largest ship then afloat. The prospect of the journey must have been quite exciting to men who had seen little outside the industrial cities around Sheffield. Being so large, the ship took six battalions on board, all of 32 Brigade plus two battalions from the 34th – almost 6,000 soldiers in rather cramped quarters. As the battalion history noted, it would have been 'a fine bag for an enemy submarine'. At 1.45 p.m. on 3 July, the ship slipped away from the berth to begin its journey to the eastern Mediterranean. The risk to troopships from German submarines was real:

> We sailed about mid-day on Saturday, the 3rd July, and were escorted by two destroyers to a point between the Scilly Islands and Cape Ushant at about 5 a.m. on the Sunday morning. Ten minutes after their departure a German submarine fired a torpedo at us, she missed us by a few feet astern – the torpedo being diverted by our immense wash. Shortly after passing Gibraltar another German submarine was sighted, but luckily for us she was engaged in taking in fuel oil at the time.[21]

One officer recalled being woken at 5.40 a.m. 'by a flustered steward' and by the time that he and others were on deck, many in pyjamas, 'all that was to be seen of the fight was a very dim curl of smoke over the horizon behind us'.[22] A little of the magic of the trip, especially once through the Straits of Gibraltar, is captured by Lieutenant Priestman in the letters to his mother. As they passed the Rock, they sailed close to the African shore, which he described as 'simple dream country'. There were 'funny little Moorish houses and mosques' and the rocks and mountains made him think of 'brigand caravans and pirates and all sorts of jolly things'.[23] His letter also hints at the more relaxed time the officers would have had on board compared with the men; 'To lie in a deck chair and watch all these exciting things slide past is really quite enjoyable. We are all in shorts and helmets now and my knees are brick-red to-night!' They may not have had the comfort of a deck chair, but the men were probably equally excited by the views of foreign and exotic lands.

The army hated idle hands, and 6,000 men on a ship needed to be given a routine to keep them busy. The 12th battalion[24] diary gives an insight into how its soldiers were kept occupied on the way to Egypt in December 1915:

20   Wylly, *6th Battalion History*, p.117.
21   Wylly, *6th Battalion History*, p.117.
22   Priestman, E.Y., *With a B-P Scout in Gallipoli* (Naval & Military Press reprint of 1916 original), pp.103-4.
23   Priestman, *B-P Scout*, p.113.
24   TNA WO 95/4590, war diary, 12/York and Lancaster.

Reveille 6 a.m.
Muster parade 10 a.m.
Lights out 9.30 p.m.
Guard mounting 8 a.m.
Troop-decks cleared 8.30 a.m.
Troops allowed below 11 a.m.
Troop-decks cleared 1 p.m.
Troops allowed below 6.30 p.m.
Physical training daily
Marching order parade once per week.

Although they were not involved on the Gallipoli peninsular, the 12th, 13th and 14th battalions of the York and Lancaster Regiment were serving in the Egyptian theatre at this time. All three were part of the Suez Canal defence force. The 12th sailed from Devonport at 11.45 a.m. on 21 December 1915 on SS *Nestor* (a Blue Funnel Line ship), arriving at Alexandria on 4 January. The three battalions remained in Egypt until early March 1916. The 12th (with some of the 14th) sailed on HMT *Briton* from Port Said on 10 March, arriving in Marseilles on the afternoon of the 15th – all three battalions were destined for the Battle of the Somme.

On 10 July, 6/York and Lancaster disembarked at Mudros Bay on the island of Lemnos, some 40 miles south-east of Cape Helles. Between their arrival and their later landing at Suvla Bay, the men would be subjected to the normal army 'buggering about' that was often the result of poor planning and organization. In between orders given and rescinded for their embarkation, the men were inoculated against cholera, an important precaution given the problems they would have with water on the peninsula. Finally, at 6 p.m. on 22 July, 28 officers and 864 other ranks boarded S.S. *Uganda* for the journey to the island of Imbros, only some 10 miles off the west coast of the peninsula. Before leaving, they had been re-joined by a draft of men who had been left behind at Lemnos, bringing their strength up to 29 officers and 928 ORs.[25]

The troops waiting at Imbros had trained as infantrymen, but that had not included any of the skills that would be needed to participate in an amphibious landing on a defended beach. On 31 July, they practiced 'embarking on lighters and effecting a landing'. For the intended operation to be successful, certain basic prerequisites needed to be in place; full briefings for brigade, battalion and company commanders; maps of the area over which the troops would be fighting; sufficient ammunition and water to hand for the men; a clear artillery plan to support the infantry; clear lines of communication and control. Aspinall's Official History[26] is replete with examples of poor staff work, resulting in the men on the ground having little of the above.

25 Wylly, *6th Battalion History*, p.118.
26 Aspinall-Oglander, C.F., *Military Operations Gallipoli*, Volume 2 (Uckfield, *Naval & Military Press*, Reprint of 1931 original).

The officers who were expected to lead their men ashore had been kept in the dark regarding the plans for the attack. Throughout the days of preparation, there had been an obsessive focus on secrecy by Hamilton. On the night of the landing 'many of the officers of the 11th Division had never seen a map of the area in which they suddenly found themselves, and had little or no idea of what was required of them'.[27] Little wonder that there was confusion on the beaches; 'not until the forenoon of the 6th August' were the regimental officers told of their departure for the peninsula. Additionally, they had to wait until they were aboard the lighters taking them to the shore 'before the subordinate leaders were given any inkling of the task that lay in front of them'.[28]

The battalion history summarises Hamilton's plan for the operations that began on 6 August:

1. A feint was to be made at the head of the Gulf of Saros, as if to take the Bulair Lines in flank and rear.
2. A strong offensive was to be made in the Helles area against Achi Baba with the hope of attracting the Turkish reserve to Krithia.
3. The Anzac Corps was to endeavour to gain the heights of Khoja Chemen Tepe and the seaward ridges.
4. A simultaneous and new landing was to be effected in Suvla Bay.

If then the Anafarta Hills could be seized (the Turks were believed to have only five battalions in the vicinity of the bay),[29] and the right of the Suvla Bay force be linked up with the left of the Australians, the British would hold the crest of the uplands running through the western end of the Peninsula, cutting the Turkish communications and leading to the capture of the Achi Baba and the Pasha Dagh tableland.[30] Wylly's battalion history provides a description of the terrain at Suvla and an appreciation of the task facing IX Corps:

> The hinterland of Suvla Bay consists of a rectangle of hills lying north of the Asmak Dere watercourse, and connected towards the east with the outflankers of the Khoja Chemen Tepe system. The north side, lining the Asmak Dere and breaking down into flats two miles from the sea, is a blunt ridge, rising as much as 800 feet, of which the western part is Yilghin Burnu, called by our troops Chocolate Hill. The eastern side of the rectangle is a rocky crest, rising in one part to nearly 900 feet, and falling shorewards in two well-marked terraces. Between the three sides of the hills, from the eastern terraces to the sea, the

---

27 Aspinall, *Gallipoli*, p.140.
28 Aspinall, *Gallipoli*, p.232.
29 Aspinall, *Gallipoli*, p.128.
30 Wylly, *6th Battalion History*, p.119.

ground is nearly flat. Along the edge of Suvla Bay runs a narrow causeway of sand, and immediately behind it is the Salt Lake, partly dry in summer, but easily converted by rain into a swamp. East of this the hills and flats are patched with farms and low jungle, mostly dwarf oak, and on the edge of the terraces the scrub grows into something of the nature of woodland; everywhere the plain is seamed by dry watercourses. In the Suvla Bay hinterland are the two villages of Big and Little Anafarta.[31]

What is not obvious from the description was how big a problem would be the supply of water to the fighting troops, all of it would have to come ashore from the lighters and it would be desperately needed in that hot climate.

Because of the later controversy over the various failures at Gallipoli – reference has already been made to the Dardanelles Commission – it should be mentioned here that one of the causes of confusion at command level was the purpose of the Suvla Bay landings. Were they to be part of an aggressive move by IX Corps on the left flank of the Anzacs, or were they merely to establish a port through which supplies could be landed to support future operations? One historian argues that Stopford had told GHQ that his corps could not help the Anzac attack on Koja Cimen Tepe [Khoja Chemen Tepe], although he did aim to capture Chocolate Hill and W Hills, preferably at night.[32] Both of these heights were believed to have Turkish guns on them, which could fire into the flank of the Anzac assault. Stopford believed that it was 'improbable that I shall be able to give direct assistance to the GOC, Anzac, in his attack on Hill 305 [Koja Cimen Tepe]'. Whether or not the Suvla Bay landings were primarily aimed at the securing of a port, Hamilton would put Stopford up as the scapegoat for the failure of the Anzac assault – he claimed that Stopford had not been sufficiently aggressive.

Major-General Hammersley's 11 Division was to land on the evening of 6 August, the three brigades landing on different beaches (Map 6). Immediately the researcher becomes confused. In the report of the Dardanelles Commission, 32 Brigade was 'to land at Beach C'. All the maps show that this beach was south of Nibrunesi Point.[33] Travers states that '32 and 33 Brigades [...] landed at A and B Beaches respectively'.[34] Prior is different again; 'The 32 and 33 Brigades would land at night on two adjacent beaches (B and C) outside the bay'.[35] In those three accounts, the brigade lands on all three beaches. A fourth, and very recent account, has both the 32nd and 33rd Brigades landing together on B Beach.[36] The point at which the brigade went ashore is obviously important to the researcher as it is difficult to follow the written accounts of the

31 Wylly, *6th Battalion History*, pp.119-20.
32 Travers, T., *Gallipoli 1915* (Stroud, Tempus, 2004), p.181.
33 *Dardanelles Commission*, p.167.
34 Travers, *Gallipoli*, p.189.
35 Prior, *Gallipoli*, p.192.
36 Erickson, E.J., *Gallipoli. Command Under Fire*, p.199.

Gallipoli – the 6th Battalion at Suvla Bay 67

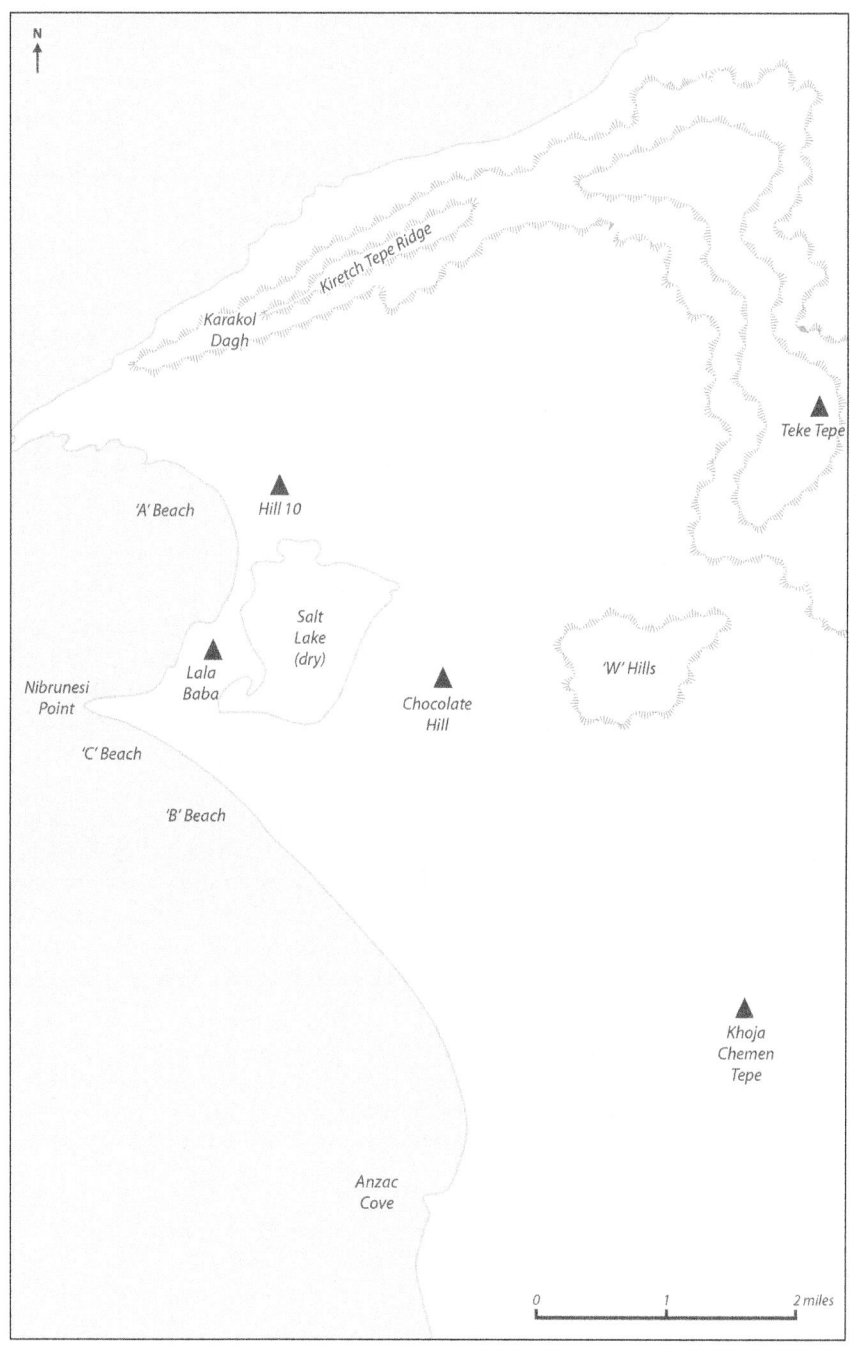

Map 6 Suvla Bay, August 1915.

action, if the start point is in dispute. Could Hamilton help, after all, it was his operation? In his Last Despatch, he stated that 'the 32nd and 33rd Brigades [landed] at B and C beaches, the 34th at A beach'.[37] Unfortunately, the battalion history only causes further confusion by declaring that 'the 32nd Brigade was to land at Suvla Point',[38] which lay at the very north of Suvla Bay and outside all three beaches. In his history of 6/York and Lancaster, Wylly includes a map on which he draws the landing point of the battalion as being on the beach immediately to the west of Lala Baba. He seems not to have noticed that this is not at Suvla Point (which he had stated was the landing point and had marked on his map), nor is it on any of the three beaches. This author believes that Aspinall's Official History is correct; 32 and 33 Brigades both land on B Beach, with 32 on the left of 33. In a footnote, Aspinall makes a point that the other historians seem to have missed:

> B and C Beaches were practically adjoining. The northern half (C Beach) was to be reserved for disembarking horses, guns and vehicles, as the shore was more steep-to there. All the dismounted troops were to land on the southern half (B Beach).[39]

After embarking in two lighters, and then transferring to the destroyer *Racoon*, the battalion set off as part of a convoy of 7 destroyers and 7 motor-lighters containing 32 and 33 brigades, 500 men in each vessel. All battalions had embarked 750 men, the remainder staying behind as first reinforcement drafts. The lighters were to be towed by the destroyers to within 500 yards of the beach at which point they would cast off, land their men and then return to pick up a second load of 500 soldiers from the destroyer. This meant that the two brigades would be disembarked in two waves.[40] Once ashore the plan called for Lala Baba, Suvla Point, the crest of the Kiretch Tepe ridge and the Turkish piquet posts on Tekke Tepe, to be gained by daylight on 7 August. Following the taking of these objectives, there would be attacks on the Chocolate and W Hills. Based on incorrect intelligence (the southern slopes were 'little more formidable than those on the northern side',[41] being only a few strands of rusty wire), it was decided that the attack on these hills would be from the north of the Salt Lake. On the evening of 6 August:

> The battalion left [Imbros] harbour at 8 p.m. with the rest of the 11th Division, making for Suvla Bay, whence at 11.30 that night the 6th Yorkshire and the 9th West Yorkshire Regiments, having made good the landing, advanced to and

37 Hamilton, I., *The Tragic Story of The Dardanelles. Hamilton's Final Despatch* (Naval & Military Press, Reprint of 1916 original), p.86.
38 Wylly, *6th Battalion History*, p.120.
39 Aspinall, *Gallipoli*, p.224, footnote 1.
40 Aspinall, *Gallipoli*, p.225.
41 Aspinall, *Gallipoli*, p.141.

"A" Beach. Suvla Bay. August 1915. (IWM Q 57866)

took Lala Baba, moving on to the further slope of that hill; by 12.30 a.m. on the 7th the 8th West Riding and the 6th York and Lancaster had also landed and were moving forward in support, the battalion in four lines at two hundred yards interval. So far no opposition had been met with, and the Brigade was assembled during the early hours of the 7th on the reverse slopes of Lala Baba, remaining in position until dawn, with the two leading battalions holding the crest line and the remaining two in support.[42]

The men of 6/York and Lancaster had got ashore relatively unscathed and pushed on 'through sweet, sickly-smelling scrub' and while the first two battalions had had contact with the Turkish defenders of Lala Baba, the 6th had arrived 'without a casualty';[43] they were one of seven battalions on Lala Baba who 'had not yet been

---

42   Wylly, *6th Battalion History*, p.120.
43   Priestman, *B-P Scout*, p.168.

in action'.⁴⁴ As soon as it was light (around 05:30) on 7 August, the battalion moved forward 'in two lines of double companies' in support of 9/West Yorkshire, towards Hill 10, to the north of the Salt Lake and approximately 2,000 yards from Lala Baba. All four companies, A and B in the first line, C and D in the second, came under heavy shrapnel fire from the direction of the Anafarta Sagir ridge. The movements of the battalions and brigades of 11 Division are a little confusing; Wylly stated that the units of 32 Brigade 'had become rather mixed up',⁴⁵ but Hill 10 was 'reached by the Battalion at 6.15 a.m.' This implies that the whole of 6/York and Lancaster had made it to the hill although Travers asserts that there were only 'a few soldiers from 32 Brigade'.⁴⁶ There is little wonder that historians have found it difficult to track the activities of individual units. The Official Historian stated that 'the situation in Suvla Bay was verging on chaos', and that 'little of the situation was as yet known at 11th Division headquarters, and nothing of it by the Corps commander'.⁴⁷

There is a special significance to the previously mentioned attack by 6/Yorkshire on Lala Baba; it was the first attack made by any unit of the New Army in the Great War.⁴⁸ Aspinall went on to state, that it would have 'tried the mettle of highly experienced troops'. As, indeed, it did; all the officers – except two subalterns – and one third of the men who made the attack, were casualties. The battalion commander, Lieutenant Colonel Chapman, was killed while following them. Chapman has no known grave but is remembered on the memorial at Azmak Cemetery, Suvla. In the advance to Hill 10, 6/York and Lancaster lost Major Hill and Captain Mott; both were killed. They are buried in separate cemeteries, the Major at Lala Baba and the Captain at Hill 10.

Having reached Hill 10 the plan called for an advance against the rear defences on Chocolate and W Hills, both of which lay to the east of the Salt Lake. The scarcity of maps has already been mentioned, and this must have been exacerbated by the different spelling of many of the Turkish place names, as well as the British habit of giving these same features English names; Chocolate Hill = Yilghin Burnu. At 10 a.m. on 7 August, the brigade reorganized in the rear of Hill 10, before clearing the enemy from the Chanak Cheshme Ridge, a little to the north of the hill. It is a sad fact that British command and control on Gallipoli was poor. Stopford was attempting to direct operations from a motor-launch in the bay and while this would be possible with modern communications, it was bound to be inadequate when commanders on the ground relied on runners. According to Wylly, at 10.50 a.m. Hamilton received a message from Stopford that 'two battalions [of the] 33rd holding Yilghin Burnu [Chocolate Hill]'.⁴⁹ Stopford's Corps then 'remained more or less inactive' for the

44 Aspinall, *Gallipoli*, p.244.
45 Wylly, *6th Battalion History*, p.121.
46 Travers, *Gallipoli*, p.191.
47 Aspinall, *Gallipoli*, p.245.
48 Aspinall, *Gallipoli*, p.236.
49 Wylly, *6th Battalion History*, p.121.

rest of the day – a point of criticism for the Dardanelles Commission. Then, around 3 p.m. (in spite of the earlier message stating that Chocolate Hill had been taken) 33 Brigade 'was to advance against Yilghin Burnu, with the 34th in support and 32nd in reserve'. These orders were later changed so that 33 Brigade were to make the assault, with 32nd in support, 'By 7 p.m. the lower slopes of Chocolate Hill had been reached by the Battalion, and an hour later the hill was captured'.[50] Following this action, the battalion withdrew to a position in reserve on Hill 10.

The orders and counter-orders associated with the capture of Chocolate Hill, demonstrate the difficulty of piecing together the movements and involvement of individual units in any specific action. Accounts were written up by commanders and adjutants, after the event, from the memory of the survivors, as well as any written signals and orders that had been received by the various unit headquarters. The picture would necessarily be a confused one; pity the poor soldier trying to describe his role in the battle when he got home. The report of the Dardanelles Commission[51] indicates how each of the brigade commanders had a different appreciation of the taking of Chocolate Hill. General Hill, 31 Brigade, believed his men were in possession of the heights at 5.30 p.m. General Maxwell, 33 Brigade, ascribed its capture 'solely to the action of his two battalions' and gave the time of its capture as 7.20 p.m. General Sitwell, 34 Brigade, stated that he had been in 'telephonic communication' with two battalions of 33 Brigade 'which reported at 11.30 p.m.' that Chocolate Hill had been carried at 9.30 p.m. The reason for this lack of awareness and, by implication, a lack of control and 'grip' on the part of the brigade commanders, is spelled out in the Commission's report:

> None of the three Brigadier-Generals concerned in the attack on Chocolate Hill […] accompanied the troops. [They were] about two miles distant from Chocolate Hill, and remained there. In view of the distance and the nature of the country they can have seen but little of what was going on, and though no doubt they may occasionally have been in telephonic communication with some of their battalion commanders, the latter's outlook was limited and their responsibility was confined to what concerned their respective battalions. In the absence of superior military control and guidance on the spot, a force of inexperienced troops, unacquainted with local conditions and consisting of a number of battalions drawn from five brigades […] must have been lacking in cohesion and co-operation, and the evidence discloses the confusion and delay which resulted from this cause.[52]

50   Wylly, *6th Battalion History*, p.121.
51   *Dardanelles Commission*, p.172.
52   *Dardanelles Commission*, p.172-3.

Throughout the day's action, and the confusion of the brigade commanders, Lieutenant-General Sir Frederick Stopford (GOC IX Corps) remained aboard the destroyer *Jonquil* in Suvla Bay 'where he considered himself to be in the best position to communicate with General Headquarters and with his subordinate commanders on shore'.[53] Although he had 22 battalions ashore, facing only 1500 Turks (equivalent to one and a half battalions), 'the IX Corps had accomplished nothing'.[54] Erickson argues, convincingly, that the Ottoman army created a fighting force that 'arguably possessed greater combat effectiveness than its opponents in 1915'.[55]

These first days on the peninsula were followed by movement and sporadic action as the British tried to extend their hold on the hinterland behind Suvla Bay. On 8 August the 2 officers and 162 ORs who had remained on Imbros, re-joined the battalion. Two days later 6/York and Lancaster, as part of 32 Brigade, was retired to divisional reserve in the area around Lala Baba. As the battalion history recorded, the losses suffered had been heavy, but the figures given by Wylly are not definitive. As has been stated elsewhere in this book, casualty statistics are notoriously unreliable, so much depending on when the count was taken. Initially the number of dead was recorded as three officers and eight men, six officers and 57 ORs injured and an additional 207 men and one officer missing. Sadly, this did not give the true picture. The Helles Memorial has the names of 35 officers and men of the battalion who had been killed by the end of the day, 10 August. Many of those who had initially been classed as 'missing' were in fact dead. It speaks to the nature of the fighting and the terrain that all those who fell in those first few days had no known grave, save for two officers. By the end of August, 114 men from the battalion would be dead, but without a grave marker.

Throughout the remainder of their time on the peninsula, the battalion had 182 men killed in actions similar to that of 21 August. On that day the brigade was assigned to attack Hill W (Ismail Oglu Tepe), east of Chocolate Hill, on a two battalion front; 6/York and Lancaster on the left, with 6/Yorkshire on their right. The objective of the assaulting battalions was the Turkish trench on the lower slopes of Hill W where, having taken it, they would dig in and allow the two following battalions to pass through and advance on the Turkish trench beyond.[56] The attack began at 3 p.m. 'and came at once under very heavy shrapnel fire at point-blank range, causing many casualties'. One of the battalion subalterns described the attack in a letter to his mother:

> Can you picture the feelings of all of us as we watch the minute-hand slowly creep towards three? Ten minutes only now. Now only seven. And what of us when that hand shall have touched the half-hour …? [Finding themselves in a ditch after the assault started, he crawls along it to ascertain their position.] Ten

---

53 *Dardanelles Commission*, p.173.
54 Aspinall, *Gallipoli*, p.275.
55 Erickson, *Gallipoli: Command Under Fire*, p.95.
56 Wylly, *6th Battalion History*, p.124.

yards along, the way is blocked by the body of a young officer – he looks not more than nineteen, and quite happy, for his work has been well done.[57]

Priestman's letter probably did little for his mother's nerves as he went on to recount that, 'we lost all our officers but six that day, and I'm lucky, I suppose. Two-thirds of the battalion have "gone under"'. In spite of the losses, both trench objectives were taken and an hour after it started, the attack had come to a 'standstill'.

On the following day, the battalion was withdrawn to behind Chocolate Hill. Only five officers and 287 ORs (out of the 646 who had started the operation) answered roll-call in the reserve area on C Beach. For the soldiers, hundreds of miles from home and with only infrequent opportunities for leave, mail was very important. Priestman gives us an indication of just how much the men looked forward to news from their families, especially if they had just been in action:

> When, next day, we gathered on the beach behind the hills (all who were left of us) and found letters from home waiting for us, I'm not going to deny that all the little home topics you sent me to read helped on a reaction which was bound to come, and that I cried over them like a great silly kid! But a shamefaced comparison of notes later on revealed the surprising fact that I wasn't the only one.[58]

One of those who died that day was Private James Dillon who, like so many who fell at Gallipoli, has no known grave. James was the son of Margaret and James Dillon; he also had a sister, Marie, three years older than him. At the time of the 1901 census they lived in Solly Street; there is a street of the same name today in the centre of the city. James's father was listed as a 'colliery beltman (above ground)', but he may have been dead when his son was killed as the son's service record[59] names his mother as his nearest relative. James enlisted on 29 August 1914 at the age of 19 and, like many young soldiers, struggled with service discipline. It should be noted though that all his 'offences' were committed before sailing for Gallipoli. Like many of the charge-sheets of WW1 soldiers, the crimes look trivial, if not petty.

Offence	Punishment	Date awarded
Outstaying his pass by 2 hours	4 days Confined to Barracks (CB)	16/10/14
Dirty on church parade	2 days CB	30/03/15
Disrespectful to an NCO	3 days CB	03/04/15
Making an improper remark to an NCO	168 hr. detention	22/04/15

57 Priestman, *B-P Scout*, pp.183-4.
58 Priestman, *B-P Scout*, pp.185-6.
59 A microfilm record in The National Archive, Kew.

He was killed one week short of a full year's service.

The losses in the brigade had been such that the remaining men were reconstituted into two composite battalions and remained in this configuration until large, fresh drafts arrived in September, allowing the battalions to 'recover their individuality'. In that month 10 officers and 652 ORs arrived to swell the ranks – almost all the men who had sailed from Imbros for the 6 August landing had now been replaced. It was very difficult for soldiers to maintain long-time friendships when the 'churn' in the ranks was at such a high rate. One of the men who arrived in these new drafts was the author's grandfather, Private Patrick Dillon. Patrick's documents show his service in the Egyptian theatre as starting on 5 September, the day before his son – and this author's father – was born.

The months of September and October were spent by the battalion in positions on the Karakol Dagh, around Jephson's Post, about one mile north of Hill 10. After the excitement of the landings, these months slipped into the routine of 'nothing to report', although there was still a steady loss of men to Turkish snipers. The conditions under which the troops operated on Gallipoli were very different from those of France and Flanders. Many of the trench lines, like the Western front, might be only yards from those of the enemy, but the areas behind the men were very narrow and stopped at the sea. Drinking water was a constant problem, made worse in the summer by the high temperatures of the eastern Mediterranean. In winter, it could be bitterly cold. Like their colleagues in France, fatigues were a constant part of camp routine and the men must have been heartily sick of 'constructing winter quarters and defences in reserve area', or 'strengthening and extending existing trench line'. The rocky terrain would not have helped; 'the ground is rocky making trench construction a matter of very hard work'.[60] Trench systems used huge volumes of sandbags and these had to be filled by the men. In October, the battalion filled and moved 14,000 of them, with a further 55,000 the following month. This was hard graft, and all on only one gallon of water per man, per day (for all uses), and this also had to be man-handled on carts from the beach.

In spite of the heat, lack of bathing facilities in the line and tight control of water, the health of the men through the month was assessed as 'fair', with 'colitis of a mild type and catarrhal jaundice' being the most frequent diseases.[61] Although bathing was not possible while in the trenches, the proximity of the sea provided other opportunities while the battalion was in reserve. Priestman noted that 'the great advantage of our present position is that the hill we are on runs down to the sea, and every day we can get a dip, so long as we stay here. After a week or two in the trenches we certainly need plenty of bathing; and I caught two of the minor horrors of war [lice] in my shirt yesterday'.[62] By November the weather had turned, with the 28th and

60 TNA WO 95/4299, war diary, 6/York and Lancaster.
61 WO 95/4299.
62 Priestman, *B-P Scout*, p.210.

29th being particularly bad, 'very wet day. Snow and severe frost at night. Ordinary work stopped'.[63] The harshness of the weather to which the men were exposed was recognised in a Special Army Order of 2 December: 'The conditions prevailing were probably more severe than any to which our troops in France and Flanders were subjected during last winter'. It was at times like these that the ability of the officers to maintain the morale of their units was tested. Priestman summed up their role as being 'to fortify the men by feigning valour he didn't possess', while the duty officer on his daily rounds of the trenches had to ensure that 'half a dozen sentries were as wakeful and as miserable as himself'.[64]

It is a sad fact that huge numbers of the young officers, on whom the army depended, were killed leading their men in battle. Priestman had self-deprecatingly written that he feigned valour, but he proved otherwise on 19 November. The battalion history records that heavy losses were suffered on 18 November in an 'endeavour to establish a new post in advance of the line',[65] 2/Lieutenant Priestman and eight men were killed. His patrol of around 30 men was sent out to gain some higher ground near Jephson's Post but, while entrenching, they were rushed by the Turks. While some of the men made it back to their lines, Priestman was among those who did not. The following night another patrol discovered the bodies of Priestman, Regimental Sergeant Major Warr, and others, in the trench they had tried to hold. Both men are buried in Hill 10 Cemetery, as are 38 others from the battalion who fell during the months after the landing on 6 August. Strangely, the cemetery records indicate that Warr died on the 18th, Priestman on the 19th – the day that their bodies were found.

By the time of Priestman's death, the end game had started for the Allies on Gallipoli. There would have to be a withdrawal, no matter how it might be viewed throughout the Empire. Stopford, who had tried to command operations from a destroyer in the bay, had been removed by Hamilton:

> The senior commanders at Suvla had had no personal experience of the new trench warfare; of the Turkish methods; of the paramount importance of time. Strong, clear leadership had not been promptly enough applied.[66]

Hamilton went on to state that it was 'for these reasons he had replaced Sir Frederick Stopford by Major-General de Lisle'. However, Hamilton could not escape censure for the failure to make progress on the peninsula. On 14 October, he was recalled and a week later General Sir Charles Monro was ordered to take over. In his written instructions to Monro, Kitchener told him to report 'fully and frankly' on the military position and to evaluate whether or not 'it was better to evacuate Gallipoli or to make

63   WO 95/4299.
64   Priestman, *B-P Scout*, p.271.
65   Wylly, *6th Battalion History*, p.126.
66   *Dardanelles Commission*, p.192.

another attempt to carry it'.[67] The Secretary of State for War did not have to wait long for his reply, Monro telegraphed him 31 October:

> On purely military grounds, therefore, in consequence of the grave daily wastage of officers and men which occurs, and owing to the lack of prospect of being able to draw the Turks from their entrenched positions, I recommend evacuation of the peninsula.

In coming to this decision Monro had also given thought to how this might be seen by the Empire; 'I think loss of prestige caused by withdrawal would be compensated for in a few months by increased efficiency'. The Turkish 'prop' would remain standing.

In contrast to the attempts to clear the peninsula, the withdrawal (like Dunkirk) was a masterly example of good preparation and staff work. With the trench lines sometimes 'no more than twenty paces distant [from each other]' more than 80,000 men and supplies had to be removed across open beaches 'in the face of an enterprising enemy'.[68] All units went to great lengths to disguise their leaving from the Turks. As the numbers in the trenches reduced so those remaining lit all the usual fires to make it appear that all positions were still occupied. Additionally, mines were laid in front of the lines (these would be made active by a sapper as the rest of the men pulled back), existing wiring was strengthened and the trenches improved in case they had to be defended. The move back to Imbros was phased and by the night of 18/19 December, the battalion was reduced to 360 of the 'fittest and best men'.[69] On the two nights of 18 and 19 December, the final parties withdrew, each man carrying 'filled water bottles, packs, blankets, water proof sheets, 220 rounds of SAA [Small Arms Ammunition] and 1 day's iron ration'.[70] Only one man was killed during the operation. The sequence of trenches by which the men withdrew read like an A-Z of London; 'Shaftesbury Avenue, Piccadilly Circus, Hyde Park Road and Cannon Street'. During the morning of 20 December, the battalion was once again all together, on Imbros.

The men of 6/York and Lancaster had their first experience of overseas service on the Gallipoli peninsula, taking part in a failed operation, which was badly led. Like Private James Dillon, many died a long way from England, fighting an enemy who was not German. By the time they left 181 of their colleagues had died there, most with no known grave.

---

67 *Dardanelles Commission*, p.197.
68 Wylly, *6th Battalion History*, p.126.
69 WO 95/4299.
70 WO 95/4299.

Cemetery[1]	Number of dead
Helles Memorial	130
Hill 10 Cemetery	40
Green Hill Cemetery	7
Lala Baba Cemetery	1
Twelve Tree Copse Cemetery	3

Note
1   Data from CWGC web site.

The heavy casualty count for August is demonstrated in the following table, which gives the strength of the battalion and the brigade on the first and last days of the month.

Date	6/York and Lancaster		32 Brigade	
	Officers	Men	Officers	Men
1 August	28	913	112	3,679
31 August	4	337	19	1,167

The soldiers had to deal with the constant loss of friends and colleagues and their response can seem a little 'black', but the squaddies in Afghanistan would understand. Priestman cites one soldier who, while writing to inform a family of the loss of their son, said he was very sorry to tell them that he was 'killed in action on the 18th [but] we have divided the parcel you sent him amongst us; kind regards'.[71]

The withdrawal of 11 Division was not to Britain, the men were destined to spend some months in Egypt, protecting the Suez Canal – but not until they had spent some weeks on the Greek islands of Imbros and Lemnos. The battalion eventually sailed for Alexandria in the *Ascanius*, making landfall on 2 February before proceeding to camp at Sidi Bishr. The War Office was very concerned that the Turks, released from having to face the Allies on Gallipoli, would turn their attentions to the Canal, a strategic lifeline between Britain and India. To the powers that be, Egypt was considered an ideal spot for the troops from Gallipoli; their presence would reinforce those already doing garrison duty along the canal, while the climate was considered a good one in which exhausted men could recuperate:

> The formations were very weak, and thousands of men were in the trenches who would in any other campaign have been in the hospitals. […] For the purpose no

71   Priestman, *B-P Scout*, p.233.

better situation than Egypt could have been found. Its climate from November to March is as healthy and invigorating as any in the world. Hard work on digging trenches, in the stimulating air of Sinai, with ample food, was an excellent recipe for the restoration of troops debilitated by exposure and nervous strain.[72]

The description could almost have been written for a travel brochure. With the author's grandfather among them, the men of 6/York and Lancaster moved first from Sidi Bishr to Port Said on 10 February and then on the 24th to El Firdan.[73] For those troops who came from Gallipoli, as well as those direct from Britain, the sights, smells and 'pushy' Egyptian market-sellers would have been a world away from the Yorkshire cities they were used to. Naïve young men could be taken advantage of by wily natives, as was pointed out in general orders: 'Arab quarters placed out of bounds to all ranks'; '33% of men allowed on pass daily until 8 p.m. – NCOs 9 p.m.'; 'Men warned against buying sweets, sweet drinks or food from hawkers as instances had occurred of men in other battalions being drugged'.[74]

Much of their time in Egypt (February to June), was spent on working parties and patrolling the Canal Zone. The men also had their first experience of camels, the local beast of burden that was used extensively for moving wooden posts and barbed wire. On 3 February 57 camels carried 116 coils of wire and 112 bundles of sandbags, all to be used in building up the canal defences. Camel and mule trains feature in the war diaries as enormous quantities of material were moved for perimeter defence; one such train had 514 coils of wire and 206 wooden posts, and all had to be installed by the soldiers in the heat of the desert. The terrain also presented challenges to tented encampments. On 24 January, a violent storm blew up during the night and 'a great number of the tents were blown to the ground and it [was] quite apparent that the standard pattern of short tent-pegs [were] useless in sand in the event of a storm'. New tricks had to be learnt.

Sadly, most of the men who served in the war spoke little of their experience when they returned home. The author's grandfather was no exception; he left only a few pages in a hand-written diary. There are no entries covering any of the fighting, only mundane activities such as that for 27 March 1916:

[A] boiling hot day reveille at 5 a.m. & off digging by 6 about 3 miles to walk & trench digging till 11. We went with our coats on this morning for it was cold but coming back it was a scorcher. [On the following day] we had our clothes fumigated'.[75]

72 Macmunn, G., and C. Falls, *Military Operations, Egypt and Palestine* (Nashville, IWM, 1928), p.87.
73 Wylly, *6th Battalion History*, p.127.
74 TNA WO 95/4590, war diary, 14/York and Lancaster.
75 Diary, Private P. Dillon.

The opportunity to put on clean clothes did not come around very often and one can imagine how welcome it would have been in that climate. The battalion diary has only one reference to bathing facilities during their time in Egypt (others may have gone unrecorded): 7 March 'bathing parade'.

While their time in the desert was pretty much free of the risk of being killed, that was offset by a regime of physical labour and boredom and it was at times like these when discipline could suffer. According to his diary, Dillon was court martialled while in Egypt: 'I was in a bell tent [he was supposed to be on guard] when the Captain came & put me on a charge of quitting my post'. He was lucky, had they been in the trenches, and so 'in the face of the enemy', the offence risked a sentence of death. However:

> [O]n the 22nd [March] Wednesday my C.M. was washed out & I got 8 days C.B. [Confined to Barracks]. This was a surprise & a lenient sentence & I took my first punishment with a good heart & to make it better [it] only meant the 22nd & 23rd two days for we were to fall in at 6 p.m. for the draft'.[76]

Dillon's punishment was cut short as he was among those sent to El Firdan to dig trenches. On Easter Monday, 1916, my grandfather received a letter with a small photo of his son (this author's father), who was born the day after he arrived in the Egyptian theatre – this photo was the first time he had seen him; 'what a beauty he is' was his diary comment. The family still have that original photo.

Although the men of the battalion would have been volunteers, not all were able to accommodate themselves to the discipline, routine and separation from family. The reaction to these stresses could often have fatal consequences, as it did for 20401 Corporal H.R. Bean. Sadly, one life lost, in the context of a world war, was not going to get a great deal of attention. Bean 'was found dead in rear of 35th Field Ambulance Lines, from the effects of a gunshot wound in the head'. A court of inquiry sat the same day and concluded that he 'intentionally shot himself during temporary insanity'.[77] Today the case would warrant a deeper investigation. Had he not died from the gunshot he may well have been court martialled for 'self-inflicted injury', a serious offence under military law. Bean is buried in the CWGC cemetery at Ismailia.

While Private Dillon and his mates in 6/York and Lancaster were filling sandbags in Suez, Sir Douglas Haig was planning a 'Big Push' on the Western front. The 12th, 13th and 14th battalions left Egypt for France in March 1916. On 26 June, the 6th battalion followed them. They boarded trains at El Firdan for Alexandria, where they boarded the *Oriana* two days later (and all had the opportunity for baths).[78] As Dillon cryptically recorded in his diary, 'cannot say wherefore'. The troops were probably

---

76 Diary, Private P. Dillon.
77 TNA WO 95/4588, war diary, 6/York and Lancaster.
78 Wylly, *6th Battalion History*, p.128.

aware (the rumour mill would have been working overtime) that their destination was Marseilles, which they reached, via Malta, on 3 July. They had at least managed to miss the first day of that great battle on the Somme, unlike the three battalions who left in March. There is no indication in his diary that Dillon was aware of the events of 1 July.

On 16 July, in the area of Duneville, the battalion had their first spell of duty in the trenches on the Western front. Three days later, they had their first death in France. The entry in the war diary is short and to the point: 'Private Beswick killed, by rifle grenade – first battle casualty. Great number of rats'.[79] On the following day, L/Corporal Fruin and Private Turnham were both killed 'by explosion of hand bomb by raiding party of enemy'. All three are buried in Agny Military Cemetery. For some reason, they all have the date of their death recorded one day later in the CWGC database, than that in the battalion war diary. Fruin and Turnham both have the same grave reference, D18. The significance is that while both bodies were positively identified, the effect of the grenade was such that it was not possible to identify which remains belonged to which man. In cases like this, both soldiers are buried in the same grave and are named on the one headstone.

We now board our Tardis and travel back to the summer of 1915, to meet 10/York and Lancaster. This battalion was to have the unlucky experience of going straight from the training camps of Buckinghamshire, into Sir John French's Battle of Loos.

79   TNA WO 95/1809, war diary, 6/York and Lancaster.

5

Unfavourable ground – the Battle of Loos

This chapter introduces the 10th battalion of the York and Lancaster Regiment to the account of the war. While Private Patrick Dillon and his comrades were struggling with the conditions on the Gallipoli peninsula, 10/York and Lancaster were preparing to move from Britain to France. The battalion came into existence on 23 September 1914 and joined 63 Brigade of 21 Division, the following month. The other three battalions in the brigade were; 8/Somerset Light Infantry (SLI); 12/West Yorkshire; 8/Lincolnshire. Until August 1915, the division was based at Halton in Buckinghamshire, before moving to Witley for final training.[1] After just a month, the division sailed for France, where the Allied armies were 'embarking upon operations on a very much larger scale than had hitherto been attempted'.[2]

On the morning of 10 September, the men marched to Milford where, at 10.30 p.m., they left in the *Duchess of Argyll* for Boulogne. Arriving in the very early hours of the following morning, they had a few hours rest in a camp at Ostrohove before proceeding to Norbécourt for ten days of training. After this brief introduction to France, and with the experience of the officers and men limited to the training camps in England, the division was plunged into the centre of the battle of Loos – a decision that would later be criticised. At 6 p.m. on 20 September the battalion set out by route march for St. Omer, they would be on the road for the next five days. On 25 September, they arrived at Vermelles and went 'straight into action'.[3] However, before following 10/York and Lancaster into battle we should step back and ask, "why Loos?"

The expedition to the Dardanelles, in the early part of 1915, had been expensive in men and failed in its result; the 'props' under Germany were still standing and the Westerners were convinced in their argument that the enemy would only be defeated on the Western front. Joffre proposed a French attack in Artois, around Vimy, with the BEF making a supporting attack on his northern flank. The battle, officially

---

1   This author spent his first 3 years in the RAF as an apprentice at RAF Halton, 1963-5.
2   Wylly, *10th battalion history*, p.216.
3   TNA WO 95/2158, war diary, 10/York and Lancaster.

lasting from 25 September to 13 October, is important to our narrative for a number of reasons. Up to that point, it was the largest land-battle Britain had fought; the BEF used poison gas for the first time; Sir John French's control and use of the reserves was heavily criticised; Sir Douglas Haig later replaced Sir John French, as Commander-in-Chief. In his excellent account of the battle, Nick Lloyd commented that Loos had 'failed to attract much scholarly attention. It remains a 'forgotten battle'.[4] The events of that September became the storyline to Alan Clark's polemic, *The Donkeys*, in which bunglers and butchers commanded the battle. Robert Graves (who was there) referred to it as a 'Bloody balls-up'.[5] Many mistakes were made by the senior commanders, but that does not excuse Clark's hyperbole; 'Again and again they [the men] were called upon to attempt the impossible, and in the end *they were all killed*. It was as simple as that'.[6] [My emphasis.] They were not all killed, and it was not that *simple*, war rarely is. Whatever criticism is directed at Clark's book, his point that mistakes were made is a valid one and they directly affected 10/York and Lancaster.

In his account of the war, Basil Liddel Hart referred to Loos as the 'Unwanted Battle',[7] an epithet that has stuck for good reason. Sir John asked Haig, whose First Army would be making the assault, to submit a report on the proposed attack. The conclusions were far from encouraging. The area around Loos and Lens was dotted with coal-mine workings, miners cottages and slag heaps, all of which made for 'very carefully sited' German defences,[8] which would break up an infantry attack. In Haig's view, the ground was 'not favourable'. French, however, was under considerable pressure to support Joffre's offensive. The British attempts to force the Dardanelles had failed, the Allied troops put ashore on the Gallipoli peninsula were unable to move far from their beach-heads and the Russians had taken a drubbing by Austro-German troops at Gorlice-Tarnow. The British C-in-C was in the unenviable position of having to press ahead with an assault, which, because Haig and his commanders believed it to be unwise, would be 'very half hearted; for everybody who knows the ground is sure success is impossible'.[9] Not least among those pressuring French was Kitchener, who believed that the situation in the eastern Mediterranean and Russia required Britain to help France, even if 'by so doing we may suffer very heavy losses'.[10]

The situation in which French found himself was not a comfortable one but he acknowledged the need to be seen to do something; 'I have decided that in the end it is necessary to leave the direction of affairs in the hands of the Generalissimo'.

---

4   Lloyd, N., *Loos 1915* (Stroud, Tempus, 2006), p.13.
5   Graves, R., *Goodbye to All That* (London, Penguin, 1960), p.127.
6   Clark, A., *The Donkeys* (London, Pimlico, 1991), p.11.
7   Liddel Hart, B.H., *History of the First World War* (London, Papermac, 1997), p.193.
8   Sheffield, G., and J. Bourne, *Douglas Haig. War Diaries and Letters 1914-1918* (London, Weidenfeld & Nicolson, 2005), p.25.
9   Holmes, *The Little Field Marshal*, p.298.
10   Edmonds, *1915, Vol. 2*, p.129.

He would leave it to Joffre to 'tell me what he wished me to do and I *will do it*'.[11] Sir John's effective capitulation did not impress Haig, in his view First Army were to be asked to attack across unsuitable ground and French had 'put himself and the British Forces unreservedly in Joffre's hands!'[12] At this point (early August) French was only committing to assisting Joffre's Tenth Army (on Haig's right flank) by 'neutralizing the enemy's artillery, and by holding the infantry on its front' – this was not an all-out bayonet charge over No Man's Land. He did not want First Army involved in an attack against objectives, 'which are so strongly held as to be liable to result in the sacrifice of many lives'.[13] Unfortunately, for Sir John, the lack of success on other fronts (as well as the need to support the French), caused Kitchener to call for something more robust than French's 'artillery plan'. The British C-in-C was directed (on 21 August) to 'take the offensive and act vigorously'.[14] Against his better judgement, he was to launch an unwanted battle, on unfavourable ground, with inadequate infantry and artillery and against the advice of his army commander. Sir John French would be rightly criticised for some of the decisions he made during the first days of the battle, but Kitchener must bear a heavy responsibility for pushing him into an offensive he did not fully believe in.

Joffre's plan, by attacking both flanks of the German salient around Noyon (which stretched from the Somme in the north to Reims in the south), would straighten the line on that sector of the front. The French Second and Fourth Armies were to strike the southern flank, on either side of Reims, while their Tenth Army (assisted by the BEF's subsidiary attack at Loos) struck the northern boundary of the salient. If the plan was successful then it might allow for dreams of a dramatic breakthrough and 'exploitation' to become a reality. If the assault broke the German line, might it not go far enough to cut off the enemy's transportation links on the Douai plain? In tune with the desire for a war of movement, the plan included 'strong detachments of cavalry, supported by infantry in motor buses', rushing through the gap created by the infantry. Having achieved this, why not follow it with a general Allied offensive to compel the Germans 'to retreat beyond the Meuse and possibly end the war'.[15] It would take another three years of desperate fighting before such grandiose schemes stood a chance of becoming a reality.

Haig's First Army was to attack the German front between the La Bassée Canal in the north and Lens in the south, with two corps: on the left was I Corps under the command of Lieutenant-General Gough (this formation included 1/York and Lancaster in 28 Division), and Lieutenant-General Rawlinson's IV Corps on the right. The boundary between the advances of the two corps was the west-east road between

---

11   Holmes, *The Little Field Marshal*, p.297.
12   Sheffield and Bourne, *Haig*, p.133.
13   Edmonds, *1915, Vol. 2*, p.125.
14   Edmonds, *1915, Vol. 2*, p.129.
15   Edmonds, *1915 Vol. 2*, p.113.

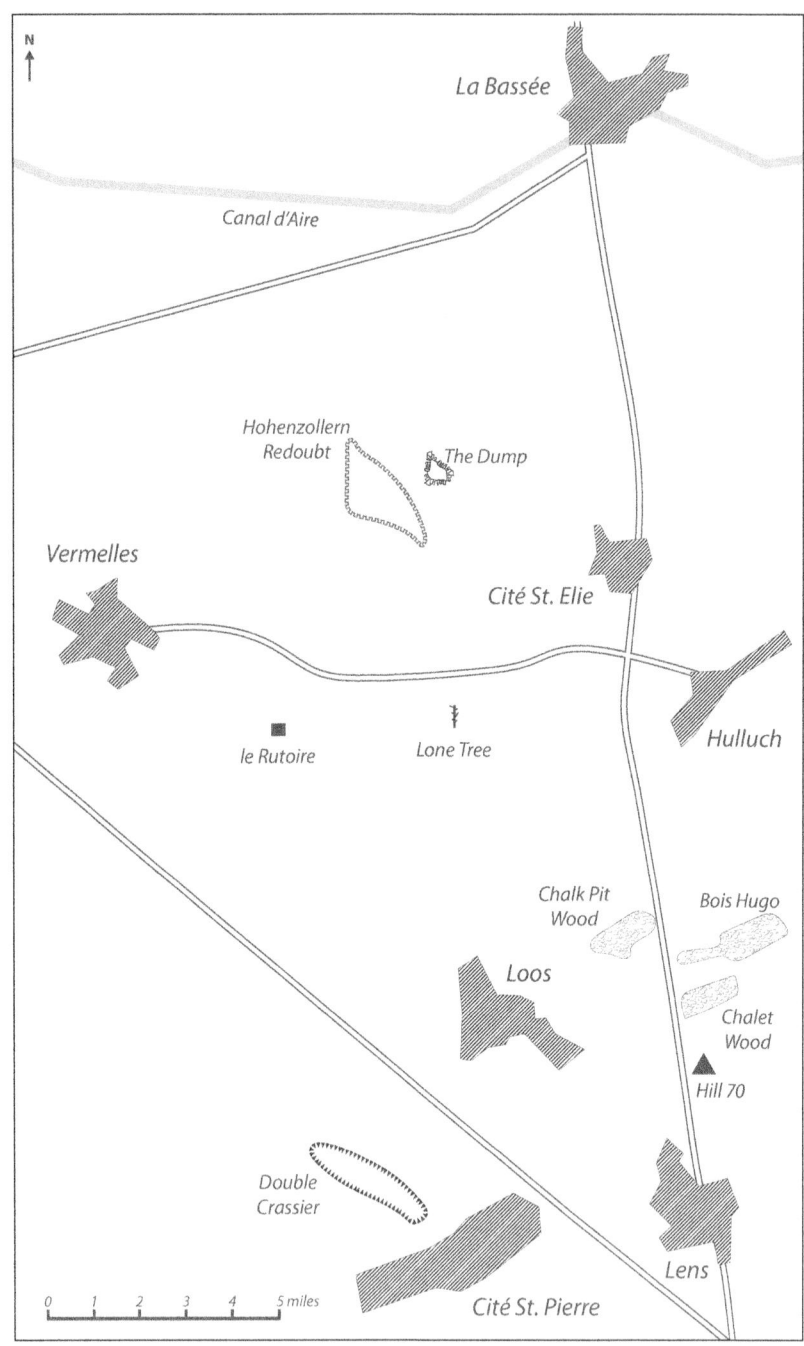

Map 7 Loos, September 1915.

Vermelles and Hulluch. In reserve was XI Corps, Lieutenant-General Haking, with 10/York and Lancaster in 21 Division. The control and timing of the use of the reserve was important to the outcome of the battle – and Sir John French's career. No Man's Land on this north-south front varied between 200 and 400 yards, with the narrowest section in the north on either side of the Cambrin-La Bassée road. At the northern and southern extremes of the British line the troops were faced by mining villages with their pit-heads, slag heaps and rows of small miners cottages, many of them with cellars providing good defensive positions. To cite the Official History:

> A more unpromising scene for a great offensive can hardly be imagined; and on the 25th September 1915 the surface was a barren prairie of rank grass, intersected by trenches whose white chalk parapets defied concealment.[16]

In the centre, on either side of the corps boundary, the ground was largely flat and free of obstructions, until reaching the German second line and the small towns of Cité St. Elie and Hulluch. The slightly higher ground of the German positions, as well as the vantage points afforded by the pit-head winding-gear towers on their side of the line, afforded the Germans excellent observation such that 'every battery brought to within 3,500 yards of the German front trenches could be located'.[17] Little wonder that Haig had declared the ground to be unfavourable.

In spite of the outrage expressed by the British at the German first-use of poisonous gas on 22 April, Haig incorporated the weapon into his planning for Loos; he hoped that it would make up for a deficiency in heavy artillery, but the plans would be weather dependent. Edmonds recounts the episode of Haig asking his ADC to light a cigarette at dawn on the morning of the attack, and watching the direction in which the smoke drifted to help him make his decision; 'seldom have the vagaries of the wind been watched with such tense anxiety'.[18] However, before we get to the battle it is necessary to review the issues that surrounded the use of Haking's XI Corps, which was to constitute First Army's reserve at Loos.

Haig was the Army commander for the battle; he would dispose of his corps and divisions in the first and supporting waves of the attack. Ordinarily the general in command would hold back sufficient forces to form a reserve, which he could then commit to the battle to either reinforce a break-in to the enemy line, or help to strengthen a sector of his front that was coming under particular enemy pressure. In the case of Loos, the question of who controlled the reserve was open to some confusion, which then led to its being in the wrong place when it was needed. On 7 August, Haig was informed that the troops available for the operation would be 'those of your own Army, plus the Cavalry Corps and two divisions held in general reserve under the

---

16 Edmonds, *1915 Vol. 2*, p.144.
17 Edmonds, *1915 Vol. 2*, p.146.
18 Edmonds, *1915, Vol. 2*, p.168.

Loos. Looking towards Cite St. Auguste. (IWM Q 41998)

orders of the Commander-in-Chief'.[19] Haig had committed the six divisions available to him to the battle; he had no reserve of his own. On 26 August, French addressed a conference, at which Haig was present, where he stated that eight British divisions would be employed in the attack; 'six divisions for the assault and two divisions in general reserve'.[20] French was implicitly acknowledging that Haig would be using all six of his divisions and that consequently the only reserves available to the Army Commander were the two in XI Corps. That being the case they had to be close to the front if they were to be of any use as a reserve – they had to be able to be inserted quickly into the battle-space where they were needed.

The problem was exacerbated by French and Haig having different views of exactly what kind of battle they were fighting. The situation was summarised by Nick Lloyd; 'while French wanted a more limited attack, with the reserves being employed *once* success had been achieved, Haig's 'all-out' plan called for the reserves to be used to *ensure* this initial success'.[21] This difference in approach influenced the two men in their view of how far forward the reserves should be when the battle started. For Haig, they should be 'up' to take part in the battle and ensure success, whereas French

19   Edmonds, *1915, Vol. 2*, p.273.
20   Edmonds, *1915, Vol. 2*, p.273.
21   Lloyd, N., *Loos*, p.63.

wanted them in a position to move to any part of the front where they could exploit any breakthrough. Lloyd takes the argument further and suggests that as Sir John was reluctant to get into the intricacies of Haig's plan – Haig's diary has the comment that he did not see how the C-in-C could control operations from a chateau twenty-five miles from his C.G.S. and Staff[22] – then he would use the reserves to influence how Haig used his army. Instead of insisting on Haig carrying out his (French's) plan, Sir John 'tried to compel him to do so by keeping back the infantry reserve'.[23] Initially, French planned for them to be some 20,000 yards behind the front line but, following Haig's lobbying, he agreed that on 25 September they would be 'between 5,000 and 7,000 yards' back.[24]

Their distance from the start line was not the only issue that would be picked over in post-battle reports, and by historians. Edmonds makes the point that, as the reserves might have to take part in 'open warfare' in the event that the attack was a success, it should consist of seasoned troops.[25] Because of other dispositions that French had had to make to form Third Army, he did not feel that he could remove any more experienced units from the line to form a First Army reserve: he had to use two of the New Army divisions, 21st and 24th. The involvement of these new formations gave French no cause for concern, he believed that they would have the enthusiasm to 'have a go' and that, unlike battalions who had already spent time in France, they would not bring with them the 'sedentary habits of trench warfare'.[26] This view was at variance with his comment in January of that year; 'I feel quite sure [that to put such inexperienced troops] straight into the field under commanders and staff who are inexperienced in up-to-date European warfare might easily become a positive danger'.[27] Haking, the corps commander, was considered by Haig to be a 'thruster' – ideal for pushing troops forward. While a lecturer at Staff College he had put his philosophy into print; 'There is only one rule that can never be departed from and will always lead to success, and that is always to push forward, always to attack'.[28] Poor staff work was to cause problems for the reserve divisions when they were moved forward to take their place in the battle, but this was hardly surprising given that the new corps headquarters included officers who had previously neither worked together nor served on a corps staff.[29]

As we have already seen, 10/York and Lancaster (after two weeks training in France) spent five days on the march to take up their reserve positions at Vermelles. The troops

---

22 Blake, R., *The Private Papers of Douglas Haig 1914-1919* (London, Eyre & Spottiswoode, 1952), p.104.
23 Lloyd, *Loos*, p.65.
24 Lloyd, *Loos*, p.66.
25 Edmonds, *1915, Vol. 2*, p.139.
26 Edmonds, *1915, Vol. 2*, p.140.
27 Edmonds, *1915, Vol. 2*, p.2734, footnote 1.
28 Senior, M., *A Dutiful Soldier. Lieutenant General Sir Richard Haking XI Corps Commander 1915-18. A Study in Corps Command* (Barnsley, Pen & Sword, 2012), p.26.
29 Holmes, *Little Field Marshal*, p.301.

may well have had the enthusiasm that French was looking for, but they and their regimental officers were new to battle, and it would show. Haig, meanwhile, was still objecting to French's plan for their use. In his diary for 19 September he noted that the reserves would not be near Lillers until the 24th; 'This is too late!'[30] In a subsequent meeting on 22 September (only three days before the battle) French told Haig that he would 'release the XI Corps to support me on the first possible moment', but only a day later Haig believed that they would be 'close up in the places where I have arranged to put them, and will go forward as soon as any opportunity offers'.[31] As Sheffield noted, this was 'the beginning of the confusion over the control of the Reserve'.[32]

One of the lessons learnt from Neuve Chapelle and Aubers Ridge was that a successful infantry assault required a heavy and effective artillery barrage to cut the wire, damage defences and kill the defending troops. Haig had insufficient guns and ammunition:

> [T]o prepare an assault on a frontage of more than two divisions, but it was anticipated that, in combination with gas, there would be no need for a thorough bombardment, and that there were enough guns to prepare and support the simultaneous assault of six divisions.[33]

As well as insufficient weight of fire, the four day barrage was less effective than hoped for; the weather was not good for artillery spotting; some batteries were fresh from the UK and were not capable of the accuracy required for wire cutting; the German dug-outs were too deep for the British shelling to cause them a problem. Captain Dunn, Royal Welch Fusiliers, remarked that in his sector of the front (a little south of the La Bassée Canal) 'I did not like to hurt the gunners' feelings by saying how little sign there was of cut wire'[34] – it did not augur well for the attack.

For the opening of the battle, Haig placed a great deal of reliance on his use of gas, indeed he believed that it 'ought not to be launched except with the aid of gas!'[35] Haig's situation on the night of 24 September must have been similar to Eisenhower's on the night of 5/6 June 1944; both were hanging on the forecasts from their meteorologists. Haig's man was Captain Gold, on loan from the RFC, and he predicted that from midnight to midnight the wind would be 'southerly, then changing to southwest or west, probably increasing to 20 miles per hour'.[36] At 9 p.m. on 24 September, based on Gold's observation, Haig decided that the troops who were to attack in the morning should move up to their jumping off trenches. The final decision for the attack would

30 Sheffield and Bourne, *Haig*, p.149.
31 Sheffield and Bourne, *Haig*, p.152.
32 Sheffield and Bourne, *Haig*, p.151, footnote 1.
33 Edmonds, *1915, Vol. 2*, p.164.
34 Dunn, J.C., *The War the Infantry Knew 1914-1919* (London, Abacus, 1994), p.150.
35 Sheffield and Bourne, *Haig*, p.149.
36 Sheffield and Bourne, *Haig*, p.152.

be made early the next day. On 25 September, with the smoke from his staff officer's cigarette drifting towards the enemy trenches, Haig ordered release of the gas to be at 05:50, with the men going over the top at 06:30. The effect of the gas was, at best, variable. On some sectors of the front it hardly moved as the wind dropped, while in others it blew back to the British trenches: 'What wind there was caused it to drift along the line from right to left and to fall back into the trench. Men in the front line got mouthfuls of it, and some became panicky'.[37] It should have been no surprise that a weapon, which would be so dependent on the vagaries of the wind, would prove to be a little unpredictable. On 7 Division front, in the centre of the line, the gas 'hung about, in places it blew along the front and, despite gas-masks and all precautions, put out of action many of the assailants. [...] The carefully concealed "accessory" [gas] was far from the conspicuous success on which so much depended'.[38]

In the hope that the gas would provide some surprise, and would veil their advance, the troops went forward, heavily weighted down with sandbags, iron rations, grenades, picks and shovels, as well as their individual rifles and ammunition. Communications on the battlefield were rudimentary and so each platoon had a 'large disc on a pole to indicate [their] position to the artillery'.[39] With gas now a weapon to be used by both sides, each man had to have a crude respirator with him to give a level of basic protection; they were little more than a 'flannel bag' with 'talc-covered eye-holes'.[40] With all his equipment, and the width of No Man's Land, the soldier going over the top would have walked steadily forward, rather than attempting to run. It took the lead battalions of 7 Division twelve minutes to reach the opposing trenches,[41] during which time they suffered heavily.

As the battle progressed, Haig received messages that led him to infer that 'First Army was on the crest of a wave of victory';[42] Puits 14 and Hill 70 were reported to have been taken; Cité St. Auguste was about to be attacked; Hulluch was reported as captured; 7 Division was in Cité St. Elie and 9 Division was 'pressing on to Haisnes'.[43] But all of these messages were erroneous, success was overstated and losses were rarely mentioned. Wishing to take advantage of this 'wave of victory', Haig wanted to use his reserve to exploit the situation. At 2.35 p.m., he ordered Haking to 'push forward at once between Hulluch and Cité St. Auguste and occupy the high ground between Harnes and Pont à Vendin, both inclusive, and secure the passages of the Haute Deule canal at those places'.[44] However, the reserves were not sufficiently far forward.

---

37 Dunn, *The War the Infantry Knew*, p.153.
38 Atkinson, C.T., *The Seventh Division* (Milton Keynes, Naval & Military Press, 2009), p.205.
39 Edmonds, *1915, Vol. 2*, p.173, footnote 2.
40 Edmonds, *1915, Vol. 2*, p.173.
41 Atkinson, *The Seventh Division*, p.206.
42 Edmonds, *1915, Vol. 2*, p.282.
43 Edmonds, *1915, Vol. 2*, p.282.
44 Edmonds, *1915, Vol. 2*, p.283.

We come now to the control of XI Corps on the morning of the assault, and the poor staff work that led to 10/York and Lancaster (with the rest of the reserve troops) arriving tired, hungry, and confused on the field of battle. As we have seen in the previous paragraph, Haig believed he was in a position to exploit success and at 8.45 a.m., he made an urgent request for the reserve to be assigned to him, as 'reserves must be pushed on at once'.[45] In response, French ordered Haking to move his corps forward, but still under GHQ control. It was not until 11.30 that morning that the C-in-C visited Haig and in that meeting he told the Army Commander that he (French) was going to visit Haking and put XI Corps under First Army – the question has to be asked, why did he not telephone? This caused further delay as it was not until 13.20 that Haking informed Haig that 21 and 24 Divisions were now under First Army control.

It takes good staff work to co-ordinate the movement of infantry divisions from a rear area to the front, during a battle. These formations were made up of approximately 12,000 men, transport, horses and artillery, and when on the march a division took up miles of road. Haking's corps staff did not have the experience to move these bodies of men across the rear of an army already in battle. When French ordered XI Corps to move forward at 09.30 on 25 September he instructed Haking to 'arrange move in communication with First Army accordingly'; at that time the C-in-C still retained control of the reserve and yet he passed the responsibility for clearing the roads for the corps' movement from GHQ to First Army and XI Corps HQs. The result was that the troops from 21 and 24 Divisions did not arrive in their allotted areas until the early hours of the 26th. By midnight on 24/25 September, 10/York and Lancaster had marched 41 miles to get to the battle area but the last few miles were congested, the road was heavily shelled and 'in a terrible condition of mud and shell holes'.[46] This battalion 'lost' the rest of the brigade for an hour and a half in the early hours of the 26th. Not unnaturally, troops marching into battle get hungry; Napoleon (or Frederick the Great) remarked that 'an army marches on its stomach'. Unfortunately, this aphorism was overlooked in the movement of XI Corps. The post-battle report of 63 Brigade observed:

> Rations arrived just at the time of departure, no arrangements had been made for using the cookers on the march. There would have been ample time to have allowed the men to have had their dinners before leaving the bivouac. [...] It was found afterwards that many men had put their rations in their packs and consequently when these latter were discarded [before going into the attack] the food also was lost.[47]

---

45   Edmonds, *1915, Vol. 2*, p.280.
46   TNA WO 95/2157, war diary, 63 Brigade.
47   WO 95/2157.

Not for the first time the men were blamed by senior officers for issues which came down to poor planning, staff work and leadership. According to Major-General Forestier-Walker (GOC 21 Division) there should have been 'no difficulty regarding food. Only such men as had lost, or previously eaten, their iron rations, could have gone hungry'.[48] In 1926, while compiling his Official History, Edmonds received a letter from Brigadier-General Maurice of French's GHQ staff:

> GHQ should have made arrangements for assisting the march of [the] newly-formed divisions. I think now this was a bad oversight on my part. The reason or excuse for it was that we were pressing Sir John up to the last to hand those divisions over to Haig as soon as they came into his area and we didn't know from hour to hour what the decision would be.[49]

A rare instance of a senior commander declaring, *Mea culpa*.

By the end of the day, 25 September, the gains that had been made were much less than the original expectation. The Hohenzollern Redoubt, in the north, had been taken, as was ground to the east of it in an area known as The Dump. In the centre of the line, 7 and 9 Divisions had advanced on either side of the Vermelles-Hulluch road, while in the south the 1st and 15th Divisions occupied ground around the Chalk Pit and towards Hill 70. However, the new positions were not contiguous, the German second line had not been reached and many men had been lost. During the night of 25/26 September, the enemy took the opportunity to reinforce his second line, ready for the second day of the battle, and the introduction of the British reserve divisions into the fray.

After a night of some confusion, it was time for the reserves to move forward to the positions from which they were to attack the second German line on Sunday, 26 September. The information given to the commanders of the two divisions gave the impression that the enemy had been heavily defeated 'and was everywhere retiring', consequently they believed that, in the early hours of the Sunday morning, 'little more was required than a long march in pursuit of an already retiring and demoralized enemy'.[50] The Chief of the General Staff had told them that 'in no conceivable circumstances' would the new divisions be put in 'unless and until the Germans were absolutely smashed and retiring in disorder'.[51] This perception was reinforced by Haking ordering that the men should carry their greatcoats. The advance during the dark hours of Sunday morning was towards the Lens-Hulluch road, but it was not an easy one for these raw troops. Without food, with regimental officers who had inadequate maps and had to rely on compass bearings and with incorrect intelligence regarding

---

48　TNA WO 158/262, Battle of Loos: 21st Division's report.
49　Lloyd, *Loos*, p.93.
50　Edmonds, *1915, Vol. 2*, p.284.
51　Edmonds, *1915, Vol. 2*, p.284.

which side held Hulluch and Hill 70, there was a great deal of confusion. Edmonds was sympathetic to their situation:

> Without having been in action before or having seen a shot fired, these troops were actually confronted with a difficult situation on unknown ground, without guidance from the commanders and staffs who had been in the sector and had studied its features for months past.[52]

By dawn on the Sunday, 63 Brigade was in the vicinity of the Chalk Pit, with 10/York and Lancs and 8/Somerset L.I. to the left of the pits, 8/Lincoln and 12/West Yorkshire on the right, extending towards Bois Hugo (Map 7). Although there had been heavy rain during the night, this had stopped and by 4 a.m., the sky was clear, 'and as it got light a thick mist formed, which cleared suddenly about 9 a.m. At 07.00, the brigade was told that 'an advance on a large scale' would commence at 11 a.m., towards the enemy trenches (the German second line) which were 'about 1,000 yards' in front.[53] While the battalion was in position on the Lens-Hulluch road, and before the start time for the attack, the York and Lancs were ordered to send two companies to move through the wood by the Chalk Pit, this was apparently misunderstood, and the whole battalion moved forward. Coming under enemy fire, the battalion fell back. The Brigade Major who wrote the 63 Brigade after-battle report was critical of the battalion's performance, however, it must be said that there was a great deal of confusion over the day's events, which is apparent in most of these reports. According to 63 Brigade, the battalion exhibited 'a certain amount of reluctance to remain in the trenches under shell fire'. Additionally, 'very little effort had been made by this Battalion to improve and deepen the trenches which they had occupied since about 3.30 a.m.' As a result of the poor entrenching efforts there had been more casualties than necessary, a situation that could have been improved had officers and NCOs 'insisted upon the men digging themselves in properly'.[54] Sadly, many of the reports written after the battle, frequently by officers who were not on the front line with the soldiers, contain a rather glib criticism of those who were trying to manage the situation.

For the York and Lancaster men, fresh from the UK, being under fire would have been horrific. The viewpoint from a hastily dug trench is limited and determining exactly who was firing which shells at them would have been difficult. The report by the divisional commander states that 63 Brigade during the morning 'began to be shelled by the enemy, and the more forward trenches by our own guns'.[55] The corps commander, Haking, was dismissive of the idea of the troops being shelled by their own artillery:

52 Edmonds, *1915, Vol. 2*, pp.284-5.
53 WO 95/2157.
54 WO 95/2157.
55 WO 158/262.

I am doubtful about this, the line of advance of our attacking troops would be clearly seen by the Artillery Observing officers, and although the Artillery of the 21st Division had had very little experience in fighting I think they were good enough to prevent a mistake of this kind being made. Troops that have failed in an attack are very apt to believe that they have suffered from their own shell fire when really it was the enemy's, and many cases of this nature have been investigated and it has been found that there was no real foundation for the allegation. [Once again, the troops are blamed.] It is of course extremely difficult to discover whether they are being shelled by their own artillery or by the enemy, especially when, as in this case, the attack is in a salient and hostile shells are coming from both flanks and perhaps almost taking them in reverse.[56]

Haking's response is written from the assumption that everyone had a clear picture of what was happening; they did not. The 63 Brigade report again; 'The absence of information of what was happening elsewhere was nothing short of disastrous, as no-one knew what anyone else was doing'. The artillery observers were presumably relying on platoons raising their 'disc' (mentioned earlier), but as that would have given the men's position away to the enemy, they were unlikely to have been used. When 10/York and Lancaster followed 12/W Yorkshire and 8/Lincolns towards the Chalk pit, they believed the position to be in enemy hands, they thought they were fired on by the enemy, so the leading battalions fixed bayonets but did not fire back. It was then ascertained that 'the pit was in British hands'. Although the night had been clear, 'the unexpected arrival of the 63rd Brigade *en masse* had very nearly led to its being fired on'.[57] Haking cannot avoid responsibility for these inexperienced troops going forward without a clear picture of the ground held by friendly units – if 63 Brigade were unaware that the pits were in British hands, why would the artillery know where the forward troops were?

By 10 a.m., the situation had become quite messy for 63 Brigade. The whole of 10/York and Lancaster had moved to Chalk Pit Wood (rather than the two battalions that should have gone) and suffered many casualties from the Germans in Bois Hugo. In the action around the wood C Company had lost all its officers including the commander, Captain Abbott. This officer was shot and died while being carried back; presumably, his body was then dropped as the men carrying him retreated to the trench and the rest of the battalion. Abbott has no known grave but is remembered on the Loos Memorial. Because of the strong German presence in that wood Brigadier-General Nickalls (63 Brigade commander) requested support from 64 Brigade, who sent 14/Durham Light Infantry (DLI) forward. At this juncture, with the brigade under heavy fire, but support on its way, Nickalls was killed; 'his loss at such a critical moment was irreparable'.[58]

56   WO 158/262.
57   Edmonds, *1915, Vol. 2*, p.291.
58   Edmonds, *1915, Vol. 2*, p.320.

It was at this point that a disorganised retreat set in. It appears to have started when 12/W Yorkshire (whose CO had just been wounded) came under enfilade fire: 'completely surprised and suffering many casualties, the majority of the men left the trenches and ran back towards the Lens road'.[59] The route to the rear for the men of the West Yorks, was through the lines of 10/York and Lancaster who 'rose as the retreating men reached them and joined in their rearward movement',[60] efforts to rally them were not successful. At the same time as these troops were pulling back, 14/DLI were advancing to their support and, seeing men coming towards them in long greatcoats, mistook them for Germans and fired on them. Luckily the mistake was quickly recognised. With 63 Brigade pulling back, and 14/DLI advancing, 'the unique spectacle was presented of the larger portion of the Regiments of the Brigade retreating through portions of advancing Battalions'[61] who were coming to their aid. Sadly, it cost the Durham men dear; the battalion commander and 16 other officers, together with 220 Other Ranks were casualties of the German machine guns.

Various attempts were made to rally the men but, having lost a good number of officers and men, little was gained and by 7 a.m. on 27 September the division was relieved and the battalion pulled back into billets at Rély. The first blooding of 10/York and Lancaster, fresh from the training schools of the UK, was 'nasty, brutish and short'.[62] Some three weeks after the assault, the GOC 21 Division submitted his comments on the events of that day; the soldiers had been exhausted during the night march to their start lines; the commander of 63 Brigade had been lost at a critical point; the men had believed that they were being shelled by their own guns and casualties had been high. However, when full allowance was made for these circumstances, it was his considered opinion that the men of 12/W Yorkshire and 10/York and Lancaster 'did not behave with credit. Although 12/W Yorks had lost their Commanding Officer and their left flank was exposed, 'they appear to have retreated without sufficient cause'.[63] The 63 Brigade report was no less damning: 'It is not understood how the order to retire came to be given, apparently it emanated from the Officer Commanding West Yorks Regt.'[64] The NCOs came in for particular censure:

> During the retirement, Regimental Officers and N.C.O's did not give much assistance in trying to rally the Men (there were a few exceptions in the case of Officers but the N.C.O's were useless).

The terms used to blame the men for the lack of success completely ignore the responsibility of those making the criticism for ensuring that the staff work is adequate to

---

59   Edmonds, *1915, Vol. 2*, p.320.
60   Edmonds, *1915, Vol. 2*, p.320.
61   WO 95/2157.
62   Apologies to Thomas Hobbes' *Liviathan*.
63   WO 158/262.
64   WO 95/2157.

the task, that the men are sufficiently trained and have the required equipment, and that senior commanders display leadership. Without these, morale suffers and that indicates a failure of leadership.

Retreats are qualitatively different from orderly retirements, they tend to be uncontrolled, with every man looking out for himself as he tries to get back to a safe place, and this would have been especially true of men who had had no previous experience of battle. In these circumstances, it is not surprising that some soldiers lost, or cast aside, their rifles in their haste to get back, or that they might want to lend assistance to wounded comrades. Unfortunately, both of these actions were viewed poorly by authorities who considered them to be examples of a lack of fighting spirit. The GOC 21 Division observed:

> Over 300 men of the three Infantry Brigades returned without rifles. Each of these cases has been separately investigated. […] I regret to say that a considerable number of men abandoned their rifles without excuse, under circumstances which tend to show that these men were demoralised.[65]

As the Divisional Commander of men taken direct from the UK to the battlefield, never having had to face the enemy, Forestier-Walker appears to recognise no irony in the fact that he is responsible for the morale of his division. Haking claimed to have asked 'several' of the men who had discarded their weapons, why they had done so, 'almost all told me the same story, viz., that they had helped to bring back a wounded man and had to leave their rifle behind'.[66] Haking's solution to the problem would become a staple of many Operation Orders for the rest of the war:

> I am quite sure that a large number of unwounded men came back, many without their rifles and equipment, on the excuse of assisting a wounded soldier, probably a man who was quite able to walk back himself. I think the most stringent orders should be issued to new formations that no wounded soldiers are to be helped to the rear by unwounded men, that those able to walk or crawl back must go by themselves, and that those unable to move must be taken back by Regimental stretcher bearers as opportunity offers.

The various reports were read by Haig and his comments were forwarded to GHQ. Although it is outside the scope of this book, it is worth mentioning that Haig (along with others) was actively undermining the authority of Sir John French with the War Office and the King, and the failures at Loos were grist to their mill. In one communication to the King, Haig stated that 'it was not fair to the Empire to retain French in

---

65 WO 158/262.
66 WO 158/262.

command'.[67] Haig's summary, laying stress on the newness of the divisions as a cause of failure, should be read against this background:

> These divisions went straight into a battle which would have tried experienced troops, and I am of opinion, although neither staff nor troops are wholly free from blame in one respect or another, that the failure of the operations of these divisions was due to the fact that they were new formations, that both the corps and divisional staffs were recently formed, that the troops were untried, and in some cases insufficiently and even entirely untrained in bombing.[68]

The battle of Loos continued until mid-October, although with little involvement by 10/York and Lancaster. Their baptism of fire was not a glorious one, but their march into battle was no ringing endorsement of the administrative skills of Haking or his corps staff officers. These soldiers were the pawns in the struggle between French and Haig over the control and deployment of the general reserve. On 10 December 1915, Haig replaced French as Commander of the BEF.

The men of the 10th battalion were not the only ones from the York and Lancaster Regiment to fight at Loos: 1/York and Lancaster joined the fray on 28 September. We first met this battalion in April, following the Germans' use of gas at Second Ypres. These men were Regulars, and had experience of facing the enemy in a fire-fight; this would serve them well in the fight to hold the Hohenzollern Redoubt. This strong point, about one mile north of the Vermelles-Hulluch road, had been captured from the Germans on 25 September, but three days later the enemy was making serious attempts to re-take the position. In the early hours of 28 September, the battalion was ordered to move from Noyelles to Vermelles, where it came under the orders of 85 Brigade. When we look at British trench maps from that conflict the trench lines appear to be clearly defined, each with a name. For the soldiers at the front, moving forward across ground which has been pounded for some days by the artillery of both sides, especially at night when relieving another battalion, those lines on the map lose their clarity. When units were unfamiliar with the trenches they were about to occupy, it was normal for the battalion being relieved to provide guides to assist the incoming troops to find their way. The guides provided to lead 1/York and Lancs lost their way; it was 5 a.m. before the battalion had completed the relief, something that was always done under the cover of night, not at dawn. For the next two days the men would put their experience to good effect.

Early on the morning of 29 September, Captain Buckley and 2/Lieutenant Ellison led a bombing party over the top 'and delivered an attack, returning when the supply of bombs was exhausted'.[69] The action in Dump Trench, as well as Big and Little

---

67 Senior, *Haking*, p.55.
68 WO 158/262.
69 WO 95/2275.

Willie trenches became a soldiers' battle. British and German troops were fighting it out at close quarters, in the same trenches, with grenades and bayonets. The trenches quickly became congested with troops going forward, others going back as they were relieved, and wounded men doing the best they could for themselves. In this confusion, Major Robertson and Captain Forster gave the order to 'charge'. The Germans were driven back, but at a cost. These two officers, together with two others, were killed, and three more were wounded. Robertson has no known grave and is remembered on the Loos Memorial; Forster (a Major on the CWGC site) is buried at Loos Cemetery. Attacks continued through the day and at 5.30 p.m. the order was given to 'fix bayonets' (a guarantee to the soldiers that the fight would be at close quarters) and 'Capt. Lucas gave the order to charge'. The battalion diary says nothing other than that a German bombing party was put out of action. During that one day the battalion had 101 casualties; 6 men killed, 20 wounded, 21 missing, 4 missing – believed killed and a further 50 'wounded and missing'.

Hard as the fight had been, there was no let-up on the 30th. Attacks and counter-attacks continued through the day, until they were relieved by the Northumberland Fusiliers. A further 76 of their number had joined the casualty statistics. Out of a 'trench strength' of 783 men on 10 September 177 had become casualties in just 48 hours at the Hohenzollern, a 'wastage' rate of 23%. However, the battalion proudly recorded that, 'throughout the two days fighting no part of a trench was given up by our men, although regiments on our flanks did leave portions which we had to retake'.[70]

Those days in late September, 1915, demonstrate how two units, taking part in the same battle, could come away with very different stories. Those from the 10th battalion advanced at night (hungry, tired and with little idea where they were), to see no more than Chalk Pit Wood and a disorderly retreat. The men of the 1st battalion were restricted to a section of the Hohenzollern and three adjacent trenches. Readers of military history should remember that the account of the battles they have access to in official histories, as well as those that fill the shelves of our bookshops, are probably unrecognisable to those who fought there – their view of the battle would have extended little beyond the ground occupied by their own company. Soldiers of 10/York and Lancaster could be forgiven if they called Loos the Battle of Chalk Pit Wood, or the men of the 1st Battalion, the battle for Big and Little Willie trenches.

One of the soldiers from 10/York and Lancaster, who died at Loos, was Lance Corporal James Dillon, this author's great-uncle. He is remembered on the Loos Memorial at Dud Corner Cemetery, along with 116 other members of the York and Lancaster Regiment who were killed in those first days of the battle and have no known grave.

As well as the 1st and 10th battalions, the 8th and 9th (in 23 Division) also played a small part. 23 Division 'played only a subsidiary part in the battle; only if success

---

70 WO 95/2275.

Dud Corner cemetery, Loos. (Photo J. Dillon)

Memorial to Private James Dillon, Dud Corner cemetery, Loos. (Photo J. Dillon)

had been more complete would it have been called on to play a more important rôle'.[71] Although this division was on the periphery of events, Sandilands acknowledges the size of the task facing the British soldiers at Loos:

> No one who has studied the field of Loos, where troops of the New Armies were engaged in their first big battle, can fail to be impressed by the magnitude of the task set them, or to realise the determination and valour that enabled the troops to accomplish what they did.[72]

Unlike Forestier-Walker, Sandilands implies that the reasons for failure did not lie with the soldiers:

> The success gained [on the 25th] was due to the spirit of the troops engaged; failure to exploit the success was due to causes for which the troops were in no way responsible.

Officially, the battle continued until 4 November, 'but the failure of the attack on 13 October effectively brought the battle to an end';[73] it was time for the recriminations. Haig, as we have seen, was briefing against Sir John French whose position 'which was weak before Loos, was now untenable'.[74] Haig took command of the BEF at noon on 19 December 1915.

For 10/York and Lancaster, the battle of Loos had been a traumatic introduction to the war in France. Historians might record the battle as lasting seven weeks but for the battalion it was all over in a couple of days. Not surprisingly after the heavy losses, the men were taken out of the line and spent the next few months in the area around Armentières. On 15 November, the battalion took over trenches 'on its own'.[75] The next few months were relatively quiet, during which the men took their share of trench duty. Finally, on 20 March, the battalion moved from Armentières and transferred to XV Corps, Fourth Army; they were 'preparing to take part in the great Battle of the Somme'.[76]

---

71 Sandilands, H.R., *The 23rd Division 1914-1919* (Uckfield, *Naval & Military Press*, Reprint of 1925 original), p.33.
72 Sandilands, *23rd Division*, p.32.
73 Lloyd, *Loos*, p.213.
74 Holmes, *The Western Front*, p.74.
75 Wylly, *10th battalion history*, pp.219-20.
76 Wylly, *10th battalion history*, p.220.

6

"There was no wavering" – The Somme

"The Somme"; the name of this battle has almost become a synonym for the First World War – for many in Britain, it is the only battle from that conflict to which they could put a name. Over the last century, *The Somme* has become a byword for futility; Caporetto holds a similar meaning for the Italians. The losses suffered by the British infantry on 1 July 1916 made it the bloodiest day in the history of the British Army. At the end of that day, based on unit roll-calls, 61,816 men were not there to answer their names, this figure was later adjusted to 57,470 as some of those thought to be 'missing' made it back to the lines. The dreadful statistic contained 19,240 officers and men killed. The official historian summed up the day as a 'disastrous loss of the finest manhood of the United Kingdom and Ireland [for which] there was only a small gain of ground to show, although certainly the greatest yet made by the British Expeditionary Force'.[1] It was a day on which the machine gun was king. As the war progressed, so the artillery came into its own and became the major killer but on 1 July, 'about 60 per cent' of the casualties were due to German machine guns.[2]

In December 1916, Lloyd George became Prime Minister. During the remainder of the war (and in his memoirs), he was heavily critical of the military commanders for the great loss of soldiers' lives in attritional, frontal attacks against heavily defended positions. This criticism was aimed particularly at the Chief of the General Staff, Sir William Robertson, and the Commander of the BEF, Sir Douglas Haig. Both men bear a heavy responsibility for the way they prosecuted those attacks, though we should remember that they were also learning how to fight total, industrial war, 'on the job'. However, politicians cannot simply slip from under, they were involved in the decision making process and they had the authority to remove the senior commanders if they believed they were not up to the job. They did not do that. The Somme had its genesis in a meeting held at Chantilly in December 1915. One of the decisions

---

1 Edmonds, J., *Military Operations France and Belgium, 1916, Volume 1* (Uckfield, Naval & Military Press, Reprint of 1931 original), p.483.
2 Holmes, *Western Front*, p.127.

taken was for an Anglo-French assault on the Western front in 1916, with the French playing the major part. Preparations for this battle became a regular topic of War Committee meetings in the months prior to the attack. Lloyd George, as Minister for Munitions, kept the council apprised of gun and ammunition production while Kitchener (in his civilian role as War Minister) introduced his recruitment drive for the New Armies, 'without which there could have been no Battle of the Somme'.[3] In February 1916, the Germans launched a massive offensive at Verdun, where the German Commander-in-Chief, Erich von Falkenhayn, intended to 'bleed France white'. As the battle progressed, with enormous losses on both sides, the plans for the Anglo-French offensive agreed at Chantilly, had to change. Instead of the French, the British became the major participants and Haig was to direct it rather than Joffre. In March, Lloyd George was asked whether or not the army would have sufficient munitions 'in May and June'; his answer was 'yes'.[4] As the minister responsible for ensuring that the army had the weapons it needed, he knew that his reply related to the planned summer offensive. On 7 April, in response to a question from Haig, Robertson replied that the C-in-C had Cabinet approval for the combined operation.[5] Lloyd George (still as Minister for Munitions) was party to that decision for the offensive to go ahead; he also concurred with the Prime Minister's comment that the way in which it was carried out 'must be left to the General on the spot'.[6]

The Somme has frequently been portrayed as a battle launched to take the pressure off France at Verdun, this is not correct. As we have seen, the proposal for the Anglo-French offensive came out of the Chantilly conference two months before Falkenhayn launched the German army against the French fortress. That said, the French problems did lead to two changes of plan; first, the date for the British attack was brought forward from Haig's preference for August; second, while the number of British divisions remained substantially the same as in the original plan, those from France decreased, so causing Haig's force to increase relative to Joffre's. It is also worth pointing out here that *The Somme* is something of a misnomer for the British; the river was on the far right of their sector, with the French Sixth Army occupying both banks. None of Haig's soldiers fought anywhere near the river.[7]

The attack was to be carried out by Sir Henry Rawlinson's Fourth Army, which held the line north of the Somme, with the French on their right. The British front stretched south from Gommecourt in the north to Beaumont Hamel, it then ran south-east, across the Albert-Bapaume road to Fricourt where it turned sharply east, past Mametz to Maricourt and the French left flank. Prior to the battle, this area had been relatively quiet, and the gently rolling countryside was not scarred by the

---

3   Prior, R, and T. Wilson, *The Somme* (London, Yale, 2005), p.5.
4   Prior and Wilson, *The Somme*, p.23.
5   Edmonds, *1916, Vol. 1*, p.13.
6   Prior and Wilson, *The Somme*, p.28.
7   Roberts, A., *Elegy. The First Day On The Somme* (London, Head of Zeus, 2015), p.34.

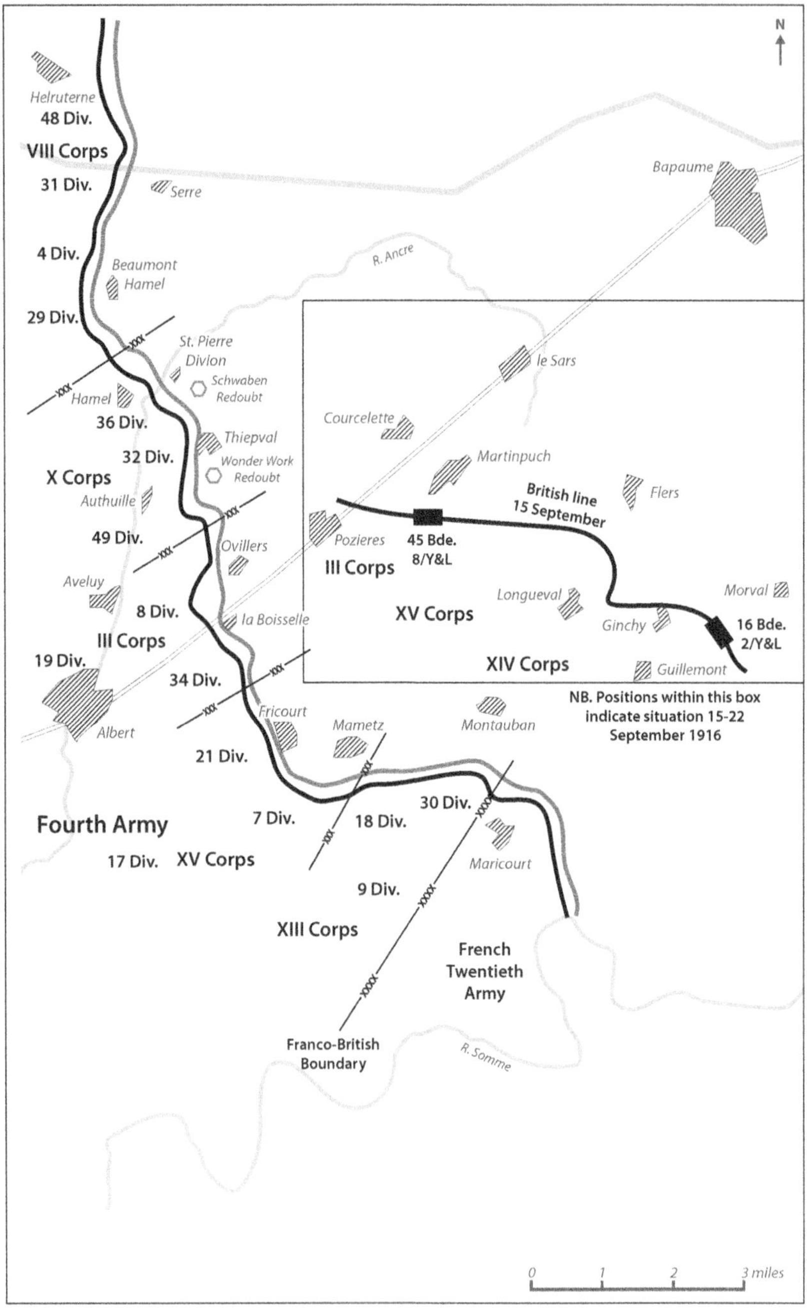

Map 8 Battle of the Somme: Primary map denotes British front on 1 July 1916. Inset relates to Flers/Courcelette, 15 September 1916.

slag-heaps and mine-heads of Loos, it also had better drainage than the Ypres Salient and Passchendaele. This would be more 'favourable ground' than that which had faced 10/York and Lancaster in September 1915; on 1 July, this battalion would be in action opposite the small town of Fricourt. Although there had not been action on this part of the front on the scale seen around Ypres, the Germans had not been inactive. A great deal of effort had gone into strengthening their defences. Their front line trenches were backed up by a second line some 2,000 to 4,000 yards behind the first, the whole reinforced with deep bunkers, strong points like the *Schwaben Redoubt*, and belts of wire from 15 to 30 feet wide. As the army commander, it was the job of Rawlinson and his staff to produce the plan for the attack, but Haig would also have to sign off on it before it went ahead.

We have already seen (at Aubers Ridge) that Rawlinson favoured a progressive attack, moving forward to the second objective after the first had been consolidated – 'bite and hold'. Haig, on the other hand, was more in favour of 'pushing on' vigorously for objectives that were deeper into enemy territory, even beyond effective artillery support. The argument over who was 'right' has been well covered by historians and this account will not go over that ground; suffice to say that there was a difference of opinion between the two men over the way in which the Somme battle should be prosecuted. Rawlinson's plan of 3 April anticipated having 17 infantry divisions available, 'of which 10 were to attack, 2 to remain on the defensive, and 5 to be in corps or Army reserve'.[8] He intended to use them in a two-step, bite and hold attack, knowing that such an approach would come up against Haig's more aggressive stance:

> I daresay I shall have a tussle with him over the limited objective for I hear he is inclined to favour the unlimited with the chance of breaking the German line.[9]

Haig's diary entry for 5 April expressed his view of Rawlinson's more cautious approach:

> I studied Sir H. Rawlinson's proposals for attack. His intention is merely to take the Enemy's first and second system of trenches and 'kill Germans'. He looks upon the gaining of 3 or 4 kilometres more or less of ground immaterial. I think we can do better than this by aiming at getting as large a combined force of French and British across the Somme and fighting the Enemy in the open.[10]

Rawlinson was concerned the New Army divisions did not have the steadiness and experience of the old Regulars and consequently he did not want to overreach his

---

8   Prior and Wilson, *Command on The Western Front*, pp.141-2.
9   Prior and Wilson, *Command on The Western Front*, p.141.
10 Sheffield and Bourne, *Haig*, p.184.

objectives. By the middle of April, he was indicating that his better judgement was giving way to Haig's views:

> It is clear that D.H. would like us to do the whole thing in one rush and I am quite game to try but it certainly does involve considerable risks [...] It will be difficult unless we start a panic.[11]

Prior and Wilson speculate that his acquiescence might have been down to a previous incident between Rawlinson and Haig. At Aubers Ridge Rawlinson apparently laid blame on another officer for his own failings, with the result that Sir John French had said that Rawlinson should be sent home. Haig spoke up for him but had to convey the message that any future attempt to blame subordinates for his own failings would result in the loss of his corps. Haig passed this on, 'making it clear whom Rawlinson had to thank for the retention of his command'.[12]

Rawlinson accepted that he had to aim for the deeper objective of the enemy's second line on the first attack, even though it would probably mean that the new divisions would find it difficult to maintain their cohesion. Much depended on the lengthy artillery bombardment cutting the enemy's extensive wire defences. Unfortunately, much of the German second line could not be seen from the British positions, making artillery spotting difficult, except by air. The depth to which the troops were expected to advance on the first attack gave rise to a further problem: more targets would have to be engaged in the initial bombardment. The effect of this was to reduce the weight of shell that could be brought down on the front line, the wire in front of it, and the machine gun teams sheltering in their dugouts. Rawlinson knew from Neuve Chapelle and Aubers Ridge that the artillery plan was fundamental to the success of the infantry advance, but it would prove to be inadequate on a number of levels. The German defences were deeper and stronger than those they had assaulted at Aubers Ridge and Loos. Additionally, while the attack frontage was 20,000 yards, the length of trench that required shelling was much longer because it included the German second line and the communication trenches in between.

While Rawlinson and his staff made their plans for the assault, the battalions of the York and Lancaster Regiment went about their training and other duties before moving forward to their assembly positions. The 8th battalion (part of 8 Division) opposite the fortified villages of Ovillers and La Boisselle, took turns in the trenches with 9/York and Lancaster; out of the line they were billeted in Albert. Hot baths in mid-May were a welcome diversion, with a further 400 men being able to soak at Millencourt on 11 and 25 June.[13] Sport was a major diversion when the men had time away from the fire-step: on 13 May, 8/York and Lancs played 2/Scottish Rifles

---

11 Prior and Wilson, *Command on The Western Front*, p.148.
12 Prior and Wilson, *Command on The Western Front*, p.71.
13 TNA WO 95/2188, war diary, 8/York & Lancs.

in the semi-final of the Divisional Football Cup. Unfortunately, they did not play well and lost 5 goals to nil. On the following day, their officers performed no better, losing against their colleagues in 11/Sherwood Foresters. On a more sombre note, the battalion joined a memorial service in Millencourt 'in conjunction with service at St Paul's in memory of the late Earl Kitchener of Khartoum' – the man whose face on the recruitment posters had encouraged so many of them to join the fight. In 1914, 'K' had appealed to the men going to France to be on their guard against excess in drink and women, he would have been disappointed (but probably not surprised) that many men ignored the warning. On the day of the service Sergeant Bain, 8/York and Lancaster, was arraigned before a Field General Court Martial 'for drunkenness', the war diary does not record the verdict.

In the days before a battle, soldiers' thoughts may have turned towards things spiritual. It is often said that there are no atheists on the battlefield, but neither were there so many who wanted to give up their Sunday mornings to go to church. Richard Holmes asked 'what hope and faith moved this vast assemblage of the proud and the profane, the cynical and the contemptuous, that constituted the British army in France?'[14] When the men were out of the front line, church parade was a frequent Sunday ritual and while many attended of their own volition, many more were there because it was a 'parade'. On 14 May, there were 'about 300 on parade' out of a battalion strength of a little fewer than 1,000. No doubt, many of their colleagues were on 'fatigues' or 'work parties'. Even in the weeks before a major assault, there were routines in place for keeping the men busy, fit and clean. With a large number of men living together in confined spaces, with infrequent access to baths and clean clothes, cleanliness and sanitation become very important. Battalion diaries often contain the entry 'internal economy', a euphemism for the inspection of a whole variety of items and activities, which had the potential to adversely affect the health of the men: cooking facilities; billets; horse-lines; latrines. Often these would be carried out on a competitive basis, one company or platoon against another, and they were taken seriously by the men.

Time spent out of the line should have been spent resting and training but too often the men were used to augment labour and working parties. Although the army did have labour battalions, frequently made up of West Indians and Chinese, there were insufficient of them for the jobs that needed doing. Only one week before the 'Big Push' the men of 14/York and Lancaster made up large working parties digging assembly trenches for the attack, as well as carrying parties taking rations, water and ammunition to the front:

> The whole of the available strength of the Battn was employed on this work & it was impossible to carry out any further training. The men were obliged to walk about 12 miles daily getting backwards and forwards to their work & it

14 Holmes, *Tommy*, p.503.

undoubtedly placed them under a very heavy physical strain. Had it been possible to obtain motor lorries for conveying the men to & from their work they would have proved most useful.[15]

The following series of diary entries indicates how, in the last days before they were called on to rush German machine guns, the men of 12/York and Lancaster were kept busy but hardly in a way that would better prepare them for what was coming:

> 20 June: men allowed to rest and clean themselves up [there is no record in the diary of the troops having had access to baths in the previous months].
> 21 June: Battn. provided carrying parties from Colincamps to trenches for ammunition etc.
> 22 June: Battn. provided carrying parties from Euston Dump to front line for gas cylinders. Also digging parties [...] working all night 22/23. 6. 16.
> 23 June: working parties supplied to trenches. 1 OR killed.
> 24 June: Quiet day.
> 25 June: Divine services during the day.
> 26 June: Battn. move off to training ground to re-practice assembly and assault [...] The Division Commander spoke a few words of encouragement to the Batt., prior to its going into action.

Although the battalions appear to have done little training in the days before the attack, there was a comprehensive schedule in May and the first half of June. Commanders did try to prepare their men for the various phases of the coming assault, but it was largely based around how to form up in the assembly trenches, how to cross various obstacles and how to advance behind an artillery barrage. The obvious component that was missing was an enemy firing live bullets. Given this omission, the training always seemed to be completed successfully. On 17 May, 8/York and Lancaster practiced an 'attack on enemy trenches' while the following day 'raiders carried out a practice raid by night'. To make the exercises more relevant, training areas were often marked out with tape and flags to represent the ground over which the troops would be advancing, as on 8 March at Franvillers:

> The Brigade practiced the attack on a flagged course representing the front over which the 70th Bde will probably attack – from the NAB to FARM DE MOUQUET in front of AUTHUILLE WOOD. The attack was practiced in all its phases – 8th KOYLI on the right, 8th Y&L on the left with 9th Y&L in support and 11th Sherwood Foresters in Reserve. Front line battalions advanced in 4 waves the first halt being the enemy's 3rd line, followed by the taking of 1st,

---

15 TNA WO 95/2365, war diary, 14/York & Lancs.

2nd & 3rd objectives. Trench mortars, machine guns, Lewis guns & Bombing parties all took part.[16]

The whole exercise was repeated the next day and then all the officers went over the course again after the practice, to enable them to become familiar with the objectives. Sadly, the real attack on 1 July went nothing like that. In order to shorten the distance the men would have to advance when the whistle sounded, the first waves of the brigade were to leave the front trenches during the pre-attack bombardment, they would then lie out in no man's land until zero hour, hoping that their move had not been spotted by the Germans. If the plan worked, the troops would reach the German wire before the enemy re-appeared on their parapet, complete with machine guns. As preparation, the battalion trained 'in assembly in "NO MAN'S LAND" to take up a position of readiness prior to the Assault'. Additionally, on 17 June, the men were taken to observation posts from which 'all ranks viewed the ground over which [the] future advance will be made'.

Senior commanders held the strong opinion that active raids and patrols into no man's land had a beneficial effect on morale and strengthened the 'fighting spirit'. These aggressive tactics allowed the battalions to gain intelligence on the troops to their front, gauge their preparedness and inspect the enemy wire. In some places the gap between 9/York and Lancaster trenches, and those of the Germans, was only 60 yards.[17] One such raid was carried out by 2/Lieutenant Riley with a sergeant and six men from 8/York and Lancs. The area to be covered was close to 'The Nab'. This was a point in the German line in front of the battalion, which included a cross-road they believed to be used by the enemy. The following is taken from Riley's pencil notes:

> We proceeded up the road parallel to our front as far as the cross roads at [map reference]. When within about 50 yards of cross roads we saw a number of men come across NO MAN'S LAND, cross the road and take up a position behind the bank. Not sure whether it was one of our own patrols or not we approached nearer and challenged – on receiving no reply we opened fire and threw bombs. They retaliated with bombs – 2 of these failed to explode and we brought them in. Every member of my patrol was hit – one fatally. Sergt. [unreadable] & I brought in Pte Hughes and on our return to our trenches sent another party to bring in the man who was killed (Pte Metcalfe). The enemy patrol was about 15 strong and I am sure we inflicted casualties as great as ours.[18]

16   WO 95/2188.
17   WO 95/2188.
18   WO 95/2188.

The British were convinced that the Germans used The Nab as a listening post, and so sent a number of subsequent patrols to try to deny it to them; not all were successful. On 20 June, a patrol from 9/York and Lancaster recorded the result as

> disastrous. [...] Our machine gun Sgt – an excellent NCO – being killed, two of the detachment being wounded & some of the Trench Mortar men were also wounded. The enemy was not encountered but he found a most excellent use with his machine guns from his front line for dealing with our patrol.[19]

Raiding was becoming such an essential part of trench routine that 9/York and Lancaster formed a special raiding party of 2 officers and 50 men with the aim of training them 'in the many arts of raiding'. Experienced NCOs were the backbone of the army and once lost, were hard to replace. Company Sergeant Major Ellis, 12/York and Lancaster epitomised these old Regular soldiers. On 3 May, the company telephone dugout was hit by a German 'mine', Ellis and five men were killed:

> Stiff, sturdy, and manly, the sergeant-major was one of the best-liked men in the Battalion, and always was a notable figure. He represented the best type of the British soldier, and the traditions of the British Army were matters of great moment to him. [...] A Sheffielder by birth he joined the 2nd Battalion of the York and Lancasters over a quarter of a century ago, and was in South Africa from 1891 to 1897 [...] with the Mounted Infantry in the Matabele war. [...] He stayed with the regiment in India until the end of 1898, when he went to the Indian Volunteer Staff.[20]

Ellis later saw fighting in the Boer War with Lumsden's Horse and stayed in South Africa until 1901 when he was selected to go to Australia. At the end of that war he returned home and joined the battalion in Dover; he followed this with service in Malta and was then on the permanent staff of the Hallamshires until 1911. A civilian when war was declared, he then joined the York and Lancaster Regiment and is now buried in Sucrerie Cemetery only a few yards away from Private McKenzie, the battalion's first man killed. McKenzie was described in the diary as 'a quiet lad', killed by a rifle grenade; he was 'reverently buried in a small cemetery behind the line'.[21]

In the days immediately prior to the 1 July attack, all battalions in the front line would have been trying to assess the effect of their own artillery on the enemy defences, specifically the wire. They could not see how deep the German dugouts were, but they could gain intelligence on whether or not the wire had been cut. If the defences were

---

19   WO 95/2188.
20   Sparling, R.A., *History of the 12th Service Battalion York & Lancaster Regiment* (Uckfield, Naval & Military Press, Reprint of 1920 original), p.37.
21   Sparling, *12th Battalion*, p.35.

intact then the task of the infantry would become that much harder; attempting to cut a way through, in the teeth of a hail of bullets from the enemy's machine guns, would not have a happy ending. Cutting the wire was not an easy task for the gunners, it required shrapnel shells to be delivered with great accuracy, and fused to explode close to the wire. High Explosive (HE) shells exploded on impact or, after traveling a short distance into the ground, tended to move the wire rather than cut it. By 1916, ground commanders were beginning to depend heavily on the reconnaissance efforts of the RFC but while aircraft were ideal for spotting changes in the enemy trench lines and wire defences (backed up by aerial photographs), they could not determine whether or not the wire was cut. The only reliable method of making that assessment was by direct visual observation: this required patrols to go out between the lines, at night. Unfortunately, this was no panacea as the slow movement of the patrols (they needed to avoid observation) meant that they could only inspect a limited amount of the enemy line. Additionally, it was summer, the nights were short, the enemy was alert and it took time for the men to crawl from their trenches to the enemy's and back again. In one analysis[22] of the reports of 50 patrols sent out prior to the attack, around half reported the wire as uncut, the rest were a mix of 'cut' and 'cut in places'.

When analysed by individual corps, the situation regarding the enemy wire was inconsistent along the front, with VIII Corps (which included 12/York and Lancs) producing 'far more negative than positive reports'. As well as patrols between the lines, battalions also sent out trench raiding parties to bring in prisoners for interrogation. Sadly, the intelligence gleaned was scarce and contradictory. Haig was particularly critical of the intelligence gathering efforts of VIII Corps, calling in the corps commander to express his dissatisfaction. Haig's criticism was that during the bombardment period the corps had failed to break into the German position, they 'had no experience of the fighting in France and [had] not carried out one successful raid'.[23] Only 12 Germans were taken prisoner by Fourth Army between 25 and 30 June and on this small sample (75% on the front of just one corps), Rawlinson and his staff determined that 'most of the dug-outs in the [enemy] front line had been blown in or blocked up'.[24] One has to agree with Prior and Wilson that such a determination bordered on 'irresponsible' and brave men would go into battle that day believing that the destruction of the German defences was more complete than would prove to be the case.

Before we sound the whistle and send the troops 'over the bags', it is worth spending a moment to review the ground in front of the five corps that made up Fourth Army's front line (see Map 8). In the south, on the right of the army, and with the French on their right, was XIII Corps (18 and 19 Divisions). Like XV Corps on their left, they had the advantage of higher ground and a view over the German defences. XIII

22 Prior and Wilson, *The Somme*, p.64.
23 Edmonds, *1916, Vol. 1*, p.308.
24 Prior and Wilson, *The Somme*, pp.66-7.

corps had the most success (in terms of ground gained) on 1 July, with losses on a much small scale than the rest of Fourth Army. As well as the advantage of ground, this corps benefited from the priority given to counter-battery fire, so nullifying the effect of German artillery. The York and Lancaster Regiment did not have a battalion in this corps. On the left of XIII Corps was the XVth, which included 10/York and Lancaster (63 Brigade, 21 Division) on the left flank of the corps. The corps front was bisected by the river Ancre; to their right was the village of Mametz, faced by 7 Division, and to their left, Fricourt faced by 21 Division. Here, the British had the rising ground of the Morlancourt-Maricourt ridge behind them, providing good observation over the German lines. Additionally, the shape of the front at this point allowed British guns to provide enfilade fire from the south. As the two villages to the divisional fronts were heavily defended, the plan was for the initial attack to by-pass both of them. They could then be taken out by follow-on troops.

Moving further north we come to III Corps, to the right front (opposite 34 Division) of which was the village of La Boisselle and on their left was Orvillers (faced by 8 Division, which had both 8 and 9/York and Lancaster in 70 Brigade). Both of these fortified villages lay at the southern end of the Thiepval ridge. Behind them, the British troops had little cover and the Germans, with the advantage of height, were able to observe them moving to their start lines. This disadvantage was compounded by the width of No Man's Land in this sector: between Ovillers and La Boisselle – Mash Valley – the men were expected to cover an 800 yard gap, while coming under German machine gun fire from both flanks. The German strong point at Thiepval – now the site of the impressive Memorial designed by Sir Edwin Lutyens – 'overlooked practically all the first belt of ground over which the divisions of the III Corps had necessarily to advance'.[25]

The next corps on the left was the Xth, with the formidable task of advancing towards heavily defended Thiepval and Mouquet Farm ('Mucky Farm' to the Tommies); the ridge in front of them rose to between 140 and 160 meters. The two divisions forming the corps front were 32 on the right and 36 (the men of Ulster) on the left, with 49 Division (1/4 and 1/5 York and Lancaster of 148 Brigade) in corps reserve. The position would be a tough nut to crack. On the southern end of the Thiepval spur was the *Leipzig Redoubt* with fields of fire over the British line between the woods of Authuille and Thiepval. Between *Leipzig* and Thiepval, but on the reverse slope, lay the *Wonderwerk Redoubt*. North of Thiepval, and with good lines of fire towards the village and over most of the spur, was the triangular system of trenches of the *Schwaben Redoubt*. Lastly, where the spur sloped down to the River Ancre, was the defended village of St. Pierre Divion. There was a little good news in that the woods along the Ancre – Thiepval, Authuille and Aveluy – allowed assembly positions and communication trenches to be constructed out of sight of the Germans.

25 Edmonds, *1916, Vol. 1*, pp.371-2.

Last, but not least, we come to VIII Corps, on the left of Rawlinson's attack front. Facing these troops (which included 12, 13 and 14/York and Lancaster in 94 Brigade, 31 Division), were the fortress-villages of Serre and Beaumont Hamel, with the *Quadrilateral* mid-way between both and forming part of the German front line trench system. The three Pals battalions of the York and Lancaster Regiment would suffer terribly while trying to overcome the German defences at Serre. Others have written comprehensive histories of the Battle of The Somme, this account limits itself to 'how went the day' on 1 July for the York and Lancaster battalions.

We start with the men of 10/York and Lancaster who had such a torrid time at Loos. On the left front of XV Corps was 21 Division, a little north of the defended village of Fricourt, with 63 Brigade in the centre of the divisional front. The brigade was to form a defensive flank facing Fricourt village, while 64 Brigade on their left advanced towards Bottom Wood, behind Fricourt, and linked up with 91 Brigade from 7 Division on their right. At 9 in the evening on 30 June, the 63rd moved forward to take up its position in the assembly trenches a little north-east of Becordel and west of Fricourt. Although the battle is commonly referred to as starting on 1 July, it actually began with the seven-day artillery bombardment that commenced on 24 June. The massive shelling of the German lines was due to continue until the planned date for the infantry assault on the 29th, by which time the British hoped that the enemy would be incapable of resistance. In the event, bad weather intervened and necessitated a 48 hour postponement of Zero Hour until 1 July.

The intensive – postponed – bombardment of the German front line began at 6:25 a.m., 1 July, and at 7:28 a.m., three mines were exploded in front of Fricourt. The intention was to distract the enemy as well as to form deep craters. It was hoped that these would make it difficult for the enemy machine gunners to direct enfilade fire against 63 and 64 Brigades.[26] Although the men of the 10th had been 'issued with rum at dawn'[27] –the effect may well have worn off by the time the whistle went – the infantry attack did not commence until some hours later, at 7:30 a.m. 4/Middlesex and 8/Somerset L.I. were the lead battalions of 63 Brigade:

> At 8.30 a.m. 10th York and Lancs and 8th Lincoln Regt advanced from Assembly Trenches and passed through the 4th Middlesex Regt and 8th Somerset L.I. respectively, coming under very heavy machine gun fire from FRICOURT and FRICOURT WOOD. After very hard fighting (in which heavy casualties occurred) the Battalion consolidated in LOZENGE ALLEY and later in DART LANE. Battalion remained in this position till about 2.0 p.m. third day when it moved to SUNKEN ROAD and took up station in DINGLE TRENCH, with H.Q. in SUNKEN ROAD.[28]

26 Edmonds, *1916, Vol. 1*, pp.348-9.
27 Mortimer, IWM Doc. 7449.
28 WO 95/2158.

In an attempt to help the infantry, the corps artillery implemented an early form of the 'creeping barrage'. The fire of the heavy guns did not 'creep' – this technique had still to be developed – but lifted, at designated times, to fire onto the next barrage line. The creeping was effectively a sequence of 'fire and lift'; the guns moving their barrage line forward at a rate of 50 yards every minute. If the troops arrived at any point ahead of the barrage then they were to 'wait under the best cover available and be prepared to assault directly the lift takes place'.[29] As was so often the case with new tactics, reality fell short of expectations: insufficient guns were allocated and the infantry were not able to keep up with the artillery plan.

The two brigades of 21 Division had done well, advancing about one mile from their start positions. However, 34 Division on their left (and part of III Corps), had not kept pace with them. With their left flank 'open' until units from divisional reserve could be sent forward, the advance was stopped. Although 63 and 64 Brigades had not reached the objectives set for them (most were too optimistic), it was decided to launch 22 Brigade (7 Division) against Fricourt. Suffice to say that this attack, together with that of 50 Brigade on their left, was not successful, though many men died trying. Fricourt was still in German hands at the end of the day. Mametz, however, was taken and considerable ground gained around and behind the village.

At the close of day, 1 July, the front line of XV Corps had changed considerably. Advances had been made on both flanks: 2,550 yards on the right and up to 2,000 on the left, but the centre, opposite Fricourt, had barely moved. The Germans remained in occupation of this strong point, with a deep salient into the British line. For these gains, the corps had suffered over 8,000 casualties, the largest coming from 21 Division – 4,256 men.[30] One more battalion of the York and Lancaster Regiment should be mentioned before we leave XV Corps: 7/York and Lancaster was a Pioneer battalion in 17 Division, which started the day in Corps Reserve. These men did not take part in the fighting, but were used in their pioneer role for strengthening defences. On 3 July, two platoons were assigned 'to act as burial party on [the] battlefield'.[31]

When 10/York and Lancaster came out of the line and took stock of their losses of the previous three days, they counted seven officers and 53 men as killed or died of wounds, six officers and 237 men wounded with a further 25 men listed as missing.[32] Mortimer referred to it as 'two days of hell'.[33] One of those wounded was Private 17489, M. Dillon;[34] while the nature of his wound is not known, it was sufficient for him to be medically evacuated to England on 3 July – a 'Blighty one'. The battalion was relieved by 12/Manchester on 4 July and proceeded to Dernacourt. A few days later 63 Brigade was moved from 21 to 37 Division, where the battalion had two spells

29   Edmonds, *1916, Vol. 1*, pp.349-50.
30   Edmonds, *1916, Vol. 1*, p.368.
31   TNA WO 95/1995, war diary, 7/York & Lancs.
32   WO 95/2158.
33   Mortimer, IWM Doc. 7449.
34   The author takes a particular interest in all those with the same family name.

in the trenches, 11-14 July and 25-31. Both of these passed relatively quietly, except for the night of 13/14 July when 'gas [was] emitted from our trenches, raid taking place on our left'.

While the 10th Battalion was waiting to go forward on the Ancre, the 8th and 9th of the York and Lancaster (70 Brigade) were to the north of them, on the extreme left of III Corps. The corps front was occupied by 8 Division on the left and 34 on the right; the boundary being close to the Albert-Pozières road and Mash Valley. The fortified village of La Boisselle was on the left of the 34 Division sector and to the north of it, in the centre of 8 Division, was Orvillers. The jumping-off position for 8/York and Lancaster (the left-most battalion on the corps front) was at a point where the British line made a right-angle to the west to go around the *Leipzig Redoubt*. In this position, the battalion had Authuille Wood behind them, The Nab directly in front, and enfilade fire from *Leipzig Redoubt* on their left. One can only imagine the thoughts of the men as they surveyed the ridge in front of them. The battalion's final objective lay to the east of Pozières – a straight-line advance of some two miles, with two other intermediate lines 'to be consolidated as soon as captured'.[35] Directly behind 8/York and Lancaster, in the second wave, was their sister battalion.

The troops of III Corps had a formidable task before them. On the right, 34 Division was to 'attack and capture' the German positions around Fricourt and Sausage Valley and then continue advancing to a line some 800 yards short of the enemy at Pozières-Contalmaison. At the same time, 8 Division on their left, to the north of the Albert-Pozières road, was to take the 'western slope of [the] Orvillers spur and the village'.[36] The enormity of what they were expected to do was summed up by Edmonds:

> The two assaulting divisions had thus to capture two fortified villages and six lines of trenches, and to advance into the German position to a depth of roughly two miles on a frontage of four thousand yards – a formidable task.[37]

When the barrage ceased at zero hour, the men of 34 Division rose up and went forward. Unfortunately, a German listening post had picked up a British telephone conversation, which gave details of the timing of the assault and they were ready; 'in a matter of ten minutes some 80 per cent of the men in the leading battalions were casualties'.[38] By the end of the day, the difference between the plan and the facts on the ground was obvious. Units had had their line of advance changed by the ferocity of the fire from defended positions, strong points such as *Scott* and *Sausage Redoubt* were by-passed rather than attacked; 34 Division gains were minimal.

---

35 WO 95/2188.
36 Edmonds, *1916, Vol. 1*, pp.372-3.
37 Edmonds, *1916, Vol. 1*, p.373.
38 Edmonds, *1916, Vol. 1*, p.377.

Unlike 34 Division, the 8th had all three of its brigades in the front of the assault (34 had one brigade in reserve). On the right, the 23rd was to attack Mash Valley and continue advancing for one mile, over rising ground, to Pozières. On their left, 25 Brigade was to take Villers while on the far left the 70th (with both York and Lancaster battalions) was to advance along Nab Valley, all the way to Mouquet Farm. Although there were only 1,800 Germans opposing the 9,600 men of 8 Division,[39] events would prove how overly ambitious was the plan. Each of the British battalions moved forward in four lines of companies, 50 paces between them, on a frontage of 400 yards. The advance, over open ground with little cover, was described by the Germans as being 'at a steady easy pace as if expecting to find nothing alive in our front trenches'.[40] However, they were occupied and as soon as the bombardment lifted, the enemy had established a firing line of machine guns and rifles. The Germans were presented with easy targets; 'all along the line men could be seen throwing up their arms and collapsing, never to move again'.

In the early hours of 1 July, 8/York and Lancaster were to send out 'their two leading waves in front of our wires. They will be formed up in previously selected positions marked out by stones or sandbags and by rope. The leading wave will be about 200 yards from German trenches, 2nd wave 60 yards behind 1st wave'.[41] Many of them would be killed by German machine gunners when the barrage lifted. A reading of the Operation Orders for the day cannot help but give the impression that the German defenders were expected to offer little resistance, and conform to the British battle plan: the two leading waves would 'move over ground without stopping to 3rd German line'. Having taken the first objective (which they did not), the brigade would move quickly to the second 'across the open for about 1300 yards. The leading troops should be able to reach a point close to the 2nd position to be consolidated [2nd intermediate line], in 15 minutes *if only a slight resistance is met with*'.[42] [My emphasis.] Commanders must plan to win, but the assumptions for 1 July are staggering. There was sufficient experience, from previous assaults, to recognise that German resistance would be tenacious. Had the ordinary soldiers read the Operation Order in detail (only the officers would have had copies), they would have been somewhat worried by one item: hand grenades were 'not to be used indiscriminately, as they are difficult to replenish'. Not what men who were expected to rush machine gun nests would have wanted to read.

The following is the 1 July entry in the war diary of 8/York and Lancaster. It is all the more powerful for being written in a matter-of-fact style, and with a complete lack of hyperbole:

39   Edmonds, *1916, Vol. 1*, p.385, footnote 2.
40   Edmonds, *1916, Vol. 1*, p.393.
41   WO 95/2188.
42   WO 95/2188.

Being the leading Battn on the left of the 70th Bde, in the attack near Ovillers the Battn assaulted as per Appendix 1 [the operation order]. The attack was timed for 7.30 a.m. & for an hour previous to that hour the guns delivered an infernal bombardment to which the enemy replied. At the time the assault commenced our front line trenches in the NAB were heavily shelled but the casualties were very few. No smoke was liberated on our front as the wind was unfavourable. The first wave left our trenches in perfect order & to time & were at once met by an exceptionally heavy fire from front and both flanks. Most of the men were killed or wounded, but the remainder continued the advance. In spite of the heavy fire the remaining waves advanced to the attack but before getting halfway to the enemy trenches were mown down by the machine guns. About seventy men reached the enemy trenches & some of these eventually reached the enemy's third lines of his front system of trenches. Here they remained fighting for some time until all were killed or taken prisoners – one returned. The remainder were held up in the enemy front line & considerable fighting took place here until almost all were killed – only three returned. Many of the enemy were killed by our men both in his trenches & when he marched across the open to counter attack. The supporting Battn (9th York & Lancs) were also caught by the machine guns as they advanced to the attack & suffered so many casualties that only an odd man or two reached the German line where our men so badly needed support. The same happened to the Reserve Battn (11th Sherwood Foresters). The Battn as it went over the parapet numbered 680 NCOs & men & 23 officers. Of these only 68 men returned. All the officers were casualties, 18 being killed & missing & 5 wounded. The CO & Adjutant were among the killed. In the evening the Bde was withdrawn upon being relieved by the S.W.B.[43] [South Wales Borderers]

The men of 8 and 9/York and Lancaster did not advance far that day, very little ground was taken, and even that was recovered by the Germans before the day ended. Plans were laid for another attack that evening, but these were wisely shelved. At around 7 p.m. that evening, 9/York and Lancs were making arrangements for those men who made it back from the action:

GS wagons & limbers were sent patrolling the roads between Long Valley & Crucifix Corner, under orders to pick up any men who were on their way to rejoin the Bn in Long Valley. 180 returned up to 10 p.m. Strength of Bn going into action, 25 Officers, 736 other ranks.[44]

On 2 July, the adjutant recorded that another 3 officers and 180 men had turned up. During all the post-battle confusion, it would have been difficult for stranded men to

43 WO 95/2188.
44 WO 95/2188.

find their way back to their units and their comrades. The following day, all the survivors were paraded so that a count could be made of those remaining. On 1 July III Corps suffered over 11,000 casualties and of these 5,121 were from 8 Division (1,927 were dead).[45] According to the Official History, the 8th and 9th battalions suffered 597 and 423 casualties, respectively. Based on the numbers that their diaries recorded as having gone 'over the top' that day, their respective casualty rates on 1 July were 85% and 55.6% – truly dreadful. On the other side of the equation, the German 180th Regiment, which faced 8 Division, suffered a total of only 280 against the British loss of 5,121.[46]

The two battalions (or what remained of them) were taken out of the line on 2 July and entrained at Dernancourt station for their move to the rear. Between then and 25 July the troops spent their time training and welcoming new drafts to bring them back up to battalion strength. By this point, many of those young men who had sailed for France in August 1915 – eager to do their bit before the war was over – were dead.

We come next to X Corps and the 1/4th and 1/5th battalions of the York and Lancaster Regiment, both of them in 148 Brigade, 49 Division (in corps reserve in Aveluy Wood). The corps was to attack on a two division front, the 32nd on the right (facing the fortified village of Thiepval) and the 36th (Ulster Division) on the left. The Ulstermen had a particularly difficult challenge. From their assembly trenches in Thiepval Wood, the ground rose to the ridge and the enormously strong *Schwaben Redoubt*, while their advance would come under enfilading fire from the village of Thiepval on their right. The men of Ulster did their country proud that day, advancing further than any other division but in doing so, they suffered dreadful casualties.

Rawlinson's plan called for X Corps 'to capture the whole of the Thiepval spur and plateau in its first onslaught'[47] – a massive task. By 10.10 a.m., or only two hours and forty minutes after starting the attack, the two leading divisions were expected to have reached the German line between Mouquet Farm and Grandcourt – an advance of some 3,000 yards against a formidable system of trench-works, redoubts and machine guns. Needless to say, the bravery of the troops was not sufficient to achieve the objectives of the Staff Planners. At 10.30 a.m., by which time the lead brigades of 32 Division were supposed to have reached the Mouquet Farm-Grandcourt line, many of the men were dead, although some had made it to the *Leipzig Redoubt* and the outskirts of Thiepval village. Poor communications led the corps headquarters staff to believe that Thiepval had been captured and so they directed the artillery to leave it alone for the rest of the day.[48] The inability of 32 Division to make much progress in the face of the German machine guns meant that the right flank of the Ulstermen was seriously exposed. In spite of this they had taken the *Schwaben Redoubt* and the

45 Edmonds, *1916, Vol. 1*, p.389.
46 Edmonds, *1916, Vol. 1*, pp.393.
47 Edmonds, *1916, Vol. 1*, p.397.
48 Edmonds, *1916, Vol. 1*, p.403.

trenches behind it but, unless supported (or their flank covered by 32 Division), they would be unable to hold their exposed position. When and where to use his reserves is a decision that a commander makes based on his knowledge of the situation on the ground; when that information is lacking, poor decisions are made, if any are made at all. By midday, the troops of 49 Division, the corps reserve, had not been deployed. The 1/4th and 1/5th York and Lancaster were in Aveluy Woods, 'undisturbed by the enemy [and] left to draw what conclusions we could from the noise and the confused stories of the constant stream of wounded which passed by us'. Grant's battalion history has that smack of bravado and jingoism that is to be found in so many of the accounts written after the war: 'We had expected a day of chances and real activity; it proved to be a mere straining at the leash until the chance of seizing the enemy by the throat had vanished'.[49]

At 1.30 p.m. 1/5 York and Lancaster were ordered to move along the right bank of the Ancre to support 108 Brigade (36 Division), who were facing the strong German position at St. Pierre Divion. The move must have taken some time, as the next diary entry was three hours later. The battalion was moving through Thiepval Wood, which had been 'very badly knocked about and bodies, kit and equipment strewed the tracks and trenches'.[50] In the end, the move came to little and by 'about midnight the last of the 108Bde were withdrawn into dugouts in Thiepval Wood'. 1/4th York and Lancaster did not set off until 8.30 p.m. – 'some twelve hours later than we had hoped!'[51] Ordered to attach themselves to 107 Brigade in Thiepval Wood, they did not get there until it was very dark and they had difficulty finding their way. Once in position they were told to 'hold the old British front line around the edge of the [Thiepval] Wood'. Confusion on the ground was the order of the day; those in command were unaware of whether or not the old German trenches were occupied by British troops, as well as being uncertain regarding the situation around Thiepval. As a result, 'the night was one of nervous uncertainty, of orders issued and cancelled'.[52] It was not until the very early hours of 3 July that both York and Lancaster battalions went forward to occupy the old German trenches, which had been captured on the first day of the assault.

The total confusion as to the true position on the ground was poor reward for the bravery of the men of 36 (Ulster) Division who had captured the *Schwaben Redoubt*. Isolated in their forward position, and with no help appearing, the senior officer in the redoubt (a major) decided, at 10 p.m., that the situation was untenable and gave the order to retire: 'The withdrawal was carried out in good order without interference by the enemy until the Ulstermen were well clear, when they were followed by rifle fire'.[53]

---

49 Grant, *Hallamshires*, p.38.
50 WO 95/2805.
51 Grant, *Hallamshires*, p.38.
52 Grant, *Hallamshires*, p.39.
53 Edmonds, *1916, Vol. 1*, p.419.

At the end of that first day of the battle, the three divisions of X Corps had suffered 9,643 casualties, of whom 5,104 (almost 50%) came from the Ulstermen.[54] The men of the 1/4th and 1/5th York and Lancaster had suffered less than other battalions from the regiment who had been involved in the first wave of Fourth Army's attack; only 590 casualties were recorded for the whole of 49 Division – a consequence of its being the corps reserve. The reserve troops on this sector of the front, as at Loos, had been used poorly, and came in for criticism from Edmonds:

> The piecemeal employment of the 49th Division by X Corps headquarters had accomplished nothing.[55]

A similar opinion was recorded in the battalion history of 1/4th York and Lancaster: 'The great mistake seems to have been the splitting up and frittering away of our Division at the critical time on the afternoon of the 1st'.[56] There was a frustration among the reserves that they had not been allowed to do more to help and, in one letter, the writer commented that, on reading of their involvement that day (1 July), 'you will see that it amounts to very little, and that is the disappointing part of the business. We went into action seven hundred and fifty strong, and came out three hundred and seventy, and yet we have nothing to show for these very big losses'. The 1/4th recorded 222 casualties for the first three days of July while the 1/5th listed 307 for the first eight days. Once again, the contemporaneous record of casualties does not accord with the post-war statistics.

The Hallamshire's historian may have expressed some frustration at being left to 'strain at the leash', but the 1/5th had an opportunity on 6 July to 'attack, occupy and consolidate' part of the German line. The following is from their war diary for that day:

> 3:30 a.m. Five bombing squads and a party of snipers set off from GORDON CASTLE [a point in their trench]. The whole operation was under the direction of Major Shaw 2nd in command. The CO accompanied the party to the front line. The 1/4th KOYLI were holding points A15-A18 [map references] and the entry to the trenches was to be made under cover of their occupation. On arrival it was found that 1/4th KOYLI had been attacked during the night and their hold on the trenches was precarious; bombs having run out. Our bombing squads were divided into 3 parties; 2 squads to right, 2 to left and 1 in reserve. Right party found enemy in possession of strong point of A15 and were unable to dislodge him, finally last man came back when last bomb had been thrown. The left party could make no progress from A18 and had to man the trenches,

54 Edmonds, *1916, Vol. 1*, p.421, footnote 1.
55 Edmonds, *1916, Vol. 1*, p.416.
56 Grant, *Hallamshires*, pp.41-2.

soon after what was left of the party returned across the open. The CO Lt. Col. Shuttleworth Rendall DSO was wounded early on and taken to a German dugout. It was impossible to bring him back when the trench was evacuated. Major GT Shaw was killed later on.

Total of party going out was 7 Officers 80 OR
Total of party returned was [Officers] Nil 22 OR
1 officer killed, 2 wounded, 1 wounded and missing, 3 missing.[57]

This account demonstrates that raids could be as dangerous as an attack, and equally frustrating in their failure to achieve the objective. Lieutenant Colonel Rendall, who had been left wounded in the German dugout, obviously died of his wounds; he is buried in Lebucquiere Communal Cemetery Extension near the village of the same name, 8 kilometres east of Bapaume. He was attached to the York and Lancaster battalion from the Duke of Cornwall's Light Infantry. Major Shaw, attached from 2/Northamptonshire Battalion, has no known grave and is remembered on the Thiepval Memorial.

Having been denied the opportunity to take part in the 'real' events of 1 July, the battalions spent the following three months in and out of the line between Thiepval Wood and the Leipzig Redoubt, with alternate periods 'enduring bombardment in shelterless trenches and of finding working parties of the most strenuous description'. At the same time, new troops arrived to bring the battalions back to full strength, and that meant that a great deal of training had to be fitted into the routine:

Owing to the great number of new and inexperienced officers and men the battalion require[d] very strenuous training to give it that confidence and efficiency necessary to a battalion in the line. About 30% of the men have had only 3months previous military training and are lacking in all drills and especially discipline. Much however is being done to remedy this while the battalion is holding a quiet part of the line.[58]

The brigade, together with the men from 1/4th and 1/5th battalions, moved from the Somme in October and the battle officially dragged on into November with the battalion historian grudgingly commenting that; 'While the last stages of the Somme Battle of 1916 were in progress the Hallamshires were destined to read of the great progress made, as they sat in trenches just north of the battle area'.[59] While the Hallamshires may have felt cheated of the opportunity to take a front line role on 1 July, three of their sister battalions in VIII Corps, on the very left of Rawlinson's

57   WO/95/2805.
58   WO 95/2805.
59   Grant, *Hallamshires*, p.50.

front, were to be almost wiped out in front of the little village of Serre. While the Devonshires are said to still hold their trench near Mametz, the six cemeteries in front of Serre are still held by the Pals from 94 Brigade.

Lastly the narrative moves from X Corps to VIII Corps, on the extreme left of Rawlinson's front, all three of its divisions in the attack line. On the left of the corps 31 Division faced the heavily defended village of Serre; 94 Brigade on the left (with the three York and Lancaster battalions); the 93rd on their right, opposite the southern side of Serre; the 92nd was in division reserve. In the centre of the corps line 4 Division had the strong point of the Quadrilateral to their front, and on the right flank of the corps was 29 Division, which had been heavily involved in Gallipoli. This last division was faced with the formidable obstacles of Beaumont Hamel, Hawthorne Ridge and 'Y' Ravine. The corps commander, Lieutenant-General Sir Aylmer Hunter-Weston, has come in for much criticism[60] for his performance at Gallipoli. In that ill-fated adventure against the Turks, Hunter-Weston commanded 29 Division, before being promoted to lead VIII Corps at Helles. In July 1915, he was invalided back to England; his health had been 'undermined by the incessant strain of the past twelve weeks, [and] was struck down by sun-stroke'.[61] As we saw earlier, Haig was critical of VIII corps for failing to put out sufficient raids to assess the state of the German wire on their front, his opinion also extended to the capabilities of Hunter-Weston's staff. In Haig's view 'the majority [were] amateurs and some thought that they knew more than they did of this kind of warfare because they had been at Gallipoli'.[62] Haig was not alone in believing that the fighting on the Western front was more difficult than in other theatres. His comment on Gallipoli was similar to the view held by him and Rawlinson towards the mountain warfare on the Italian, Isonzo front.[63] The corps had been reconstituted in France in March 1916, with Hunter-Weston in command; 29 Division being the only one it retained from Gallipoli.

One of the features of the VIII Corps attack confirming Haig's poor opinion of their staff work related to the firing of a 40,000 lb. mine in front of Hawthorn Redoubt. The divisional commander's timing for the explosion was overridden by VIII Corps; it was to be fired ten minutes before the general attack. This had an unfortunate effect on the artillery plan. The intention had been for the *divisional* batteries targeting the redoubt to lift their fire onto the German rear trenches at the time the mine was blown, so that the attacking troops would not be hit by their own shells as they rushed the new crater. Unfortunately, the fire plan was implemented by *all* the corps batteries. The consequence was that all the enemy troops were alerted to the start of the assault by the blowing of the mine, and the ten minute interval following the explosion gave them time to get back on the fire-step and man their machine guns. It was a disaster.

60   Travers, *Gallipoli* and Prior and Wilson, *Gallipoli*, are particularly critical.
61   Aspinall, *Gallipoli, Vol. 2*, p.112.
62   Sheffield and Bourne, *Haig*, p.194.
63   Dillon, *Allies are a Troublesome Lot*, p.59.

All four battalions of 94 Brigade were those close-knit units that became known as 'Pals'. Each had been recruited in small, local areas and many of the men who joined knew each other before answering Kitchener's call. The premise behind their formation was that the men, all coming from the same local area or industry, would have a higher *esprit de corps* than those raised by normal recruitment. The downside was that when these units suffered heavy casualties they fell disproportionally on the families in a small area. The four Pals battalions of 94 Brigade were; 12/York and Lancaster (Sheffield 'City' Pals); the 13th (1st Barnsley Pals); the 14th (2nd Barnsley Pals) and 11/East Lancashire (Accrington Pals). Sheffield, Barnsley and Accrington would come to have cause to remember 1 July 1916. Along the brigade's front were the remnants of four small woods, which had been named after the four apostles; running south to north they were Matthew, Mark, Luke and John. The first two flanked the Accrington Pals, with Luke and John doing the same for the Sheffield battalion. Today, Matthew has gone but Luke and John are still there, sites for CWGC cemeteries and the last resting place of many who fought that day.

First World War battles required a lot of preparatory work. To enable the attacking troops to move forward quickly, lanes had to be cut through their own wire and then marked with ribbons to allow the men to find them. Extra communication and assembly trenches were also needed and because the Germans had the advantage of higher ground, all this work was visible to their observation posts. The trench digging, together with the preparatory barrage, would have warned the enemy of an impending attack – the only question was, 'when'.

Following the postponement of the attack by 48 hours, zero hour was now set for 07.30 on 1 July. In preparation the men started to move forward to their jumping off positions during the evening of the 30 June, and early hours of 1 July; 'hot tea and rum' was sent round to help them on their way.[64] By 02.40, the first and second waves of A company, 12/York and Lancaster, were in position in the assembly trenches but the heavy rain before the postponement had water-logged many trenches:

> [I]n places the water was well above the knees. This caused great fatigue to the men and consequently delayed assembly of [the] Battalion in the trenches at least 2½ hours.

However, the Germans (having been alerted to the coming attack) began shelling the battalion lines heavily around 4 a.m.:

> [I]t would appear likely that the enemy was warned of the attack by observing gaps cut in our own wires and tapes laid out in No Man's Land, thus obtaining at least three and a half hours warning of the attack'.

---

64 WO 95/2365.

One consequence was that all the battalion telephone lines had been cut by 6 a.m., in spite of them having been laid six feet down. As a result, runners had to be used to tell the gunners that they were firing short and killing their own men in the trenches before they had even begun the attack.

The day went badly for Hunter-Weston's VIII Corps. On the right of his front, the mine under Hawthorn Redoubt – in 29 Division's sector – had been fired early, contributing to that division's 5,240 casualties. Edmond's comments are stark:

> By 7.35 a.m. nothing remained of the Borderers [2/South Wales Borderers] but some scattered individuals lying within a hundred yards of the German trench.[65]
>
> [T]he Lancashire men [1/Lancashire Fusiliers] were mown down directly they showed above the dip in which the lane lies, and only a party of about fifty reached the low bank beyond it.[66]
>
> The battalion [1/Newfoundland Regiment] suffered over seven hundred casualties, and was literally annihilated, losing every one of its officers.[67]

To the left of 29 Division, the 4th had some success, but not to the extent expected. All along Fourth Army's front communications were chaotic and confusing. Unable to get a clear picture of the situation on the ground, commanders released reserves to support failure, or (in some cases) failed to release them at all. Edmonds summarised the situation in the centre of VIII Corps front:

> It seemed certain that a considerable portion of the 4th Division had successfully broken through the German front position, and this was confirmed by reports from the 31st Division on the left. It is now known that a large number of men who had thus penetrated the enemy's front were shot down by Germans, who came in behind them from the trenches on either side, which the 29th and 31st Divisions on the right and left had failed to capture.[68]

On the left flank of VIII Corps, 31 Division were ready to play their part in Haig's big push. In spite of the shelling in the minutes prior to the attack – and with some of the British shells falling on their own trenches – the first waves of A and C companies from 12/York and Lancaster moved out into No Man's Land at 07.20, to lie down about 100 yards in front of their own line. The second waves did likewise and lay down 30 yards behind them. At zero hour, the men rose up to go forward, only to be met by a withering fire from the German machine gunners, who had regained their

---

65 Edmonds, *1916, Vol. 1*, p.433.
66 Edmonds, *1916, Vol. 1*, p.435.
67 Edmonds, *1916, Vol. 1*, p.436.
68 Edmonds, *1916, Vol. 1*, p.441.

parapet in the ten minute artillery lull following the explosion of the mine in front of Hawthorn Redoubt.

At 7.30, as so many others were doing along the front of Fourth Army, the men of 12/York and Lancaster and 11/East Lancashire rose up from their positions in No Man's Land, to begin their assault on the German lines. The advancing troops 'were immediately met with very heavy machine gun and rifle fire and artillery barrage. The left half of 'C' Coy was wiped out before getting near the German wire, and on the right the few men who reached the wire were unable to get through'.[69] The artillery barrage had failed to cut the wire:

> As soon as our barrage lifted from their front line, the Germans, who had been sheltering in Dug-outs, immediately came out and opened rapid fire with their machine guns. Some were seen to retire to the second and third lines. The enemy fought very well throwing Hand grenades into his own wire.[70]

Brave men can only do so much; they were no match for the massed fire of the machine guns. Behind them were both battalions of the Barnsley Pals, in the third and fourth waves. They suffered so heavily that, 'by the time they had reached No Man's Land [not even the German lines], they had lost at least half their strength. Whole sections were wiped out'. In spite of the barrage during the preceding five days, and many optimistic reports to the contrary, 'the German front line wire was found to be almost intact'. 12/York and Lancaster again:

> A few men of both "A" and "C" Coys managed to enter the German trenches on the right of the attack, but in all other parts of the line men were held up, being shot down by the Germans in front of them. The few survivors took shelter in shell holes in front of the German wire and remained there until they could get back under cover of darkness.

In the opinion of the officer writing this, 'the failure of the attack was undoubtedly due to the wire not being sufficiently cut'.[71]

By late evening, brigade HQ believed that about 150 men of the battalion had penetrated the German line in front of Mark Copse, and were still there. In an attempt to verify this, and to make contact with them if they were in fact in the enemy line, two patrols were sent out. Unfortunately, the wounded men that the patrols encountered in No Man's Land said that they believed those who had made the German line were by now casualties, and were unable to offer any resistance – 'Patrols consequently

69 WO 95/2365.
70 WO 95/2365, war diary, 12/York & Lancs.
71 WO 95/2365.

withdrew'. At the end of the day, the 12th battalion recorded 17 officers and 468 other ranks as casualties, and they had hardly even made it to the enemy trenches.

Following the East Lancashire troops (their gallantry is given due note on the 'pals' website)[72] were those from the 1st Barnsley Pals; 698 other ranks and 23 officers:

> The advance was carried out in perfect order under a terrific hostile artillery bombardment and machine gun fire; Major Guest and all his Officers, as well as those of the 'clearing party', being killed or wounded before reaching the First German line. Although this advance had to be carried out under a perfect tornado of fire all ranks advanced as steadily as if on a drill parade.[73]

Proud as the officer was of his troops when he wrote this, it was that steady advance that made the job of the German machine gunners so much easier. Communications had broken down, and HQs were receiving overoptimistic assessments of the infantry's advance. As a consequence, units were being sent to support troops in positions that were still held by the Germans. At 9 a.m., C and D companies of 13/York and Lancaster were ordered forward to support men that the headquarters believed were further forward than was actually the case. Their orders were as follows:

> [A]dvance to & hold the 1st & 2nd German Lines respectively, as a support to our first 4 waves who were then thought to have succeeded in reaching the German 4th line. While these two companies were moving forward they were stopped by verbal orders from the Brigadier who had now received information that all our preceding waves had been decimated and had consequently not reached their objectives. C & D companies were then ordered to re-organise in MONK TRENCH [about 500 yards behind the British front line] and Lt. Col. Wilford was ordered to collect what men he could of any units and organise the defence of this trench as our second line as a German counter-attack was feared.

One can only imagine the confusion; far from reaching the German fourth line, the men were now trying to stabilise a position 500 yards behind their own front line, against a possible German attack. There is little wonder that individual soldiers on the Somme would have had no idea of what was going on outside the bounds of their own platoon or company.

By 11 a.m., driven back to their own lines, a mix of stragglers and men from A company were 'holding our original front line trench which had been practically levelled to the ground'. At the same time, C and D companies, together with a mix of men from other units, were holding Monk Trench. The battalion remained in these positions for the rest of the day, 'subjected to a very heavy bombardment with heavy

---

72 Andrew Jackson's *www.pals.org.uk*.
73 WO 95/2365, war diary, 13 York & Lancs.

H.E. and shrapnel which lessened at dusk'.[74] When muster was taken on the evening of the attack, 13/York and Lancaster had only 280 men of all ranks in the trenches. Those who remained then spent the following hours collecting the dead and wounded from their lines and, where possible, from No Man's Land. Much of the work was done under a continual fire from German guns; 'several wounded & unwounded managed to return from NO MAN'S LAND under cover of darkness from shell craters in which they had been hiding'. With the return of these men, many of whom would have been initially recorded as 'missing', together with the 5 officers and 45 other ranks who had not been part of the attack, battalion strength on 5 July was 15 officers and 469 men. Relieved in the line by 6/Gloucesters, they marched to their billets at Louvencourt, arriving at 5 in the morning. Of the 23 officers and 698 Other Ranks who had taken part in the attack, 12 officers were casualties (6 of them dead) and 274 of the men (40 dead), a total of 286, or 40 per cent.[75]

The third of the York and Lancaster battalions to form the attack on 94 Brigade front was the 14th (2nd Barnsley Pals). Advancing behind the men of the Sheffield battalion, their orders give an indication of the excessive optimism of the planning staff; 'should it be necessary they will also assist the first two waves of the 12th York & Lancs, *if resistance is met*'.[76] [My italics] Like all the others, they were expected to sweep to their objectives against little opposition. The operation order required the troops to go forward in three 'bounds', following the artillery 'lifts'. Once occupied, the enemy position was to be:

> [H]eld at all costs. The word "Retire" will not be used. All men will be informed that should they hear the word "Retire", they may be quite sure it has been shouted by the enemy.

As at Loos, the supply of water to the men at the front was a recognised necessity, but it was also a problem: how could you get water to the soldiers while they were under fire? Battle conditions not unnaturally brought on thirst, physical activity and fear will do that. When the adjutant wrote the operation order, he meant well by requiring the troops to conserve their water, but his directive was unlikely to be followed: 'NO water will be drunk until after the assault, and then only on orders from the Company Commanders'. Most of the officers became casualties and even if they lived through the ordeal, they would have had far more to worry about than the state of the men's water-bottles.

The 14th battalion began the move to the front during the evening of 30 June, stopping en-route to have some hot tea. They reached their assembly trenches by 04.30 on 1 July. The men now had three nervous hours to wait while they 'were very heavily

---

74   WO 95/2365.
75   WO 95/2365.
76   WO 95/2365, war diary, 14th York & Lancs.

shelled by the Germans'. In some places, the trench 'was completely levelled, and so much exposed that it appeared to form part of No Man's Land'. The adjutant's post-battle report gives some indication of why the day did not go as planned: before the clock had moved to zero hour, '30% of the assaulting, consolidating and clearing parties became casualties before reaching our parapet'. After all the rehearsals of moving forward from assembly trenches, it all went wrong on the day. The enemy, who had been assumed to offer little resistance, had not read the script and insisted on pouring in shells together with machine gun and rifle fire. If the men had gone forward to the front as directed, they would have suffered 'casualties amounting almost to annihilation'. It was not until 40 minutes after zero, at 08.10, that 'a line of men got over the parapet and advanced in quick time across No Man's Land. [...] The men advanced in good dressing to [the] middle of our wire, when they came apparently under machine gun fire and commenced to fall. No men of those on the left got further than a yard or two beyond our wire'.[77] The attack was stalled; the battalion could not even move its headquarters forward within its own trench system. 'No further movements were made in connection with the attack, all subsequent operations being in reference to the holding of our trenches'.

The casualties within 2nd Barnsley Pals were less than those in the Sheffield and Accrington battalions, but most were lost before they even reached No Man's Land; 11 officers (2 killed) and 265 ORs (24 dead). The three days following the attack were taken up with holding their own lines, although 'the front line trenches were practically non-existent', and with bringing in the dead. The wounded, lying out in No Man's Land had a hard time, made only a little easier by the fine weather. Some did not make it back to their lines until 3 July. On 4 July, the weather broke and heavy rain resulted in the badly shelled trenches becoming full of water. That night the Barnsley men, with the rest of the brigade, retired to billets in the rear.

The battle continued until November, lessons were learnt and ground was gained, but that first day was a disaster for 94 Brigade and the four Pals battalions of Sheffield, Accrington and Barnsley. The consequence of recruiting the men from these narrow areas was hard-felt by the local communities when the casualty lists were published. As evening drew on, on 1 July, VIII Corps 'had nothing to show for its very heavy losses except a footing in and near the Quadrilateral, and this had to be abandoned next morning'.[78] It was not until the evening of 3 July, and after some cooperation with the Germans, that most of the wounded had been removed from No Man's Land, and not until 4 July, that the area could be declared cleared. VIII Corps suffered a greater loss than any other corps that day, over 14,000.[79] In 31 Division, 37 per cent of the casualties were dead. In marked contrast, the three German regiments that had faced

77 WO 95/2365.
78 Edmonds, *1916, Vol. 1*, p.449.
79 Edmonds, *1916, Vol. 1*, p.450.

Hunter-Weston's corps lost only 1,214 men. Edmonds summarised the brave efforts of 31 Division:

> Only a few isolated parties of the 31st Division were able to reach the German front trench, where they were in the end either killed or taken prisoner. The extended lines started in excellent order, but gradually melted away. There was no wavering or attempting to come back, the men fell in their ranks, mostly before the first hundred yards of No Man's Land had been crossed. The magnificent gallantry, discipline and determination displayed by all ranks of this North Country division were to no avail against the concentrated fire-effect of the enemy's unshaken infantry and artillery, whose barrage has been described as so consistent and severe that the cones of the explosions gave the impression of a thick belt of poplar trees.[80]

The first day of the Battle of the Somme has become popular shorthand for the futile sacrifice of 'a generation' at the hands of bungling generals who directed the conflict from the comfort of their chateaux – in fact, forty-seven brigadiers and lieutenant-colonels were casualties that day.[81] Many mistakes were made, as there had been at the smaller battle of Loos in the previous September, and many men died unnecessarily as a result. While it is of little consolation to those who died that day, lessons were learnt and the British army did discover better ways of coordinating their infantry and artillery. Whether or not the reader agrees with Gary Sheffield's premise of the 'Learning Curve' – Prior and Wilson[82] appear sceptical with their comment that 'sharper eyes than ours have detected a 'learning curve' in the performance of the Commander in Chief during the Somme battle – Haig's army did develop 'all arms' tactics, which did lead to an eventual Allied victory in 1918. Sadly, Loos and the Somme had to happen first. The old Regular Army had almost gone by mid-1915 and the fight had to continue with volunteers and conscripts who did not have their earlier colleagues' depth of experience, training and discipline. It is a sad fact, if a country has only a small standing army, then the soldiers and their commanders are not equipped to fight a large-scale industrial war; they end up 'learning on the job'. Edmonds reminds us that 'of the corps commanders on the 1st July only two had commanded as much as a division in peace time, and of the twenty-three divisional commanders in the field only three had commanded as much as a brigade before the war'.[83] Rawlinson, who commanded IV Army, had half a million men, five corps and 16 divisions, yet only nine months previously he had been a corps commander at Loos. Politicians took Britain into the war, not the generals, they were also responsible for the size

80 Edmonds, *1916, Vol. 1*, pp.442-3.
81 Roberts, *Elegy*, p.204.
82 Prior and Wilson, *The Somme*, p.222.
83 Edmonds, *1916, Vol. 1*, pp.491.

of the army in those early years of the twentieth century. Unfortunately, the politicians (especially Lloyd George) have done a good job of deflecting on to the military commanders much of the responsibility that by 'constitutional tradition [...] remained the province of the civilian heads of government'.[84]

When German regimental historians looked back on the battle of the Somme they did not see it as a futile British sacrifice, one of them lamented that the tragedy of that battle was that the German army lost its 'best soldiers, the stoutest-hearted'.

> The Somme was the muddy grave of the German field army, and of the faith in the infallibility of the German leading, [...] The German Supreme Command, which entered the war with enormous superiority, was defeated by the superior technique of its opponents.[85]

For the men of the York and Lancaster Regiment who fought on that July day, it was not an enormous battlefield with 17 divisions, it was a narrow front of some 200-400 yards in which their 'mates' were killed and wounded in enormous numbers and where (until they read about it later in the papers) they had no real conception of what had gone on outside their own battalion. For individual soldiers, battles are much smaller and more personal than many histories represent them.

---

84   Prior and Wilson, *The Somme*, p.1.
85   History of the *27th(Württemberg) Division* in Edmonds, *1916, Vol. 1*, p.494.

7

"A process of trial and error" – the tanks at Flers-Courcelette

In British First World War folk memory, the 'Battle of the Somme' is synonymous with the dreadful losses during the infantry assault of 1 July. In reality, the battle was a series of conflicts along Fourth Army front, lasting until the middle of November. One such was the Battle of Flers-Courcelette, 15 September 1916. The significance of that date is that it marked the entry of the tank onto the battlefield. Sir Douglas Haig has been criticised as a 'cavalryman', reluctant to adopt change, and yet he incorporated the first British use of gas into his battle plan for Loos, and here at Flers he introduced another new weapon, against the advice of some of his staff.

The story of the development of the tank is not a topic for this book as it is well covered elsewhere. Of particular note is Trevor Pidgeon's two-volume account[1] of this new weapon and its introduction to the battle-field in September 1916. These new machines would have struck the viewers as enormous, lumbering leviathans. In side-view they were lozenge shaped, a little over 26 feet long and 14 wide, weighing 28 tons and with a caterpillar track going the whole way round each side of the body. They came in two variants, 'male' and 'female'; the former was armed with two 6-pounder Hotchkiss guns mounted in side 'sponsons', as well as three Hotchkiss machine guns; the female carried four Vickers machine guns in its side sponsons, together with one Hotchkiss machine gun on the front. Each tank required a crew of eight; a commander, a driver, two 'brakemen' and four men on the guns. Steering was more an art-form than a science, it required differential braking of the drive tracks – to go right, stop or slow the right track and speed up that on the left. To do this, the driver would pull a lever to decide which way he wished to turn the tank; the brakemen (in the rear of the vehicle) would then disengage the appropriate gearbox to stop one of the tracks. Given its solid metal construction, lack of suspension, and the noise from the massive internal engine and gearboxes, it was a most uncomfortable war-machine for its crew of volunteers. With its lack of manoeuvrability and a speed of only 2-4 mph, it was a far-cry from modern, armoured vehicles.

---

1   Pidgeon, T., *The Tanks at Flers Volume 1 & 2* (Cobham, Fairmile Books, 1995).

Mark II (Female) Tank. (IWM Q 64483)

6 pounder gun on 'Male' tank. (Photo J. Dillon)

In spite of these limitations, it had the potential to assist the infantry in that critical phase of the battle – crossing No Man's Land and getting through the wire to the enemy trench. The size and weight of the vehicle allowed it to trample and crush wire defences, and to ride across a trench. The 6-pounder and multiple machine guns meant that it could attack strong points and enfilade trenches as it rode over them. However, its ponderous movements and its large profile made it a target for enemy gun batteries. Although the machines gave the appearance of affording a great deal of protection to their crews, they were vulnerable to armour piercing bullets, which could produce terrible injuries. In the days of Nelson's wooden ships, if a cannon ball penetrated the ship's side it tore off large splinters of oak, which then sprayed the area below decks with large, deadly splinters of wood. In the same fashion, when the sides of the tank were penetrated by high-velocity armour piercing bullets they caused shards of red-hot metal to separate from the inner plating and ricochet around the interior of the vehicle.

The proponents of the tank believed that it could act as a 'force multiplier' on the battle-field, but only if used in large numbers. Additionally, the surprise and morale effect that could be expected from its first appearance in battle would be maximised if it were used in volume. Unfortunately, the manufacturers could not produce them at the rate needed to put hundreds in the field in September 1916; only 49 were available to Fourth Army. Haig was advised not to use them that month, as their number would not be sufficient to produce a game-changing effect. The C-in-C however was keen to employ any new weapon that might give him an advantage; 'I shall use what I have got […] and it would be folly not to use every means at my disposal in what is likely to be our crowning effort for this year'.[2]

The tanks that were to be delivered to France started shipping from Thetford on 13 August; the 49 available machines were then taken by train to be in their assembly areas two days before the attack started. These new vehicles were extremely noisy when moving under their own power, and the RFC was detailed to fly sorties over their assembly areas to mask the sound of their movement to the front. The use of the tank in the coming battle was a secret but Haig gave the men who were going into battle a hint that he had a trick up his sleeve; the soldiers should know that not only did they have a 'superiority of at least four to one in infantry', they also had the advantage of a 'new weapon of war'.[3] Unfortunately, the new weapon, being new, had problems: of those machines sent to France only 36 made it to their start line;[4] 27 went on to reach the German front line, 19 to the First Objective, 11 to the Second and 6 the Third.[5]

---

2   Edmonds, J., *Military Operations France and Belgium, 1916, Volume 2* (Uckfield, Naval & Military Press, Reprint of 1931 original), p.235.
3   Edmonds, *1916, Vol. 2*, p.300.
4   Edmonds and Pidgeon have 36 while Liddell Hart states 32.
5   Pidgeon, *The Tanks at Flers, Vol. 1*, p.205.

On the left and right flanks of Fourth Army were the British Reserve Army and the Sixth French Army. The village of Courcelette, which lent its name, along with Flers, to the official name of the battle, lay in front of the Canadian Division on the extreme right of the Reserve Army (see Map 8). Rawlinson's Fourth Army consisted of three corps and they were, from left to right, III, XV and XIV Corps. The 8th and 9th battalions of the York and Lancaster Regiment were detached from 23 to 15 Division (III Corps), the first into 45 Brigade and the second into the 46th. Both battalions were in Brigade Reserve for their respective brigades. In 16 Brigade, 6 Division, in the centre of XIV Corps (on the army's right flank), was 2/York and Lancaster. They were in front of the village of Guillemont, half way between Ginchy on their left and Leuze Wood on their right. The three battalions of the York and Lancaster played rather different roles in the battle, which started on 15 September; we will begin with the 8th and 9th, in 15 Division.

Seconded from 23 Division, theirs was a support role, primarily as 'carrying parties'. On 12 and 13 September, 8/York and Lancaster had to provide three large fatigue details; two were of 150 NCOs and men, the third was considerably larger, nearly half the battalion – 320 NCOs and men.[6] During the day of the attack, the soldiers were carrying rations, rifle ammunition and grenades to those in the line. Their brigade also had to handle 'about 500 prisoners'. The experience of these two battalions was quite different from that of 2/York and Lancs, who were on the front line for 16 Brigade, and this is reflected in the casualty statistics. The 9th had 113 casualties against 333 in the 2nd battalion. These figures were further broken down to record the numbers suffering from 'shell shock', interestingly there were 14 in the battalion doing the support role, with only 8 amongst those in the front line. It begs the question; does fighting take their mind off being shelled?

By 23 September the men of 9/York and Lancaster had been relieved and had the opportunity to take baths – always welcome. It was during this period away from the front line that their war diary records one of the grim tasks that is frequently overlooked in the histories of the conflict; battlefield clearing duties. Someone had to bring in the dead and see to their burial. On 23 September, Lieutenant Colonel Addison's body (the battalion's previous CO) was found in No Man's Land, near Aveluy Wood. It cannot have been pleasant to gaze on the faces of men they had fought alongside, especially after they had been lying there for three months. Each man must have had a strong sense of 'there but for the Grace of God'. Lt. Col. Addison (formerly of Royal Irish Rifles), the son of a general, is buried in Becourt Military Cemetery along with one Private from the same battalion and one from 10/ York and Lancaster. A similar job fell to 8/York and Lancaster on 19 September, when they had to send out burial parties under Reverend Clarke to 'recover and bury bodies of our officers, NCOs and men killed on July 1st'.[7] One soldier, on similar duties in

6   WO 95/2188.
7   WO 95/2188.

November, noted that 'the men who had been there since 1st July were only bones and khaki'.[8] The battalion buried the bodies of Captains Edmundson, Smith and Stewart, as well as Lieutenants White, Baker Stephenson and Spencer, together with 29 Other Ranks. The burial parties noted the map reference of the plot for the grave registration service. All of this information was used by the Imperial (later, Commonwealth) War Graves Commission for the beautiful cemeteries we see today. Having recovered the bodies, all could now have their own headstone, rather than just their name on a memorial to the missing: Edmundson at Adamac Military Cemetery; Smith, Stewart and Stephenson at Blighty Valley Cemetery; White, Baker and Spencer at Lonsdale Cemetery. All three cemeteries are located near the village of Authuille and Aveluy Wood.

Unlike the 8th and 9th battalions (in Brigade Reserve), 2/York and Lancaster was in an attacking brigade with the villages of Morval and Lesboeufs to their front, some 2,500 yards from their start line. In the middle of the front of 6 Division, between 16 Brigade on the right and the 71st on the left, was the German strong point of the Quadrilateral (there were many strong points along the whole British front with the same name); this was only 2-300 yards in front of the British line. As was so often the case the advance expected of the infantry was overly ambitious. For Rawlinson to gain all his objectives XIV Corps were required to advance 5,000 yards, while 2/York and Lancaster were expected to make 3,500 yards. The timescale for this leap forward was also 'aggressive'; the final objective was to be reached 'before noon',[9] after which the cavalry would exploit the break through. The right flank of Rawlinson's army was occupied by XIV Corps, commanded by Lord Cavan. We last met Cavan at the battle of Loos, commanding the Guards Division and we will come across him again in 1917 as commander of the Italian Expeditionary Force (which included the 8th and 9th battalions of the York and Lancaster Regiment). After the war, Cavan went on to become Chief of the Imperial General Staff, after the assassination of Sir Henry Wilson by the IRA.[10] The three divisions making up XIV Corps were; 56 on the right, 6 in the centre (including 2/York and Lancs) and the Guards (Cavan's old command) on the left.

Even though 2/York and Lancaster was to be a part of the attack on 15 September they spent a large part of the preceding days (described as 'quiet) occupied on carrying parties. The use of the infantry as labourers, even so close to a battle, is a recurring theme in unit war diaries. At 2 p.m. on 14 September, the battalion received orders 'to take part in general attack on 15th'; their final objective was a line to the east of the village of Morval – a line they would not reach. At 10 p.m. that evening the men began their move up to their assembly positions, south-west of Guillemont, which they reached a

8   Mortimer, IWM Doc 7449.
9   Edmonds, *1916, Vol. 2*, p.291.
10 Wilson, R., and I. Adams, *Special Branch. A History: 1883-2006* (London, Biteback, 2015), p.128.

little over an hour later.¹¹ Similar moves were made all along the front 'with little loss or confusion, and most of the troops arrived in time for a few hours sleep. All were fed, and in some cases a rum ration was issued'.¹² When the attack began, the York and Lancaster men were to go forward behind 1/Buffs. The battalion would be led off by A and D companies, each with a frontage of 250 yards, B and C would follow at a distance of 100 yards. The Official History states that Zero Hour was set as 06.20 a.m., at which time the infantry was to advance behind a creeping barrage, the latter advancing at 50 yards per minute. By 06.50, the barrage would lift 'to enable the infantry to occupy this objective'.¹³ At 07.20, the infantry and tanks 'advance together to the assault of the Brown Line', the second objective and by that time the barrage was to be advancing at 100 yards every three minutes. There is an old saying that the first casualty of an attack is the battle plan, and 15 September was no exception. When 2/York and Lancs left the trenches, at 07.20, they would have expected the lead battalions to be on the first objective, going forward to the second but, at 08.45 the battalion was held up; 'found 8/Bedfords in their original position'.¹⁴ The Bedfords were in the first wave of the brigade attack which had obviously now stalled because of machine gun fire from the Quadrilateral. For some reason the planners had believed this strong point would fall to the Bedfords at the first rush. But what of the tanks, and their debut on the battlefield?

Sixteen of the new machines had been allocated to XIV Corps, three each to 6 and 56 Divisions, while ten went to the Guards. Because the tanks had been rushed to Haig in the last days before the battle, as well as a need for secrecy, there had been no opportunity for the infantry to exercise with this new weapon. Some of the problems soon became apparent. Due to their noise, and a lack of portable wireless sets, communication between tank commanders and the infantry was extremely difficult. In an attempt to overcome the problem 'simple flag and lamp codes were arranged [...] to signal 'out of action' and 'am on objective' – some of the crews even carried pigeons.¹⁵ Although the infantry had learnt how to advance behind an artillery barrage, tank crews had no such experience. A means had to be devised whereby the new weapon was not shelled by British guns. To this end, the artillery plan was modified such that corridors, 100 yards wide in front of each tank, would not be shelled by the batteries. This had an unintended consequence for the infantry. The tanks were to move 'aggressively' against German strong points, but these were not shelled by the artillery who were leaving clear lanes for the tanks' advance: 'What the tank lanes managed to accomplish was the creation of clear fields of fire for German machine gunners'.¹⁶ These barrage-free corridors were seen from the air by Cecil Lewis who was flying above the lines, in the area of Flers:

11   WO 95/1610, war diary, 2/York & Lancs.
12   Edmonds, *1916, Vol. 2*, p.303.
13   Edmonds, *1916, Vol. 2*, p.295.
14   WO 95/1610.
15   Edmonds, *1916, Vol. 2*, p.297.
16   Prior and Wilson, *The Somme*, p.232.

"A process of trial and error" – the tanks at Flers-Courcelette 135

Mounting for Hotchkiss machine gun behind the 6 pounder. Photo also shows exit door for the gunner. (Photo J. Dillon)

> When we climbed up to the lines, we found the whole front seemingly covered with a layer of dirty cotton-wool – the smoking shell-bursts. Across this were dark lanes, drawn as it might be by a child's stubby finger in dirty snow. Here no shells were falling. Through these lanes lumbered the Tanks in file, four to each lane. By 6.20 they had reached the front line and the barrage began to roll back as they advanced, the infantry with them.[17]

The tanks, back home in England, had demonstrated their abilities to mount obstacles and demolish the wire, but the training grounds of Thetford were not the same as the shell-pocked terrain of No Man's Land. In addition, they had had to travel considerable distances, under their own power, at night, just to get to the assembly areas;

17 Lewis, C., *Sagittarius Rising* (London, Greenhill Books, 19913), p.142.

breakdowns were almost inevitable with these new, untried vehicles. Of the three tanks allocated to 6 Division, two broke down and took no part in the battle. Similarly, two of the three 56 Division machines failed to make the British front line through mechanical failure; a further five of the ten assigned to the Guards also did not make it: an inauspicious start for the new weapon. However, one of the three operating with 6 Division, C22 commanded by Lieutenant Basil Henriques, had some success. While there is some dispute as to exactly how far forward C22 was able to progress, it is believed that they may have made it into the Quadrilateral. Having got there, they then came under fire from armour piercing bullets. At this point Henriques 'discovered the sides weren't bullet-proof' and that 'to save the tank from being captured [he] had better withdraw'.[18] With only one tank appearing on the front line to support 6 Division, it is not surprising if the troops seemed to be almost unaware of their existence. There is only one reference to them in the war diary of 2/York and Lancaster; at 09.50 a.m., 'one tank appears out of action in front of QUADRILATERAL'.[19] This may well have been C22 as it is the only one thought to have made into that German position, before it made its way back to the lines.

We return to 2/York and Lancaster; the battalion had been held up by the lack of progress of the battalions in the first wave (1/Buffs and 8/Bedfords), trapped by the cross-fire from Bouleaux Wood on their right and the Quadrilateral on their left. At noon, they received orders to attack a position close to the Quadrilateral with their advance commencing at 13.30 p.m. Twenty minutes before their start time, they requested artillery support to cover them until 2 p.m. However, at 13.20 they were told to cancel the attack and by 5 in the evening new orders told them to relieve the Bedfords and Buffs in the line, which they did by 7 p.m. Having only just taken over the trenches, one company had to be detached to 11/Essex who were about to have another go at the German strong point; this commenced at 7.35 p.m. As often happened, hastily prepared assaults tended to fail. The battalion diary records that at 7.50 p.m., 'attack on Quadrilateral failed. Attack on both sides lost direction and missed objective'. At the end of the first day, 2/York and Lancaster had advanced about 300 yards but was tied down by German fire from both flanks. In the original plan, they should have reached the east side of Morval. The day had gone somewhat better for XV and III Corps with the villages of Flers and Martinpuich in British hands.

The 16th was a 'quiet day' with 16 Brigade tied down and unable to advance and the 17th was spent preparing another advance. At 05.50 on the morning of 18 September, the battalion provided bombing parties to support an attack on the Quadrilateral. This was short and sharp and by 06.00 it was recorded as 'successful' with the additional booty of three captured machine guns and 51 prisoners. Opponents in war will often complement the other side's soldiers; in the fight for the Quadrilateral, 2/York

---

18   Pidgeon, *The Tanks at Flers Vol. 1*, p.84.
19   WO 95/1610.

and Lancaster had suffered 'comparatively small loss' against a 'magnificent defence'.[20] Any euphoria at having finally removed the Germans from their strong position may have been dulled by the rain, which fell for the rest of the day while the men were employed 'digging continuously'. The employment of the infantry as navvies never seemed to stop.

Having been relieved from their duties in the line, the men would have been pleased that on 20 September they were 'changing worn boots and clothing as far as possible'. However, only three days later, word came down that they were to go back to the front to take part in an attack on the 25th. By 23.30 on 24 September, the battalion was in its assembly positions only to find out that they had a long wait ahead of them, zero hour would not be until the afternoon of the 25th. The battalion history records an amusing interlude in the trenches:

> The most forward position of the line [...] consisted of 250 yards of one of the main German trenches, which was held by the Germans on both flanks for some distance. Fortunately we were in possession of the communication trench leading up to it, and during the three nights after taking over, considerable excitement and amusement were caused by the occasional arrival of German ration parties at our part of the trench, having failed to hit off the part occupied by their own troops.[21]

The divisional objective for 25 September 'was the ground between the north end of Morval and the road which passes through the centre of Les Boeufs'. So, ten days after the assault began, they were still trying to get Morval, a village which should have fallen 'by noon' on that first day. At 13.00 the battalion HQ moved forward into dugouts in No Man's Land followed by the men leaving their assembly trenches 'in artillery formation', behind 1/Buffs. The attack was over very quickly. At 14.35, the troops moved forward again 'to the assault under cover of a creeping barrage'. Only 30 minutes later, they were able to declare 'all objectives gained'.[22] During the afternoon, there was sporadic activity by the enemy troops and aircraft, but nothing serious and on the following day, the battalion pulled back. Before the men reached their billets at Meaulte, south of Albert, they had the unpleasant task of clearing the battlefield; on the 28th and 29th a party of one officer and 75 men had to bring in bodies for burial. And so, as the battalion history states; 'Thus ended for the present, the share of the Battalion in the Somme fighting'.

We will close out September on the Somme with one last action by 8/York and Lancaster. Before leaving the area for the Ypres Salient, the battalion was ordered (at midnight on 28/29 September) to attack and take Destremont Farm. The farm was

20 Wylly, *2nd Battalion History*, p.357.
21 Wylly, *2nd Battalion History*, p.358.
22 WO 95/1610.

about 800 yards south of the village of Le Sars, on the road from Courcelette. An attempt had already been made by 11/Sherwood Foresters, but this had been repulsed 'by heavy machine gun [&] rifle fire'. As an assault was planned on Le Sars, the Germans at this position had to be neutralised:

> The attack was launched promptly at 6.00 a.m. & was entirely successful, despite the fact that almost 800 yds of open ground had to be traversed by our men. The men charged with great spirit, cheering when just approaching their objective. The enemy offered very little resistance & fled in disorder, leaving a number of dead & one machine gun, which was brought back by our men. The farm was immediately consolidated & one platoon commanded by 2nd Lieut. J.V. Medley left as a garrison.

During the rest of the day, the position was heavily shelled and the garrison suffered casualties, Medley among them. A measure of how 'hot' the farm became can be gauged by the fact that after Medley, a further five officers had to be sent, in turn, to command the men there. Before the brigade left the line for billets in the rear, 'watches [were] put back 1 hour – summer time being cancelled'.

Military histories of the war tend to concentrate on the battles fought, but these occupied only a small part of a soldier's time. While 8/York and Lancaster were disputing ownership of Destremont Farm, Private Smithson (of that battalion) was facing a Field General Court Martial at the headquarters of 11/Sherwood Foresters; his offence was being 'absent without leave'. Although the battalion was close to the front line, he was not charged with desertion. Contrary to popular mythology, not all men who were absent were charged with desertion or cowardice, nor were they all executed. Being 'absent' did not carry a death penalty (if found guilty), nor was it the same as desertion. The latter charge requires it to be proved that the man had the 'intent' not to return to active duty; he needed to have thrown away his weapon, or changed out of uniform. While the war diary does not say what happened to Smithson, it is highly likely that, if he was found guilty, then he was probably awarded Field Punishment Number 1. This involved being tied to a fixed post – not always a wheel, or in the crucifix position as some writers would have us believe – for two hours a day, for a number of days. The intention was to humiliate, but it was not crucifixion. The penalty is likely to have been carried out when they returned to Ypres on 18 October, rather than at the front. On a lighter note, the battalion played football against 9/South Staffords on 28 August; no result was given in the diary. On the day before this match, the battalion marked a special event:

> Today was [the] anniversary of the Battn. arrival in France. Dinner held to celebrate it by all those remaining with the Battn. who came out with it.

From the original complement of 29-30 officers, only eight were named as still being with them. No doubt, there were a few toasts to 'absent friends'.

"A process of trial and error" – the tanks at Flers-Courcelette   139

The battle of Flers-Courcelette saw the introduction to the battlefield of the Tank. Those who had promoted the new weapon had had high expectations that it would be a 'game changer' – but only if used *en masse*. Haig, in his willingness to try a new technology, accepted the risk of employing the lumbering land-ships in sub-optimal numbers. While his decision has been criticised he had a responsibility to try to assist the infantry in their fight against the German wire. In fairness, with such a new vehicle, there would have been problems even if used in volume. The tank was not yet mechanically robust enough to fight for prolonged periods and their crews had not had the opportunity to operate them in battle conditions. At some point, they had to be baptised; 'it may be said that in perfecting and exploiting a new weapon it is wise to proceed by a process of trial and error both on the testing ground and in the field: one can rarely expect to arrive at sound tactical methods by theory alone'.[23] The new machines, and the men who crewed them, would have opportunities in 1917 and 1918 to demonstrate that the tank would take its place in the all-arms battles that were to follow.

For many in Britain 'the first day of the Somme became the necessary image of the war', it was an image that 'possessed the status of an established fact'. However, the Somme was more than just 1 July; it cannot be distilled into a single image. The experience of the Pals at Serre, where battalions almost ceased to exist, was quite different from that of 2/York and Lancaster on 15 September, or the 8th battalion at Destremont Farm at the end of the month – and yet, they were all participants in the Battle of the Somme.

---

23   Edmonds, *1916, Vol. 2*, p.365.

8

April 1917 – the Battle of Arras

As the battle of the Somme drew to a close, and the conflict dragged on towards 1917, for those men who had joined the army in August 1914 (and had managed to survive) the winter of 1916 was their third Christmas away from home. Sadly, many of the battalion war diaries have no record of the Christmas season being treated any differently from other days, even when the unit was out of the front line. The men of 9/York and Lancaster were in billets near Ypres on Christmas Day, but it does not appear to have been very festive. The only note in the diary is that 173 men were supplied for working parties, as they were the day before and the day after. New Year's Day, and the following week, were spent on such festive activities as; box respirator drill, bayonet fighting, guard duties, musketry and – most galling of all – 'saluting drill'. However, 2 January 'was observed […] as Xmas Day' and the following day the men were able to have baths at Poperinghe.[1]

In 8/York and Lancaster, the men appear to have had more opportunity to celebrate the festive season. They were in the trenches on Christmas Day and New Year's Eve, but had withdrawn to billets in Winnipeg Camp, Vlamertinghe by 1 January 1917. Having come straight from the trenches, they had a parade in the morning followed by football against the Sherwood Foresters; the match was a draw, 1-1. The following day the team did less well against the KOYLIs, where they could only manage one goal to their opponents four. However, it was not sport for all; while the match was in progress, one officer and 120 of their colleagues found themselves on working parties. The best day was 3 January: following a parade in the morning, the men had their 'Xmas Dinner & Concert' in the cinema during the afternoon and evening. No doubt, they all thoroughly enjoyed the interlude from trench duties and working parties. On 5 January, the men were reminded of the health issues attendant on life in the line; they had their feet inspected, were able to go for baths and also undergo an 'inspection for scabies'. Medical officers had a constant battle with hygiene and the consequences of the dirty conditions of the trenches and took the opportunity of the periods in

1   WO 95/2188.

British troops eating their Christmas dinner in a shell hole, Beaumont Hamel, 25th December 1916. (IWM Q 1630)

billets to assess the condition of the men. Three days later, with the festive season behind them, the battalion was back in the routine of trench warfare.

With Christmas and New Year behind them, the account now jumps from 8/York and Lancaster in the trenches at Vlamertinghe, to the regiment's 10th battalion at Arras, the first major battle of 1917. The battalion was part of 63 Brigade, 37 Division and on 9 March, the 37th transferred from I Corps (around Loos) to VI Corps in Third Army in preparation for the coming offensive. VI Corps was commanded by Lieutenant-General Sir A. Haldane and contained the 3rd, 12th, 15th and 37th Divisions.[2] We first met the battalion, as part of 21 Division, at the disastrous battle of Loos, and again opposite Fricourt during the 1 July attack on the Somme. On 8 July 1916, 63 Brigade left the 21st to join 37 Division and become part of the battle of Arras. This author has a particular attachment to this battle, as he believes his grandfather fought there, having moved from the 6th battalion.

By the end of March 1917, with Revolution beginning in Russia, Germany having pulled back to the Hindenburg Line (and devastated the ground they gave up), and Lloyd George having become Prime Minister in Britain, the stage was set for a

2 Wylly, *10th Battalion History*, p.226.

few changes in the prosecution of the war. In France, Joffre had been replaced as Commander-in-Chief of their armies by General Robert Nivelle who had made his name during the Verdun campaign. Lloyd George, heavily critical of the way in which the military had prosecuted the war to that point, lacked the courage to sack Haig, on the grounds of 'who will I put in his place?' It was Lloyd George's strong opinion that the C-in-C wasted soldiers' lives unnecessarily: '[He] does not care how many men he loses. He just squanders the lives of these boys'.[3] Given the losses in the French army, it is curious that he considered the solution to be the subordination of the BEF commander to a French general. Seduced by Nivelle's conduct at Verdun and his proposal for a new offensive (which was intended to last only 48 hours), Lloyd George pushed for Haig to report to Nivelle.

The whole issue of the command of national armies on the Western front is beyond the scope of this book; suffice to say that Robertson and Haig were strongly opposed: 'We ought not to have *signed* the document'.[4] As we have seen the relationship between the Prime Minister and his military chiefs was not good; Robertson referred to him as 'an awful liar'[5] and 'an under-bred swine'.[6] Robertson was himself from a working class background where his father was a village tailor and postmaster. An agreement was reached whereby, for the period of the Arras offensive, Haig would conform to Nivelle's requests for the support that the British army were requested to provide to the French. Unfortunately, the French commander wrote a letter to Haig in terms that cast him (Haig) as Nivelle's subordinate, rather than as the C-in-C of the British army – 'it is a type of letter which no gentleman could have drafted'. Sufficiently annoyed by its tone, Haig sent a copy to the War Committee asking them 'whether it is their wishes that the C-in-C in command of this British Army should be subjected to such treatment by a junior *foreign* Commander'.[7] Lloyd George had gone out on a limb with his support of Nivelle and his spring offensive, the French came close to sawing it off. In March, the French government that had backed Nivelle's plan was supplanted by one that 'seriously doubted his promise of a decisive victory'.[8] Whatever the French government's reticence, Nivelle was to have his offensive, supported to their north by the BEF. In essence, Haig's attack was to take place some days prior to Nivelle's in order to draw off German divisions from the French sector.

The British army had learnt hard lessons in the battles up to April 1917 (and would continue to do so for the rest of the war), and while the losses of the Somme had been dreadful they were not all futile. The army and its commanders were – sometimes too

3   Wilson, T., *The Myriad Faces Of War* (Cambridge, Polity Press, 1986), p.441.
4   Woodward, D.R., *The Military Correspondence of Field-Marshal Sir William Robe*rtson (London, Army Records Society, 1989), letter from Robertson to Haig, 3 March 1917, p.156.
5   Woodward, *Robertson*, p.155.
6   Woodward, *Robertson*, p.213.
7   Sheffield and Bourne, *Haig*, p.274.
8   Wilson, *Myriad*, p.445.

April 1917 – the Battle of Arras 143

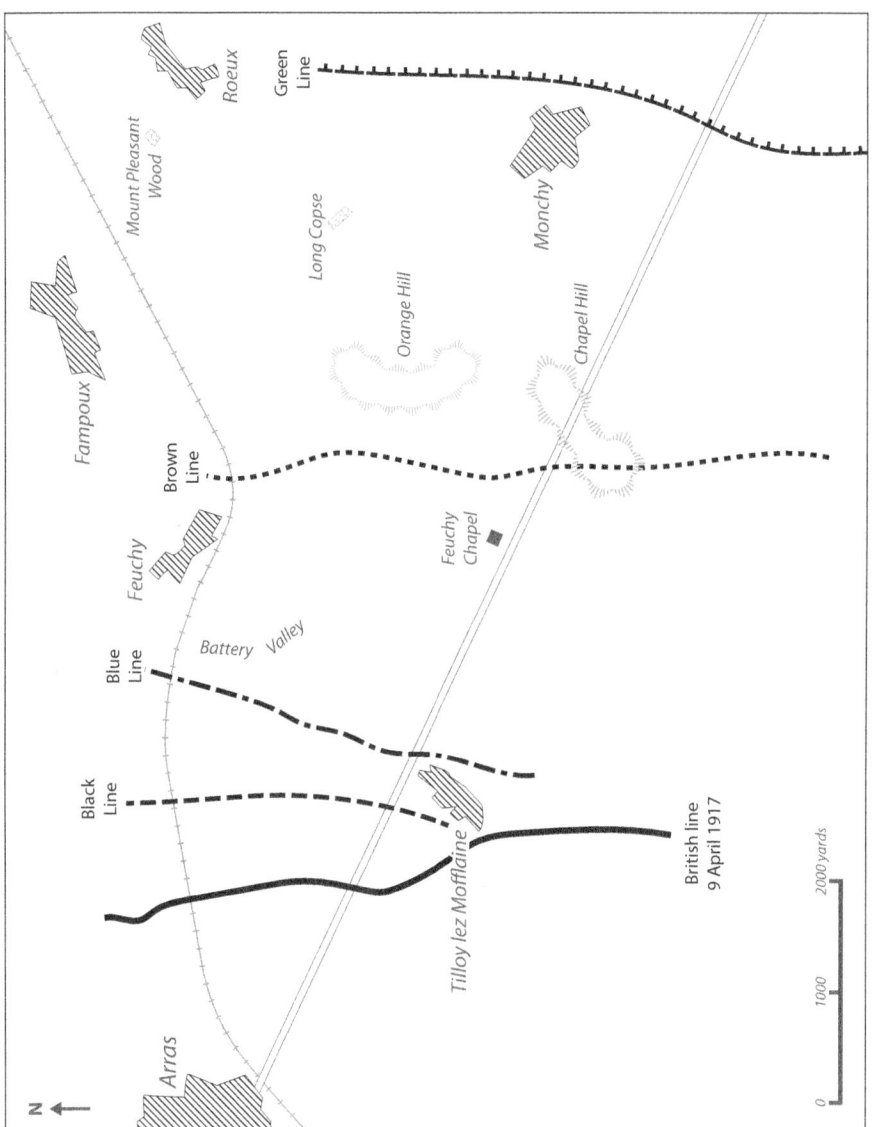

Map 9 Battle of Arras, April 1917.

slowly – progressing up the 'learning curve'. The benefits were most apparent in the development of artillery as the paramount weapon of the war. Not only had it been recognised that the number of guns (especially heavy calibre and howitzer) per yard of trench was important, but the effectiveness with which British gun batteries could suppress those of the enemy would have a vital effect on a battle's outcome. Artillery spotting and 'ranging', as well as 'firing off the map' – no need to pre-register the guns – became increasingly important. One development, which deserves more space in the histories than it gets, was 'sound ranging'. The scientists had produced equipment that allowed gun batteries 'to follow the path of single British shells to their destination and correct the range accordingly'.[9] Not only would counter battery fire be more effective but also it would become easier to lay down a creeping barrage – one that the infantry would have sufficient confidence in to follow closely behind it.

For the British, the spring offensive would start on 9 April and last until mid-May. Haig would use three of his armies; the First under General Sir Henry Horne (which included the well-respected Canadian Corps) would attack Vimy Ridge; on Horne's right was General Sir Edmund Allenby's Third Army attacking east from Arras towards the fortified village of Monchy le Preux; lastly on the right flank was Gough's Fifth Army attacking towards Bullecourt. Our focus will be on 10/York and Lancaster, 63 Brigade, 37 Division, VI Corps, Third Army. Although the operation lasted until mid-May, this account confines itself to only a few days in April.

Today, Vimy Ridge is crowned by the magnificent Canadian memorial. Standing proud on the ridge edge, this white structure can be seen for miles around. To quote Hew Strachan:

> The Canadians breasted the crest at 1.18 p.m. [on 9 April], having penetrated 4,000 yards of German defences. The capture of Vimy Ridge was a national triumph for Canada, a more auspicious coming of age than the mismanaged landings at Gallipoli had been for Australia.[10]

The ten divisions of Third Army were spread along a front of approximately 15 miles. Running west-east, and just north of the town of Arras, was the River Scarpe that formed the corps boundary between XVII and VI corps. A couple of miles south of the VI-VII corps boundary the front turned south-east to the River Sensée. With four divisions on the line and one in reserve, VII Corps had the same length of front as the other two corps to the north with their six divisions in the line and one each in reserve. Behind these was XVIII Corps (four divisions) in army reserve. VI Corps, in the centre of Third Army's line, had (from left to right); 15, 12 and 3 Divisions in the front line and 37 behind in corps reserve. Their objective was 'the capture of the German third line system from Feuchy Chapel to Feuchy and the high ground about

---

9   Wilson, *Myriad*, p.450.
10 Strachan, H., *The First World War* (London, Pocket Books, 2006), p.240.

Canadian war memorial, Vimy Ridge. (Photo J. Dillon)

Monchy-le-Preux'.[11] Once these divisions had commenced their attack on the third line, the 37th was to leapfrog through to take Monchy on the same day; this would be done by the 111th and 112th Brigades. Behind these, in divisional reserve, was 63 Brigade (including 10/York and Lancaster) 'ready to afford assistance to either of the other brigades of the Division should these demand it'. If VI Corps achieved its

11 Wylly, *10th Battalion History*, p.226.

ambitious objectives, then it would have advanced some four and a half miles but it would still be two or three miles short of the fortified German line from Drocourt to Quéant. Without a comprehensive plan for the follow-on exploitation, against a heavily defended German line, 'the battle would still be less than half won'.[12]

French plans for their offensive against the Chemin des Dames experienced a number of delays and, as Haig's was to start a week before Nivelle's, this meant delays for the British. On 5 April, a day after the start of the preliminary bombardment, Haig was asked to delay his start by 48 hours. While not wishing to put it off for two days, he could see the benefit to Third Army of an additional day's bombardment. Accordingly, he moved zero hour from Easter Sunday, 8 April, to Easter Monday, the 9th.[13] Nivelle eventually opened his offensive at 6 a.m., 16 April, on the Aisne.

In previous battles, the troops have frequently had to assemble in trenches very close to the front, sometimes crawling out to lie down in No Man's Land. In the case of Arras the British were able to make use of the unique system of caves and tunnels below the town; a result of quarrying for the local stone. These workings provided ideal assembly areas for an army of 30,000, providing them with electric lighting, water, and even a light railway. 'By this means the attacking infantry could be brought right up to the jumping-off point, unobserved by the enemy'.[14] 37 Division, who were not due to leave the front line until part of the way through the events of 9 April, spent the night of the 8th to the west of Arras; 10/York and Lancaster was in hutments at Duisans where 'fighting equipment was completed and all arrangements made for going into action the next day'.[15]

The attack frontage of VI Corps (whose start position was to be some 2,000 yards east of Arras) was shaped like a wedge (see Map 9). The wider arc was the Green Line, or fourth objective, to the east of the village of Monchy; to reach it required an advance of 7,000 yards. The southern boundary of this 'wedge' was a line running to the south of the villages of Tilloy lès Mofflaines and Guémappes. The northern boundary was the River Scarpe. A little over half-way from their start point to Monchy was the Brown Line (third objective) which ran almost due north from the village of Wancourt to Feuchy on the southern bank of the Scarpe. Once again, troops advancing on foot across shell-pocked ground were expected to fulfil a plan that was too ambitious. At 03.30 on 4 April the 'greatest assembly of artillery yet made by the British army'[16] began shelling the enemy. Utilising the new techniques for gun ranging and the fall of shot the British guns began counter-battery fire. The RFC flew a great many sorties but was inferior in numbers and aircraft to their German opponents; losses were many, and the month became

12 Harris, J.P., *Douglas Haig and the First World War* (Cambridge, CUP, 2008), p.305.
13 Falls, C., *Military Operations France and Belgium, 1917, Volume 1* (Nashville, Naval & Military Press, Reprint of 1940 original), p.182.
14 Wilson, *Myriad*, p.454.
15 TNA WO 95/2529, war diary, 10/York and Lancs.
16 Harris, *Haig*, p.306.

known among the aircrew as 'Bloody April'. Tanks, the new weapon introduced in the previous September, were available in greater numbers, though still not as many as would have been liked – forty were allocated to Third Army. Unfortunately, the new machines had still not developed to the extent that they were yet reliable. Ten tanks had been allocated to operate near the Harp stronghold, south of Tilloy, an area that had been very heavily bombarded and consequently of the ten which had started, 'seven were bogged' and the remaining three put out of action, 'two by shells and the third by bombs thrown under the tracks'.[17] The new weapon still had some way to go to make a difference.

The day of the assault dawned bright and cold with freezing temperatures and snow on the ground. Because of their role as brigade reserve, in a division that formed the corps reserve, 10/York and Lancaster had little involvement in the first day's action. The Operation Order, issued five days before the attack, was a little vague as to how the battalion, and the brigades it was supporting, were to attack their fourth objective:

> No details as to the manner in which this attack will be carried out or the time at which it will be possible to launch it, are yet available.[18]

The next appendix in the diary (undated) gives no further clarification: 'It is still uncertain what part the Brigade may have to take in the course of operations'. No doubt, the battalion officers would be thrown back on their own initiative and 'cross that bridge' once they got there. By 1 p.m., the battalion was in the reserve trenches, finally reaching Battery Valley (half way between the second and third objectives) by 'about 3.40 p.m.'. This was a considerable advance and quite different from 1 July. At the end of the first day, Haig wrote to the King:

> Your Majesty will be pleased to hear that I found the troops everywhere in the most splendid spirits and looking the picture of health. […] the fact that the Army was *advancing* made everyone happy! […] The attack was launched at 5.30 am, and has progressed most satisfactorily. […] Our success is already the largest obtained on this front in *one* day.[19]

Great as was the advance, the infantry had not reached the Green Line, their fourth objective for the day, which should have been attained by 'Zero plus 7 hours'; 12.30 p.m. On VI Corps front, things could have gone better. At one point, with darkness approaching, the two lead brigades of 37 Division, 111 and 112, became muddled and lost direction; the former was actually moving in 12 Division's space, rather than that of its own division. Had this mix-up not occurred then the official historian believes that

---

17 Falls, *1917, Vol. 1*, p.212.
18 WO 95/2529, war diary, 10/York and Lancs, Appendix 8.
19 Sheffield and Bourne, *Haig*, p.278.

Monchy might have been taken that night.[20] That village did not fall to the British until 11 April. By the evening of 9 April, VI Corps had only managed to penetrate the Brown Line (third objective) on the front of one of its three divisions. 10/York and Lancaster spent part of the night in an old German communication trench in the area of Battery Valley, moving out again at 3 a.m. The priority for 10 April was for both VI and VII Corps to take full possession of the Brown Line – the Wancourt-Feuchy line. For that to happen, the strong point at Feuchy Chapel, to the west of the Brown Line on the Arras-Cambrai road, had to be taken as the machine guns there could enfilade any attacks on the Wancourt-Feuchy line. The redoubt fell to the attacks of 3 and 12 Divisions.

In the early hours of 10 April, the battalion moved out of Battery Valley to the junction of a railway and a sunken road in the very north of their sector, south of Fampoux. At his point, they made contact with mounted troops from 9 Division (XVII Corps) on their left on the River Scarpe. The battalion must have been somewhat on their own up to this point, as the battalion commander, in his post-battle report, stated that they had 'got in touch with the 4th Battalion Middlesex Regt., who were 1,000 yards on my right rear.'[21] Around noon, the battalion received orders to move forward, probably to Lone Copse Valley, but heavy machine gun fire from Mount Pleasant Wood (to their left front) was making this difficult. At this point in the narrative, it is worth quoting from the Official History to try to get a picture of 37 Division's situation, remembering that the three brigades making up the 37th were the 111th, 112th and 63rd:

> Each brigade was to carry out more or less the role allotted to it on the 9th April; that is, the 111th to capture Monchy le Preux, and the 112th and 63rd to cover its flanks. As, however, the 63rd was now established on Orange Hill [i.e., through and to the east of the Brown Line] and through the gap, whereas the other two were not, the sequence of events was to be altered and the 63rd was first of all to push on and gain all the ground it could between Monchy and the Scarpe.[22]

We have seen, however, that the forward movement of 10/York and Lancs was not going to be easy because of the fire from Mount Pleasant Wood. To reach Lone Copse Valley the other three battalions of 63 Brigade had to 'dribble small parties forward from one shell-hole to another'. However, the York and Lancaster 'found [themselves] unable to advance at all'. In fact the battalion did make it, but not until 8 p.m. that evening. They remained there until the middle of the morning, 11 April.

The third day of the battle saw the York and Lancaster men coming under a lot of fire, but making only little progress. At 11.15, they moved from Lone Copse 'in the direction of Bois des Aubepines'. This wood lies some 1,500 yards north-east of

20   Falls, *1917, Vol. 1*, p.225.
21   WO 95/2529, war diary, 10/York and Lancs, Appendix 10.
22   Falls, *1917, Vol. 1*, p.249.

Monchy and is the most eastward of three woods; from west to east, Arrow Head Copse, Twin Copses and the Aubepines. All three can be clearly seen on Google map, as can the previously mentioned Lone Copse and Mount Pleasant Wood. As the battalion moved across a spur to the west of Monchy, they came under

> [H]eavy frontal and enfilade M.G. Fire and had severe casualties in the leading Coy. I [the battalion C.O.] then trickled the remainder of the Bttn over the Danger Zone and got into and occupied the German practice trenches [north-west of Monchy]. These I consolidated.

They remained there until 12 April. In the meantime, Monchy was taken by a mix of infantry from 111 and 112 Brigades, cavalry from 8th Cavalry Brigade and the assistance of six tanks. Of these six, three were to go to the north and three to the south of Monchy. Two of those on the northern side broke down before they got there, the third was finally hit by British guns, but the crew got out. On the south side, all three were hit, either by British or German guns, and a number of their crew members were killed. With the capture of Monchy, two days later than planned, the troops had captured 'the last organized line of defence short of the Drocourt-Quéant line'.[23]

On 12 April, 10/York and Lancaster 'was relieved from ground won from [the] enemy near MONCHY-LE-PREUX by 17 Division. This battalion relieved by 10th West Yorks and proceeded to ARRAS by route march. Billets in HOSPICE-DES-VIEILLIARDS'. Those three days in April were summed up in the battalion history:

> VI Corps had captured the villages of Feuchy and Tilloy, the strong redoubts of the Harp and the Railway Triangle, had gained some thirty-six square miles of ground and taken two thousand prisoners and sixty guns.[24]

Strangely, the history made no mention of Monchy.

At this point, the men of 10/York and Lancaster might have believed that they were finished with Arras and its surrounds, but they would have been wrong. After a few days in the rear at Manin, a few miles west of Arras, orders were received on 20 April for 37 Division to join XVII Corps north of the River Scarpe, near Fampoux, relieving the 4th Division. To make up for men lost earlier in the month the York and Lancs was joined by 200 Other Ranks from 34 Infantry Base Depot, Étaples. The battalion was to be engaged again before the month was out but we should first mention a mini mutiny on the part of some of Allenby's generals.

Haig wanted Gough's Fifth Army to attack astride the Bapaume-Cambrai road 'with the objective of piercing the Hindenburg Line in the direction of Marcoing',[25]

---

23 Falls, *1917, Vol. 1*, p.253.
24 Wylly, *10th Battalion History*, p.227.
25 Sheffield and Bourne, *Haig*, p.284.

a little south-west of Cambrai. However, Haig also noted in his diary that Gough would not attack the front at Bullecourt-Quéant 'until Allenby's advanced guards are across the Sensée River'. For Allenby's men this would have been an advance against stiff opposition, in grim weather, and without any special artillery preparation; 'it was, to say the least, an extremely demanding goal'.[26] Three major-generals commanding front-line divisions, met to protest Allenby's order to advance as Gough had requested. Their protest was passed on to Haig:

> This collective protest by a group of divisional commanders going over the heads of their Army commander to GHQ was an extraordinary procedure. Yet, [...] the protest seems to have succeeded.[27]

Haig's later order of 15 April took account of some of the generals' points and according to Harris; these represented 'a fairly dramatic change of Haig's plans within twenty-four hours'. As a result, Haig's follow-up attack did not take place until 23 April. The Official History comments that, 'Sir Douglas Haig, as almost always, deferred to the wishes of the commanders on the spot'.[28]

The renewed operation was postponed until 23 April, with Third Army advancing on either side of the River Scarpe and XVII Corps on the north side of the river. Following their recent move to XVII Corps (to relieve 4 Division) the 37th 'had thus had little time for reconnaissance of ground entirely unknown to it',[29] which would have been unsettling for brigade and battalion commanders. On the left of the corps front was 37 Division (with 51 to their right), with their line of advance towards Oppy in the north and Plouvain in the south. The men of 10/York and Lancaster, with the rest of 63 Brigade, would be on the right of the divisional front, 111 Brigade on their left and the 112th in divisional reserve. By April 1917, it was becoming the norm for infantry assaults to go ahead under the cover of a creeping barrage. The Operation Order for 23 April stressed 'the vital necessity of following up the barrage as closely as possible. If this is not done, the enemy have time to get their machine guns in action. Leading waves should keep within 50 yards of the barrage'.[30] The planned rate of 'creep' was 100 yards every 4 minutes. On reaching their final objective, the troops were to 'immediately push forward Lewis Guns and covering troops whilst remainder dig in and consolidate before counter attack is delivered'. The new weapon on the battlefield, the tank, had so far not been the game-changer that its exponents had hoped (for reasons mentioned in the previous chapter). This last phase of the Arras offensive was little different.

---

26 Harris, *Haig*, p.317.
27 Harris, *Haig*, p.317.
28 Falls, *1917, Vol. 1*, p.379.
29 Falls, *1917, Vol. 1*, p.396.
30 WO 95/2529, Appendix 11.

While 22 of the machines had been salvaged or repaired after their involvement on 9 April, only two were available to 37 Division on 23 April. The Operation Order and the 10/York and Lancaster diary make no reference to them. At this stage of the war, the tank had made little impression on the ordinary soldier attacking the German lines.

At 11.15 p.m. on the night of 22/23 April, 10/York and Lancaster started its move forward to relieve 4/Middlesex in Honey Trench. The assembly area was effectively just 'a line of shell holes'[31] but, in spite of this, the men had taken up their positions by 1 a.m. When the whistle blew, at 4.45 a.m., 'the battalion went steadily forward and met with heavy frontal and enfilade machine-gun fire'. However, the morning did not progress as planned. During the battle the battalion commander, Lieutenant Colonel Ridgway[32] (originally from 1/North Staffordshire Regiment) was killed and command devolved to junior officers, this would have contributed to the morning's confusion. The officer drawing up the post-battle report stated:

> Very soon after the battle opened units of the Brigade became mixed up, and no information reached me from officers of the Battalion. I sent out patrols to get in touch with the companies, but no reliable information was brought back.

According to the Official History, 'The 10/York & Lancaster lost the barrage, and failed to reach the first objective'.[33] With their C.O. dead and only junior officers left in command, the battalion was sorely stretched.

Unsure of what was happening, the temporary commander sent out patrols to try to get in touch with other units, however 'these only met scattered parties' which were collected up and put themselves under the command of the O.C. 8/Lincolns. At this point, all they could do was form a support line in an available trench, where they remained throughout the night of 23/24 April. The report gives little information of what was happening at that time other than that three officers and 38 men remained in that position 'during the 24th until ordered to withdraw to Hudson Trench and Sunken Road about 9.45 p.m.'[34] Too often in this narrative of the war the point has to be made that, while extensive planning went into the arrangements for the first days of offensives, insufficient thought was given to the follow up exploitation. Time and again, Haig and his commanders intended that the advance should continue past the initial objectives, but the required movement of ammunition, the re-positioning of gun batteries and the replacement of casualties did not allow this to happen. The point is well put by Falls:

31 WO 95/2529, Appendix 11.
32 Buried in Cabaret-Rouge British Cemetery, Souchez.
33 Falls, *1917, Vol. 1*, p.397.
34 WO 95/2529, Appendix 13.

It seems certain [...] that had the bulk of the British divisions been fresher more would have been accomplished. It was not only the strain and shock of battle which had worn out the troops; preparatory work, carried out for the most part by night, in foul weather, upon churned-up ground, and often under heavy fire, had also contributed to their fatigue.[35]

The following is an account of being wounded on 25 April by one soldier of 10 York and Lancaster:

The first shock was quickly overcome and I proceeded to bandage the wound with my field dressing. [...] The shrapnel had penetrated deeply into the flesh of my thigh but fortunately had just missed the bone. [He then had to crawl about 150 yards] but it seemed more like 150 miles. [He made it back to the lines but because of the heavy shelling, he could not yet be evacuated.] There I was, sure of a trip to England and a rest from the mud of Flanders, unable to move, in a trench that might at any minute be knocked to pieces with a shell. [He was eventually evacuated to Arras and put on a hospital train for Étaples; in the train he had a bed.] A bed, the first I had experienced for many months – a real bed with white sheets.[36]

Carter was later commissioned and joined 2/York and Lancaster as a 2nd Lieutenant in September 1918.

Once again the infantry battalions assigned to the attacking waves, were also expected to provide large numbers of working parties before taking part in the assault: 'A period of the War had been reached when the infantry, the sole source of man-power for all odd jobs, was being excessively "milked"'.[37] As well as being utilised as a source of manual labour, battalion strengths were shrinking because of battle casualties and sickness, while drafts of new men (often straight from training school) were insufficient to make up the losses. In the case of 37 Division, 'the drafts had not arrived; battalions went into action on the 28th April not much above 200 strong; and companies had only one or two officers'. 10/York and Lancaster was in action again on the 28th under the command of Lieutenant R.N. Wilkinson. At 11.30 p.m. on 27 April, the battalion left Hudson Trench for the assembly trenches, getting there at 03.55 on the morning of the 28th; the attack was launched 30 minutes later with 10/York and Lancs in support of 8/Lincolns. However, as in the previous attack on 23 April – although by now without their Colonel, fatigued and suffering casualties – little progress was made. One hour after the assault began the remnants of the battalion were isolated and under heavy machine gun fire. A little before mid-morning they retired to trenches held by 111 Brigade, remaining there

---

35 Falls, *1917, Vol. 1*, p.401.
36 Carter, C., Private Papers, IWM Doc. 7988.
37 Falls, *1917, Vol. 1*, p.414.

until 4 a.m. on the 29th. It was time for 10/York and Lancaster to withdraw from the events around Arras and they 'proceeded by bus to billets at Manin'.

The events on the north side of the Scarpe had not gone well for 37 Division and the men of the York and Lancaster battalion; the division had been reduced to a 'shadow' and 63 Brigade was 'virtually destroyed',[38] with 'little to show' for the loss. Falls' summary may have been a fair assessment of the gains made on the 23rd and 28th of April, but on the 9th, the assault had taken a good deal of ground from the Germans: the Canadians had done magnificently at Vimy Ridge, while the Third Army had done well to the east of Arras. The gains made after 12 April, except by First Army, were on a much smaller scale. During the month of April, 10/York and Lancaster lost six officers killed and 17 wounded as well as 72 men sick, 37 killed, 391 wounded and 119 missing – a total of 642 from the strength of 956 on 31 March: 67 per cent of all those on the battalion roll. The CWGC database indicates that three soldiers with the Dillon surname were killed during the Arras offensives: Private R. Dillon, 8/Argyll and Sutherland Highlanders, was killed on the first day (9 April) and is buried in Roclincourt Valley cemetery; Private Arthur Howard Dillon, 2/King's Own Scottish Borderers, was killed on 20 April; Private John Thomas Dillon, 10/York and Lancaster, was killed on 21 April. John and Arthur have no known graves and are remembered on the Arras Memorial to the missing.

By the end of April, there would have been very few men who had been with the battalion since its move to France; there had been 600 new arrivals in the drafts of May and June. Although they saw little action in those two months the war diary shows that they spent a great deal of time on route-marches from one French village to the next, before ending up on 28 June in the front line, this time at Wytschaete in the Ypres salient. At some point in 1917, the author's grandfather joined the battalion from 6/York and Lancaster, the family believe that he fought at Arras, but have no documentary evidence. According to the battalion history, 10/York and Lancaster continued its rotation through the front line, but took no part in any later 'great' battles. By January 1918 the York and Lancaster Regiment was experiencing difficulties in recruiting enough men for the number of battalions it had in the field, at the same time the army was reducing the number of battalions per brigade from four to three. As a consequence, on 28 January 1918, 10/York and Lancaster was disbanded and the men moved to other battalions; Private Patrick Dillon was one of those who were moved to 2/York and Lancaster.

While 10/York and Lancaster was rebuilding its strength and preparing to move to Wytschaete, plans were afoot in Sir Herbert Plumer's Second Army for an assault on the high ground of Messines Ridge, south of Ypres. Our narrative now relocates to the Salient and the British attempt to literally blow the Germans off their defensive line. To that end, we re-join the 8th and 9th battalions of the regiment; we last met them during the action around Flers-Courcelette in September 1916.

38 Falls, *1917, Vol. 1*, p.428.

9

"We shared in the great victory" – Messines Ridge

Nearly three years into the war (which many predicted would be over by the first Christmas) our story moves 70 kilometres north of Arras to a ridge of high ground south of Ypres: Messines Ridge. For any of the soldiers who had gone out with the original BEF – there would not have been many still alive by spring 1917 – they could have been forgiven for thinking that the front lines in the Ypres salient had not moved very far. To the south of the Belgian town, the German line arched westwards, along the Messines Ridge, forming a salient from Hill 60 in the north to Ploegsteert Wood in the south. With Flanders being so flat, the term 'ridge' was a relative one: it was only 40 metres above sea-level. However, that was enough to give those who held it a great advantage in terms of observation and defensive strength; not to mention dryer ground in which to dig trenches. For the British, the taking of the Messines Ridge would not only give them the higher, drier ground, it would also remove the German salient and straighten their line. The task fell to General Sir Herbert Plumer, commander of Second Army.

Short, rotund and with a large moustache, Plumer was the very caricature of a 'Colonel Blimp', but only in appearance. A soldier's pen portrait of him is left to us by Norman Gladden who was with the Northumberland Fusiliers at the Somme, Ypres and Italy. Gladden's description gives us an inkling of how the troops viewed their senior commanders:

> He was a short, venerable-looking man, remarkably spruce for his age and keen in appearance, the type not inclined to overlook any sort of slackness on the part of the leaders. He had a great reputation among the troops, whom he always treated with consideration.[1]

---

1   Gladden, N., *Ypres 1917. A Personal Account* (Abingdon, Purnell, 1967), p.83.

Soldiers appreciated commanders who treated them as more than just navvies and bayonets, and were capable of determining which of them were leaders rather than just martinets:

> We were all delighted that afternoon to see our battalion leaders eclipsed by a much greater personality and power and being decisively put in their place, as they were so much in the habit of putting us in ours.

Gladden's comment that 'it was not authority but its misuse that made us savage' summed up how many of the troops felt towards their officers, the NCOs and their often seemingly arbitrary enforcement of discipline.

In November 1916, Haig tasked Plumer with the planning of a 1917 offensive in the Ypres sector. However, as the C-in-C was pre-occupied with Arras, the fall-out of Nivelle's failed offensive on the Chemin des Dames, and Third Ypres (Passchendaele) later that year, he intended to leave the detail of what came to be the battle for Messines Ridge, to Plumer. Assaults against heavily defended positions presented the attacking commander with a major problem: how could he achieve surprise. For centuries, siege warfare had employed the digging of tunnels, and the laying of mines to blow up the defences from below. This was the tactic adopted by Plumer.

Individual battles of the First World War are frequently remembered for particular events or weapons; flame-throwers at Hooge; gas at Second Ypres; the casualties on the Somme; tanks at Flers and Cambrai. The signature of Messines Ridge was the detonation of 19 large mines under the German line – some claimed to have heard the explosion in London. Not all the mines exploded; at least one is known to be still there. The digging and tunnelling needed for this engineering feat were substantial with approximately one million pounds of explosive having to be taken underground by the British, Canadian and Australian tunnelling companies. The underground war was dirty and dangerous, each side working in silence, listening for the other and sometimes having to fight in the tunnels. Those wishing to read more on the topic should try Simon Jones' book, *Underground Warfare 1914-1918*. With our focus on the York and Lancaster men, the two mines with which we are concerned are those at Hill 60 and The Caterpillar, both on the left flank of the attack (Map 10).

At the time of his planning for Messines, Plumer was less ambitious than Haig. Previous chapters have shown how the C-in-C frequently set objectives that the infantry could not achieve. This tendency was exacerbated by the inadequacy of the planning for the exploitation phase that would be necessary to follow through on Haig's expectations. Plumer did not want that to be the case at Messines, he intended to limit the objectives and to make the assault in timed waves, with pauses in between to allow for the consolidation of ground gained. As Second Army's preparations progressed, so Haig's involvement – some might say, interference – became more influential. In early May he told Plumer that:

[Their] objective is now to capture and consolidate up to the range of our guns, and at once to push on advanced guards to profit by Enemy's demoralisation after the bombardment. No delay should take place in doing this.[2]

Haig did not only visit the army commander, he also took himself off to meet those who would have to carry out Plumer's plan. On 22 May, he visited the X Corps commander, General Morland, whom he found 'greatly improved since July last year on the Somme'. However, while he considered the spirit in the corps to be 'fine', he also felt that 'the leaders have been on the defensive about Ypres so long that the *real offensive spirit* has to be developed'.[3] There would be no lack of it once the assault started. Continuing his visitations, Haig considered the OC 19 Division to be 'very nervous and fussy', while General Russell (New Zealand Division) was 'a most capable soldier with considerable strength of character'. By this time Haig, who wanted the whole ridge captured in one go, had persuaded Plumer to extend his objectives. Originally, Plumer intended that the German Oosttaverne Line, some way beyond the ridge summit, should only be a target if the initial attack had gone well; it had now become a formal objective 'making operations for Z-day more ambitious and much more complicated'.[4]

The Second Army front contained three corps; II Anzac in the south, opposite the village of Messines; IX Corps in the centre, opposite Wytschaete; and X Corps in the north. While X Corps had no defended villages on their front, they did have a railway, a canal and a deep cutting (*Damm Strasse*). The two mines in their sector, at Hill 60 and the Caterpillar, were close to the boundary of 23 and 47 Divisions. On the very left of X Corps was 23 Division, with both 8 and 9 York and Lancaster battalions in 70 Brigade. Because of the shape of the salient, the men of 23 Division would have a shorter distance to their objectives, between 300 and 800 yards, than those in the centre who would have to advance 2,000 yards. The Germans had modified their system of defence, having learnt from earlier battles; deep areas of their forward zone were now thinly held, but contained strongpoints and machine gun nests to slow down an attacker's advance. Haig, in a discussion with Plumer, said that the enemy now fought 'not *in* but *for* his first position. He uses considerable forces for counter-attacks'.[5] At Messines, this forward zone area stretched back to the summit of the ridge while behind it was the bulk of the infantry who would meet the attackers that had managed to get past the machine gun posts. Some of these positions were 'small concrete forts, partly above and partly below ground, armed with machine-guns, they presented a strong defence against infantry attack'[6] – their shape reminded the British soldiers of a chemist's 'pill-box', and the name stuck.

2   Sheffield and Bourne, *Haig*, p.293.
3   Sheffield and Bourne, *Haig*, p.295.
4   Harris, *Haig*, p.343.
5   Sheffield and Bourne, *Haig*, p.293.
6   Sandilands, *23rd Division*, pp.155-6.

"We shared in the great victory" – Messines Ridge 157

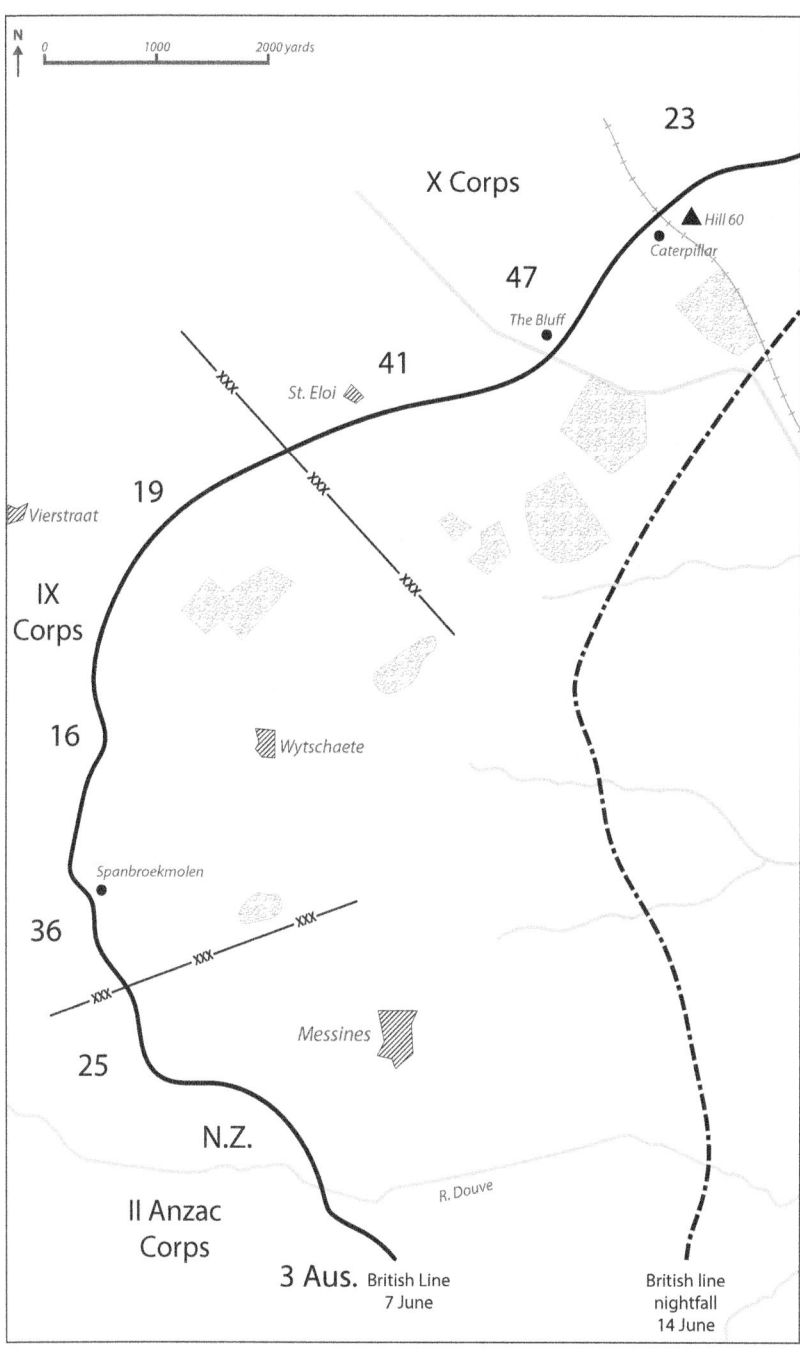

Map 10 Messines Ridge, June 1917.

In his account of his experience of the war Gladden had commented on Plumer's consideration for his soldiers and one of the manifestations of that was the training of the troops before their attack up Messines Ridge: 'meticulous organization and forethought marked every stage of the preparation'.[7] In the weeks prior to the attack, the battalions took advantage of their time out of the trenches to practice for the coming offensive. These simulations were done on ground marked out with tapes and flags to represent the British and German trench systems. 8/York and Lancs did this on four days in May; one of them was in conjunction with a 'contact aeroplane' to allow them to practice using visual signals. Their sister battalion did the same on three days. Logistical preparations were also extensive with light railways being used to transport ammunition and stores to the front, pipelines were also laid to carry the 150,000 gallons of water needed each day by each corps. Richard Holmes described it as a 'teed-up' battle, one in which the 'preparation and planning were first-rate, and briefing and rehearsal had been comprehensive'.[8] In his divisional history, Sandilands relates how Lieutenant Oakley (8/Yorkshire), a 'celebrated' artist, had 'constructed a model of the Caterpillar and Hill 60 from maps and air photographs, showing the hostile trenches, railway, and the general detail of the ground'. Study of this prior to the attack enabled NCOs and officers to feel that 'they knew the German trench system as well as their own'.[9] However, it was not all work and training. The diary of the 9th battalion mentions one event that would have been very welcome to young officers away from home: 'The Bn Hqr mess entertained four nurses of the 3rd Canadian C.C.S. to tea'. For men starved of the company of young women one can imagine the fight among the young officers to escort the visitors.

In spite of the many accounts of how involved the units were in training and preparing for the coming offensive Gladden, whose company supplied work patrols assisting with the mine at Hill 60, states that they were unaware of their involvement until two days before it was launched:

> Rumours had been going about for some days that important moves were pending. But rumour was always active in this way and I doubt whether any of us in the rank-and-file had allowed it to sink in. After all, secrecy was still part of official policy. [...] Thus the news broke upon us with a shock. On the day after the morrow a great attack was being launched in which our battalion would take a foremost part.[10]

The rumour-mill was an active part of soldiers' lives and a direct consequence of the policy of keeping everything secret from the men on the grounds that they might

7 Liddell Hart, *First World War*, p.324.
8 Holmes, *The Western Front*, p.160.
9 Sandilands, *23rd Division*, p.150.
10 Gladden, *Ypres*, p.57.

give away information if captured by enemy patrols. Sandilands refers to 'canteen rumours' borne of the 'incurable optimism' of the British soldier and 'prominent among their main promoters were the officers' servants'[11] who were keen to claim inside knowledge as a result of their close association with their officer charges. Speculation had it that the 23rd would be part of an 'army of pursuit' in the coming operation. As Sandilands relates, this 'high-sounding title possessed an optimistic flavour, suggesting a hunt of demoralised masses of Germans with all the sting taken out of them'. Gladden was right to state that the authorities seemed unaware of the insidious effect of ill-informed speculation and did not realise how worthwhile it would have been 'to organise an active news service to keep us in the picture'.[12]

A constant problem for commanders was how to stay in contact with the men, once they had commenced their attack. The enemy shelling, in the days prior to the attack, kept 23 Division Signal Company constantly engaged 'in an endless struggle to dig and maintain buried-cable routes'.[13] Although these cables were normally laid six feet down, enemy shells still broke them. Without portable wireless sets, other means had to be found to allow battalion commanders to know how far their troops had advanced: one solution was the RFC. The instructions for 9/York and Lancaster stipulated how they should operate with a 'contact aircraft':

> The contact aeroplane [...] will be distinguished by three broad white bands on the fuselage [a scheme repeated for the D-Day landings in 1944] & by the attachment of a black board on the left lower plane [wing]. This contact aeroplane will call for flares by firing a white light & sounding a Klaxon horn. Leading infantry will light flares approximately at the following times – Zero + 30 minutes; Zero + 1 hour; Zero + 4 hours 30 minutes; Zero + 5 hours. Infantry must however ensure that the aeroplane is calling for flares before lighting up. It is recognised that in confused fighting it is difficult for bodies of troops to know if they are actually the leading troops & it must not be assumed that there are no other troops in front. Isolated bodies out of touch on their flanks should light flares when called on to do so. The colour of the flares issued are green. A wireless aeroplane will be up throughout the day for the purpose of looking out for counter attacks. A red light fired from this aeroplane will denote an impending counter attack N[orth] of the canal – the position and direction of enemy movement will be communicated by this plane through the artillery to the Brigadier concerned who will warn Battalion Commanders concerned.[14]

---

11 Sandilands, *The 23rd Division*, p.142.
12 Gladden, *Ypres*, p.86.
13 Sandilands, *23rd Division*, p.146.
14 WO 95/2188, Instruction No. 2.

When historians criticise commanders for their bungling during the battles on the Western front, they would do well to bear in mind how difficult it was for those individuals even to know where their men were once they had gone 'over the bags'. How were troops in battle to hear a Klaxon over the noise of the aircraft engine, as well as the tremendous sound of an artillery bombardment?

After all the preparations, it was time to move the troops forward to their assembly positions on the night of 6 June, ready for the 'off' the following morning. The 9th battalion noted that they had suffered no casualties during what was often a dangerous period for the troops. If the enemy had any indication of the time of an attack then it was normal for them to shell communication and support trenches with the intention of causing as many casualties as possible, before the attack could get going. Just such a scenario had killed many of the men from the Pals battalions in front of Serre on 1 July 1916.

At 3.10 a.m. on 7 June, 'our artillery opened up a terrific barrage on the Hun front line & simultaneously the mines under HILL 60 and the CATERPILLAR were blown'.[15] The British troops must have been impressed with the scale of the explosions, especially given their own proximity to the mines. Major Henry, commanding 1st Australian Tunnelling Company, 'having fired the mines under the Caterpillar and Hill 60, had opened a bottle of champagne to drink success to the 23rd Division';[16] the reader can probably picture the scene. The divisional history describes what came next:

> Simultaneously, those far back behind the British front saw the whole sky lit by the flashes of guns and bursting shells, then heard a dull roar like the continued roll of mighty drums, as the artillery opened the heaviest barrage yet put down in the course of the war. [...] one minute later the infantry advanced.

The effect of the mines on the German defenders must have been traumatic: 'some defenders were simply vaporized by the blast'.[17] In addition, the mines did not go off simultaneously (as intended), the last one detonating some 19 seconds after the first. It would be unusual if this 'rolling thunder' effect did not cause its own panic among the defenders. According to Sandilands, the Germans were 'quick to reply', with their barrage coming down only two minutes later, 'but by then our men had reached the German front line at nearly every point'. Edmonds gave his enthusiastic picture of the assault in the Official History:

> In that rosy dawn a host of British and Dominion troops were surging forward behind the cloud of smoke and dust of the deep barrage up the great breast of

---

15   WO 95/2188, war diary, 9/York & Lancs.
16   Sandilands, *23rd Division*, p.154.
17   Holmes, *The Western Front*, p.159.

Spanbroekmolen Crater – Pool of Peace. Left after the detonation of the largest mine at Messines Ridge. (Photo J. Dillon)

the Messines-Wytschaete Ridge; over a hundred battalions, about 80,000 men, were moving up the slope, and every man among them had a pre-arranged and carefully rehearsed task.[18]

By 03.30, only 20 minutes after the attack started, 'with the exception of a short length of trench on the extreme left of the attack, the whole objective of the first phase had been captured'.[19] 23 Division, and the York and Lancaster men, were helped by the fact that they were only required to advance 300 yards to their objective. The cutting of the wire by the massed guns of the artillery had been a success, while the efforts of the 12 tanks allocated to X Corps seemed to go unnoticed. The diaries of both battalions of the York and Lancaster make no mention of them but Gladden made a passing reference; 'we crossed a track about which clung a strong reek of petrol

18 Edmonds, J., *Military Operations France and Belgium, 1917, Volume 2* (Uckfield, Naval & Military Press, Reprint of 1931 original), p.61.
19 Sandilands, *23rd Division*, p.155.

as though a tank had recently passed this way. [...] As it happened, this was the only trace of a tank that I was to come across throughout the operations'.[20] In all, 72 tanks were part of Second Army's assault that day.

All along Plumer's front, the initial attack had gone well, but how had the two battalions of the York and Lancaster Regiment fared? The extreme left of the corps front was held by 70 Brigade with 11/Sherwood Foresters on the left and 9/York and Lancaster on their right. This brigade would be the pivot about which the corps would swing in their advance:

> At zero + 1 [minute] the first wave consisting of B Coy [9/York & Lancs] on the left and A Coy on the right went over, and were followed by D Coy (moppers up) & C Coy in support at short intervals. The attack progressed very favourably and by zero + 30 the Bn had reached its objective and began consolidating.[21]

The move forward was actually more complicated than the statement in the diary would have us believe; the Operation Order gave more detail. Each of the two companies in the first wave, A and B would use 2 of their 4 platoons. These would in turn form up in two lines, 15 yards apart. Behind these came D company in one line, followed by the second wave consisting of the remaining 2 platoons from each of A and B companies, again in two lines, 15 yards apart. The whole was followed up by a 3rd wave (C company), 'in lines of sections in file', this third wave to be not more than 100 yards from the second. In effect, this would mean that the three waves of 9/York and Lancaster would form a front nearly 200 yards deep. Once the enemy line had been taken, the battalion had to dig a fire step (the original German one would have been facing the 'wrong' way) and commence wiring for telephone communications back to battalion HQ. During this initial phase, the battalion suffered 'few casualties'.

A few minutes after reaching their first objective the second wave of 70 Brigade was to pass through the first two battalions, with 8/York and Lancaster leap-frogging the 9th battalion and reaching the brigades final objective. Having got this far, only a few hundred yards, the battle for Messines Ridge was almost over for 9/York and Lancaster. The battalion 'remained on its objective until the evening of the 9th' and during that period, they were heavily shelled and 'sustained many casualties': 4 officers (including the CO) were killed and 6 of them wounded; from the Other Ranks, 39 were killed, 211 wounded, another 9 died of wounds and a further 18 were missing – a total of 287 casualties from the one battalion. Their Commanding Officer had been Lieutenant Colonel Bowes Wilson, he had 'gone forward to watch the course of the battle'[22] but, in trying to see how his men were doing, he was killed around 7

20   Gladden, *Ypres*, p.60.
21   WO 95/2188, war diary, 9/York & Lancs.
22   Sandilands, *23rd Division*, p.158.

in the morning. He is buried in the Railway Dugout (Transport Farm) cemetery, 2 kilometres south-east of Ypres. Captain D Lewis took over temporary command of the battalion.

Battalion war diaries vary greatly in the level of detail they accord to their involvement in combat operations; 8/York and Lancaster give away little regarding the events of 7 June:

> We shared in the great victory by the 2nd Army. Zero hour 3.10 a.m. The 9th Y & L took their objective in fine style, and at 6.50 a.m. we left their new line to attack the final objective. This we took with a strong-point about 50 yards in advance of the right flank, also the KNOLL, an eminence in NO MAN's LAND in front of our centre.

Given its commanding position, it was essential that the battalion drove the Germans off the Knoll. Having done that, and consolidated their position, they waited for counter attacks, which did not materialise. Their 'leapfrog' through the 9/York and Lancs position was successful, but like their sister battalion, not without casualties: one officer killed; two were 'believed killed'; six officers wounded; among the men, 300 were 'estimated' to be casualties. It was always difficult to obtain accurate numbers for the men who were lost in the immediate aftermath of a battle. The participation of the two York and Lancaster battalions was almost complete, although the battle would not 'officially' end until 14 June.

'By 9 a.m. British troops were established along the length of the Messines-Wytschaete Ridge from the [River] Douve to east of Mount Sorrel'.[23] From their new positions, the British observers could see deep into the German rear areas, a rare privilege for them in the Ypres Salient. As the men dug in along the ridge they, and their commanders, prepared to receive the expected counter attacks, but it was not until almost mid-morning that reports came in to indicate that the Germans were repositioning for such a move. The rest of the day passed with no indication in their diaries that either battalion had more to do than consolidate their positions. On the night of 8/9 June, both units came under heavy enemy bombardment but by the 10th they were both relieved from their front line duties and were pulled back into billets in the rear. Messines was another example of battalions taking part in the initial stages of a major attack, but not being in the line to see the final results; one hopes that they would have been told that Second Army did achieve a notable victory between 7-14 June, with the new British front line being considerably advanced – see Map 10.

Once in the rear the battalions reverted to routine; absorbing of new drafts; training; inspections and 'internal economy'. On the evening of 11 June, the commanding officer of the 8th battalion 'gave a dinner to those officers who had been all thro [sic] the attack, in Poperinghe'; only nine attendees are named in the diary. As it was

23   Edmonds, *1917, Vol. 2*, p.71.

summer, cricket was on the sports agenda: on 17 June, the 9th battalion beat the 8th by 70 runs to 49; between 19 and 25 June, 8/York and Lancs played three more matches against other units, winning two and losing one. Even in infantry battalions, officers frequently had horses, 'chargers', which gave an excuse for Divisional Horse Shows. To allow the men to also participate, there were awards for the heavy horses of the artillery and transport sections. On 25 June, the 8th battalion took first prize for 'Heavy Draught Pairs', while the CO's horse, George, came third in the Jumping Class (owner up) – this meant that the CO had to ride his own horse. All entertainments and sports provided an excellent 'safety valve', not only for any tensions that had built up during combat, but also for any friction that may have built up between the men and their officers and NCOs. One example of how these shows gave an opportunity for the men to laugh at their officers is recounted by Sandilands in the history of 23 Division. General Babington (Divisional Commander) was one of those judging the jumping on 25 June and he declared that Captain C [no name given] 'must go again, because he amuses the troops':

> Captain C played up in generous fashion. Midst the wild enthusiasm of the soldiery the first fence was negotiated in excellent style. Then the unexpected event occurred. At the second fence, a post and rails, the horse stopped dead, and, to a howl of delight from the crowd, Captain C, sportsman and great horseman as he was, described a graceful parabola over the fence, landed on the far side with a thud reminiscent of the explosion of the Hill 60 mine, and rose smiling, with his eyeglass still firmly attached to the peak of his cap. For the troops it was the star turn of a great day![24]

The entertainment that the men probably appreciated most was on the evening of 18 June: 'Concert in METEREN YMCA by the Tivolies from Poperinghe'. These concert groups were made up of soldiers, some acting as women, and they were immensely popular. As well as the Brigade Commander and some of his staff, this one was attended by 'practically the whole battalion, with many other officers of the 70th Brigade. An excellent programme was submitted'.[25]

On those few days in June, Plumer's Second Army had achieved a significant victory in the Ypres salient, one which Sandilands (hardly an unbiased observer) described as 'the most overwhelming success yet attained in trench warfare'.[26] Yet to the ordinary soldier, the perspective could be a little different. In his account of the Northumberland Fusilier's efforts, close to Hill 60, Norman Gladden makes some telling statements. In the first, he reminds us that the individual troops rarely had a complete picture of the operation: 'in such battles the participants rarely got more than a worm's-eye view of

24   Sandilands, *23rd Division*, pp.163-4.
25   WO 95/2188, war diary, 8/York & Lancs.
26   Sandilands, *23rd Division*, p.160.

what was going on';[27] the infantry man was no more than a 'pawn' in a game that was 'both outside his range of vision and beyond his understanding'.[28] Gladden's second comment reduces Plumer's victory to one rather closer to a soldier's viewpoint: 'On the night of the 9th our relief came in unheralded. There was but a bare strip of trench to be handed over, a ditch in a poor hygienic state'.[29]

Battles, such as that at Messines, were occasions when ordinary men, many of them conscripts, demonstrated leadership and bravery, acts which the army recognised through the award of medals. For the two days, 7-9 June 8/York and Lancaster's diary recorded the following; one officer received the Distinguished Service Order (DSO) and four were awarded the Military Cross (MC); among the NCOs and men there were six Distinguished Conduct Medals (DCM); twenty-one Military Medals (MM) and two received bars to their existing MM.[30] Before moving on to Third Ypres (Passchendaele) and the mud that came to be synonymous with the Salient, Edmonds' comment on Messines makes a fitting close to this chapter:

> A great victory had been won by General Plumer's Second Army, and with a swift completeness beyond that of any previous major operation of the British Armies in France and Flanders. [...] After two years of patient endurance, the ambition to remove the Germans from the dominating southern face of the Ypres Salient had been realized and the aim of months of intensive labour and preparation was achieved.[31]

---

27 Gladden, *Ypres*, p.60.
28 Gladden, *Ypres*, p.66.
29 Gladden, *Ypres*, p.72.
30 Officers awards are a 'Cross' while the men receive a 'Medal'; a bar denotes winning the same award on two occasions.
31 Edmonds, *1917, Vol. 2*, p.87.

10

"The ground is like a bog in this low-lying country" – Passchendaele and Third Ypres

The second half of 1917 was to occupy the BEF in another of those long drawn-out operations, which epitomised attritional warfare. The sequence of battles that lasted from 31 July to 10 November is often listed under the one rubric, Third Ypres. Over time, however, this period of bitter fighting in the mud of Flanders is frequently referred to by the name of just one of the villages – Passchendaele. The water-logged state of those Flanders' fields has become the paradigm for the Western front: 'Without mud, it wouldn't be the First World War'.[1]

The third year of the conflict was a difficult one for British commanders and politicians. As well as the dreadful human cost, the war's end seemed to most people (soldiers and families alike) to be still some years away. The upheavals in Russia, and that country's exit from the Entente, meant that German divisions could be moved from the east to the Western front, with a consequential increase in pressure on the British and French armies. The outlook was also gloomy when viewed from the Italian theatre, where General Cadorna was having no real success with his many assaults against the Austro-Hungarians across the River Isonzo. To add to Allied problems, large elements of the French army had mutinied following the failed Nivelle offensive on the Chemin des Dames. Robertson had told Sir Henry Wilson that there was a growing British belief that 'the French are not now really out for business'[2] and Haig was questioning whether 'the French intend to play their full part'.[3] At the same time, Lloyd George, concerned at what he saw as the Army high command's disregard for soldiers' lives, was pushing his strategy of removing Germany's props. It was against this background that Haig was attempting to get War Cabinet approval for another Western front offensive in the second half of 1917.

1 Todman, D., *The Great War. Myth and Memory* (London, Hambledon Continuum, 2005), p.41.
2 Woodward, *Robertson*, p.182.
3 Sheffield and Bourne, *Haig*, p.294.

The arguments for and against Haig's proposed operation, which he believed had been agreed 'as long ago as 23 November 1916',[4] were still being aired in the War Cabinet while the preliminaries for Third Ypres had already begun: General Trenchard's RFC began its air offensive on 11 July, with the artillery bombardment beginning on the 16th.[5] As Haig commented in his diary:

> The fact is that the Cabinet does not really understand what preparation for an attack really means!

Approval was finally given on 21 July for a major attack starting just ten days later. However, the 'go ahead' was conditional. The offensive would be reviewed 'during its execution' if it appeared probable that the results 'would not be commensurate with the effort made and the losses incurred'. Should events not go to plan there might be a 'cessation of the offensive and the adoption of an alternative plan'.[6] This less than ringing endorsement was followed up by a telegram, on 25 July, from the War Cabinet to the Commander in Chief. This stated that he could depend upon their wholehearted support and that, if and when 'they decide again to reconsider the situation, they will obtain your views before arriving at any decision as to the cessation of operations'.[7] In this hesitant way, the series of battles designated as Third Ypres began.[8]

In his biography of Plumer, Powell quotes the historian John Terraine; 'The decision to entrust the main offensive in the Flanders battle to the Fifth Army under General Gough must be regarded as Haig's greatest and most fatal error'.[9] Based on his recent success at Messines and the fact that Gough had problems working with his own staff, the better man would have been Plumer. As the offensive developed and Gough ignored a central tenet of Haig's attack plan, the C-in-C 'decided to pass the main role in the battle back to Plumer'.[10]

As with all battle plans, that for Third Ypres went through a number of iterations before it was finalised. At Messines, the attacking divisions halted on the ridge, after taking the initial objectives, and while the attack was a great success, the pause precluded a follow-up as it allowed the Germans the time to gather reinforcements. Haig and Gough were determined that their Third Ypres offensive would exploit any early success by continuing the advance after the early gains. The attack would be pressed to at least the third objective but, because the fourth was 'beyond the effective support of the majority of the field batteries, the attack was not to be pressed to this

---

4   Sheffield and Bourne, *Haig*, p.304.
5   Edmonds, *1917, Vol. 2*, pp.134-5.
6   Edmonds, *1917, Vol. 2*, p.105.
7   Edmonds, *1917, Vol. 2*, p.106.
8   Powell, G., *Plumer. The Soldiers' General* (Barnsley, Pen & Sword, 2004), p.199.
9   Powell, *Plumer*, p.202.
10 Powell, *Plumer*, p.210.

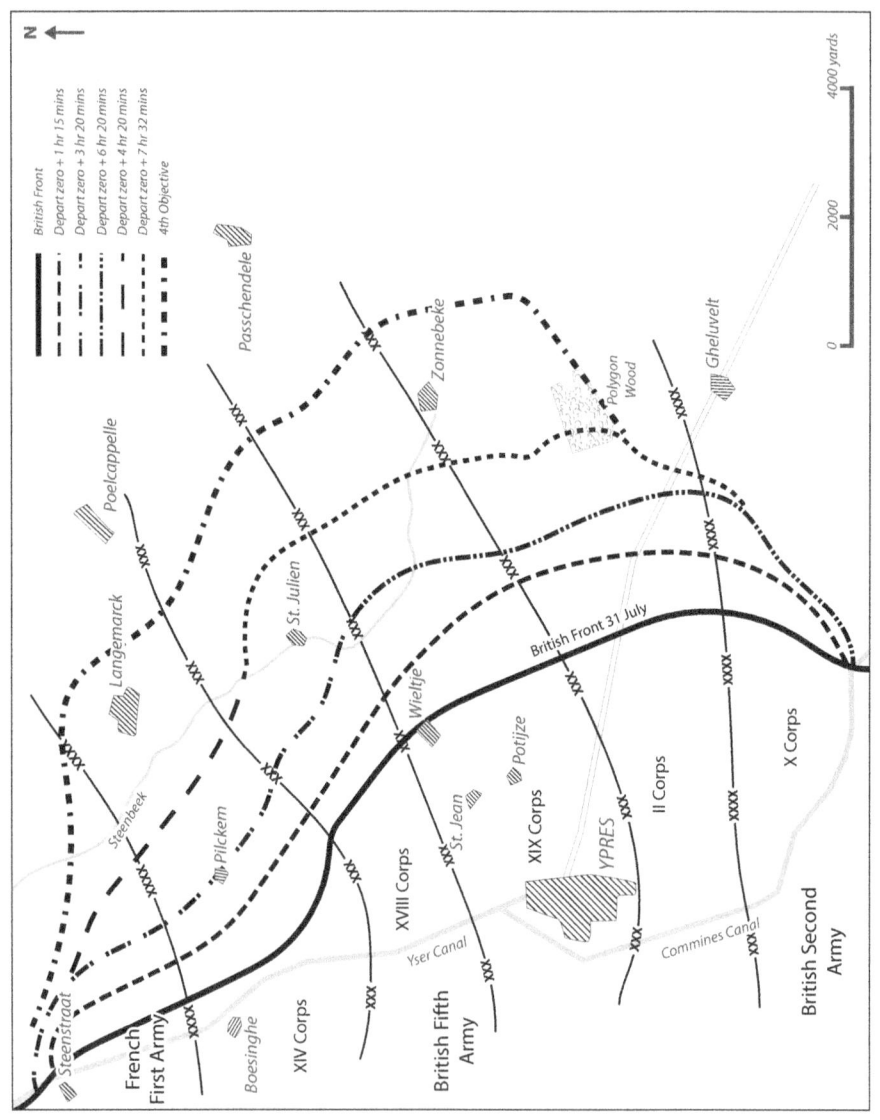

Map 11 Third Battle of Ypres: 31 July 1917 objectives.

final line 'if the enemy seriously contested the advance'[11] towards it. Even now (mid-1917), senior British commanders were still suggesting – against all evidence to the contrary – that German defences might not be 'seriously contested'. In spite of objections from the head of the Operations Branch at GHQ, Haig (on 28 June) 'allowed the Fifth Army scheme to stand'.[12] However, the C-in-C reminded Gough that 'the main battle would be fought on and for the high ground west of Gheluvelt' and that the advance further north 'should be limited until the right flank was firmly established upon it [the Gheluvelt plateau]'.[13] It was Gough's mistake in relation to this part of the plan that led to Plumer taking over that section of the front, and where we will see most of the York and Lancaster involvement in this operation.

As we have seen in the previous chapter, the German defensive systems had developed beyond those used at the start of the war. Their first line was thinly held with the second and third lines on reverse slopes, pillboxes and other strong-points were strategically placed to give covering fields of fire. As July moved into August, so the weather over Flanders became wet and inauspicious for an assault across low-lying farmland. The rain and low cloud not only caused the ground over which the British had to advance to become water-logged; it also made it difficult for the RFC to provide aerial artillery spotters. As a result, the barrage was less effective than planned and the start date was put back to 31 July. It was the rain and mud that came to epitomise Third Ypres – Passchendaele – in popular memory'. In his diary Haig noted how bad the weather had been on the first day of the attack; 'A terrible day of rain. The ground is like a bog in this low lying country'.[14]

The attack began at 03.50 a.m. on 31 July, this should have provided the soldiers with the dawn light of a summer's morning but the bad weather and low cloud made it quite dark. The assault did not make the ambitious objectives set for it. The greatest gains were in Cavan's XIV Corps area, some 3,500 yards towards Langemarck, while on the right II Corps averaged between 1,000 and 500 yards; Haig's concern over the Gheluvelt plateau had been realised. The C-in-C informed the War Cabinet, on 4 August, that the day had been 'highly satisfactory'[15] – the ground gained for men lost was much better than the first day on the Somme. However, Fifth Army could not advance beyond the *Steenbeek* (this small river marked the day's advance in the north and centre) until II Corps on the right, 'had both gained and consolidated the greater part of Gheluvelt plateau'.[16] As Haig had told Gough at the beginning, 'the main battle' would have to be fought at Gheluvelt.

From the point of view of this narrative, we jump forward to the month of September, and the activities of the 8th and 9th Battalions of the York and Lancaster

11 Edmonds, *1917, Vol. 2*, p.128.
12 Edmonds, *1917, Vol. 2*, p.129.
13 Edmonds, *1917, Vol. 2*, pp.129-30.
14 Sheffield and Bourne, *Haig*, p.309.
15 Edmonds, *1917, Vol. 2*, p.177.
16 Edmonds, *1917, Vol. 2*, p.181.

Men of the 2/4th York and Lancaster Regiment in their trench cookhouse, January 1918. (IWM Q 8443)

Regiment (23 Division). After their participation in the events at Messines Ridge, both were now to take part in the action around Gheluvelt. The weeks prior to 20 September, the Battle of the Menin Road, were taken up with the many items of army routine that filled the men's time in between major battles. On 6 and 7 September, 8/York and Lancaster had the chance to take baths, while the battalion band played at Brigade headquarters. The day was not quite so relaxing for Private L. Mitchell; he was tried by a Field General Court Martial, although the diary gives no indication of the offense or the verdict. On the 8th and 11th the battalion played football against teams from 70 Brigade, drawing the first and winning the second. Time and again, we see football being played by battalions only days before or after they are in action. The diary for the 9/York and Lancs has an entry to show that on a number of days in September they practiced for the attack 'on flag courses'; by now this form of preparation had become normal procedure. Having moved up to the front, the 8th battalion raided the enemy lines on the morning of 18 September. An officer and 40 men 'raided the enemy lines for about 300 yards in depth [...] 14 prisoners were taken, one being subsequently shot for trying to escape'.[17] The officer leading the raid was

17 WO 95/2188.

wounded, along with two of the men, while a third man was killed. Rather surprisingly, given that they would be going into action the following day, the men of the 8th battalion had the opportunity on 19 September for baths, before relieving 11/Sherwood Foresters in the line.

Before we come to the attack itself, one or two points from the Operation Order are worth highlighting. Battle Police had the role of preventing 'stragglers'; if men wandered too far back from the fighting then they were in danger of being deemed to have deserted. In the coming attack, all stragglers who were sent to the rear would be given a certificate by the MO, which they had to produce when they reached their battalion's Transport Line; 'Loss of this certificate makes a man liable to the charge of desertion. This is to be brought to the attention of all ranks'.[18] Wounded men were always a problem; their comrades might leave the action to see them back to an Aid Post, or they would need to be brought in once the battle was over. For 20 September:

> Every unit must look on itself as being primarily responsible in getting its own wounded back to the Regimental Aid Posts [RAPs], aided by such assistance as can be given from the rear. If a unit is relieved before all its wounded are in – guides should be left at the R.A.P. so that every assistance can be given to the incoming unit in locating [the] area where most of the wounded lie.

Having covered a number of topics directly relevant to the organisation of the coming battle, the Operation Order then went on to include an item that seems a little incongruous and having little to do with the coming fight. A cheque for £23 from the Divisional Comforts Fund was to be 'distributed among units'. £5 was allocated to each battalion, whose CO was given a 'free hand as to the expenditure of this amount, for the benefit of the men'. Given that a battalion was approximately 1,000 men, it would have been interesting to know how the £5 was spent, and what 'benefit' the men noticed. It also seems an odd item to appear on the Operation Order for a coming battle.

Norman Gladden (whom we have met previously) was in 23 Division with 11/Northumberland Fusiliers (68 Brigade) and he gives us a description of the division's march to the front. Reveille had been sounded at 04.30 on 18 September, but it was not until mid-morning that they were on their way through territory where 'great changes' had taken place 'since the recent battles'.[19] Gladden could see that the gradual move eastwards of the British line had been beneficial: 'The low ridges, now occupied by our own troops, stood up clearly before us, and it still seemed somehow wrong to be walking there in broad daylight'. The surroundings changed, however, as they got closer to the front; 'All around us stretched a morass in gradations of grey and black which looked like some petrified inferno from Dante'. The landscape

18 TNA WO 95/2186, war diary, 70 Brigade.
19 Gladden, *Ypres*, p.125.

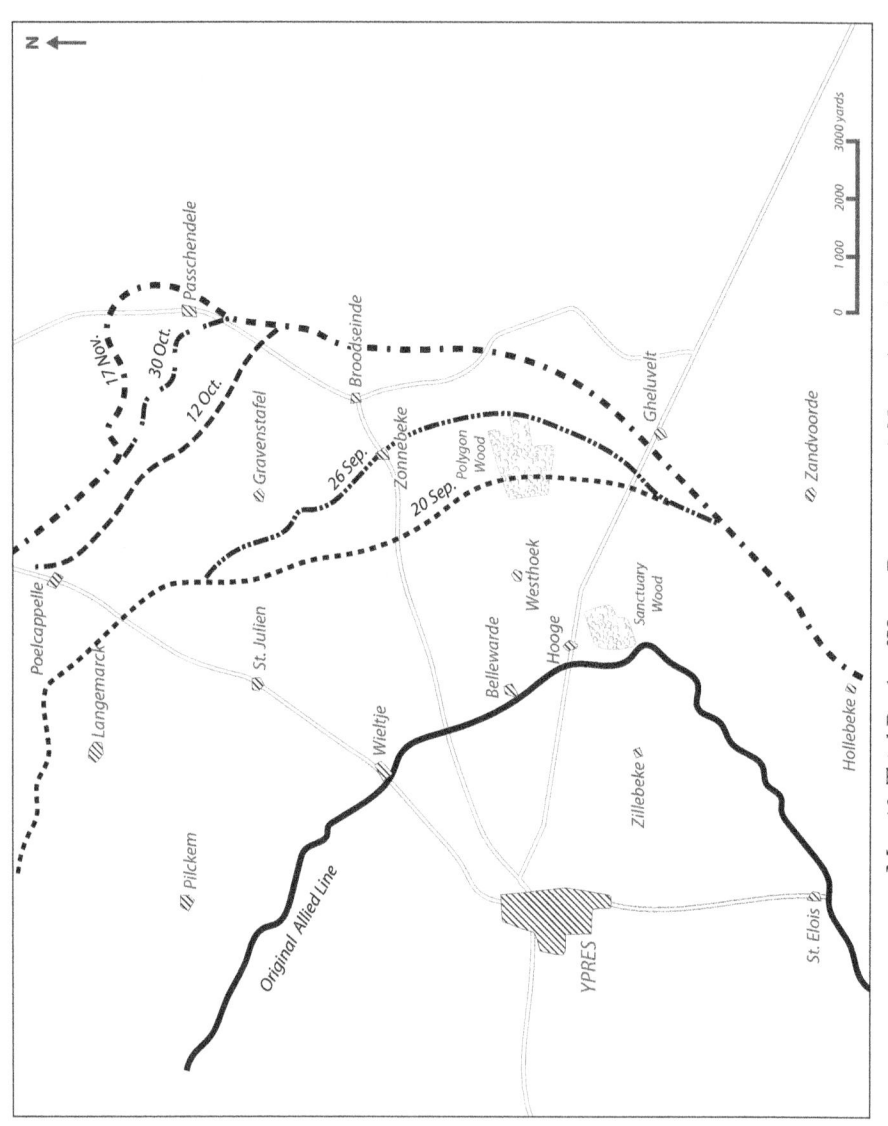

Map 12 Third Battle of Ypres: Progress to 17 November 1917.

took on the features we are used to seeing in the old black and white photographs of Passchendaele – waterlogged shell holes almost touching one another, passable only on the wooden 'duckboards'.[20] Once at the front, Gladden's battalion moved out into No Man's Land to be ready for the whistle; he thought it incredible that 'the Germans did not smell a rat'. In his recollection of the ensuing battle he commented on how little the individual soldier was aware of overall events – 'I did not at that moment realise how in this much wider battle the incidents on a small sector of the front might bear little relation to what was happening elsewhere'.[21]

Having failed to take sufficient note of Haig's emphasis on the importance of taking the Gheluvelt plateau, the 'harooshing' Gough[22] was reduced to a secondary rôle. As he had at Messines, Plumer ensured that the attack, which he was now to command, would not suffer from a lack of planning and preparation. To support the infantry he had assembled a massive numerical superiority in guns, while behind them was a 'new deep organization of supports and reserves'.[23] The attacking divisions, advancing on a 4,000 yard front, had the benefit of a barrage that was planned to be 'of an extent and weight beyond all precedent'. The British guns were to bombard an area 1,000 yards deep, the aim being to obliterate the objectives of the advancing troops. Beyond that, the heavy artillery, using counter-battery fire, were to 'neutralize with gas and H.E. Shell any German batteries which might open fire'.[24] Advancing over relatively dry ground – there had been three weeks of dry weather – the troops would follow closely behind a creeping barrage; up to the German outpost line, this would go forward at a rate of 50 yards every two minutes, thereafter the guns would lift by 100 yards every six minutes. The artillery barrage was so successful – although Gladden referred to it as 'a wave of inconceivable confusion'[25] – that, even though many of the German pillboxes were not destroyed, the men inside were sufficiently demoralised by the intensity of the shelling that they quickly surrendered.

Plumer allocated four divisions: 1 and 2 Australian (I Anzac Corps) on the left, north of the Hooge-Gheluvelt road; 23 and 41 (X Corps), to the south of the road. With its left flank on the road, 23 Division was to advance towards Inverness Copse and Dumbarton Wood, and then on to a line of dug-outs north of Kantinje Cabaret, on the Menin road.[26] The division had two brigades in front, 69 on the left, with 68 on their right and 70 (with both York and Lancaster battalions) in divisional reserve. In similar fashion to Messines Ridge, Plumer intended the attack to take place in stages,

20 Gladden, *Ypres*, p.125.
21 Gladden, *Ypres*, p.131.
22 Griffith, P., *Battle Tactics of the Western Front. The British Army's Art of Attack 1916-18* (London, Yale, 1998), pp.87-8.
23 Edmonds, *1917, Vol. 2*, p.253.
24 Edmonds, *1917, Vol. 2*, p.254.
25 Gladden, *Ypres*, p.130.
26 Edmonds, *1917, Vol. 2*, p.256.

rather than in one giant leap. There were to be three 'bounds', 'each to be captured by fresh troops, and each one shorter than the one before'.[27] The lead battalion of each attacking brigade – 68 and 69 – would advance 800 yards, after which there would be a 45 minute halt for the next battalion to move forward and pass through to the next objective, 500 yards ahead. These two moves were then followed by a two-hour pause to allow the remaining two battalions of each brigade to come forward before making the final 300 yards to the last objective.[28]

Zero hour, 20 September, was set for 05.40, by which time it would 'probably be light enough to see two hundred yards ahead'.[29] In the event, overnight rain (similar conditions to those on 31 July) had made the ground slippery for the battalions as they moved forward to take up positions – 9/York and Lancs suffered about 20 casualties in this phase – and the day dawned with a thick mist and poor visibility. The lead brigades of 23 Division made good progress, but not without heavy casualties: 9/Green Howards (69 Brigade) had eight of their 16 officers either killed or wounded, including two company commanders. The leading units had advanced rapidly, by-passing strongpoints that were to be dealt with by the 'moppers-up'. While this system had the advantage of allowing the leading troops to take ground quickly, it had the potential for these men to find themselves being fired on from the rear by the enemy forces that had been by-passed – this happened to 69 Brigade. However, 60 of the Germans who had fought back in this manner were subsequently killed by the moppers-up groups. Norman Gladden, 68 Brigade, mentions a similar occurrence in his memoir:

> It was from the shelter of this rubbish [near Tower Hamlets] that German snipers had begun their deadly work after the advancing groups had passed. During the day mopping-up parties, especially assigned to the task, crossed out into the waste and disposed of those Germans who had persisted in offensive action after the ground had been lost.[30]

Edmonds summed up how the 23 Division troops might have felt on reaching their objective:

> A fresh breeze from the south-west rolled away the mist, […] the value of the morning's achievement was apparent. The sight which met the eye brought that thrill of victory always hoped for but so seldom experienced in previous offensives.[31]

---

27   Powell, *Plumer*, p.214.
28   Powell, *Plumer*, p.214.
29   Edmonds, *1917, Vol. 2*, p.252.
30   Gladden, *Ypres*, p.137.
31   Edmonds, *1917, Vol. 2*, p.258.

The soldiers who took part were aware that events on the ground had not gone as cleanly as the 'paeans of victory' would indicate in the newspapers – 'we seemed to be getting lost [...] we had no idea how far we were from the Germans or who was ahead of us'.[32] In spite of that, 'we, who knew how it had all happened, were inconsistent enough to feel elated at having taken part in a military victory'.[33] Everyone likes to win.

The men of 70 Brigade, in divisional reserve, might not have experienced that same 'thrill of victory'. Both York and Lancaster battalions played little part in the fighting that day. One of the roles of the reserve units was to act as carrying parties for those at the front; one officer and 90 men of 8/York and Lancs were assigned to carry rations forward to the fighting troops. This support role is reflected in the low casualty rate for the battalion; only 3 men were killed and four were wounded. By 23 September the operation on the Menin road was a resounding success, save for a remaining German strongpoint on the Tower Hamlets spur. The Menin Road was also an opportunity for the tank to make an impression on the battlefield and possibly improve on their effectiveness in their previous outings. Unfortunately, the four machines allocated to the attack on 20 September did little more than reinforce the view that the new weapon was a 'work in progress': one failed to reach the start point, and the 'pace of the infantry was too fast for the other three across such broken ground'.[34] Of these three, one received a direct hit and the other two were used for transporting ammunition and engineering material. The Tank Corps would get their chance to show their machines to better advantage at Cambrai in November.

For the men of the York and Lancaster battalions, those September days were memorable more for carrying parties than for the storming of German positions. However, taking their turn to rotate through the front line trenches, they were on the receiving end of German counter attacks on 30 September and 1 October. The last day of September dawned in a thick mist:

> 4.30 a.m. intense bombardment helped on with minenwerfer & smoke-bombs: 5.15 a.m. enemy discovered in large numbers advancing against our trench especially on our right: mist still very thick: enemy used bombs and flamenwerfer. Heavy fire with rifles, Lewis & machine-guns and bombs was opened on them & none reached our trench: S.O.S. sent up but was not seen at Batt. H.Q. owing to mist: an orderly arrived with the first news at 7.20 a.m. About 6 a.m. enemy again attacked but was driven off: took 2 prisoners, 1 flamenwerfer & a machine-gun: 60 or 70 dead were left in front of our trenches: the attack was repulsed entirely with the fire of the infantry: the artillery did not barrage our front: a wire fence, put up during the previous night by a pioneer battn helped greatly

32 Gladden, *Ypres*, p.134.
33 Gladden, *Ypres*, p.137.
34 Edmonds, *1917, Vol. 2*, p.256.

to impede the enemy. A short barrage was put down on our lines at 10 a.m.: the remainder of the day was normal.[35]

For the rest of the month the two battalions slipped back into the routine of rotating into and out of the front line. Their spell in the rear provided the opportunity for the men to be issued with clean clothing, take baths and otherwise try to delouse themselves. To that end, on 30 October, the battalion's blankets were "Iodenised";[36] this was presumably a reference to the use of iodine for delousing the men's bedding. The diary for that day has another interesting entry regarding the fitness of the men. It was in the interest of the unit commanders that the men under them should be physically capable of filling the role of a fighting soldier, but not all men would meet that standard all the time. In those cases where a medical officer believed a man in his unit might be unfit for the front line, he could send them before the divisional Director of Medical Services (DMS) medical board. If the board felt the man was not fit to return to the line they could declare him to be PB (fit for Permanent Base) or PU (Permanently Unfit).[37] On 30 October, 20 men were sent to the ADMS 'for inspection for PB', but there is no mention of the outcome. The following day was one of those rare occasions when the troops got close enough to see the man who was commanding them in battle. Along with the rest of the brigade, the soldiers of the 8th and 9th battalions of the York and Lancaster Regiment were 'inspected by and marched past F.M. Sir Douglas Haig'. It may be coincidental, but the review by the C-in-C was followed later that day by 'smartening up drill under company commanders'. These periods out of the line were also opportunities for new drafts of men to bring the battalions up to full strength after they had been in the line. No doubt, 'old sweats' in the unit would have wanted to show their precedence over the 'new boys' and the diary gives a hint of that: 'The new draft were beaten at football by 5 goals to nil by a *weak* team from the rest of the battalion'. [My emphasis.]

When battalions first deployed overseas to take part in the war the adjutant often included in the war diary events that were out of the ordinary, especially if they involved the death of one of its soldiers. As the war moved on, and death became part of everyday life, the details became scarcer. One example is the diary of 8/York and Lancaster for 25 October:

> L/Cpl [Lance Corporal] Archibald, 34822, accidentally shot – died of wounds.
> Battalion route march. Kit inspection – clothing, rifle & ammunition etc, baths.

The accident merits little more mention than the kit inspection. On the following day a court of inquiry was convened (4 officers from the battalion), 'to investigate the

---

35 WO 95/2188, war diary, 9 York & Lancs.
36 WO 95/2188, war diary, 8 York & Lancs.
37 TNA WO 95/4245, war diary, 48 Division, ADMS.

circumstances under which L/Cpl Archibald met his death. No finding is given in the diary but he was given a funeral, 'with full military honours', on the same day. By according him that formality it is unlikely that the board determined that he died by his own hand. Archibald, 23 years old and from Glasgow, is buried in Quelmes Churchyard where he is one of three military graves.

Death was a constant for the men, but it was not always accidental, self-inflicted, or a result of enemy action. Under military law, there were occasions (most frequently, desertion) when the army was entitled to take away a man's life. If a sentence of death was passed by a court martial, and confirmed by the C-in-C, the soldier was executed by a firing party formed of men from his own battalion. On 26 October, the diary of 8/York and Lancaster states that there was the 'Promulgation of sentence of Court Martial on 32559 Pte. [Private] Nicholson'. Once again, little information is given. Discipline in the army had two purposes: it was to punish an offender, but it should also deter others. To that end, the 'promulgation' is likely to have taken place in front of the assembled battalion – there was a parade that morning for the men to attend the firing range. It would also have been announced in Routine Orders through the whole of the BEF. Nicholson would have been informed that day that the sentence would be carried out on the morning of the following day, the 27th:

> Sentence of Death on 32559 Pte. Nicholson duly carried out. Battalion route march. Practice football match.[38]

While the battalion diary gives little detail regarding Nicholson's offence and subsequent trial by court martial, the facts are contained in the WO 71 series of files at Kew. The following is taken from Nicholson's file.[39] In a mass army, there will always be some men who should not have been there; Charles Nicholson was probably one of those. One of twins, who both joined the army, he did not take to military discipline. He had previously been awarded 90 days Field Punishment No. 1 for desertion – on that occasion he had avoided a capital sentence, but it would no doubt count against him when he did it again. In addition, at the time of his second desertion offence, he was under a suspended sentence of two year's imprisonment, with hard labour, for being Absent Without Leave (AWOL). He was not in a good place. At that stage in the war, the Suspension of Sentences Act had been passed so that men who were given prison sentences were returned to their units, with the intention that they should serve their period of incarceration when the war was over.

Although the court martial papers for Nicholson's trial are short on content, it is incorrect to say that those soldiers who were executed had no 'due process', or that sentences were handed down by 'kangaroo courts'. The court martial was held on 8 October 1917. On 25 August 1917, the sergeant who was supervising the soldiers on

38 WO 95/2188.
39 TNA WO 71/619.

field punishment told them to rejoin their companies as they were about to go back into the line. A little later, Lieutenant Duffy (Nicholson's platoon commander) was waiting with No. 4 platoon to go into the trenches. Giving evidence at Nicholson's trial, Duffy stated that 'while we were waiting some enemy aeroplanes came over and dropped bombs near us and the men took cover. When the platoon fell in again the accused was absent'.[40] Later that day Nicholson was detained just before midnight 'for being out after 9 pm without a pass, [he] said he didn't know where he was, and had been away from his platoon since about 3 pm'. Nicholson had been detained at Reninghelst, some 5 kilometres behind his platoon front; his only plea in mitigation was that 'when the bombs dropped I got nervous. I can't say anything else'. In military law, the difference between 'desertion' and 'absence' is in the soldier's 'intent': was it his intention to avoid his military duty? In Nicholson's case, the 5 kilometres that he had walked from his platoon would have indicated his 'intent' to remove himself from the line. If he had merely been absent from his platoon and found within the company bounds he would have been unlikely to be found guilty of desertion. A finding of desertion was not, of itself, sufficient reason for a death sentence. The offence becomes a 'capital' one if it is committed 'in the face of the enemy'. Those men caught deserting from their units in Britain, or while in training camps in the rear areas were not deemed to be facing the enemy and so, while guilty of desertion did not necessarily suffer the ultimate punishment. Frequently they were sentenced to imprisonment or their offence was changed to Guilty of Absence – this was used extensively in Italy to avoid the death sentence.

Having been tried and found guilty, the court martial board sentenced Nicholson to Death; the papers were then sent up the chain of command for confirmation of the sentence, where his previous offences would have counted against him. On 22 October, Haig added his signature; Nicholson was shot at 06.10 on 27 October. He was not buried in a cemetery close to the place of execution; his body was moved to the Pas de Calais where it was interred in the Longuenesse (St Omer) Souvenir Cemetery. For Nicholson's parents, there was a double tragedy. As well as being notified that their son had been shot as a deserter, they were also told that his twin brother, John, was killed in action – just two days after Charles's trial. Much has been written on the subject of the 346 soldiers who were executed by firing ssquad during the First World War, rather than add to the argument I will close with words from Richard Holmes:

> It was indeed a hard law, but it was, in general fairly applied. But like so much else about this war the issue divides head from heart, and if my head applauds the logic of capital sentences, they still break my heart.[41]

---

40 WO 71/619.
41 Holmes, *Tommy*, pp.569-70.

The 8th and 9th battalions were not the only representatives of the York and Lancaster Regiment in Haig's Third Ypres offensive. In July 1/4th and 1/5th battalions, both part of 148 Infantry Brigade, were in 49 (1st West Riding) Division, XV Corps, Fourth Army; as such, they were part of the coastal defences on the left flank of the Franco-British armies, covering the beaches from Dunkirk to Nieuport. The two months spent there were not as quiet as 'coastal defence' might lead the reader to believe. The war diaries show that the Germans shelled the front line on a regular basis, frequently using gas. The worst of the attacks were in July with that on the 21st being particularly notable: the Germans used 'shells containing a new kind of gas, now known to all the world as "mustard" gas on account of the peculiar smell and the colour which it stained everything with which it came into contact'.[42] Two days later the lines were again heavily shelled with the result that 13 men were killed and a further 59 wounded or gassed. However, the location also had its advantages; 'August and September were in some respects a real summer holiday' – apart from the shelling. Sea bathing was 'delightful' and the men 'played football every evening in spite of the heat'. By early September the troops were in 'comfortable billets' at Bray Dunes and, because they were in Army Reserve, could devote themselves 'entirely to training and enjoyment'.[43] There are constant references in the battalion history to the glorious weather that summer and, with the opportunities to go shopping in the local towns 'the men could buy anything from a bathing dress to a tin whistle'. However, this interlude from the 'real' war did not last; troops were needed at Third Ypres. At the end of September, 49 Division was transferred into II ANZAC Corps in Plumer's Second Army from where it would become involved in the battles in front of the village of Passchendaele.

By 6 October, both battalions were at Vlamertinghe ('a badly wrecked village'),[44] about two miles west of Ypres, ready to go forward into the line. At that time the battalion strength was 43 officers and 1016 men. One of the problems for battalion commanders was knowledge of the ground over which they were to attack; this was especially the case when units were moved from one area of the front to another, with the assault following shortly after. Both 1/4 and 1/5 York and Lancaster were expected to go into battle only three days after reaching the rear area of Ypres; they had not yet gone into the trenches. In an attempt to get some familiarity with the sector on which they would be fighting, small parties of officers and men were sent forward on reconnaissance patrols. The diary of one battalion gives an indication of the problems that can arise with a move to an unfamiliar area:

> Party of 1 Officer & 10 OR per Coy were sent forward to reconnoitre & to learn the way up to the front so that they could lead the Bn. up when required. [This

---

42 Grant, *Hallamshires*, p.74.
43 Grant, *Hallamshires*, p.76.
44 Grant, *Hallamshires*, p.82.

party received no further orders & so failed to meet the Bn. & took no further part in the battle;[45] they were 'a distinct loss to our fighting strength'.[46]]

At brigade and battalion level, preparation for the coming attack was necessarily brief; 1/4th did not receive their Brigade Orders until 3 a.m. on the morning of the 8th. As the troops were still west of Ypres, they had to march through that town to fields near Potijze, about a mile and a half east of Ypres. At 6 in the morning, 8 October, they set out for 'the muddy fields of Potijze and Wieltje'. Once there, the rest of the day was spent preparing to go forward and to take their place in the battle. In an attempt to reduce officer casualties – the Germans could recognise them by their different tunics – 'Officers were dressed in the ordinary S.D. jacket, trousers and puttees exactly like the men, except that they wore their badges of rank on the shoulder straps and a two-inch square of white cloth sewn on the back of the jacket to enable our men to recognise them easily'.[47] At 4.45 that afternoon, the battalions began the move to the assembly positions. Once again, we see how tired the troops would become, before ever going 'over the top'. The distance to the assembly points was only seven kilometres, 'as the crow flies', but it was not to be that easy. Because of the winding nature of the country lanes, seven kilometres became twelve:

> Owing to the heavy rain which fell almost continuously during the march & to the state of the track the assembly position was not reached until 4 a.m. [9 October], and by this time the men were very weary.[48]

The 1/5th battalion found the going equally difficult:

> The march up to the assembly position, & forming up, were both rendered extremely difficult & exhausting owing to the state of the ground. Very wet weather for a week previous had produced mud of great depth, whilst the whole area of operations consisted of shell-holes, mostly containing two or three feet of water. In spite of this, only five men of the battalion fell out on the way up. The state of the ground caused the 1/5th K.O.Y.L.I [who should have been following] to be late in getting up & they took no part in the action.[49]

After a march of eleven and a quarter hours, the men arrived at their assembly positions only one hour and twenty minutes before they had to go into battle, over ground which was unfamiliar to them – they were 'soaked with rain and nearly exhausted'.

45 WO 95/2805, war diary, 1/4th York & Lancs.
46 Grant, *Hallamshires*, p.82.
47 Grant, *Hallamshires*, p.83.
48 WO 95/2805, war diary, 1/4th York & Lancs.
49 WO 95/2805, war diary, 1/5th York & Lancs.

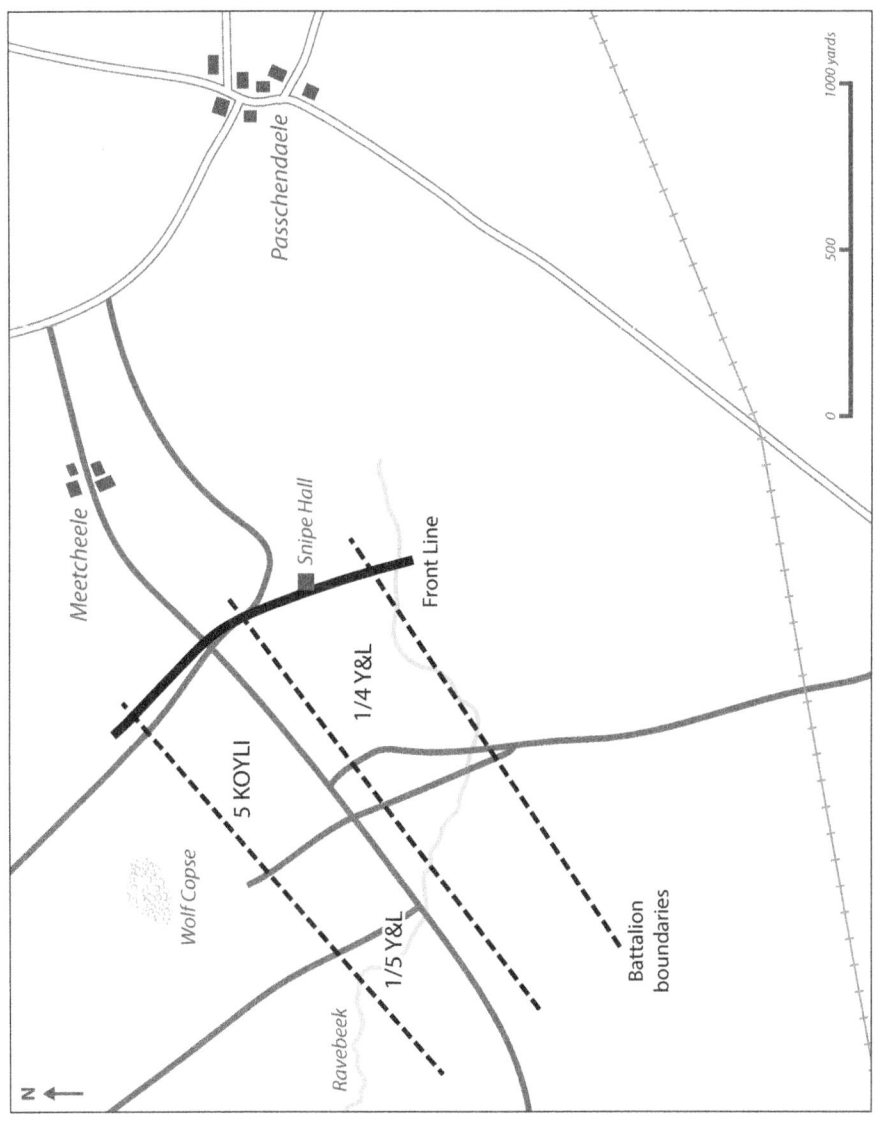

Map 13 Action of 1/4th and 1/5th York & Lancaster, Third Battle of Ypres, September 1917.

Zero hour was set for 05.20 on 9 October. 49 Division was to attack with the 66th on its right and the 48th on the left flank; two of the division's three brigades were to lead. 146 Brigade took the left front, with 148 on the right. The plan of attack for 148 Brigade had three battalions going forward with the fourth (1/4th KOYLI) in brigade reserve. Of the leading three, 1/4th York and Lancaster took the right front while, to their left, the 1/5th York and Lancaster was detailed to take its first objective and then allow 1/5th KOYLI (who should have been behind them) to 'leapfrog' through to the second objective. As we have seen above, 1/5th KOYLI were held up on the march forward. The brigade start point was approximately 2,500 yards, south-west of Passchendaele – in official parlance this was the Battle of Poelcappelle.

Both battalions had to advance across low-lying, water-logged ground, up a gradual slope towards a farm at Meetcheele. One of their first obstacles was the Ravebeek stream where 'the mud was anything up to waist-deep'.[50] In the post-battle report, the artillery barrage was criticised as being unsatisfactory but the blame was laid on the atrocious weather and the mud, rather than the gunners. According to the 1/4th battalion report, the only dead Germans that they came across in the advance were a result of rifle fire, not shelling. Having said that, 1/5th York and Lancs do say that the men kept 'very close up to the barrage'. After advancing about a mile, 1/5th battalion claimed to have reached their first objective by 6 a.m., both battalions found that they were coming under very heavy machine gun fire from Wolf Copse (on their left) and Snipe Hall (on their right). The KOYLI battalion that should have followed 1/5th York and Lancs, and then leapfrogged through, had not made the advance from the assembly area (as we saw above) and so the 1/5th pressed on as far as they could beyond their own objective, until halted by the German machine guns. Both battalions were held short of their final objective by the enemy pillboxes, which were on the ridge crest near Meetcheele, 1,000 yards west of Passchendaele. With no further advance possible, they consolidated their positions and remained there until they were relieved on the evening of 10/11 October. Before leaving the front line trenches it would be appropriate to give credit, as does the 1/4th battalion history, to those who had to keep the troops in the line supplied:

> How Lieutenant Philip Branson and his transport men were able to bring up rations and stores through the mud and shell-fire is a mystery. It seemed perfectly impossible that they could survive the shelling even if the ground had not been so awful, yet, in the fading light of each afternoon, these gallant men – and gallant mules – were streaming over the ridges towards the front line.[51]

Having been relieved from the line, the men still had a tiring journey to their rest area. Initially they had to march all the way back to Vlamertinghe, through the night,

50   WO 95/2805, war diary, 1/5th York & Lancs.
51   Grant, *Hallamshires*, p.85.

arriving at 5 in the morning. Only five hours later, they were on the move again. They finally arrived at a camp near Winnizeele, about 28 kilometres west of Ypres, at 5 in the evening. Tents were allocated to the men and then 'everyone at once went off into the sleep of utter exhaustion'. The 1/4th York and Lancasters had been reduced to 33 officers and 688 men by the time they made camp. Casualties in both battalions had been high for the two days, 9 and 10 October:

> 1/4th: killed, 4 officers and 42 men; wounded, 5 officers and 110 men; missing, 1 officer and 48 men.
> 1/5th: killed, 7 officers and 58 men; wounded, 1 officers and 249 men; missing, 2 officers and 51 men.

During the following days, the battalions could take stock. The wet conditions had taken their toll on the men's feet: 'Every man was suffering more or less from trench feet, for we had been lying in water-logged shell-holes for nearly two days'. This particular medical condition was very debilitating and while treatment and preventative measures could be taken in the line, many soldiers had to be hospitalised. In 1917, trench foot was the second highest cause of non-battle casualties in France and Flanders: Venereal Disease came first with 25.6%; trench foot accounted for 11.4%.[52] There is little wonder that battalion diaries have quite frequent references to 'foot inspections' as part of the routine when in the rest areas. In spite of the casualties, the heavy marches to the line and the ravages of trench foot, the troops were in surprisingly good heart – according to the war diary:

> After the attack on the 9th & 10th inst the battalion was very weak in men, but morale was good, & the men who were left seemed very pleased with themselves. The second tour in the line still further reduced the strength [95 casualties from 18-22 October], but although not properly recovered from the 9th, the work done on this tour called forth the warm praise of both the Army and Corps Commanders.

The series of battles that made up the Third Ypres campaign ground on to an official end in mid-November. Four battalions of the York and Lancaster Regiment played a part; two in 148 Brigade and two in the 70th – it is highly unlikely that those in one brigade would have had any idea of what was happening in the other. The battalions went into and out of the line, with the men having little knowledge of what was happening outside their own few hundred yards of trench. To appreciate the view of the soldiers it is worth bearing in mind a comment by one who was there: 'The truth

---

52 Mitchell, T.J., *Medical Services. Casualties and Medical Statistics* (Uckfield, Naval & Military Press, Reprint of 1931 original), Table 17, p.164.

is that each of those fighting men in all the armies on all the fronts experienced his own personal war[,] which differed in its unique essence from those of all the others'.[53]

Mud has become a byword for Passchendaele and most of the photographs that are used to illustrate accounts of that battle reinforce the popular image, but those conditions should have come as no surprise to those planning the offensives. Flanders is a low-lying area of rich farmland, with a high water table. It should have been obvious that the field drainage systems would be utterly destroyed by the ferocious artillery bombardments of both sides. In spite of the appalling conditions, the Passchendaele Ridge eventually fell to the Allies; a success that the official history accorded to the 'unfailing staunchness' and 'infinite courage' of all those involved. One of those was Private Stanley Butwright, 1/8 Royal Warwickshire Regiment. I was made aware of his story after a chance meeting with his great nephew, Andrew Wegg (see Appendix II).

For the men of the 1/4th and 1/5th battalions, the next few months were spent in the Ypres Salient, but for their mates in the 8th and 9th, change was in the air. On 28 October, a warning order was received: 'The Division complete will be in readiness to move by rail forthwith; destination unknown'.[54] In Italy, a combined force of Austrian and German divisions had routed the army of General Cadorna at Caporetto. It was necessary for the French and British to send troops to support their southern ally.[55] We will re-join both battalions in chapter 13.

53 Gladden, *Ypres*, p.12.
54 Sandilands, *23rd Division*, p.209.
55 Dillon, *Allies are a Tiresome Lot*.

11

"Steel monsters" – the tanks at Cambrai

The mud of Passchendaele may well be the enduring memory of the autumn months of 1917, but it was not the last battle of that year to involve the York and Lancaster Regiment. In mid-November, the BEF's Third Army launched an 'all arms' offensive, which British histories remember as the Battle of Cambrai and in which tanks were to play a major part. So far, we have seen the new weapon used only in small numbers, but for Cambrai the attacking divisions would be supported by 476 of the lumbering beasts: 378 were fighting tanks; 54 carried supplies; 32 were fitted with grapnels for pulling away the German wire; two carried bridging material to assist a cavalry breakthrough; nine were fitted with wireless and one more carried telephone cable.[1] The new fighting vehicle was to take a more prominent place on the battlefield.

In August 1917 there was a plan for a tank 'raid' south of Cambrai in which the aim was to 'demoralize and disorganize' the enemy, rather than to 'capture ground' – the game-plan was to "advance, hit, retire".[2] As was so frequently the case, plans changed. By October, with Haig's Third Ypres offensive sinking in the mud of the Salient, the tank 'raid' had gestated into a Third Army assault which might 'redeem British prestige'.[3] Six divisions, from III and IV Corps of General Byng's Third Army, were to attack two German divisions defending six miles of front from the St. Quentin Canal in the east to the Canal du Nord in the west. The primary objective was to 'break the enemy's defensive position by a *coup de main* with the help of tanks,[4] the cavalry would then pass through the break 'to exploit the success gained by the infantry'.[5] In the planning of the attack, great reliance had been placed on the ability of the tanks to smash through the German wire and on the artillery to deliver an accurate barrage, without prior registration of the guns. By doing away with the long drawn-out

---

1   Miles, W., *Military Operations France and Belgium. The Battle of Cambrai* (Nashville, Naval & Military Press, Reprint of 1948 original), p.28.
2   Liddell Hart, *First World War*, p.340.
3   Liddell Hart, *First World War*, p.341.
4   Miles, *Cambrai*, p.17.
5   TNA WO 95/3090, war diary, 2/5 York & Lancs, General Plan of Operations.

barrages of previous assaults, the enemy (it was hoped) would be surprised when the infantry attacked at Zero Hour. However, by the time that the assault started, Haig had altered the direction of the advance so that Bourlon Wood (8,000 yards to the west of Cambrai) became the focus, rather than the town of Cambrai. The C-in-C was still looking for the 'big break-through' and was hoping that Byng's force might spearhead a 'rolling up' operation, extending possibly as far as the River Sensée and Arras. In his history of the 6th Division, Marden outlines a number of factors that militated against success; limited daylight (it was late autumn); long distances to be covered by men and tanks (which were still slow and unreliable); the difficulty of getting tanks over the canal system to the west of Cambrai. Additionally, while the initial advance would roll back the German salient in front of Cambrai, it would increase the British front 'from a straight 7,000 yards to a curving 15,000 yards'.[6] With Third Ypres still tiring British divisions, the need to send men to support Italy after the Austro-German success at Caporetto and the potential for the return of German forces from the Russian front, Haig's revised plan was unrealistic.

The battle of Cambrai involved three battalions from the York and Lancaster Regiment; the 2nd battalion in 16 Brigade, 6 Division of III Corps; the 2/4th and 2/5th battalions of 187 Brigade, 62 Division in IV Corps. On 20 November, IV Corps was on the left of the attacking front, with 62 Division on its left flank; III Corps was on the right with 6 Division on the left of the corps front, joining up with IV Corps. Because of the number of tanks involved, and their close coordination with the infantry, joint training between the two arms was essential. In 62 Division, each battalion was allocated two days with the tankers, 'the steel monsters inspiring the greatest confidence amongst all ranks of the Division'.[7] The battalion history for 2/York and Lancaster notes that during the first two weeks of November, 'the battalions of the Division were exercised in attacks by infantry and tanks against trenches, and all were also shown a plan of the ground which had been drawn up on a piece of country near Bullecourt'.[8] Appendix 1 to the Operation Order outlines some of this training. Emphasis was laid on the 'Assembly of Infantry behind tanks before advancing to attack', as well as 'Advancing to the attack behind tanks'. However; 'These exercises may be carried out with or without tanks' – the soldier might be forgiven for thinking that the presence of the vehicles was an essential part of the training. The 2/4th York and Lancs, in 62 Division, had the opportunity to 'practice the attack in conjunction with tanks' on 6 November. In the event that tanks were not available, 'a man carrying a flag should be used as a substitute'.[9] The orders regarding the assembly of the troops behind the tanks go on to state that:

6   Marden, *6th Division*, p.36.
7   Wyrall, E., *The Story of the 62nd (West Riding) Division 1914-1919 Volume 1* (Uckfield, Naval & Military Press, Reprint of original), p.68.
8   Wylly, *Volume 1*, p.367.
9   WO 95/3090/2, war diary, 2/4th York & Lancs.

"Steel monsters" – the tanks at Cambrai 187

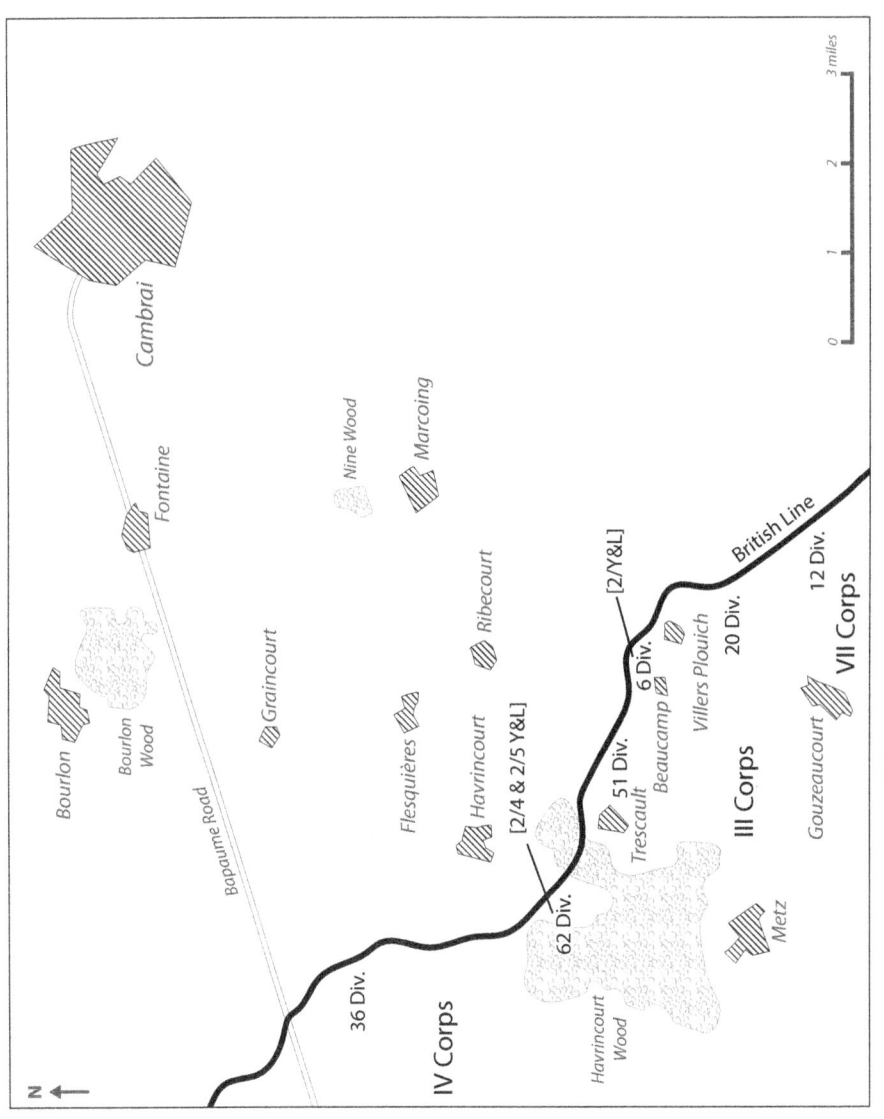

Map 14 Battle of Cambrai, November 1917.

This should be carried out as a *parade movement*. [My italics] No talking, no noise, the men at attention with rifles at the short trail. When halted the men should kneel or lie down. Before moving off, if the assembly takes place during night time, the Section Leader should first ascertain that all the men in his Section are awake.

Given the battlefield conditions along the front in France and Flanders, it is difficult to envisage the troops carrying out a *parade movement* to position themselves behind their allotted tank.

Facing the attacking divisions was the formidable Hindenburg Line, which 'embodied the latest German theory of an active defence in depth'.[10] The first line that the British troops would have to cross was the Outpost Zone with 'disconnected lengths of trench' and 'self-contained centres of resistance'. Next was the serious obstacle of the Battle Zone. Here, many of the defences ran along the reverse slopes of the spurs between the two canals. Trenches in this zone were designed to be tank-proof, some of them being 12 feet wide at the top. The British designed a novel solution to the problem: bundles of brushwood – fascines – were carried on the front of the leading tanks and then dropped into the trench to form a 'bridge' over which the tank could cross. Wire was a serious obstacle, in many places the Germans had four rows with each belt being 'about 12 yards in width and three feet high, forming a zone 100 yards in depth'.[11] Altogether, the Hindenburg Line formed a defensive system approximately three miles deep. It was for defences such as these that the tank was designed (they could either trample or rip out the wire) and 30 tanks were assigned to each assaulting brigade.

By the time of the Cambrai offensive, some of the orders to the infantry that have been referred to in previous chapters had become common-place. The men were to ignore any calls to retire as the word 'does not exist, and will not be understood or obeyed by anyone in this Division'. Troops had to send back information to their battalion headquarters: 'No information is likely to lead to no assistance – therefore when in a tight place, send back information'. Because of the worry that men might leave the firing line, 'no unwounded men, other than stretcher bearers, [are] allowed to bring back wounded men'. Water was a constant need of men in battle, especially those who were wounded, but it was a difficult one for the authorities to resolve. There was always the fear that the retreating Germans would poison any supplies, so the men had to rely on the two pints in their personal water-bottle; 'No man [was] to drink the water in his bottle without permission from his Platoon Commander'. It is difficult to see how this could possibly have been enforced. In order to ensure that the men went into battle with some sustenance a hot breakfast was issued before they left their bivouacs for the assembly areas. Rum was frequently handed out before an attack

10   Miles, *Cambrai*, p.2.
11   Miles, *Cambrai*, p.3.

(it could warm a man up as well as provide 'Dutch courage') and the orders for 2/4 York and Lancaster stipulated that it would be carried 'in empty wine bottles by the officers' and issued before the men went into battle.

All three battalions record the days prior to the attack as 'quiet', but eventually the time came to take up their positions at the front; Marden described the move forward as 'marching by night and hiding in villages and woods by day'.[12] Although the men were aware that they were to take part in a major operation, after all they had been doing training with the 'tankers', secrecy meant that they were not aware of just when they would be called on to go over the top. The 2nd and the 2/4th battalion diaries indicate that it was only on the day before the attack that they were informed of the jumping off time.

The morning of 20 November was 'fine but inclined to be misty'. 2/York and Lancaster, who would be working in cooperation with their assigned tanks to 'capture the HINDENBURG front line system',[13] went into the attack 10 minutes after Zero Hour (06.20). As part of 16 Brigade, they were in the front line of the attack, on the right front of 6 Division; 71 Brigade were on their left. In one of those 'Boys' Own' acts of derring-do the commander of the Tank Corps in France, Brigadier General Elles, attached the largest Tank Corps flag he could find to his tank 'Hilda' and spearheaded 6 Division's assault.[14] The attack went well: by 06.45, the first message had come in 'intimating the capture of the first objective – the German Outpost line'.[15] Only 90 minutes later 'all objectives had been captured & consolidation was being done'. Surprisingly the casualties were very light; 3 killed and 19 wounded with 6 machine guns, 3 Trench Mortars and 170 prisoners taken. Having encountered little resistance 2/York and Lancaster, together with 8/Bedfordshire and 24 tanks, was 'in possession of the Hindenburg front system' and by 11 a.m. 16 Brigade had taken its second objective.[16]

The two York and Lancaster battalions in 187 Brigade, 62 Division, also encountered only light opposition. By 08.30, the 2/5th had crossed their first objective and within a further two hours, the second was secured 'at the cost of less than eighty casualties'.[17] Advancing on their left, 2/4th 'was no more strenuously opposed'. Although the tanks did good work at the start of the assault 'the battalion soon outstripped them, advancing steadily for 1,400 yards up the Hindenburg front system behind a barrage which moved with remarkable precision'.[18] This diary comment points up the fact that tanks were still ponderously slow but the artillery could now lay down accurate fire, which was capable of 'creeping' forward at the planned rate. As a result 2/5 York and

12 Marden, *6th Division*, p.36.
13 WO 95/1610.
14 Miles, *Cambrai*, p.54.
15 WO 95/1610.
16 Miles, *Cambrai*, p.54.
17 Miles, *Cambrai*, p.61.
18 Miles, *Cambrai*, p.61.

Lancaster 'secured the whole of its objective'. At this juncture, all three battalions of the regiment had good cause to feel proud of their achievement that day. The sense of having done a good job was summed up by General Marden, GOC 6 Division: 'The Division had a most successful day, [...] Everything had gone like clockwork'.[19] At the battalion level, the success of the day was attributed to two main factors; the use of tanks and the insistence on secrecy. The former were deemed to have 'dealt extremely effectively with the enemy wire, which was very formidable in places, and machine guns'. Secrecy 'had been impressed on all ranks' and even when marching up to the line the destination of the battalion 'was not made known to anyone below the rank of an officer'.[20] Unfortunately, the success of 20 November did not continue through the succeeding days.

By the end of the first day, the largest advance had been made on the left by 62 Division, which had reached the village of Anneux; Third Army had advanced more than five miles – what a contrast with the Somme and Third Ypres. To their right, 51 Division, attacking Flesquières, had been held up by the defenders in that village. Consequently, 62 Division were left holding a fairly deep salient, with the Germans in Flesquières threatening their right flanks. 6 Division, on the left of III Corps, had had 'a most successful day' during which they captured 28 German officers, 1,227 men, 23 guns and between 40 and 50 machine guns.[21] However, while noting that the division had taken its objectives, the divisional commander had a criticism of the cavalry, Haig's hope for any breakthrough:

> At 3.15 p.m. the cavalry, who would have been of the greatest assistance in capturing the enemy guns holding up the 51st Division [on the left flank of the 6th], reported that they could not advance owing to snipers in Ribécourt. *The village had been in our possession since 10 a.m.*, and the 18th Infantry Brigade had passed through it at 11.30, and were now two miles beyond it.[22] [My emphasis.]

In IV Corps, 62 Division had advanced four and a half miles; 'Everywhere the attack had gone splendidly, the Tanks were a great success and the period of combined training early in November had produced just that degree of cooperation between infantry and Tanks essential to success'.[23] The divisional commander, General Braithwaite, had taken risks during the advance in that his right flank was exposed due to the slower progress of 51 Division. However, his summary was positive: 'The day was one of memorable achievement. On a front of over six miles an advance had been made varying from three miles to four', and all that in not much more than four

---

19 Wylly, *Volume 1*, p.368.
20 WO 95/3090, war diary, 2/4th York & Lancs.
21 Marden, *6th Division*, p.39.
22 Marden, *6th Division*, p.39.
23 Wyrall, *62nd Division, Vol. 1* p.90.

hours. In spite of that, the gains had 'fallen far short of the intention'.[24] Once again, wishing to see a major breakthrough of the German line, Haig's ambitions were overly optimistic. To exploit the progress made on 20 November required more reserves than were available. On top of that, the early days of tank operations were very exhausting on their crews – the environment was abominable, the machines bogged down and there was little chance of them re-grouping to provide adequate support on the second and subsequent days of a prolonged assault. In almost every chapter of this book, it has been emphasised that advancing infantry relied on close support from the artillery. While this could be planned for on the first day of an attack, it became more difficult on the following days, especially if the advance by the troops was a deep one. For the assault to continue the gunners had to move their batteries (and all the heavy ammunition) forward over the ground gained – they could not continue to provide a barrage from their original positions if the infantry had advanced four miles. Haig's insistence on capturing Bourlon Wood on day one, as preparation for a further and deeper penetration, meant that a stunning advance ground to a halt, but it would be renewed the following day.

At 7 p.m. on 20 November 62 Division received the order to 'advance [and] capture the high ground west of Bourlon Wood and Bourlon Village'. The task was given to 186 Brigade, although the two York and Lancaster battalions took no part. For all three of the regiment's battalions, 22 and 23 November were spent in the German lines, mainly trying to avoid being seen by patrolling German aircraft. It is worth pointing out that at this point the battalions that had made the greatest advance, like 2/York and Lancaster in 6 Division, were effectively behind the Germans who were still holding out in Flesquières. Recently (2016) it has been suggested that the reason for the German strength in that village was a result of information given to them by Irish POWs from 36 Division.[25] John Taylor alleges that two of six of the Ulstermen captured on 18 November were sufficiently anti-British that they divulged details of the impending attack, including the probable use of tanks. Taylor bases his assertion on the German interrogation report completed at the time.

The battle had now lasted for more than three days and had become stalled. During the initial planning, Haig had told Byng that 'he would stop the offensive after 48 hours, or even earlier, unless the results gained or the general situation justified a continuation'.[26] When the self-imposed time limit was reached, and with Bourlon Wood and the village still in German hands, Haig decided to continue. On 23 November (the fourth day), Haig noted in his diary: 'I am anxious that everything possible should be done to pass our cavalry through near Bourlon to exploit our

---

24 Miles, *Cambrai*, p.88.
25 Attar, R., 'Aggrieved PoWs betrayed plans for the Cambrai attack'. *BBC History Magazine*, October (2016), pp.11-12.
26 Miles, *Cambrai*, p.17.

success'.[27] The C-in-C appeared to have a form of 'target fixation' on Bourlon Wood in spite of the fact that he recognised the tiredness of the men: 'the 51st Division is tired and several other units are *very short* of sleep. Many men can hardly keep awake'. On the following day, 24 November, in spite of the obvious exhaustion of some of the men, Haig was still anxious that 'everything be done to exploit the success at Bourlon by utilising the cavalry'[28] – the dream of flashing sabres and galloping hooves was still alive. However, the continuation of the assault did not mean the involvement of all battalions: 'Things were comparatively quiet on the front of the 6th Division from the 22nd to the 26th, except for some shelling by the enemy and the activity of his aircraft which flew low and endeavoured to locate the positions of the troops'.[29] While 2/York and Lancaster were then able to withdraw into Brigade Reserve, their sister battalions in 62 Division were to re-join the fight on 27 November.

The attack on Bourlon Wood was to be renewed. 62 Division was to go forward with 186 Brigade on its right front and 187 (with eleven tanks) on their left; 2/5 York and Lancaster would be one of the two attacking battalions in 187 Brigade. At 02.30, the battalion moved to its assembly area over ground made heavy by the rain of the preceding days. As on 20 November, Zero Hour was set for 06.20 with 2/5 York and Lancaster on the left of the brigade front; their sister battalion, 2/4th, was in reserve and was not called on to fight. The battalion diary notes that the 2/5th 'could not keep up with our barrage' owing to the heavy ground, but they followed the tanks through the enemy barrage and 'penetrated the village'.[30] Once they were into the village they came under heavy machine gun fire from both flanks and 'stiff fighting took place'. The diary continued:

> The enemy had erected barriers which prevented progress of tanks. Owing to this and the enemy's powerful machine gun organization in the village the Bn. was unable to break through and after suffering heavy casualties was obliged to take up a position in the Brigade original front line. Enemy shelling of these positions and the approaches was heavy and methodical throughout the day.

During the night of 27/28 November, the battalions were relieved by 185 Brigade and moved to the Hindenburg support line, south of Graincourt – 'Thus ended the operations of the 62nd Division in the Battle of Cambrai'.[31] Although the Germans counter attacked on 30 November, 2/4th and 2/5th York and Lancaster were not called into action.

---

27   Sheffield and Bourne, *Haig*, p.350.
28   Sheffield and Bourne, *Haig*, p.350.
29   Wylly, *Volume 1*, p.368.
30   WO 95/3090, war diary, 2/5th York & Lancs.
31   Wyrall, *62nd Division, Vol. 1* p.119.

On 30 November, the Germans launched their own counter attack. 2/York and Lancaster, with the rest of 16 Brigade, were in reserve and were now called upon to go back into the line:

> At 10.0 a.m. orders were received that the Germans had broken the line and that this Battalion had to withdraw to DEAD MAN'S CORNER in order to form a defensive flank on the Right. Arriving in a valley after tracking [sic] a considerable distance in open country, orders were suddenly received for the Battalion to make an attack on Gouzeaucourt with the aid of tanks, this order was eventually cancelled as it had been retaken by the Guards Brigade; in place of this an attack was ordered to take QUENTIN RIDGE, this however could not be done owing to the dark and the difficulty the tanks had in crossing the Sunken Road. The Battalion eventually moved up across the Sunken Road towards the ridge and dug themselves in. Another attack was ordered for 10.0 a.m. to again capture the Ridge, but, owing to the Enemy massing a considerable number of Machine Guns our advance was stopped.[32]

While the two York and Lancaster battalions of 187 Brigade settled into their billets in the rear – the troops' spirit throughout the operation having been noted as 'excellent'[33] – the men of 2/York and Lancs were to spend the first days of December in trying to hold back the German counter attack. Ordered into action on 1 December the men met heavy machine gun fire, which forced them to return to their original positions, but not before they had 'suffered rather heavily'; two officers killed, four wounded and 'about 65 other ranks were killed, wounded or missing'. Conditions on the night of 1/2 December were miserable but 'in spite of the cold and rain the men stood the test'. The battalion remained in the line until withdrawn on 5 December. By then the British had been forced to withdraw to the Flesquières line in the face of the continued German counter attack.

Cambrai is remembered as the first battle to employ massed numbers of tanks and it is fair to say that on the opening day of the assault, they demonstrated their potential as a serious support for advancing infantry. Unfortunately, Haig's overly ambitious objectives caused the operation to stall. In the words of the 62nd Division history:

> In the first phase (20th-21st November) rested troops attacked on a well-rehearsed plan and made an immediate and record advance; in the second phase, tired and battle-worn troops, brought up from the rest area, fought well, but they were pitted against fresh enemy forces just flung into the field'.[34]

---

32 WO 95/1610, war diary, 2nd York & Lancs.
33 WO 95/3090, war diary, 2/5th York & Lancs.
34 Wyrall, *62nd Division, Vol. 1* p.120.

Haig did not bring the operation to a halt after 48 hours, in spite of the problems of pushing for a break through, instead he kept the men at it until, after two weeks, much of the ground was ceded back to the Germans: 'The results of the battle, measured in terms of ground gained or lost, showed little profit'.[35] It is sad that once again the post-battle analysis of what had gone wrong was to focus on the men rather than the commanders. The War Cabinet sought the advice of General Smuts: 'no one down to and including corps commanders was to blame', but, 'although there was no evidence with regard to them', he felt that some brigade and regimental commanders might have been in part responsible. This last comment was also held 'to apply to the troops as a whole'.[36] It was the view of the Government that, regarding the counter attack:

> [T]he Higher Command was not surprised; that all proper and adequate dispositions had been made to meet the German attack; and that it was not in the national interest that there should be a public debate "on the breakdown which undoubtedly occurred".

Better to place the blame on the troops than that the commanders should be thought to be lacking.

The battalion war diaries paint a picture of troops who did all that was asked of them, even if the 'ask' was at times confusing and contradictory – their battalion commanders obviously had pride in their men and the stoic way in which they had performed. This view is reflected by the official historian: 'That the consequences were not more serious is to the credit of the troops of all arms who maintained such a dogged resistance after the first onset had exposed the whole British salient to grave danger'.[37] The failure to capitalize on the initial success of 20 November was not down to the men but to the 'defects of the original plan of exploitation and partly in the methods employed to carry it out'.[38]

By this stage in the war, the battalions had a good leavening of 'Old Sweats', they had battle experience and they knew how to operate with massed numbers of tanks. Cambrai may have failed in its strategic aims, but it was 'of particular importance because it saw the development of new tactics destined to exercise so much influence on future warfare'.[39]

35 Miles, *Cambrai*, p.273.
36 Miles, *Cambrai*, p.296.
37 Miles, *Cambrai*, p.303.
38 Miles, *Cambrai*, p.116.
39 Miles, *Cambrai*, p.305.

12

Kaiserschlacht – the German Offensive, 21 March 1918

The men who answered the call to arms in August 1914 were concerned that if they did not join quickly then they would miss out on the fun, as it would be 'over by Christmas'. As 1917 morphed into 1918, there would have been very few soldiers in the trenches who were a part of those initial drafts. The war had dragged on for more than three years and looked like going on for some time yet. For the troops in France and Flanders there were signs that the early months of the new year would see a German offensive in the west: Russia was effectively out of the war, releasing German divisions from that front; the Americans were entering the conflict and would soon be building up their forces on the Western front; the Italians on the Isonzo had collapsed following the combined Austro-German victory at Caporetto; the British army was experiencing manpower problems, which had led to the disbandment of many battalions. It was against this background that the Germans planned and launched their Spring Offensive; *Kaiserschlacht*.

From mid-December, Haig's GHQ had been predicting a 'large-scale German offensive effort in the following spring with increasing certainty and in increasing detail'.[1] The C-in-C's diary has a number of references to his concerns in this regard; 13 December, 'we must still expect an attack!'; 19 December, 'I consider Germans will launch large attack on the Western Front early next year'; 18 March, 'we must expect an attack at short notice, and make our plans accordingly'.[2] By 19 March, 'the last pieces of evidence regarding the approaching storm' were available and Gough (commanding Fifth Army) wrote home that he expected a bombardment 'to-morrow night', which would be followed by the German infantry 'on Thursday 21st'.[3] In spite of the certainty with which an assault was viewed, when it came it was as if all were surprised.

---

1 Harris, *Haig*, p.432.
2 Sheffield and Bourne, *Haig*, pp.360, 361 & 388.
3 Edmonds, J., *Military Operations France and Belgium 1918, Volume 1* (Nashville, Naval & Military Press, Reprint of 1935 original), p.110.

The growing belief in a German offensive was translated at brigade and battalion levels into the need for raiding parties to bring in enemy prisoners, who could then be interrogated. In the weeks before they were attacked, 2/York and Lancaster, which had recently absorbed the men from two of the companies of the 10th battalion (among them was the author's grandfather), staged two raids on 7 and 14 March. Although the first had little to record, the second was a little more eventful. Three officers and 29 men went forward with the aim of 'securing an identification' for the German unit facing them. However, they were 'apparently heard' crawling through the grass: 'Fire was opened by hostile machine guns on both flanks. Creeping forward the patrol discovered a large hole containing an English rifle. Nothing further could be discovered and since the enemy was alert and still maintained his MG fire the party withdrew and entered our line after an absence of nearly 5 hours. There were no casualties'.[4] It took brave men to take part in these excursions so close to the enemy line. Although this patrol was unable to bring back any intelligence, other sources were painting a picture that proved to be accurate. The battalion history cites one example: 'On 20th March aeroplane photographs disclosed ammunition pits for seventy extra batteries opposite the divisional front, and when at 5 a.m. on 21st March the bombardment commenced, there was no doubt but that a real offensive had begun'.[5]

Although Haig and his commanders were aware of the likely German assault, they had a number of issues to contend with concerning the extent and condition of the front they would be defending. The French had been pushing the British to increase the length of their line by taking over some of the trenches held by the French army. By 4 February, Haig's sector of the front had increased from 95 to 123 miles (an increase of some 30%),[6] while at the same time brigades had been reduced from four battalions to three. Harris is not the only historian to express the view that Lloyd George had adopted a policy of denying Haig 'any surplus manpower that might incline him [Haig] to resume major offensive efforts in 1918'.[7] The result of political interference and the reduction of brigades from four battalions to three, was that '134 infantry battalions in France effectively disappeared'.[8] Haig probably had 70,000 fewer fighting troops at the start of 1918 than he had had in January 1917; a reduction of some seven per cent. Just as Lloyd George cannot avoid his responsibility for retaining Haig as C-in-C when he obviously had so little confidence in his methods, so the War Cabinet cannot wash their hands of the position Haig's army was in when the German spring offensive struck them.

The British army had experienced a great deal of fighting in 1917. Arras, Messines, Third Ypres and Cambrai had sapped strength and morale, often for relatively small

4   WO 95/1610, war diary, 2nd York & Lancs.
5   Wylly, *Volume 1*, p.374.
6   Harris, *Haig*, p.433.
7   Harris, *Haig*, p.420.
8   Harris, *Haig*, p.433.

Kaiserschlacht – the German Offensive, 21 March 1918

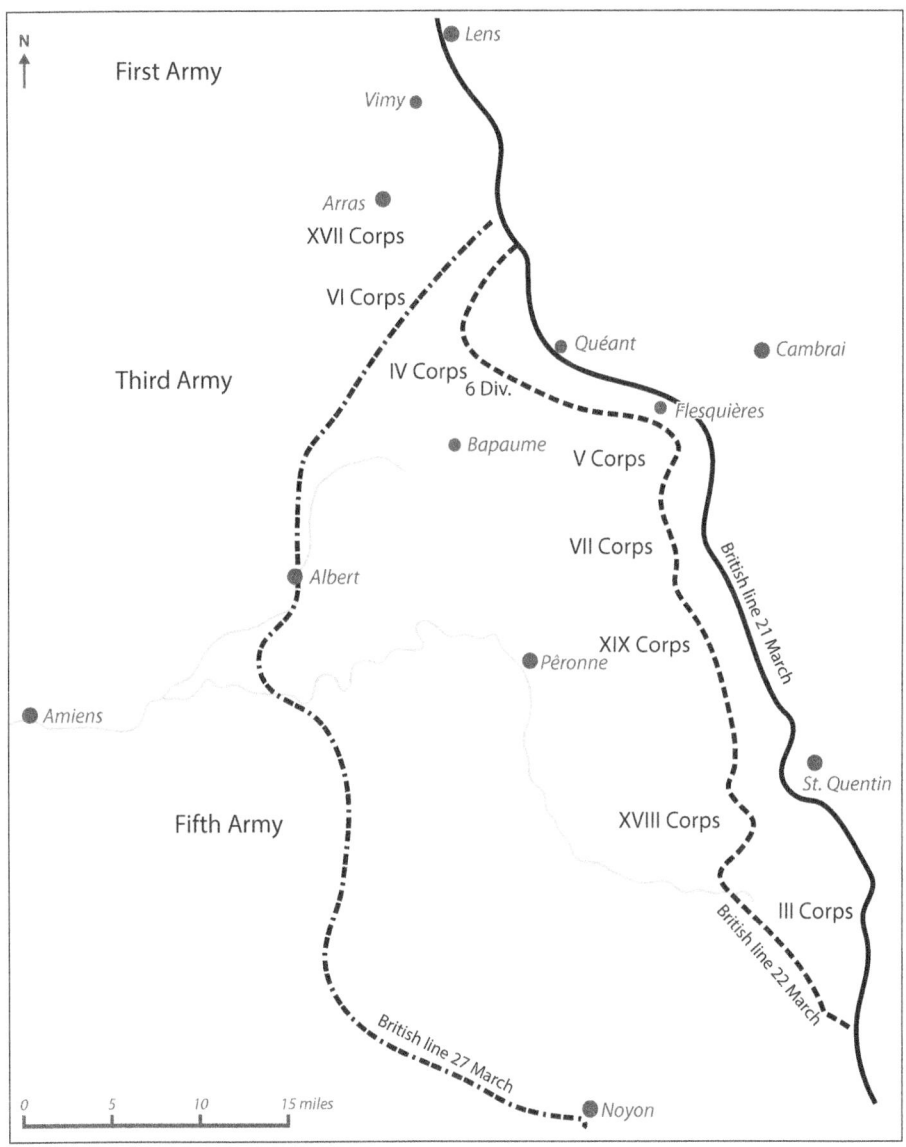

Map 15 Kaiserschlacht: British line, 21 and 27 March 1918.

gains, or for ground that was then given up because there were insufficient reserves to exploit the advantage won. But lessons had also been learnt. Haig's armies had adopted many of the principles of the German system of 'defence in depth', which were applied – to varying degrees – along their front in 1918. The British line consisted of three zones: Forward Zone; Battle Zone; Rear Zone.[9] The Forward Zone (typically about 1,000 yards deep), closest to the enemy, was lightly held by groups of men in half-platoon and platoon strength, protected by wire and machine guns; they were not in the long, zig-zag, trenches of the 1915 front line. It was the role of these men to hold up or slow down the enemy advance. The main defensive effort was sited in the Battle Zone, between one and two miles further back and anything from 2-3,000 yards deep. Situated on ground that was judged to be good for defence, and for fighting, it was in this zone that the enemy advance should be stopped. Some miles further back was the Rear Zone to which troops could retreat and hold if the enemy broke through the Battle Zone. Such was the theory. In the rear areas of both Third and Fifth Armies, the preparation had not been completed to the degree required. In mitigation, Gough's Fifth Army had taken over ground from the French as part of the extension of the British line. On this section of the front the French 'had not even indicated a Rear Zone on their maps'; there was little except a marking out of the line and the laying of some wire.[10] The situation on Third Army's front was not much better, here the trenches were 'marked by shallow digging', or 'scrapes in the ground' as Richard Holmes described them.[11] At his disposal, Haig had 58 divisions spread throughout the four British Armies: from north to south, these were; Second, First, Third and Fifth. Four battalions of the York and Lancaster Regiment were to be caught up in the Spring Offensive; the 2nd, the 13th, the 1/4th and 1/5th. The first of these is particularly relevant to this author as his grandfather was taken prisoner on the first day of the attack. 13/York and Lancs (who we last met on the Somme), became involved a week later with the Hallamshires joining in from 10 April.

In the shorthand of history, battles are frequently distilled down to one memorable – mythical? – point or event: Loos, the 'reserves'; Messines, the mines; Somme, the losses of 1 July; Cambrai, tanks. In the case of the German spring offensive, it is the collapse of Fifth Army and the large number of British soldiers made prisoner.[12] The greatest extent of the German advance was made on Gough's sector, but it should be stated that Fifth Army were holding a much longer front than Third Army, with only the same number of divisions; 42 miles with 12 infantry and 3 cavalry divisions

9 Edmonds, *1918, Vol. 1*, pp.41-3.
10 Edmonds, *1918, Vol. 1*, p.122.
11 In conversation with this author.
12 Much has been written on the discipline and morale of Fifth Army in March 1918; Englander, D., 'Discipline and morale in the British Army, 1917-1918', in Horne, J. (ed), *State, society and mobilization in Europe during the First World War* (Cambridge, 1997), pp.125-143 and Dillon, *Allies are a Tiresome Lot*, pp.118-120.

against 28 miles and 14 divisions.[13] At GHQ, it was the belief that the Germans, even if they broke through on a large scale, would not force the British into more than 'a gradual withdrawal of the troops on the front attacked' so allowing reserves to be assembled where required and 'sent into action deliberately in accordance with the prearranged plan'. As Edmonds would later record in the Official History, 'this anticipation was to be falsified on the Fifth Army front'.[14]

The poor condition of the trenches, especially on Fifth Army front, and the reduction in the number of men in each brigade had an unwelcome consequence for the men. The diary of 2/York and Lancaster records that on 5, 6 and 7 March 'very little training was carried out, owing to the large working parties which had to be found'; this was just after the battalion had come out of the line and should have been resting. In the week prior to 20 February, the battalion had been in the line but this was followed by a day of 'cleaning up and inspections' and a further five days of providing 'large working parties'.[15] In late January, General Smuts had been asked to look into the state of the army and he submitted his report to the War Cabinet. Smuts believed that the morale of the men was 'good' but there was no doubt that the men were 'tired'. The army's front-line defences needed a great deal of work to maintain them but, as the trenches were within the zone of enemy artillery fire, 'the burden falls in the main on the infantry'. The report made the point that the troops suffered 'in regard both to rest and training' and that, in the circumstances, 'the surprising feature is not that [the men] are fatigued but that their spirits are so good'. In Smuts' view, the need for rest was 'a psychological factor of the utmost importance' and taking over more of the line – from the French – ran serious risks:

> Either the defences will not be completed in time, or the essential rest will not be obtained, and the Army will not be in the state in which it ought to be to resist an attack. Moreover, any further extension of the front will cause great discontent among the ranks.[16]

Some historians have criticised the troops for the number of men who surrendered on that March morning, Smuts' report explains why many probably felt that they had had enough.

Before leaving the subject of the morale and spirit of the troops there is one further factor that affected the number of men available, and their level of tiredness. Haig and his commanders had direct control over the availability of leave. For the soldiers, many of whom were conscripts, the opportunity to travel home to see their families was 'a matter of urgent necessity for the men'.[17] However, from the standpoint of

---

13 Edmonds, *1918, Vol. 1*, p.114.
14 Edmonds, *1918, Vol. 1*, p.117.
15 WO 95/1610, war diary, 2nd York & Lancs.
16 Edmonds, *1918, Vol. 1*, pp.40-1.
17 Edmonds, *1918, Vol. 1*, p.39, fn.1.

the commanders, men on leave were unavailable for front-line duties. For the British *Tommy* the lack of leave available to him was highlighted by that afforded to the French *Poilu*. Following the serious discontent among the French troops in 1917, they now had leave once every four months. In December 1917, Haig informed the War Office that 89,304 of his men had had no leave for 12 months.[18] Withholding leave (always a 'privilege' and not a 'right' in the British army) may have helped manning levels in the trenches but, together with their employment as 'navvies', was seriously trying the resilience of the men. The importance of leave for the troops was elegantly summarised by the official censor:

> The Army lives for leave; talks and writes of leave; thinks and dreams of leave. Nothing tends more to the encouragement of good Morale than a free flow of leave; nothing is more conducive to grousing and despondency than its prolonged delay.[19]

We come now to the front that was to be held by the tired, leave-starved, men of Haig's armies (Map 15). The troops of 2/York and Lancaster were in 16 Brigade, 6 Division, IV Corps; the Division held the left of the corps front, with the 51st on their right and the 25th was in reserve. Just behind the German lines, on 6 Division front, was the small town of Quéant, about 10 miles due west of Cambrai, where we last met 2/York and Lancs. The two IV Corps divisions held a line 12,000 yards long with No Man's Land varying between 400 yards wide on the left (the York and Lancaster sector) and 'half a mile to one mile' on the right.[20] All three of 6 Divisions brigades (from left to right; 16, 71 and 18) were in the line. Each brigade had two battalions 'up' so that the division's frontage of 3,000 yards was covered by six battalions in the Forward Zone, the others being behind in the Battle Zone. The ground facing 6 Division is outlined in 2/York and Lancaster battalion history:

> The front held by the 6th Division was generally on a forward slope opposite the villages of Quéant and Pronville. [ ] The position lay stride a succession of well-defined, broad spurs, and narrow valleys (like the fingers of a partially opened hand), merging into the broad transverse valley which separated the British line from the two villages above mentioned. *All advantages of ground lay with the defence*, and it seemed as if no attack could succeed, unless by the aid of tanks.[21] [My emphasis.]

The Official History states that the Forward Zone occupied by 6 Division was 'difficult to hold, being exposed to enemy view and direct fire'. The zone had 'less depth

---

18 Edmonds, *1918, Vol. 1*, p.39, fn.1.
19 Hardie. IWM Doc. 4041, report for October 1917, p.8.
20 Edmonds, *1918, Vol. 1*, p.132.
21 Wylly, *Volume 1*, p.372.

than was the case on most other parts of the line' and due to previous divisional commanders disagreeing over the best method of defending the sector, 'the necessary work [on the defences] had never been completed'. In places, there was no reserve line with 'few communication trenches and none organized for defence against a break-in'.[22] In 2005, the author, together with Richard Holmes, walked the ground held by 2/York and Lancaster battalion to see where his grandfather was captured on that misty day in March (see Appendix I). The battalion history differs in some details from Edmonds, but drew a similar picture:

> A month's hard frost in January had militated against digging, and though there was a complete front trench and reserve trench, the support trenches hardly existed, and dug-outs were noticeable by their absence. [...] The depth from front or outpost zone to reserve or battle zone was about 2,500 yards. With only three battalions in a brigade, there was no option but to assign one battalion in each brigade to the defence of the outpost zones, and keep two battalions in depth in the battle zone. With battalions at just over half-strength, and with the undulating nature of the ground, the defence resolved itself everywhere into a succession of posts with a limited field of fire. A good Corps Line, called the Vaulx-Morchies Line, had been dug, the nearest portion a mile behind the reserve line, and this was held by the Pioneers and Royal Engineers, owing to scarcity of numbers.[23]

16 Brigade had 2/York and Lancaster on their right front, to their left was 1/King's Shropshire Light Infantry (1/KSLI) and on their right (on 71 Brigade front) was 2/Sherwood Foresters. The third of the brigade's battalions, 1/Buffs (East Kent) was in brigade reserve.

Before coming to the events of 21 March, a few extracts from 16 Brigade's 'Defence Scheme' document are relevant to the events of that day. The trench map (Map 16) shows that both 1/KSLI and 2/York and Lancs had isolated platoons in the very forward positions. About 500 yards further back was a trench-line made of Leeds Reserve and Bradford Reserve, this had to be 'held at all costs'.[24] To that end the zone had been 'tactically organised into a series of defended localities, with permanent garrisons. Each defended locality is wired and capable of all round defence'. One of these defended localities can be seen on the map, in Leeds Reserve. We will see later that this strongpoint was overrun early in the assault. The planning staff believed that the 'continuous trench line' would mean that the enemy attack would first have to be made frontally, which might later develop into a flank attack; the reverse would happen on the day. The left flank of the brigade, and so also the left of 6 Division, was also

---

22 Edmonds, *1918, Vol. 1*, p.224.
23 Wylly, *Volume 1*, p.373.
24 TNA WO 95/1607, 16 Brigade diary, Appendix IX, p.3.

The sunken road, Map 16. Taken from point 'X'; the bushes are at point 'Y'. (Photo J. Dillon)

the junction between IV and VI Corps. Corps boundaries are potential weak points, as both corps will assume that the other has got it covered. In the case of 16 Brigade, this left flank rested on a small river, the Hirondelle, and led to a cautionary note in the description of the defence scheme: 'Owing to the configuration of the ground and the general "lie" of the area held by the Brigade, the left flank (L'HIRONDELLE VALLEY) is very susceptible to such [a flank attack], providing the enemy first breaks through frontally on the Division on our left'.[25] On 21 March, the fog and the lie of the land made this valley an ideal entry point so that the heaviest weight of the enemy attack on 16 Brigade was directed 'up the Hirondelle Valley, where the enemy soon succeeded, not only in overwhelming the Forward Zone, but in penetrating into the Battle Zone defences'.[26] The brigade defence scheme included actions to be taken in the event of either a right or left flank attack by the enemy, but not one for an attack on both flanks. Unfortunately, for 16 Brigade, it was the unexpected (and unplanned for) that came to pass; the Germans advanced through Lagnicourt village on the right, and the Hirondelle valley on the left.

25   WO 95/1607, 16 Brigade diary, Appendix IX, p.3.
26   Edmonds, *1918, Vol. 1*, p.226.

Kaiserschlacht – the German Offensive, 21 March 1918   203

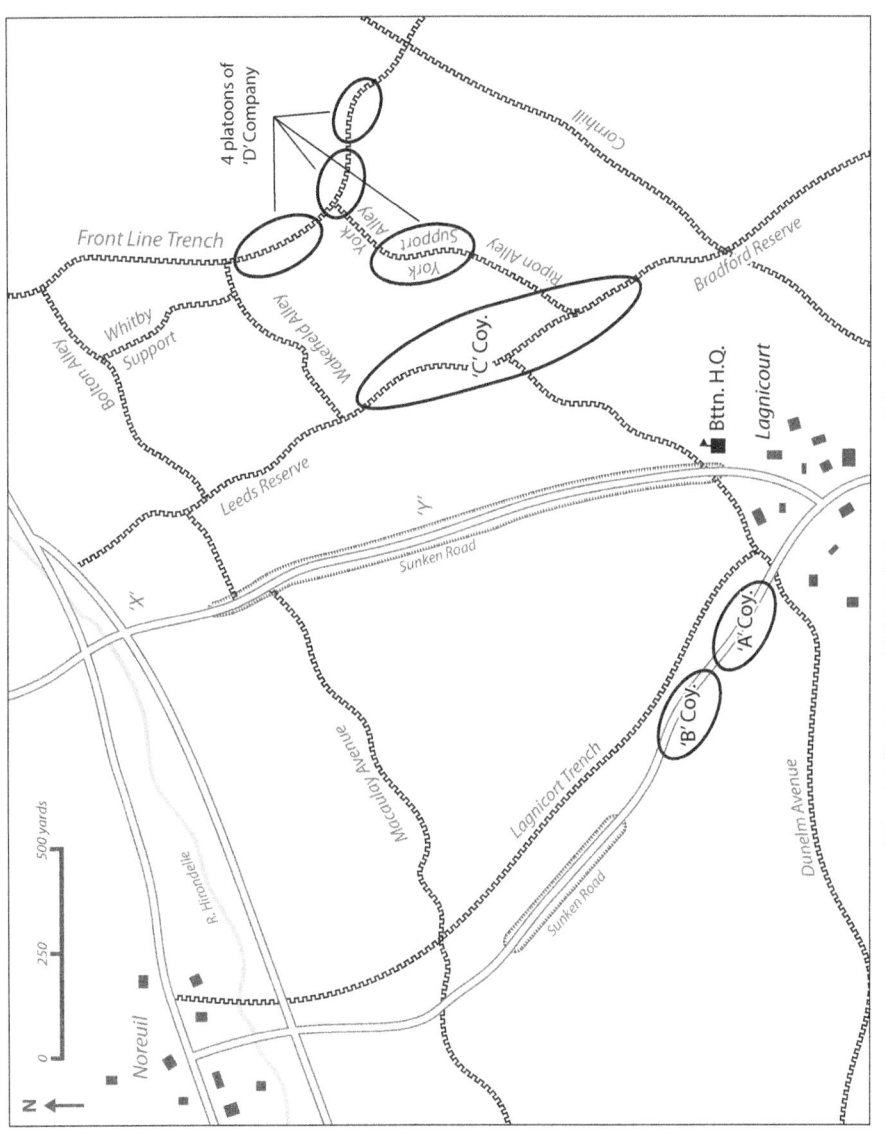

Map 16 Position of 2/York & Lancaster, 21 March 1918.

We now turn to the morning of 21 March, operation *Michael*. The German onslaught was literally overwhelming. 63 German divisions (with another 11 'position divisions' that were not part of the initial assault)[27] were pitted against the 8 of Third Army and 11 of Fifth Army.[28] This massive advantage was most apparent in front of Gough's troops where 43 German divisions faced his 11.[29] The assault was only ever going to go one way. At 04.40, the Kaiser's spring offensive, *Kaiserschlacht*, opened with a massive bombardment of the British Forward and Battle Zones. Much of the shelling was with lachrymatory (tear gas) shells, causing troops to don their respirators, and keep them on until almost 11 a.m. The weather that morning was very much to the advantage of the attackers; a heavy, thick fog added to the effect of the gas shells, making visibility very difficult for the defenders. As the sun rose, 'the fog was still thick' and remained so until the German troops began their assault at 9.40 a.m. The shallow undulations in the ground in front of the British troops, together with the fog, favoured the 'infiltration' tactics of the attackers. Many of those in the Forward Zone trenches were dead when the enemy reached them. The Germans then moved on towards and around many of the strong-points in the Battle Zone. The British troops, confused by the lack of visibility, did not know if the shadowy figures they saw were the enemy, or their mates retreating from the front. It was normal for defenders to fire S.O.S. flares when they required artillery support but again the fog helped the attackers; the artillery could not see the flares, nor could they see the defenders positions. The difficulties of the gunners were compounded by the inability of the Flying Corps to assist, due to the weather. The enemy shelling, as so frequently happened in these battles, cut most of the telephone cables to the frontline units, even though these were buried up to six feet deep. With no telephone links, and thick fog preventing aerial observation (as well as impeding the progress of runners and 'grounding' pigeons), commanders were unable to get a picture of what was unfolding at the front. The course of that first day was summed up by Major General Marden (commanding 6 Division):

> It was essentially a soldiers' battle in which units under their commanders were set to fight without hope of reinforcements against vastly superior numbers of the enemy supported by an overwhelming [sic] artillery.

Somewhere in the York and Lancaster trenches was Private Patrick Dillon; the account of the day's action is taken up by the post-battle notes of his battalion commander, Lieutenant Colonel St. John Blunt.[30] The enemy barrage commenced at 5 a.m. and was 'put down extremely heavily' on Lagnicourt trench and the sunken road behind

---

27 Edmonds, *1918, Vol. 1*, p.152.
28 Edmonds, *1918, Vol. 1*, pp.134 & 126.
29 Holmes, *The Western Front*, p.198.
30 WO 95/1610, war diary, 2nd York & Lancs.

it; this was also very close to the battalion HQ. According to Blunt, the initial shelling of the front and reserve lines was 'only a light barrage'. At 07.30, this changed and for an hour became 'intense' on the front line, lifting then to the reserve line where it remained for about 15 minutes before moving to the rear areas. Lagnicourt trench and battalion HQ were shelled until 9 a.m. this bombardment of the front trenches took a dreadful toll; 'the barrage killed and wounded practically the whole of the front line Coy., only 15 O.R. surviving and eventually getting back to the Reserve Line'. An NCO from the Sherwood Foresters had reported that the trench, which had been occupied by 'D' company (at the very front of the battalion line), was 'badly damaged and there were many dead in it'. Blunt relates that the Germans had failed to cut the wire in front of the battalion's lines, but this did not hold up their attack; he makes the interesting point that 'no infantry attack developed against my front line *from the front*'. [My emphasis.] The Germans used the lie of the land and the fog to move around the defenders and take them from both sides – the twin flank attack that the brigade defence scheme had not allowed for.

When the initial bombardment of the front line ceased it was followed up by the advance of the German infantry but, according to Blunt's record, they invested the trenches of the battalion to their right (the Sherwood Foresters), before taking on the remnants of the York and Lancaster men. This would conform to his statement –mentioned earlier – that he had not been attacked from his *front*:

> At about 8.30 a.m., as far as I can ascertain, the enemy infantry assaulted the front line of left Bn. of 71st Bde. (Sherwood Foresters) & captured the front line; they spread outwards & elements of them crossed the CORNHILL [trench] & advanced towards York Support & Ripon Av. [Both were trench names see Map 16] The remnants of the front line Coy. [of 2/York & Lancs] fought these for some time but were eventually forced back to the Reserve line. The right Lewis gun detachment in the front line engaged the enemy towards MAGPIE'S NEST [probably a strongpoint] & kept up the fire until the gun was knocked out.[31]

Blunt's report continues with a criticism of those who should have been defending the reserve line. Although he is not specific, it is difficult not to read his comments as relating to the battalion on his right; the Sherwood Foresters:

> The next phase was the attack on the Reserve Line. The enemy advanced in considerable numbers along POULTRY & reached the reserve line about 9 a.m. [Poultry was a trench that ran through the Sherwood Forester's sector of the front] Every man of both C & D Coys. [2/York & Lancs] whom I have questioned state that *no resistance was offered there & that the garrison surrendered*

31 WO 95/1610.

without fighting, being plainly visible leaving the trench with their hands up as the enemy approached. This left my right flank exposed. [My emphasis.]

With the Germans advancing (it was now about 9 a.m.), the fight moved back to the reserve line and 'the enemy quickly got into Lagnicourt [on Blunt's right, in 71 Brigade sector] in large numbers & attacked my C Coy. in flank and right rear'.[32] What Blunt is describing, with fire coming from the troops' rear, is classic German 'infiltration' (Stormtroop) tactics. Men found themselves cut off as the enemy moved around them. 2/Sherwood Foresters were joined by a Corporal and 12 men from 2/York and Lancaster who had been 'cut off by the enemy from the remainder of the battalion'. By this point, our York and Lancaster battalion had suffered heavy casualties to the four platoons in the most forward of the battalion's positions. Right at the front had been D company, with C company 500 yards behind them in Bradford Reserve. The two remaining companies, A and B, were a further 5-700 yards back in Lagnicourt trench and a sunken road, which ran parallel with it. These two companies were connected with the men in Bradford Reserve by a communication trench, Dunelm Avenue. At the same time as C company found itself being fired on from the rear (mentioned above), an attack developed on them from their left:

> [The enemy] had evidently got in the strong point between Bolton & Wakefield Avenues as part of the garrison was driven down into my company. This company [C] had suffered considerable casualties from the barrage as they came out of their dugouts when the enemy was seen advancing on the right before the barrage lifted from the reserve line.

Blunt, and the other commanders on the ground, were doing what they could to hold the situation. Before they were forced to retire down Dunelm towards the two companies in Lagnicourt trench, C company had requested reinforcement; 'A' were ordered, at 'about 8.45 a.m.', to go forward to their assistance. However, on leaving their dugouts in Lagnicourt, this company also suffered considerable casualties, but did manage to get out of the trench to the wire in front. From this position they saw 'large numbers of the enemy advancing from Leeds Reserve [and the strongpoint there]. They engaged these when the enemy shortened his barrage to the wire and killed or wounded the greater part of A Coy.'[33] Within an hour of the German infantry attack starting, Blunt had only B Company, and the few survivors of the other three, with which to try to defend his position. At about 8.45 a.m., Blunt received a message that B company 'had suffered considerable casualties, that large numbers of the enemy were advancing from Leeds reserve & that they were going to fight it out. The only survivors of this Coy. were a few men who had been left behind in the dugouts'. The

---

32   WO 95/1610, Colonel Blunt's report.
33   WO 95/1610, Colonel Blunt's report.

battalion had now been drastically reduced in numbers and somewhere in that story is the point at which the author's grandfather was taken prisoner; the war was over for Private Patrick Dillon.

The shelling of the area around battalion HQ (close to Lagnicourt trench) ceased at about 9 a.m., allowing Blunt to see that the Germans had got into Bradford Reserve (C company's trench), and was advancing through Lagnicourt village. Although the troops close to the HQ opened fire on the advancing enemy, the cover afforded by the houses in the village prevented them from stopping the Germans; 'they went through the village & continued to advance along the ridge [west of the village] and up the Vaux [sic] road'. In an effort to prevent the advancing Germans from getting behind him, Blunt had detached some men to a point on Dunelm trench, but this weakened his available garrison. After about 30-45 minutes, Blunt's men were 'driven out of Dunelm Av. & the enemy got into the sunken road by Hd. Qrs.' The Germans had succeeded in forcing a gap between the 16th and 71st Brigades. The collapse of the York and Lancaster position was almost complete. By 10.30, 'the enemy was vigorously pressing his attack home on our flanks'; an hour later 'he had entered Lagnicourt and Noreuil'. Within a further two hours, the troops holding the Battle Zone were almost cut off and by 1 p.m., their position was 'untenable'. The enemy was advancing in strength on the flanks and making 'further progress along the valleys'[34] – the only remaining option was to retire quickly to the Vaulx line (otherwise known as the Corps Line) where troops should turn and stand.

The fact that the British front was overrun that morning did not mean that there were not any acts of heroism. Buried within the post-battle report of 16 Brigade is a brief account of a last stand by Colonel Smith, commanding 1/KSLI, on the immediate left of 2/York and Lancaster. Smith was attempting to hold the very left-hand end of Lagnicourt trench, where it joined the Hirondelle Valley:

> At 1.25 pm. a message was received from the O.C. 1/K.S.L.I. timed at 12.20 p.m. stating that he was holding LAGNICOURT TRENCH with four platoons and asking for reinforcements and artillery support. The message stated they were holding on to the last. Nothing could be done to help Colonel Smith as there were no troops available for immediate counter-attack, the remnants of the brigade by this time having dribbled back to the VAULX-MORCHIES line.[35]

The Brigade Commander added a hand-written note:

> Col. Smith was to have handed over command on the night & to have proceeded to England as a 'tired officer'. He was a very gallant gentleman & those who knew him say his only wish was to be allowed to see it out to the end with

---

34   WO 95/1607, war diary 16 Brigade, report on operations of 21 March.
35   WO 95/1607.

his battn. & not to be sent home. There is some evidence to show that about noon some twelve K.S.L.I. or Buffs jumped out of Lagnicourt trench & met the enemy with the bayonet.

It would appear that the Colonel survived, probably as a prisoner, as there is no reference to him on the CWGC site.

The German penetration of the British line was comprehensive and the retreat of 2/York and Lancaster, along with many others in Third and Fifth Armies, was now well under way. With insufficient men to form all-round defence, under machine gun fire from the area of Lagnicourt trench and 'seeing no signs of counter attacks coming up', Blunt had few options. The battalion commander withdrew his remaining troops and 'the remnants of Coys. down Dunelm forming flank defences on both sides to prevent the enemy carrying out his endeavours to press from both sides'. The troops pulled back (while constantly trying to prevent themselves from being outflanked), until they reached the Vaulx-Morchies line, some 3,000 yards behind Lagnicourt trench. At this point, Blunt 'put in all my men to strengthen the garrison of that line'.[36]

While the men of 2/York and Lancaster were trying to defend their front, 2/Durham Light Infantry (on the right of 6 Division, in the Morchies sector), were similarly attempting to hold their line on the left front of 18 Brigade. The CO of the Durhams (Lieutenant Colonel Brereton) noted in his post-battle report that telephone communication was lost at an early point in the battle and he had had to resort to runners; 'I regret that both these runners were amongst the missing, I cannot speak too highly of their gallant behaviour'.[37] At about 9 a.m. Brereton noted one of those acts of 'mateship' that went largely unrecorded up and down the front:

> A wounded man was discovered out in front of the trench, and Captain Gilpin and Cpl. Robson went out to bring the man in, in spite of heavy machine gun fire. Captain Gilpin was hit in the head & Cpl. Robson in the thigh about 80 yards from the trench. Corporal Wade and L/Cpl Dairs attempted to bring them both back, but found it impossible owing to the machine gun fire.

Both Captain Gilpin and Corporal Robson died in their attempt to bring in the wounded man. Both have no known grave and are remembered on the Arras Memorial to the missing. Brereton's men were finding it harder to withdraw than 2/York and Lancaster, they had to stop their retirement during daylight and had to 'hang on till dusk, and then attempt to get back'. However, under the relentless German assault this option was also closing down.

36 WO 95/1610, Colonel Blunt's report.
37 TNA WO 95/1617, war diary, 2/DLI, Brereton's report.

The only thing to do was to fight it out, as dusk was not expected for an hour, & the position seemed hopeless. About 7-15 [in the evening] a thick mist appeared & the opportunity was seized & the order was given for everyone to get back to the Corps Line on his own. [...] there was no chance for anyone who was hit.

Brereton would no doubt have had a heavy heart as he wrote his report, detailing those who had fallen or were lost, men such as those in the front two companies – 'their orders were to hold on to the last'; of these, only one man and two wounded officers made it back. The wiring platoon had consisted of one officer and 24 men of whom 'none returned'; the same note was made of the signallers. Eleven officers had been in the reserve line – 'none returned'. All along the Corps Line, remnants of brigades were being temporarily formed into composite units.

The impact of the German assault knocked back 6 Division front by some 3-4,000 yards. The ground lost by Fifth Army was even more dramatic, in places it extended up to ten miles. Surprisingly, Haig seemed at first to be unaware of how badly things had gone. His diary for 22 March was unrealistically upbeat; 'our men are in great spirits. All speak of the wonderful targets they had to fire at yesterday'.[38] In spite of the thick fog, he also commented that the RFC had done 'wonders', firing into 'marvellous targets' where they had 'spread consternation and disorder'. The C-in-C must have been horribly out of touch with his commanders.

For 2/York and Lancaster, events had moved quickly on their front near Quéant. Having spent the night of the 21st in the Corps – or Vaulx-Morchies – line, the remnants of the battalion spent the following day in a series of defensive moves all the way back to the 'Army' or 'Haig' line – different accounts use different names:

> On the morning of the 22nd about 150 who were left in the Battalion [about 650 would have been there on the 21st] along with the remainder of another Regiment [all that were left of the Shropshire Light Infantry] had orders to make a counter attack on VAULX WOOD but owing to the deadly fire of the hostile machine guns it was impossible, they were then ordered to make a stand along the VAULX-MORCHIES sunken road. About 11 a.m. the enemy attacked the VAULX-MORCHIES line and made the garrison withdraw to a line further back. The enemy broke through on our left flank and got into the village of VAULX and started firing up the Sunken Road where the Battalion were holding on and at the same time came round on our right. The Battalion hung on to the position as long as they could, inflicting casualties on the advancing troops until they were almost surrounded when they withdrew in stages to the next Sunken Road where another stand was made. After holding on for about an hour, and the Germans still advancing, orders were sent up to withdraw to the Army line.[39]

38   Sheffield and Bourne, *Haig*, p.390.
39   WO 95/1610.

The action had become a soldier's battle with small units fighting their way back independently, while taking fire from all sides and out of communication with any headquarters staff. With the withdrawal happening all along the fronts of Third and Fifth Army, it would take until late April before the German advance had burnt itself out, and by that time the enemy had come dangerously close to the important communication centre of Amiens. Those two days in March were life-changing for Private Dillon who, as a result of becoming a POW, survived the war. The remainder of the depleted battalion was relieved on the night of 23 March and, together with the rest of 6 Division, made their way to the Ypres salient and Plumer's Second Army. During the last few days of March, casualties in the division amounted to 3,900 out of a 'total trench strength of under 5,000 infantry', 2/York and Lancaster 'suffered cruel losses' of 24 officers and 391 men, killed, wounded or missing.[40]

Although the focus so far has been on the 2nd Battalion, it was not the only unit from the regiment to be involved in trying to hold back the German offensive. The 1st Barnsley Pals (13/York and Lancaster) were near Frévillers, some 18 kilometre northwest of Arras, at the beginning of March. As part of 93 Brigade (31 Division), the battalion was out of the line and so would not have been surprised to find themselves being used as 'labour'. For the first five days of the month, the battalion supplied 340 men to 185 Tunnelling Company 'for work on the defences' in the Arleux sector.[41] As always though, sports were an important part of the men's time when they were away from the front; they enjoyed it and it kept them fit. The afternoon of 1 March, as well as all day on the 13th and 14th, the men participated in Divisional and Brigade sports and there was a divisional cross country run on 17 March, 'won by the 15th West Yorks Regt.' While 2/York and Lancaster were facing the German attacks on both their flanks in front of Quéant, 93 Brigade 'were inspected by the G.O.C. Division at TINQUES', a few miles south of Frévillers. The routine of inspections, training and working parties was interrupted during the night of 21 March as 'orders were received to move at 12 hours' notice by Bus'.[42] The move of 31 Division, from First to Third Army, was 'to be completed on the 22nd.[43] The battalion marched the 5 or 6 kilometres to Tinques, on the Arras-St Pol road, where they boarded busses for Blairville, about 10 kilometres west of Arras. Because of the enemy's success against Third and Fifth Armies, the men could not go into billets but went straight into the line that night, relieving 101 Brigade of 34 Division. By 02.00 on the 23rd, 93 Brigade was in position on the Third Army front. As a result of the German assault, the new line occupied by the brigade (between the small villages of St. Leger and Boyelles) was some two and a half miles west of where it had been prior to the attack; 13/York and Lancaster were on the left, 15/West Yorkshire on their right.

40 Wylly, *Volume 1*, p.377.
41 TNA WO 95/2360, war diary, 93 Brigade.
42 WO 95/2360.
43 Edmonds, *1918, Vol. 1*, p.253.

Kaiserschlacht – the German Offensive, 21 March 1918   211

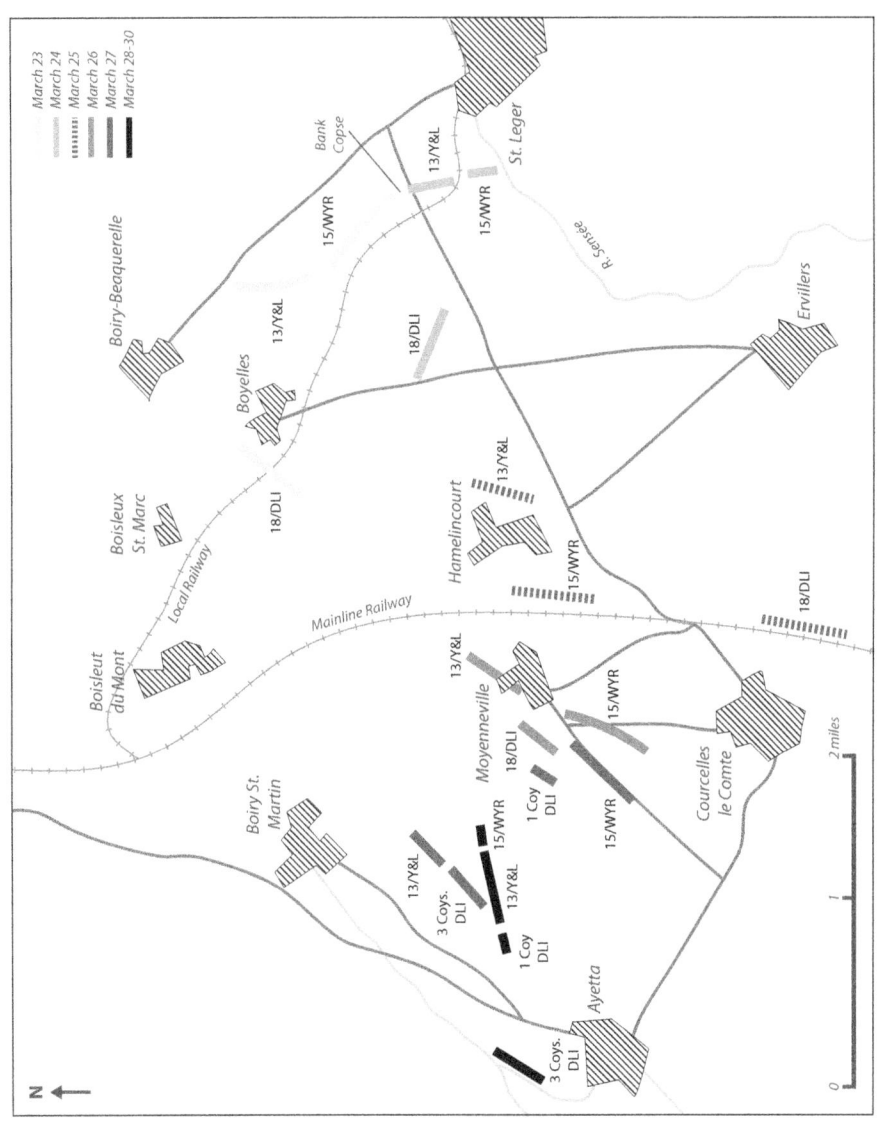

Map 17 Successive positions of 13/York & Lancaster, 23-30 March 1918.

With the German advance gaining ground, and the British falling back, the battalion's stay north-west of St. Leger was only ever going to be temporary. During the night of 23/24 March, 93 Brigade 'side-slipped' south to take over a front of 1,100 yards between Bank Copse and the Sensée River, immediately to the west of St. Leger (see Map 17). There would be more moves to come over the following days as the enemy advance continued. On the morning of 24 March, the battalion's front line was subjected to a heavy bombardment, followed up at 7 a.m. by an attack along the entire brigade front:

> He [the enemy] was completely repulsed with heavy losses by our Rifle and Machine Gun fire. In no case did he succeed in entering our trench, so no prisoners were taken. Many dead were seen lying in front of our wire. Further attacks were made at 11-0 a.m. and 4-0 a.m., the former being launched without any artillery preparation, but the only result was to add to the enemy's already heavy losses. Our casualties [93 Brigade] during these attacks were about 100.[44]

In spite of the successful stand against the attacks, the withdrawal of the brigade continued on the 25th; by then the Germans were close to Gomiecourt, to the south of the brigade. By 7 p.m. 13/York and Lancaster were in a line just to the east of the village of Hamelincourt; 15/West Yorks were to the west of the village (on the north-south railway line), with 18/DLI – in brigade support – a further 1,500 yards along the rail tracks, to the south.

The brigade moves of the previous three days, while unfortunate (no soldiers like a retreat), were made in a controlled way; the events of 26 and 27 March were to be more chaotic for the battalion. On the morning of the 26th, the brigade received orders for a further withdrawal as a result of the enemy's continued advance to their south. The intended retirement would have placed 13/York and Lancs in the village of Moyennville, with 15 West Yorks on the spur to the south of the village; 18/DLI would have been further to the west, in support. At around 11 a.m. 'it was discovered' that both the York and Lancaster and the Durham battalions were much further to the west than planned, leaving the West Yorks on their own and with their flanks 'in the air'. As the brigade diary records:

> No orders for this withdrawal had been issued [...] but it subsequently transpired that the acting Brigade Major, Captain Ramsden, who unfortunately was suffering from shell shock at the time, through being blown from his horse, had personally given these orders while visiting these Battalions, and had not informed Brigade Headquarters.[45]

44 WO 95/2360.
45 WO 95/2360.

It would seem that Captain Ramsden had 'lost it'. On the following morning, both the Brigade Commander (Brigadier General Ingles) and Captain Ramsden, 'were unable to "carry on" any longer owing to sickness': both were replaced that day. This is not the first case in the war diaries where an officer who could not 'carry on' was medically evacuated. An ordinary soldier in similar circumstances would have been deemed to be either 'shirking', or displaying 'cowardice', for which he could have been court martialled. Be that as it may, something had to be done to help the men of the West Yorks in their exposed position, the situation being made no easier by the commanding officers of both 13/York and Lancaster and 18/DLI, having become casualties. While the replacement commanders of both battalions went forward to see if they could close the gap with the West Yorks, it was deemed 'impossible owing to the heavy machine gun fire from Moyennville, which was doubtless now occupied by the enemy'.[46] In spite of the heavy enemy fire, 13/York and Lancaster was ordered by division, at around 7 p.m., 'to attack and re-capture Moyennville'. Fortunately, this order was subsequently rescinded and both the York and Lancs and the DLI were redirected to dig in as close as they could get to the village.

On the morning of 27 March, the enemy attacked 'on the whole Divisional front', but this fell particularly heavily on the men of the West Yorks – the only one of the brigade's battalions in its correct position, albeit with their flanks 'in the air'. This battalion had faced a number of attacks on the previous day, which had left the men 'extremely exhausted'. By 4 p.m. (on the 27th), 'the enemy had worked round both flanks and had brought enfilade Machine Gun fire to bear on the position'. The situation of the West Yorks was now considered 'hopeless' and the survivors needed to scramble back to safety; 'only 4 officers and about 40 Other Ranks reached our lines'.[47] The Brigade report went on to praise the efforts made by the men of the West Yorks:

> There is no doubt that the gallant resistance of this Battalion in the face of great odds materially helped to save what was at one period a very critical situation. Although they had been almost annihilated, they had inflicted enormous losses on the enemy.

The West Yorks had been assisted by one company from 18/DLI, which also suffered heavily:

> The severity of the fighting can be imagined when it is stated that the casualties of this Company alone amounted to nearly 100, practically all of whom were killed or wounded.

46 WO 95/2360.
47 WO 95/2360, diary of operations, p.3.

The events of 27 March also serve to demonstrate a point made earlier in this book; soldiers in the same brigade, ostensibly involved in the same battle and separated by no more than a mile, can have a very different day. While 15/West Yorks and one company of 18/DLI were being severely mauled by the Germans the third battalion, 13/York and Lancaster, 'were not engaged during the day, and suffered very few losses'.

The next three days were relatively quiet; 'After his efforts of the previous days, the enemy was no doubt exhausted'. With the lull in operations, fresh drafts could be moved up to rebuild the depleted battalions before they were relieved on the night of 30/31 March. Since joining Third Army, the brigade had been forced to withdraw approximately 7,000 yards from their initial position around St. Leger and had suffered 1,108 casualties.

The German offensive on 21 March was a severe shock to the British Army and it is worth noting the reasons given by the official historian, and the battalion commander of 2/York and Lancaster, for the collapse that took place on that spring day. Edmonds is in no doubt that a primary cause was the over-extension of the British line:

> Never before had the British line been held with so few men and so few guns to the mile; and the reserves were wholly insignificant. […] It needed but a glance at the General Staff situation map […] to be filled with deep and lasting apprehension of the situation. [19 of the 21 divisions had been involved in the Passchendaele battles] in which they lost a large proportion of their best soldiers whose places had been filled, if filled at all, by raw drafts and transfers.[48]

The 16 Brigade war diary records Lieutenant Colonel Blunt's comments on why he believed 2/York and Lancaster were overrun by the attackers on that foggy morning in March:

1. The extremely heavy barrage.
2. The large numbers he [the Germans] employed.
3. The lack of training in open warfare of our men.
4. The tactics of the enemy in breaking in on certain fronts and then spreading outwards thus taking our defences in flank and rear.
5. The lack of counter attacks from behind at the crucial moments.
6. The men though game to fight were tired from the enormous amount of work they had been called upon to do.

Blunt highlights the tiredness of the troops as a result of their being constantly used on 'working parties' when they should have been resting. Edmonds, while stressing that the divisions had been filled by 'raw drafts' also commented on a failure of the

---

48 Edmonds, *1918, Vol. 1*, p.254.

training programme; 'Training in the conduct of retreat, and of a retreat extending over many days, never entered anyone's mind'.[49]

The German spring offensive, while not a total surprise to the British (Haig and others' comments are mentioned at the beginning of this chapter), it was certainly an unwelcome 'wake-up call'. In November 1917, Haig and Robertson had been scathing in their comments on the collapse of the Italian army at Caporetto in the face of an Austro-German assault. The Italian retreat drew forth chauvinistic comments from the British on the stoicism of the northern races, compared with the lack of fighting spirit of the Latin race. In March 1918, the rapid collapse of the Fifth Army front demonstrated that stoicism was not enough on its own.

During the morning of 22 March, Gough (commanding Fifth Army) recognised the extent of the breakthrough the enemy had made into his Battle Zone and feared that, with no real reinforcements, his army could be heavily defeated if he tried to hold on where he was, and if the enemy made a 'serious hostile attack'. Gough authorised his three Corps Commanders to 'fight [a] rear-guard action back to the forward line of [the] Rear Zone'.[50] Unfortunately, with communications breaking down during the retreat, and with corps commanders given the authority to make independent decisions, the army lost cohesion. Lieutenant General Sir Ivor Maxse (commanding XVIII Corps), having fallen back to the Somme, realised that having the river at his back was not a good position for an army in withdrawal, and so crossed to the west bank. In so doing a large gap developed between his left wing and the right of Lieutenant General Watts's XIX Corps to his north. The consequence was a ripple effect as XIX Corps and VII Corps to their left also fell back to keep their flanks covered. Once started, it was difficult to stop. Because each corps relied on those to its right and left to give flank protection, the fall back in Fifth Army now jeopardised V Corps in Third Army, which was having its own problems in the Flesquières Salient. Maxse's withdrawal across the Somme, and the consequent problems this caused, has come in for criticism.[51] Edmonds considered it 'over hasty' and included the jingoistic comment that it did not sit well with the British soldier, whose 'habit [was] to stand and fight it out – whatever the odds might be' and that the troops would consider this as a change to 'a habit of "skedaddle"'.[52] No mention of Italians and Caporetto, but no doubt Robertson would have agreed with the sentiment.

By the end of day, 23 March, not only had Fifth Army made a considerable withdrawal, largely as a result of Maxse's decision to pull back behind the Somme, but also a gap had opened between the left flank of Gough's army and the right of Byng's. This situation was caused by the late withdrawal of 47 Division from

49   Edmonds, *1918, Vol. 1*, p.39.
50   Harris, *Haig*, p.450.
51   Baynes, J., *Far From A Donkey. The Life of Sir Ivor Maxse* (London, Brassey's, 1995), Chapter 16.
52   Edmonds, *1918, Vol. 1*, p.302.

the Flesquières Salient (on the extreme right of Third Army), which allowed the Germans to get round that unit's right wing and open a three-mile gap between the armies of Byng and Gough. The following day Haig, in a meeting with Pétain, requested that the French concentrate as many of their forces as they could on the British right; it was important 'to keep the two Armies in touch. If this is lost and the Enemy comes in between us, then probably the British will be rounded up and driven into the sea!'[53] From his side, Pétain had orders to cover Paris at all costs, he told Haig that his priority now differed from that of the British C-in-C; it was 'to keep the French Armies together as one solid whole' and only secondly, if possible, 'maintain liaison with the British forces'.[54] A crisis of confidence was building between the two allies. There then followed (24 and 25 March) a disputed sequence of events resulting in a conference at Doullens on 26 March. Haig's account of the preliminaries differ in his original and his later diary: for those wishing to go further into the topic, as well as whether or not Haig gave the French the impression that he did not believe that he could hold Amiens, Harris is a good source.[55] Probably the most important outcome of the conference was the decision to charge General Foch with the co-ordination of the Allied armies on the Western front. The situation in March 1918 had brought home the need for more central direction of the fight against Germany.

Hindsight allows us to conclude that by 28 March the worst of the crisis was over, although German attacks would continue along the British front through the first two weeks of April. For Gough, the events of late March brought his career to a halt; too many voices were raised against him and he was replaced by Rawlinson. On 28 March the *Michael* phase of the German offensive was followed (in the Arras sector), by *Mars* and then further north by *Georgette*. This last phase of the offensive, *Georgette*, struck in the neighbourhood of Armentières, a sector of the front held by British and Portuguese troops. On 6 April, Haig made the note in his diary that a 'surprise attack was to be expected against the Portuguese' (who held positions near Armentières), but that 'First Army [under General Horne] is quite alive to these possibilities and is prepared to meet them'.[56] On 9 April, following an intense bombardment, the expected attack hit the Portuguese and British front between the La Bassée Canal and Armentières; 'Thick mist made observation impossible'.[57] The Portuguese line did not hold; Haig stated that they 'ran away',[58] taking their guns with them. In the opinion of the British C-in-C, this ally was not a fighter, the 'state' of them was 'reported as bad', and the officers did not look after the men in the way that young British subalterns were expected to: 'They are very discontented chiefly because their officers have

---

53 Sheffield and Bourne, *Haig*, p.391.
54 Edmonds, *1918, Vol. 1*, p.449.
55 Harris, *Haig*, pp.453-8.
56 Sheffield and Bourne, *Haig*, p.398.
57 Sheffield and Bourne, *Haig*, p.399.
58 Sheffield and Bourne, *Haig*, p.400.

had leave to Portugal, but no men have gone'.⁵⁹ The difficulty was what to do with them? As Haig was aware, Britain did not want 'to quarrel with Portugal because they have many suitable submarine bases for the Enemy!' His problem as C-in-C was that he believed the Portuguese officers and their troops to be 'useless for this class of fighting'. Senior British commanders were frequently chauvinistic in their assessment of the fighting qualities of their allies. The line had to be held 'so it was arranged to relieve them with British troops tonight!'

Among the troops sent to recover the situation were the 1/4th and 1/5th (York and Lancaster) in 148 Brigade, 49 Division, although for this operation the brigade was assigned to 25 Division. On 10 April, they were to be 'flung into the breach caused by the Portuguese Army's collapse. We at once packed up and shortly after 9 a.m. were in lorries on the road to Neuve Eglise'.⁶⁰ On the same day as they left to plug the gap in the line, the 1/4th diary recorded how few of the original battalion members were still with them:

> On this day there were Lt Col D.S. Branson DSO, MC and 80 OR who came out with the Battn. 13th April 1915 and who have served continually with the Battn.⁶¹

Five days previously, the diarist had noted that the battalion strength was 41 officers and 939 ORs; of these 980, only 81 had sailed from England just three years earlier. On 14 April, Lt. Col. Branson would be wounded and leave the battalion; there were now none of the original officers left. Captain G. Unsworth took over temporary command of the battalion until he was replaced by Captain R.E. Wilson who returned to 1/4th on 22 April. Wilson must have been given the brevet rank of Lt. Col., as he used that rank when he signed the subsequent monthly diary entries.

The brigade reached the area of Neuve Eglise in the early afternoon, and found that there were still a few civilians in the village and 'one estaminet was actually open and doing a roaring trade in beer'⁶² – this was in spite of the fact that the Germans were only a few miles away to the east. While the French inn-keeper was ignoring the closeness of the enemy guns, some German soldiers were not giving their all for the Kaiser. The history of the Hallamshires notes an amusing incident in which one of their patrols returned to Neuve Eglise with some prisoners:

> Four Germans who had been found in the charge of one very sleepy Tommy. This man had removed his boots, puttees, and socks, and was warming his feet before a wood fire in a ruined house, with the four Huns sitting or lying on the floor

---

59 Sheffield and Bourne, *Haig*, p.400.
60 Grant, *Hallamshires*, p.106.
61 WO 95/2805, diary 1/4th York & Lancs.
62 Grant, *Hallamshires*, p.107.

about him; his rifle and bayonet were in a corner of the room, and the Germans were perfectly at liberty to kill their guard and walk back to their lines had they been so inclined![63]

Amusing as the incident was, the time the two battalions spent in the vicinity of Neuve Eglise was one of almost constant contact with the enemy. During one particularly fierce engagement, on 16 April, the battalion commander of 1/5 York and Lancaster noted an incident that, regrettably, was probably not unique:

> On approaching the farms [which the battalion was attacking] several of the enemy attempted to surrender but they were not given the opportunity and I believe some of the slightly wounded hit by covering fire of H.L.I. [Highland Light Infantry] Lewis Guns were overtaken and disposed of before they could get clear.[64]

In the first five days in this sector the 1/4th had 131 men either killed or missing, with a further 173 wounded. On 26 April alone, 4 officers were killed, 2 wounded and 1 missing, together with 17 of the men dead, 9 missing and 65 wounded – 98 casualties in the one day. Their sister battalion, 1/5th, lost even more between 11-30 April; 7 officers killed, 21 wounded and 1 missing, while among the men 99 were dead, 438 wounded and 52 missing – a battalion total of 618.[65]

One historian asserts that 'Haig's mental state was now [9/10 April] as stressed as it had been at any time since he became commander-in-chief'.[66] His pleas to Foch for the French to take over some of his line were not having the desired effect and he was raising the spectre of Britain being unable to 'continue the battle'. With the loss of Armentières, the move of the Germans around the south of Ypres and the threat to the Channel ports, the British C-in-C had again to exhort Foch to move French divisions to the area between St. Omer and Dunkirk. This plea, like the earlier one in March, was rejected by Foch. On 11 April, Haig issued his 'backs to the wall' order of the day. It was an exhortation to the soldiers under his command, as well as a statement to the people at home, of how hard the army was fighting. He demanded that every position should be held 'to the last man', there could be no retirement; with their 'backs to the wall [ ] each one of us must fight on to the end'.[67] And the soldiers did fight. Although there were more German attacks to come (Mount Kemmel and a tank battle near Villers-Bretonneux), 'Ludendorff finally called off the Lys battle on 30 April.[68]

---

63 Grant, *Hallamshires*, p.107.
64 WO 95/2805, narrative of operations, 10-19 April.
65 Figures extracted from the war diaries of 1/4th & 1/5th battalions.
66 Harris, *Haig*, p.469.
67 Sheffield, *The Chief*, p.283.
68 Sheffield, *The Chief*, p.285.

The British Army, and the folks at home, had had one hell of a scare in late March and through the month of April. Much ground had been lost but the Germans had failed to capitalise on the initial success of their spring offensives. By August, it would be the British who were taking the initiative with their attack at Amiens and the subsequent 'Hundred Days'. Despite the myth of the 'stab in the back', the German army was militarily defeated in 1918, which lead to the signing of the November Armistice.

13

Kicking away the props – Salonika and Italy

In these centenary years (2014-18), the focus of the commemorative events is almost exclusively directed at the Western front. This fixation is understandable, after all, that is where the majority of British soldiers fought and died. France and Flanders are also the locus of most of the war poems and memoirs through which the British public have formed their views of the conflict. As much as Lloyd George wanted to see the 'props' kicked from under Germany, the war was not going to be won other than by the defeat of the German army – and that would be on the Western front. The British prime minister may have stated (correctly) that all of the sideshows 'ended in victory before our triumph on the 'favoured' Western Front',[1] but that was part and parcel of his criticism of his military advisors. When it came to winning the war:

> Neither Lloyd George nor any other well-placed civilian managed to propose an actual area of operations which seemed to offer a better prospect than the Western Front.[2]

To view the conflict only through the prism of the Somme and Passchendaele is to forget that we call it a *World* War. Additionally, we do a disservice to those men whose 'corner of a foreign field' is hundreds of miles from France and Flanders.

From the perspective of this book, the fronts in Salonika and Italy also warrant inclusion because of the involvement of battalions of the York and Lancaster Regiment. Sadly, the involvement of British units in these theatres has been largely ignored in British histories of the war. This author's account of the British in Italy[3] was the first since the early 1990s, while Wakefield and Moody claimed that their

---

1 Lloyd George, D., *War Memoirs;* 6 (London, 1934), pp.3,230-1.
2 Wilson, T., and R. Prior, 'British Decision-making, 1917: Lloyd George, The Generals and Passchendaele', in Cecil, H., and P.H. Liddle (eds), *Facing Armageddon. The First World War Experienced* (Barnsley, Pen & Sword, 1996), p.94.
3 Dillon, *Allies are a tiresome lot.*

book on the British in Macedonia was the first dedicated to the Salonika campaign (in the English language), in 'thirty-nine years'.[4] In 2009, Alan Palmer published his welcome foray into the experience of the British soldiers in the Macedonian campaign with the comment that 'I fail to understand why so little attention has been given to their achievement or honour paid to their sacrifice'.[5] Unfortunately the 'Westerners' have held sway in the histories of the war, as they did in its prosecution.

The men of 1/York and Lancaster would have been at a loss to explain why they were sent to Macedonia, and what that had to do with a war against the Germans. In 1915, the Allies were concerned that Serbia, the 'cause' of the war, could not withstand further attacks by Austria-Hungary. It had been hoped that Bulgaria might be persuaded to join the Entente but having failed to defeat Turkey in the Dardanelles, the Allies did not strike the Bulgarians as being the right option for them. By mid-September, it looked as though the only way to prevent Bulgarian intervention against Serbia was to land Anglo-French forces in the Balkans, and the only way to do that was via the deep-water harbour at Salonika, in neutral Greece.

Although there were political arguments in favour of the move, opinions among the British and French commanders were split over the value of sending troops to Macedonia. Eventually, after much wrangling, agreement was reached; units would be sent to Salonika in February 1915. The timing was not good; the shelling of the Turkish forts at the Dardanelles was due to begin on 11 February. Bad weather delayed the naval bombardment, with the result that the British were not in a position to demonstrate their resolve to the Greeks. It had been a prerequisite of Greek cooperation that the Rumanians should threaten the Bulgarian border. However, the Rumanians would not move until they felt confident of an Allied victory – the Italians were not the only ones who might have been accused of 'rushing to the side of the victors'. Who knows how events might have turned out if the Allied force had landed at Salonika in February rather than October – historians love "what ifs". Palmer stated that 'the balance of the war would have been drastically altered'[6] as the Anglo-French troops would have been an 'act of reinsurance' rather than one of 'succour', as would later be the case. Greek politics of the time are not a topic for this book but their vicissitudes did influence the British and French in their Salonika operations. The Greek Prime Minister, Eleftherios Venizelos (who was in favour of working with the Allies), was forced out of office by the General Staff in March 1915 and replaced by a pro-German government; he was back in office in August of that year. The Greek position was further complicated by the differing views of the king and his prime minister towards the country's active involvement in the conflict. King Constantine wanted

---

4   Wakefield, A., and S. Moody, *Under the Devil's Eye. The British Military Experience in Macedonia 1915-18* (Barnsley, Pen & Sword, 2011 Kindle edition), locn.93.
5   Palmer, A., *The Gardeners of Salonika. The Macedonian Campaign 1915-1918* (London, Faber and Faber, 2009), p.6.
6   Palmer, *The Gardeners of Salonika*, p.27.

Greece to take a neutral stance while Venezelos was all for assisting the Entente. The prime minister lost and was out of office again until October 1915.

With political uncertainty in Greece, a failure to achieve any kind of success at Gallipoli and the need for a September offensive in France (at Loos) there is little wonder that Robertson was vehemently against any entanglement in the Balkans. Robertson later summed up his views on Salonika:

> Of all the problems which brought soldiers and statesmen into conference during the years 1915-1917 the Salonika Expedition was at once the most persistent, exasperating, and unfruitful.[7]

By autumn 1915, the Germans had decided that Serbia had to be dealt with and to that end an agreement was reached with Bulgaria for a combined operation to encircle Serbia. The French and British now had to send troops to Salonika, though it would take weeks for them to arrive. Had Serbia been blessed with a coastline then the machinations with Greece would not have been so necessary. However, with the pro-German Constantine having won out over Venizelos, any landing at Salonika would now be against the wishes of a neutral Greek government. These niceties were pushed to one side. The Allies believed that they had a right in international law to send a military force to Greece. That right was based on an early nineteenth century treaty that had been drawn up when Greece won independence from Turkey. Under the treaty, and after agreement among themselves, Britain, France and Russia had the right to land troops in Greece in case of violent upheaval in the Balkans.[8] In the event, the Allies were late to the party; the first Allied troops began disembarking 'just fifteen hours before the [German] artillery opened up on Belgrade'.[9]

The first British troops to arrive had the relatively short sea journey from Gallipoli. The troops from 10 Division had taken part in the Suvla landings in August only weeks previously and they were not off to a good start. It was late autumn in Macedonia and the men arrived dressed for warmer climes in their summer khaki. Their dispatch from the peninsula had been hurried and 'the whole landing assumed the unmistakable air of an afterthought'.[10] The weather in Salonika was very wet and the troops' misery was compounded by their camps being set up on marshy ground. The mood of the men was not improved when they found themselves practicing drill and smartness rather than being allowed to wash their clothes and keep themselves clean – 'we were well trained but filthy'.[11] Comments on the town of Salonika were also less than complimentary; 'the place absolutely stank'.[12] As well as 10 Division, the 28th was sent from France,

---

7   Woodward, *Robertson*, p.20.
8   Palmer, *The Gardeners of Salonika*, p.11.
9   Palmer, *The Gardeners of Salonika*, p.34.
10 Palmer, *The Gardeners of Salonika*, p.13.
11 Wakefield and Moody, *The Devil's Eye*, locn.199.
12 Wakefield and Moody, *The Devil's Eye*, locn.334.

including 1/York and Lancaster (83 Brigade). The battalion began their journey, by train, on 23 October; 23 officers, 709 ORs, 65 horses and 8 mules. The following day they stopped at Mâcon where the men 'had tea and were allowed to go to the buffet. Officers dined at [the] buffet';[13] a subtle difference between the ranks in the dining arrangements. At 5 p.m. on 25 October, they arrived at Marseilles and two hours later 'marched away from station to quay. Streets crowded with applauding populace'. By 8.30 p.m., they were embarking on SS *Bornu* for their journey to Salonika. The troops were not sailors and when they encountered rough seas in the Gulf of Lyon 'some officers and many men [were] incapacitated'.

This early foray into the theatre garnered little success. A move to Lake Doiran, in which they saw little of the Bulgars, resulted in a general retreat in December. The British and the French were forced back by the weather, Bulgarian attacks, mountainous terrain (with which they were unfamiliar), a lack of mechanical transport and desperately poor roads. Many of the British were suffering from frostbite and diarrhoea and by 14 December General Maurice Sarrail (French commander) and General Sir Bryan Mahon (British commander), had agreed on a complete withdrawal to Salonika.

Although the British now had troops on the ground in the Balkans, the government was having second thoughts over the whole project. At the Calais conference on 4 December, the British Prime Minister (Herbert Asquith), no doubt at the bidding of Robertson, stated that the retention of a force at Salonika was 'from a military point of view dangerous and likely to lead to a disaster. [The British military advisers] cannot therefore agree to its continued retention, and are of the opinion that preparations should be made without delay for evacuation'.[14] Under pressure from the French, Russian, Italian and Serbian representatives, Britain stepped back from its position and agreed to remain. Robertson (he became CIGS on 21 December) made his view clear to Haig when he stated that he was using 14 Division in France 'as a lever for clearing out of Salonica [sic]'.[15] In a letter to Mahon he went further; 'I am not out for any operations in the Balkans. […] Such operations would be unsound […] the day they are sanctioned I shall leave the War Office. […] I know where a decision will be got, and that certainly will not be in the Balkans'.[16] The operations did start, but Robertson did not leave over that decision.

With the build-up at Salonika, the Allies had some 150,000 troops in place, five British divisions and three French. Among the British troops were the men of 1/York and Lancaster. They arrived in the port of Alexandria (Egypt) at 10 a.m. on 3 November and after some confusion, the battalion disembarked three days later. The troops had a month of drill and training at Sidi Bishr, before embarking for Greece on 2 December. After a slow transit, they arrived in Salonika harbour on 7 December.

13   TNA WO 95/2275/3, war diary, 1/York & Lancs.
14   Palmer, *The Gardeners of Salonika*, p.49.
15   Woodward, *Robertson*, p.24.
16   Woodward, *Robertson*, p.38.

One thing a soldier learns quickly is that he will be 'buggered about' by the system: with Salonika enveloped in thick fog, which persisted for days, they did not disembark until 14 December. Once ashore they spent three days digging trenches around Salonika camp before moving to Givezne on 20 December. The battalion diary gives us a description of their new environs:

> A village of 250 houses lying in and on the sides of a valley at the confluence of two streams, about a kilometre east of the Salonika-Seres road. The inhabitants are entirely Greek – the village never contained any Bulgarians & all Turks have left the village since it became Greek territory. The Mayor (Muchtari) & the two priests expressed friendly sentiments and the former agreed to all our demands without making any difficulties. There are no roads possible to transport thro' the village, but the river bed might be employed in dry weather. There is a plentiful supply of good drinking water in the village.[17]

The point has already been made that King Constantine was pro-German and it should have come as no surprise that the Greek government resented the presence of the Anglo-French troops, frequently putting obstacles in their way. Although the battalion diary refers to the friendliness of the locals, the Greek authorities tried to prevent army patrols. On 26 December one of their 'Yeomanry' patrols was stopped by the Greeks, as were two French cars. The Greeks needed some persuasion that Allied patrols were carrying out reconnaissance on Bulgarian movements, not on the Greeks.

As in France and Flanders, so in the Balkans there was an 'argument' surrounding control of the Allied forces. The British troops, under Mahon, were formed into two corps; XII (including 28 Division and 1/York and Lancaster) and XVI. Overall command was given to Sarrail, but his control of Mahon was limited to the defence of Salonika. Any proposal for offensive use of the British troops had to be referred to London. With Serbs added to the Anglo-French contingent, Sarrail (a "wrong' un" according to Robertson[18]) commanded close to 300,000 troops – why not use them, asked the French. With his habitual focus on the Western front, Robertson was dead-set against any such use. He regretted that, at the Paris conference in late March, he had been unable to 'bring the divisions away'. He had little faith in the French commander:

> I feel that this fellow Sarrail will get us into a mess there before he has done, and I hope that Mahon will be careful and not lose any more British lives than possible in foolhardy enterprises.[19]

---

17   TNA WO 95/4914, war diary, 1/York & Lancs.
18   Woodward, *Robertson*, p.38.
19   Woodward, *Robertson*, p.45.

By mid to late April (in spite of Robertson's opposition), Britain had agreed to the participation of its troops in offensive moves up to the Serbo-Greek border. In the following month, Mahon was sent to Egypt and control of the British Salonika Force was taken over by Milne from XVI Corps. The British had also put diplomatic efforts into persuading the Rumanians to take part in the conflict alongside the Allies but, in a similar fashion to Italy, that country held out for the best deal, only joining in August 1916. By the time the Allies had their act together the Bulgarians had launched their own offensive.

During the time that the British were in Macedonia (Map 18) they were involved in numerous actions, some large (around Lake Doiran in late 1916), but many of them small and localised. The soldiers' biggest enemies were boredom and mosquitoes. Dismal hours were spent on guard duty at isolated points along the front; a world of 'goatherds and grasshoppers'.[20] The British suffered particularly badly from malaria as they were frequently based in the swampy valley of the River Struma. On one day, 16 October 1917, they had 21,434 hospital cases, approximately 20% of the total force.[21] In the April of that year, the Allied offensive had lasted only 12 days, but resulted in 14,000 casualties for no ground gained. Little wonder that the men resented Georges Clemenceau's derogatory reference to them as 'the gardeners of Salonika'.[22] One such action in which 1/York and Lancaster participated took place on 11 October 1916 and while it was small and localised, the battalion took casualties. Because of the prevalence of malaria the nominal strength of the battalion was drastically reduced, only 309 men from the battalion were fit to make the assault that was planned to follow the artillery barrage. While troops did get close to the enemy wire, and one company did manage to drive them out of one trench, there was no real success as the Bulgarians had brought up reinforcements, causing the British to withdraw in the face of heavy machine gun fire. During the action, Lieutenant Walker was injured, shot through the chest; 'one SB [stretcher bearer] was killed and 4 wounded trying to get him away. Finally he had to be left behind'. Walker may have survived, as there is no record of him on the CWGC site. One officer who did die was Captain Bedford, attached from 3/York and Lancaster. He was wounded near the enemy trenches 'but could not be brought back'. Bedford has no known grave and is remembered on the Doiran Memorial as having died on 12 October. Of the 309 men who went into the action, 98 were casualties; 6 officers and 92 men. The attack was supported by an armoured car but this was deemed to have been of 'very little use'. Although it did fire off a few rounds the NCO in charge of it 'said he could not remain stationary long owing to the tyres and heating of engine and machine gun'. As the battalion adjutant commented, 'the tyres should be solid to be of any use'. Armoured warfare still had a long way to go.

20 Palmer, *The Gardeners of Salonika*, p.143.
21 Palmer, *The Gardeners of Salonika*, p.142.
22 Palmer, *The Gardeners of Salonika*, p.145.

For those of us who have not had to fight an infantry war it can be difficult to imagine what it was like for individual soldiers, occasionally the battalion war diaries record a small vignette that gives us a little insight. One such involved 1/York and Lancaster on 13 May 1917. On that day two stretcher bearers attempted to retrieve a wounded man who lay 50 yards from the enemy wire; they were driven back by machine gun fire. Two days later, the men made another unsuccessful attempt, followed by a further two men on 17 May. In the early hours of the following day, a final, unsuccessful, attempt was made. The wounded man presumably died, he had been there more than four days, but there is one further reference to him. At 8 a.m. on 18 May the diary noted that the enemy had joined up three shell holes behind the wounded man; 'Enemy must have been using him as a decoy'. It is difficult to imagine what the man felt for those days before he died, or what his comrades felt when they realised how the enemy had taken advantage of him.

For the men of 1/York and Lancaster, Salonika in 1918 was a time of constant movement, boredom and malaria, but the British could still hold horse shows even under these circumstances. In June, the battalion provided men to set up the Divisional Horse Show at Dugout Hill. In the competition, their Commanding Officer entered his charger and won first prize in 'Class II Officer's Light Weight'. As in France, working parties were a regular part of the men's routine:

> August 19th to September 8th. Quiet with very few casualties. [...] Towards end of period men were worked very hard with RE fatigues on forward dumps and water supplies. Also gaps had to be cut and marked in our wire and paths marked out up to these gaps. Men's health obviously deteriorated.[23]

The work on the wire was in preparation for the offensive, which would bring the war in Macedonia to a close.

Overall command of the forces in the theatre had changed. In June 1918, General Franchet d'Espérey (Desperate Frankie to the British soldiers) replaced Sarrail. As well as being much criticised by Robertson, Haig also had little time for the outgoing French commander. In October 1916 he had noted in his diary that, 'it is not 'men' who are wanted at Salonika, but a 'man'! From all accounts, Sarrail, the French GOC there is quite useless'.[24] On 10 September 1918, d'Espérey received the go-ahead for a general offensive on his front; the artillery bombardment was planned to start four days later. For 1/York and Lancaster, the month prior to the attack had been one of routine; most of the time taken up with training and small patrols. At the end of August the battalion reported a strength of 17 officers and 528 ORs, 'present with battalion', while a further 196 officers and men were 'on command' for the battalion, but away on other duties – 14 were sick and 89 on leave. In preparation for the coming

23 WO 95/4914.
24 Sheffield and Bourne, *Haig*, p.248.

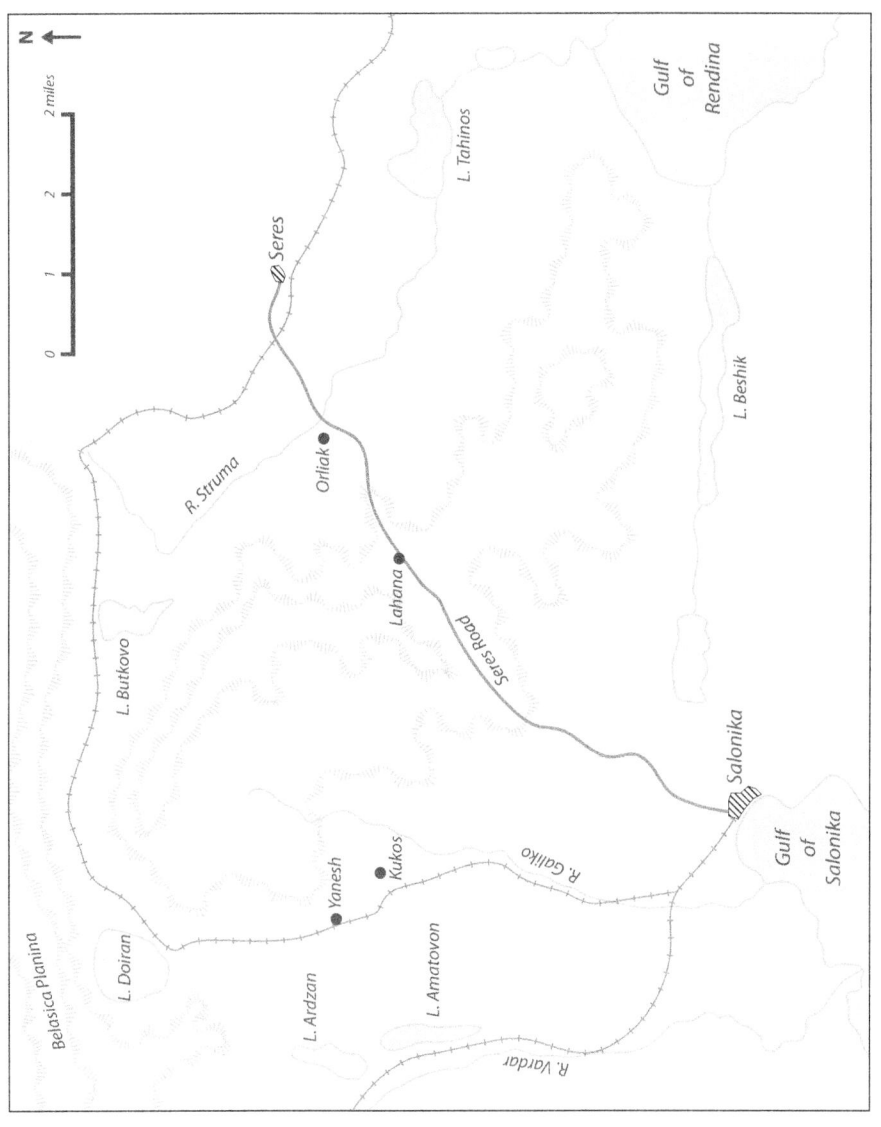

Map 18 Macedonia – Salonika and Lake Doiran.

Soldiers of 1/York and Lancaster manning trenches on the 'Birdcage Line' defences outside Salonika in 1916. (IWM Q 31608)

offensive, the battalion was on the move from late on 10 September until it arrived at Arakli at 10 p.m. on the 13th.[25] At that point, there were 15 officers and 419 ORs 'present with battalion'.

The first mention of the attack in the battalion diary is on the 18th; 'Attack commenced both sides of LAKE DOIRAN'. However, subsequent entries, up to the 23rd, indicate that the men spent all their time on the move, with no mention of any action. At 10 a.m. on 23 September, the battalion received orders to be on the right of the coming assault on Blaga Planina, a line of hills north and north-east of Lake Doiran. The attack began at 14:00, and by 19:00, the diary reported 'objective gained after slight opposition. Casualties nil'. That was the extent of the action for 1/York and Lancaster. The rest of the month was spent on the move, on difficult roads, some of which they had to stop and repair themselves. The constant marching around the rugged countryside must have worn down the men; but it was coming to

25 WO 95/4914.

an end. On 30 September 1918, at 04:10 the battalion was 'loading up mules preparatory to moving off when message received from Brigade – All operations cancelled; Convention signed with Bulgaria'.²⁶ Their strength was down to 18 officers and 315 ORs 'present with battalion'; a further 244 were 'on command' of which 84 were on leave in the UK and 63 were sick.

Although the York and Lancaster battalion had little involvement, the Allied offensive had been successful. After the artillery bombardment had opened, to the west of the British positions, the joint Franco-Serbian attack drove the Bulgarians back. The warning order for the British assault, to go ahead on the 18th, arrived in the form of a cryptic message; '508 bottles of beer will be sent to you' – zero hour was to be before dawn, at eight minutes past five.²⁷ XII Corps was attacking on territory it was familiar with from previous actions; the Coronné and the Devil's Eye – the latter so named because of its oversight of the British positions. XVI Corps was advancing to the east of Lake Doiran, towards Blaga Planina. The attacks around Lake Doiran produced little gain for great loss. The courage of the soldiers who carried out the attacks, in extremely difficult conditions, 'passed unnoticed by a public dazzled with spectacular triumphs elsewhere'²⁸ – the march to victory (the 'Hundred Days'), was underway in France and Flanders. The German and Bulgarian commanders believed that their best plan was to draw the Allies forward and then engulf them. To that end they began an orderly retreat, but one that was harried by British aircraft.

With the enemy pulling back, the way was open for d'Espérey's forces to advance, prompting his message of 22 September that 'The enemy is in retreat on the whole front'. The second largest Serbian town, Skopje, fell to a French colonial brigade on 28 September and as we have seen from the battalion diary, the Bulgarians ceased fighting on 30 September. By this time the cold, wet Balkan autumn had set in and the diary of 1/York and Lancaster records many days of cold marching; '7 October. Rained all night. Men all wet through'. Then a few days later; 'Two very heavy storms during night. Camp nearly under water'. Although hostilities had ceased on their front, the time had not come for them to go home. Like many of their colleagues in other theatres, demobilisation was a slow process and many would find themselves in an 'army of occupation' until 1919. On 31 October, they received the news that an armistice had been signed with Turkey. It would be followed on 4 November by the Austrians.

The cessation of hostilities on the Macedonian front was more important than the 'gardeners' are given credit for. Hindenburg commented that; 'As a result of the collapse of the Macedonian front' there was no longer a prospect 'of forcing peace on the enemy'.²⁹

26 WO 95/4914.
27 Palmer, *The Gardeners of Salonika*, p.205.
28 Palmer, *The Gardeners of Salonika*, p.211.
29 Palmer, *The Gardeners of Salonika*, p.226.

Macedonia had been a hard few years for the men of 1/York and Lancaster, not because of the intensity of the fighting, but because of the climate, the constant movement from one camp to another, the boredom and the sickness. In France, in 1918, there were 440.47 battle casualties for every 1,000 men in the army; in Macedonia, the equivalent number was 59.01. In the case of non-battle casualties, there was a complete reversal; 595.16 in France against 1,195.14 in Macedonia.[30] The incidence of illness as a factor in 'inefficiency' was disproportionately higher among the Salonika troops than among those on the Western front. In France and Flanders there were 1.4 men admitted for some form of illness for every battle casualty; in Macedonia there were 20.3;[31] more than 14 times as many. The culprit was malaria. In 1918, for every 1,000 men on the ration strength of the British army at Salonika, 459 were admitted to hospital with the disease. In an analysis of 1,043,653 medical records (a sample of complete records from all theatres), Macedonia accounted for 42.4% of the cases of malaria from all theatres.[32] The soldiers' experience of the war in the Balkans was quite different from that of their colleagues on the Western front.

With an armistice in the Balkans, the men of 1/York and Lancaster might have expected that they would be preparing to return home to their families, and to resume civilian employment; they were soon to be disabused of that. On 2 November, the battalion had orders 'to be ready to move at 4 hours notice'.[33] The battalion was bound for the Dardanelles but the war diary does not record the mood of the men on learning that they were not to be sailing for England. After their withdrawal in January 1916, the British no doubt wished to make a point to the Turks; the latter had ended up on the losing side. On 8 November 1918, 18 officers and 399 men embarked on H.M.S. Prince Edward, they entered the Dardanelles on the morning of the 10th and disembarked that afternoon. Two days later the Allied fleet 'entered and sailed up the Dardanelles'; something they had been denied by the Turks three years earlier. At this point, we will leave the Balkans for another Mediterranean 'sideshow' – Italy.

In the last weeks of peace, as Europe came to terms with the idea that it would be plunged into conflict over Serbia, Italy was a member of the Triple Alliance alongside Germany and Austria-Hungary. Under the terms of that treaty, Italy should have been consulted before Austria made a move against Serbia. As this did not happen, the Italian government could claim that there was no *casus foederis*, and so they declared Italy to be neutral.[34] In the ensuing months the Allies, especially Britain's Foreign Secretary (Sir Edward Grey), worked hard to convince Italy to join the Entente. Having played both sides against each other for the best deal, Italy finally declared war against Austria in May 1915; a similar declaration against Germany had to wait

---

30 Mitchell, *Medical Services*, p.167, Table 2 and p.187, Table 3.
31 Mitchell, *Medical Services*, p.169, Table 6 and p.189, Table 7.
32 Mitchell, *Medical Services*, p.291, Table 13.
33 WO 95/4914.
34 The background to this decision and the tensions it caused are explored in more detail in *Dillon, Allies are a Tiresome lot*, Chapter 1.

another twelve months. Throughout the war, senior British commanders and politicians criticised Italy's motives and commitment. There was no existential threat to Italy in August 1914; the country's leadership took the country to war for territorial gain – *Italia irredenta*; to regain the Trentino and Trieste. As the war progressed, so Italian claims increased only to be met by the charge that the Italian army was not doing enough to assist the Allies. British commanders were free with their racial stereotyping of Italians as poor fighters and that consequently their efforts did not warrant the territorial claims made by their government.

The criticism of the Italians came mainly from those, like Robertson, who saw any front other than that in France and Flanders as a distraction from the main aim – the defeat of the German army. While the tactics of General Cadorna (Italian Commander in Chief) can be questioned, the involvement of the Italian army was beneficial to the Allies. In the early months of the war, the French divisions, which had been deployed to meet any Italian move towards France (as planned under the Triple Alliance), became available for the Battle of the Marne, so halting the German advance in late 1914. Additionally, Italian divisions tied up Austro-Hungarian forces on the River Isonzo, thus making them unavailable for the Russian or Western fronts. Comments made regarding Italian fighting qualities were unfair to the Italian soldier. Measured as a percentage of the population, Italy had as many men killed as Britain – 1.6%.[35] As a result of Cadorna's many, abortive attritional assaults on the Isonzo front, Italian troops died there in their thousands. Lord Cavan, who commanded the British expeditionary force in Italy, considered the Italians to be good soldiers, but badly led by their commanders.

During 1916 and 1917, Cadorna made many requests for Britain to send troops and guns to support his offensives. In Robertson's opinion, the Italian commander was constantly exaggerating the size of the Austrian forces opposing him, as well as raising the spectre of German divisions being deployed to the Italian front. Robertson considered the Italians to be over-awed by the reputation of the German army; in a letter to Sir Henry Wilson, he made the comment that they were a 'rotten lot' who should have been capable of defending their own country.[36] In November 1917, he resented the need to send 'our good soldiers to look after their wretched country';[37] he was not shy of making his views known regarding the Italians. However, whether Robertson liked it or not, Italy was a member of the Entente and it would not be good if, at some time in the future, the country was defeated and had to sign a separate peace. Plans had to be laid for the eventuality that Britain and France might have to send divisions to the Italian front. In April 1917, Robertson sent Brigadier Crowe to Italy to draw up contingency plans for such a move.[38]

---

35   Dillon, *Allies are a Tiresome Lot*, p.30.
36   Dillon, *Allies are a Tiresome Lot*, p.35.
37   Woodward, *Robertson*, p.258.
38   TNA WO 158/23, memo Robertson to Haig, 5 April 1917.

In the early hours of 24 October 1917, Cadorna's army on the Isonzo was overwhelmed by an Austro-German attack. Criticism can be justly levelled at Cadorna for over-manning his frontline trenches (sacrificing defence in depth) and for poor communication between him, his Staff Officers and the commanders in the field. There were particular issues between Cadorna and his commander of Second Army, Lieutenant General Luigi Capello. Following the break-through, the Italian army was forced into a general retreat, only halting when it came to the River Piave.[39] The time had come for Anglo-French support to be sent to Italy. However, the Allies considered Cadorna to be a liability and his replacement was a prerequisite for any deployment of French or British troops. The new Italian Commander in Chief was Lieutenant General Armando Diaz.

While the Italians were retreating, Lloyd George told Robertson that Britain should support its ally in spite of the latter's view that there was no 'military necessity' for such a move.[40] In response to the Prime Minister's decision the War office ordered two divisions (Haig chose the 23rd and 41st) to form the Italian Expeditionary Force (IEF) under the command of Lord Cavan, commanding XIV Corps. Within days it was decided that the IEF was too small and a further three divisions (the 5th, 7th and 48th) were added. The IEF, at five divisions, was considered too big a command for Cavan and General Plumer (reluctantly) was moved from Haig's Second Army at Passchendaele to command the British troops in Italy. In spite of this change, Cavan remained with the IEF and re-took command in 1918 when two divisions (and Plumer) were sent back to France as a result of the German spring offensive in March of that year. Two of the battalions in the initial deployment were 8 and 9/York and Lancaster, both in 23 Division; we last met them during Third Ypres (Passchendaele).

The soldiers who served with the IEF had a quite different experience in Italy from that which they had endured in France and Flanders. All the divisions had arrived from the Western front, enabling them to make a direct comparison between that and the Italian theatre.[41] Almost to a man, they found that the front was much quieter on the Piave than it had been in France. One young officer remarked:

> It is deliciously amusing to read the daily newspaper reports about "intense artillery activity all along the Italian front". I was watching about 12 miles of front yesterday for two hours and didn't see a shell burst the whole time.[42]

---

39   For an excellent account of the Italian Army in WW1; Gooch, J., *The Italian Army and The First World War* (Cambridge, CUP, 2014).
40   Dillon, *Allies are a Tiresome Lot*, p.46.
41   The differences are explored in depth in; Dillon, *Allies are a Tiresome Lot*.
42   Cotton, V.E., Private Papers, IWM Doc. 93/25/1, part 2, p.146.

It did not take the men long to realise that they stood a much better chance of surviving the war on the Italian front; far fewer men were being killed because of the lower intensity of the conflict. In France there were 5 casualties for every 9 men deployed; in Italy that number dropped to 1 for every 21 men involved, the lowest in any theatre of the war. Because soldiers ran the risk of being directed to other units on their return from leave one wrote that he would rather 'forfeit all leave than go back there [France] again. I've seen quite as much as I want to see of that country. But, here, things are very different. It's like one long holiday'.[43] The war diaries of the various battalions in the IEF reflect some of that 'relaxed' atmosphere. Their entries for the time in France are concentrated on 'the war' while the months in Italy give a much fuller picture of time spent on sports, entertainment and activities less directly involved with 'fighting'.

Before leaving France, the men were given no indication of where they were moving to; one soldier wrote that they had entrained for 'oonoesware' [sic] and it was only when they got to Toulon on 10 November that 'we knew that Italy was our destination'.[44] For troops who (only a few short weeks earlier), had been in the mud of Passchendaele, the change of scene was very welcome. The mood of the men can be gauged by the items the official censor noted in soldiers' letters home, and which were included in his report to the War Office: 'On the whole, Tommy is not displeased with the change of scene'; the men thought that Italy 'was much better than Ypres'; the war on the Italian front was 'Child's play here compared with Belgium'. The whole was summed up in one letter from a soldier in 2/King's Own Scottish Borderers:

> It's a real holiday here, the best war I have been in. Our billets are good, the wine is fair, the weather grand and the people treat us A1. What could be better?[45]

The change of scenery from Flanders to Italy was enough to make the transport down there bearable. While the officers travelled in reasonable comfort on the trains, the men spent the five-day journey in cattle-trucks, each capable of carrying 8 horses or 40 men. The journey was slow, with stops at pre-arranged *haltes-repas* for meals, hot tea and latrines. Norman Gladden, a private in 23 Division (along with the men of the York and Lancaster battalion), was carried away by 'glimpses of the peaks of the Maritime Alps towering beyond, and vineyards and orchards filled with vines and fig and palm and many sub-tropical plants, which were new to me'.[46] It would all have seemed very 'exotic' to those men from the hard industrial cities of the English midlands.

---

43   Hardie, Private Papers, report Feb-July, 1918.
44   Dillon, *Allies are a Tiresome Lot*, p.50.
45   Dillon, *Allies are a Tiresome Lot*, pp.50-1.
46   Gladden, N., *Across the Piave* (London, HMSO, 1971), p.6.

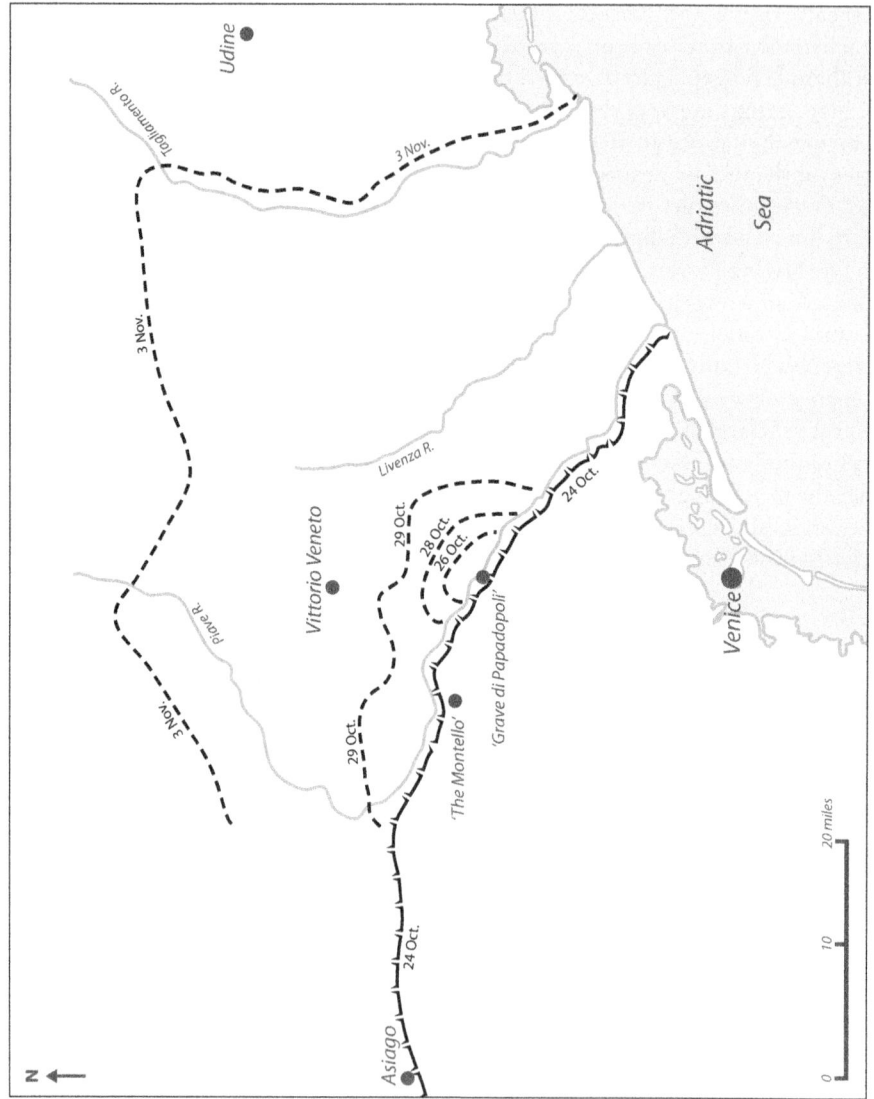

Map 19 Italian theatre showing lines of advance during battle of Vittorio Veneto, October 1918.

After their defeat at Caporetto, the Italian army had retreated to the River Piave and it was here that the British IEF took up their initial positions. The section of the front allocated to Plumer's troops was in the vicinity of the Montello, a large area of high ground close to the river. At this point the Piave is both wide and fast-flowing, especially after the winter snows have melted, but it also contains a large number of gravel 'spits' (some of which are large, like the Grave di Papadopoli) which breaks up the river's flow into a number of separate streams. The width of the river meant that the British and Austrian front lines were normally over a kilometre apart, and consequently much quieter that those in France. One of the biggest differences to strike the troops was the lower level of hostile activity in Italy:

> What must be appreciated is the difference between the warfare in Italy and France. In the former you hardly appreciated a war was on & one always motored up to the front line (I should have been sorry to have attempted it in France).[47]

The Piave may have been a quieter front than that in Flanders, but it did not mean that the British would just sit in their trenches. There was a view held by many British commanders that when troops were not displaying an 'aggressive spirit' towards the enemy they would become 'sticky' and show a reluctance to engage the enemy; the answer was to be found in raids and patrols. The battalion diaries for the IEF record many such activities to probe the Austrian defences, sometimes they were successful and returned with prisoners for interrogation. However, the diaries also paint a picture of men with time on their hands, time that the army was determined to fill. The maintenance of morale was almost more important on a quiet front than on an active one; it was harder to instil the need for discipline, fitness and fighting spirit among a body of men who regarded the front as inactive – a spirit of 'live and let live' was more likely to develop. The entries in the diaries of the York and Lancaster battalions, for November and December, demonstrate how much more 'relaxed' the war was on the Montello:

> 17 November; bathing parade.[48]
> 18 November; football.
> 26 November; inter-platoon football matches
> 27 November; B & C companies at football.

While sport played a major part in the routine of the IEF, the battalion commanders did not lose sight of the job in hand. Between 13 and 19 December, 9/York and Lancaster reported that 'our patrols were out nightly along the Piave river bed'; both battalions were actively seeking out crossing points on their front, which would allow patrols to reach the enemy lines. The point has been made in previous chapters that

---

47 Dillon, *Allies are a Tiresome Lot*, p.144.
48 TNA WO 95/4240, war diary, 8 York & Lancs.

the battalion diaries for many of the units in France had little mention of Christmas and New Year festivities – the war went on regardless. In Italy, there is a marked change. Christmas Day for the 9th battalion was marked by the 'first round of the Brigade football competition' and a concert in the medical school in Montebelluna in the evening. The 8th battalion diary gives us a much better idea of how (when they had the opportunity) the troops would go to some lengths to try to create a festive atmosphere, and replicate something of the Christmas they would have had at home:

> At 7.0 am the battalion awoke and wished each other a 'Merry Xmas Day'. All were busy putting finishing touches to decorations, etc.. At 10.30 am a Church Service was held in B Coy. billet by the Rev. Maynard. The battalion sat down at 12.30 noon to enjoy its Xmas Dinner. Each company had a room apart in its own billet which was decorated – no place being available for a whole battalion. The men thoroughly enjoyed their meal which composed of: Pork, Beef, potatoes, vegetable, Xmas pudding, beer and rum punch. At 2.30 pm an Inter-Coy. football match was played with results; A v B, B won; C v D, C won; C v B, B won the final. At 7.30 pm a concert was held in B Coys billet which was enjoyed by all ranks. Lights out at 10.0 pm.

Sickness could spread quickly in the trenches; the dirt and close proximity of so many unwashed bodies made good breeding grounds. In these conditions bathing, (when the opportunity arose) was important, as the 8th battalion's diary entry for 15 January indicates. 325 men were allocated hot baths at Venegazzu, with the rest of the battalion attending the following day:

> All NCOs and men, without exception, who were not at the baths yesterday attended and certificates were rendered by O.C. Companies to the effect that all NCOs and men in their Companies had had a bath.

As well as the baths, changes of clothing were also issued and the opportunity to be lice free, if only for a few days, must have been very welcome to the men.

The British remained in the area of the Montello, rotating in and out of the line and playing football, until late March when they were relocated to the Asiago plateau. The new position was quite different from the area of the Piave, not least because it was at a height of 3,000 feet rather than 900. At this elevation, the trenches would be warm in summer, but cold in the winter when snow was to be expected. The Asiago, approached from the Venetian plain, presented a steep climb to the plateau and the main camp at Granezza. On the forward, northern edge, of the plateau the British trenches were sited on a steep slope down to the town of Asiago. Although the Austrian lines varied from one to two kilometres away, the British front line trenches (being on the forward slope) were visible to the enemy. However, as on the Piave, the Austrians were not aggressive with their shelling, a philosophy of live and let live was more common than many history books would have us believe. Apart from patrols ('a purely passive defence policy was not followed')[49] and the periodic exchange of artillery fire – 'the general policy of the Austrian artillery for months had been one of "live and let live"'.[50]

The move to the new positions was completed on 27 March when the 9th battalion moved to huts at Granezza by lorry, but these had been left in a sorry state; 'Little work was done apart from cleaning up and improving sanitary conditions which were very bad'.[51] The battalion diaries of the IEF have frequent references to the poor standards of Italian sanitation, civilian as well as military. Private Harry Lamin (9/York and Lancaster), writing to his sister Kate, commented that 'The people out here have some funny ways and not so clean as [the] English'.[52] When 11/Northumberland Fusiliers took over a stretch of trench from the Italians, they were disgusted with the condition in which they had been left:

> It] contrasted pointedly with our own British methods of achieving good sanitary standards. There, clear for all the world to see, were their abandoned latrines: no order, no privacy, literally a field of filth.[53]

One characteristic of the British soldier (and it holds good in today's modern army) was his propensity for 'grousing'. Rather than try to stamp it out, British officers encouraged outlets such as trench journals – the best known was the *Wipers Times* – and concerts. The official censor even commented that grousing acted as a safety valve; it was good for a 'dog to have fleas, keeps him from brooding over being a dog'.[54] A frequent target of the men's ire was army food; it was boringly repetitive, too much of it came out of tins and there was not enough. In France, the troops had become accustomed, when out of the line, to the ready availability of eggs and chips to go with cheap *estaminet* wine. Unfortunately, this supplement appears not to have been so readily available in Italy. Italians ate a great deal of pasta and polenta, neither of which appealed to the British soldier; polenta was a poor substitute for Yorkshire pudding as 'in texture and flavour it resembled a batter pudding as much as chalk resembles cheese'.[55] Gladden summed up the feeling of many of the men; 'what would we not have given for a real steak and mashed potatoes'.[56]

The theatre in which the two York and Lancaster battalions were to spend the rest of the war differed from that of France and Flanders in a number of ways. Having moved from the Montello to Asiago, the terrain was an obvious contrast

---

49   Sandilands, *23rd Division*, p.244.
50   Sandilands, *23rd Division*, p.240.
51   WO 95/4240, war diary, 9 York & Lancs.
52   Lamin, B., *Letters from the Trenches. A Soldier of the Great War* (London, Michael O'Mara Books, 2009), p.152.
53   Gladden, *Piave*, pp.25-6.
54   Hardie, Private Papers, report October 1917.
55   Dillon, *Allies are a Tiresome Lot*, p.66.
56   Gladden, *Piave*, p.14.

from that of Passchendaele and Ypres. At 3,000 feet, and reached only by a switchback road on its southern slope, the Asiago plateau required short-wheelbase Fiat lorries, rather than the vehicles the army had brought with them; the drivers also had to learn to drive on the right – considered a 'bloody nuisance'.[57] The plateau was composed of limestone, not the soft plough-land of Flanders, and required rock-drills rather than shovels to dig the required trenches and dugouts. Another feature of the limestone was its tendency to produce rock splinters when subjected to artillery bombardment. Many of the British soldiers were injured by these high velocity rock shards, rather than by bullets or shells. In Mitchell's analysis of the British medical services in the First World War, he did not record injuries due to rock splinters, but he did have a category for 'accidental or undefined'; this was separate from self-inflicted or 'instruments of war'. It is highly likely that the rock-splinter injuries were included in the 'accidental or undefined' category as this would explain why in France this group constituted 16.6% of casualties while among the IEF it was 46%: a similar figure was given for Macedonia, where the terrain resembled that of the Asiago.[58]

During the period in the theatre, the IEF was only involved in two military operations that we need mention here. The first was the repulse of an Austrian attack on the Asiago in mid-June 1918; the second was the Allied offensive across the Piave in late October of that year. In the weeks prior to the Austrian attack in June, Cavan (who had taken over the IEF after Plumer, the 5th and the 7th Divisions returned to France) was pushing for an Allied offensive from the Asiago, against the Austrians.[59] In his correspondence with Robertson, Cavan expressed his exasperation at Diaz's reluctance to mount an assault, but the Italian commander had intelligence that the Austrians were about to launch a two-pronged assault. Diaz had reason to believe that one attack would be across the Piave while the other would be against the Asiago. The British, however, had been led to believe that they should not expect an infantry advance on their positions, only an artillery bombardment. To this end, the British front line trenches were 'thinned' to prevent too many casualties from the enemy guns. On the morning of 15 June, the IEF held a front of 8,000 yards; 23 Division held the right of the line, with the 48th on their left. As we have seen in previous chapters, divisions, brigades and battalions, even when 'in the line' split up their units – some would be in the forward trenches, some in support. In preparation for the Austrian offensive (which was expected to be artillery only) 23 Division had two brigades in the line and one in reserve; 70 Brigade held the right, with 68 on their left. 70 Brigade's line was held by 11/Sherwood Foresters on the extreme right, 9/York and Lancaster was to their left and 8/York and Lancaster was in support.

57 Barrett, D. (ed), *The Reluctant Tommy. Ronald Skirth* (London, Macmillan, 2010), p.127.
58 Dillon, *Allies are a Tiresome Lot*, p.94.
59 For more detail on this, see Dillon, *Allies are a Tiresome Lot*, Chapter 7.

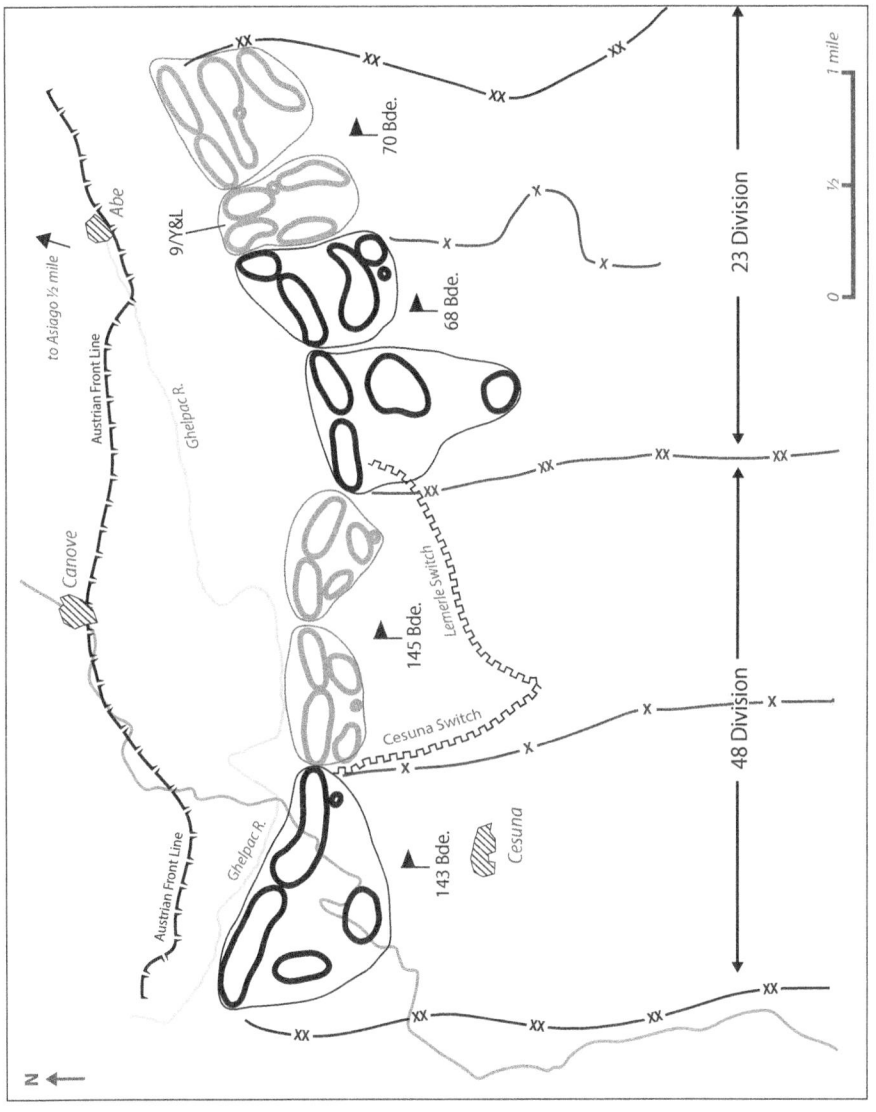

Map 20 British position on Asiago Plateau, June 1918.

The Austrian bombardment began at 03.00 on 15 June; 'Guns of both light and heavy calibre were employed by the enemy'.[60] The diary of 9/York and Lancaster records that 'lachrymatory gas' was used. Between 05.30 and 07.30, the Austrians advanced to within 100 yards of the wire on the 9th battalion front 'where he was disorganized and checked'.[61] By 10.30, the situation 'became normal' and, except for an incursion on 48 Division front, the British line had held. Harry Lamin's company (in 9/York and Lancaster) was in support of the battalion's front line and 'did not have to fire'. In a letter to his brother Jack, he gave a brief outline of the events that morning:

> The fight started about 3 oclock [sic] in the morning and Johnny Austrian started to come over about 7 o clock [sic]. Well he did get a reception I can tell you, them in the front line simply mowed them down and he got no farther than the wire. I went in the front line during the day to have a look when things had quietened down. The prisoners are the poorest lot I have seen and told us they thought that they were going to meet the Italians and where [sic] surprised to see our lads in the trenches.[62]

Lamin's account is a good example of how a battalion could be directly involved in a major enemy assault, and yet half of them (in direct support) did not fire a shot. After months of only desultory action between the two sides on the Asiago, the Austrian move caused Gladden to comment that 'Guns were firing out in front, actually out in front!'[63] He seems to have been overcome by the novelty of the situation.

The scale of the attack was considerably smaller than those the British had faced in France. By the following day 48 Division had routed the Austrian troops who had made it into their line and the IEF had restored the position to that which they had held at 3 am on the previous day. Although Cavan's force had been seriously affected by an outbreak of influenza, and so had many men off sick when the Austrians attacked, they acquitted themselves well. Total casualties for 23 Division were 'only' 556. For the men of the York and Lancaster Regiment the Austrian attack was – in comparison with those they had faced on the Western front – a relatively low key affair. On the Piave, the Austrian assault was initially more successful, though it too failed after a few days. By 23 June, the situation along the whole front had been restored to that of a week previously. With routine restored, 9/York and Lancaster was soon providing working parties, enjoying 'Divisional Baths' and carrying out 'arms drill, Company drill and Bayonet Fighting'.[64] The letters and memoirs of the men of the IEF indicate

---

60 Sandilands, *23rd Division*, p.254.
61 WO 95/4240.
62 Lamin, *Letters from the Trenches*, p.147.
63 Gladden, *Piave*, p.118.
64 WO 95/4240.

Granezza cemetery on the Asiago plateau, Italy. (Photo J. Dillon)

how much quieter their lives were in Italy, during the summer of 1918, than was the case for their colleagues in France. When they were relieved from the line, they spent time on the Venetian plain near the town of Thiene where, although the heat was something new to the soldiers, conditions could have been a lot worse, as Sandilands noted in his divisional history.

> [T]he lot of the British soldier at rest in Italy compared favourably with that of his comrades in France, let alone those other theatres of war where relaxation was taken on a patch of desert among a plague of flies and incessant dust-storms.[65]

Conditions may have been better, but that was no reason for the grousing to stop; 'I remembered the Salient and the Somme, and felt how ungrateful we were to grumble at our present lot'.[66]

Although the Italian front was relatively quiet, things were progressing differently in France where August saw the start of the Allied March to Victory on the Western

---

65 Sandilands, *23rd Division*, p.281.
66 Gladden, *Piave*, p.110.

front (the Hundred Days). Lord Cavan was losing patience with the Italian *Comando Supremo* and their apparent unwillingness to take the offensive against the Austrians. With the war progressing well in France, he suggested to the War Office that if Diaz was not going to attack then 'the time should be used for the instant transfer of good fresh divisions [from Italy] to France, which could be replaced by divisions who were tired out'.[67] Cavan was considered by Haig to be a 'thruster' and it is inconceivable that he would have considered giving up his fresh divisions, unless he believed that the Italians were content to sit on their hands on the Piave.[68] On 27 September, CIGS informed the War Cabinet that as General Diaz 'had shown clearly that he was not going to attack [...] we were replacing our present fresh divisions [from Italy] with tired ones from the Western front'.[69] By 29 September, the 7th and 23rd Divisions had moved from the Asiago plateau to the Montello, in preparation for their move back to France. Italian authorities, civil and military, were in an awkward position; they were reluctant to make a grand offensive against the Austrians, but they could not afford the war to end with their enemy still occupying the Venetian plain between the Isonzo and the Piave. The decision was taken to mount an attack in late October; they had no alternative. If the war ended with the Italian army still behind the Piave, then the country's negotiators would have no leverage at the subsequent peace negotiations. On October 7, there was a 'complete change of plan' on the part of the *Comando Supremo*, an offensive would be opened on the Piave front and 'the transfer of British troops to France had been cancelled'; the 7th and 23rd Divisions 'were to take part in the projected operations'.[70]

With the decision to go on the offensive, changes were made to the command structure; Cavan became commander of the Italian Tenth Army, which included the British 7th and 23rd Divisions (48 Division remained on the Asiago plateau to take part in an attack northwards). From their position on the Piave, opposite the *Grave Di Popadopli*, Cavan's army was to cross the river with the help of Italian boatmen (*pontieri*), for whom the British were full of praise. Once across the river, X Army was to protect the right flank of the Italian Eighth Army, which was to drive towards Vittorio Veneto (the town that gave its name to the battle); the Italian Third Army was on Cavan's right. As so often happens in war, plans do not always survive the first contact with the enemy. The armies on Cavan's left and right flanks, failed to cross the Piave on day one, leaving X Army to 'spearhead' the attack rather than act as flank cover for VIII Army. The assault had been delayed by heavy rain, but went ahead on the morning of 25 October 'in darkness, bitter cold and heavy rain'.[71] On the 23rd Divisional front, 69 Brigade was on the right, 68 to their left and 70 Brigade (with the

---

67 TNA WO 106/852, memo from Cavan to CIGS, 3 September 1918.
68 For more detail on this controversial issue see Dillon, *Allies are a Tiresome Lot*, Chapter 8.
69 TNA CAB 23/7, minutes of War Cabinet 479, 27 September 1918.
70 Sandilands, *23rd Division*, pp.293-4.
71 Sandilands, *23rd Division*, p.309.

two York and Lancaster battalions) in divisional reserve; this brigade would not enter the battle until 29 October when those in the van had made their final objective, the Monticano River. Cavan's X Army advanced rapidly [Map 19], it was a change for the troops to be involved in a war of movement after so many years of static, trench warfare. Gladden (68 Brigade) wrote that they had a 'conscious thrill of victory' with the 'novel experience of marching forward into country just evacuated by the enemy'.[72] Although the Italians would later claim that the morale of the Austrian army was 'on a very high level [...] to the end'[73] the British had a different view; 'they were not enemies of the same quality as the Germans [...] neither their discipline, training, nor morale was of the soundest'.[74] This new 'thrill' of going forward is expressed in the 7th Division history; 'this was the first time since Loos [September 1915] that the 7th Division had had the privilege of finally liberating civilians from the hands of the oppressor'.[75]

On 29 October, it was time for the men of the York and Lancaster Regiment to move forward to the front line:

> The Battalion crossed the river PIAVE at 07.00 hours, and commenced the advance towards VAZZOLA. On reaching the river MONTICANO the Battalion moved forward to support the 8th Battalion Yorkshire Regiment [also known as Green Howards, in 69 Brigade] who were held up by hostile shelling & M.G. fire.[76]

By the end of the day, the battalion had crossed the river, taken the village of Cimetta and established a line of defended posts. In their first day in the action, they had taken 'about' 150 prisoners, 10 machine guns and two small field guns; casualties were recorded as 'only 31'. The advance of 9/York and Lancaster continued on the following day, with the town of Sacile on the River Livenza as the battalion's objective. By evening they were 'manning the western side of the river [Meschio, a little to the west of Sacile] on the southern side of the ORSAGO-SACILE road'. This rapid advance, during which the battalion took another 7 prisoners, 8 machine guns and 2 small field guns, was achieved with no casualties – the British assessment of Austrian morale, rather than that of the Italians, would seem to have been the more accurate. The British advance had been rapid, and in comparison with France, had resulted in relatively low casualties. However, it had not been all plain sailing. An assault across a river, especially one as wide and fast flowing as the Piave, was a new experience for the British soldiers and engineers. The bridges, which Cavan's troops had used, became

---

72 Gladden, *Piave*, pp.192-3.
73 TNA WO 106/837, Italian report of Vittorio Veneto, p.1.
74 Atkinson, *The Seventh Division*, p.472.
75 Crosse, E.C., *The Defeat of Austria As Seen By The 7th Division* (Uckfield, Naval & Military Press, Reprint of 1919 original), p.67.
76 WO 95/4240, war diary, 9 York & Lancs.

targets for Austrian artillery, with consequences for the supply chain to the men at the front of the advance. Food and ammunition ran short, but the lack of transport hit the casualties hardest. Until the bridges had been repaired and strengthened sufficiently to bear wheeled transport, casualties had to be stretchered back to an aid station, or carried on wheeled barrows.

The war in Italy was reaching its dénouement. On 31 October, 9/York and Lancaster advanced towards Sacile:

> By 12.30 hours we had established a line along the western bank of the LIVENZA but were unable to cross to the eastern side as the bridges had been destroyed and enemy machine-guns in the Church Steeple, also snipers in houses, kept up incessant fire. After a bombardment of houses by 6" Newton Mortars, Stokes Mortars and Machine Guns, the section of 18 pounders obtained three hits on the Church Steeple, and no further trouble was caused by hostile machine guns. The pioneers then prepared a bridge over which Companies crossed the LIVENZA – almost in darkness, and by 19.00 hours our objective had been gained: an outpost line was immediately established on the whole front, touch being obtained on either flank.[77]

The York and Lancaster men 'proceeded to clear Sacile'[78] and by noon, the battalion had 'driven them [Austrians] off, captured five hundred prisoners and effected junction with the other 2 battalions of the brigade [one was 8/York and Lancaster], which had gained the objective without opposition'.[79] By the end of the day, 23 Division, whose first battle had been at the Somme on 4 July 1916, had fired its last shot of the Great War.[80] Hostilities on the Italian front came to an end on 4 August; 'The Armistice with Austria came into force at 15.00 hrs. Billets and environs were improved. A Battalion Concert was held in the evening'.[81]

As with soldiers on other fronts, the cessation of hostilities was assumed by the men to mean that they could go home. Unfortunately, an armistice was not a peace treaty, and Allied governments needed to maintain armies of occupation and be prepared in case of a German re-opening of hostilities – not a likely scenario. Many of them would not get home until 1919 and even 1920. Italian war aims extended to the acquisition of Fiume (in modern-day Croatia), a war aim demanded by the poet, aeronaut and ardent nationalist, Gabriele D'Annunzio. The Italian claim was contested and the men of 8/York and Lancaster were sent to the town as part of an international peace-keeping force; they were there until September 1919.

77 WO 95/4240.
78 Sandilands, *23rd Division*, pp.328.
79 Edmonds, J., *Military Operations Italy, 1915-1919* (Nashville, The Battery Press, Reprint of 1949 original), p.323.
80 Sandilands, *23rd Division*, pp.328.
81 WO 95/4240.

It is natural that British histories of the war concentrate on the Western front, that is where the German army had to be defeated, and it is where the iconic battles were fought that have come to represent that conflict in the British mythology of the war. Hundreds of thousands of British soldiers experienced the war on fronts quite remote from Ypres and the Somme; Salonika, the Asiago and the Piave provide us with a different perspective. Many of these men 'gave their tomorrows', just as their comrades who lie in the quiet cemeteries of the Western front, and they also deserve their place in the accounts of that World War.

14

The Hundred Days

In his foreword to one of Gary Sheffield's books on the First World War,[1] Richard Holmes wrote that 'The Western Front smoulders darkly in the middle of Britain's national consciousness, like some exhausted volcano whose once-deadly lava still marks our landscape'. Over the years, myths had solidified into 'facts' making it hard for revisionist historians to put forward more balanced assessments of the war; as Holmes puckishly commented, the British were 'mysteriously on the winning side' while the Germans 'somehow managed to lose'. After the horrors of static trench warfare, the Allied troops were soon to experience that 'conscious thrill of victory' that Gladden had noted in Italy. However, for the first half of 1918 the outlook was less than optimistic, as late as 25 July the General Staff believed that there was little chance of breaking the stalemate in France before mid-1919. The War Office was wrong, only two weeks later the 8 August attack at Amiens resulted in the Allied march to victory and the German armistice of 11 November.

Before Amiens, the war was split up (by historians) into a series of named battles – Loos, Somme, Third Ypres, Cambrai – but the weeks after 8 August 1918 were a continuous series of actions as the armies moved forward. The purpose of this account is to give some focus to the part played by battalions of the York and Lancaster Regiment in that 'march to victory', described by Paddy Griffith as 'A brilliant military attainment which deserves far more recognition than it has normally been accorded'.[2] One consequence of the concentration on the mistakes and losses of many of the earlier battles is the failure to recognise that Haig and his commanders did learn; they did adopt new tactics as the war progressed. With the benefit of hindsight, and one hundred years' analysis, it is easy to conclude that changes were needed to the way in which attacks were prosecuted. Nevertheless, the lessons were learned and those last

---

1   Sheffield, G., *Forgotten Victory. The First World War: Myths and Realities* (London, Headline, 2002), pp.xiii-xiv.
2   Griffith, P. (ed.), *British Fighting Methods in the Great War* (London, Frank Cass, 1996), p.xii.

100 days were 'a vindication of the laborious groundwork of the preceding four years'.³ Perhaps the most important change was the realisation that 'an attacker should bank his winnings after the first two or three days, and not continue gambling recklessly against a rapidly stiffening enemy defence'.⁴

Those last months of the war began at 04.20 on 8 August, a morning that Haig recorded as 'Glass steady. Fine night and morning – slight mist in the valley. An autumn feel in the morning air'.⁵ As if to demonstrate 'conceptual progress', Haig called off the battle after only three days and an advance of six miles; he did not persist, as on previous assaults, in trying to push on when the attack had run out of steam and the artillery struggled to keep up with the infantry. The battalions of the York and Lancaster Regiment took no part in the battle that 'kicked off' the successes of the following months. A sense of the optimism that fired Haig comes through in his diary entries during the battle; the Germans were 'blowing up dumps in all directions and streaming eastwards. Their transport and limbers offer splendid targets for our airoplanes [sic]'. The euphoria caused him to write a strange comment to his wife: 'How much easier it is to attack, than to stand and await an enemy's attack!'⁶ He appeared to have forgotten that the attacks at Loos, the Somme and Passchendaele had not been 'easier' than defending against German assaults.

The campaign which began on 8 August demonstrated how far British tactics had developed over the preceding four years from an artillery barrage followed by an infantry charge, to an 'all arms' battle. It was a massive concentration of force; 2,000 artillery pieces, 800 aircraft of the recently formed Royal Air Force – together with support from more than 1,100 French machines – and 534 tanks.⁷ Since the beginning of the war the air arm had made especially impressive advances, aircraft had developed to perform the reconnaissance, bombing, air-combat and artillery spotting roles. The original Royal Flying Corps (RFC) became a separate service on 1 April 1918 – the Royal Air Force (RAF) – and (by August 1918) was an essential component of Allied offensives. Unfortunately, on 8 August the RAF over-reached its capabilities. The Germans were fleeing towards the bridges over the Somme and if they could be knocked out, the retreating troops would be cut off. Major-General J.M. Salmond, who had taken over command of the RAF from Lord Trenchard, authorised the change of the bombing offensive from ground targets to the Somme bridges, 'as long as weather and light permits'.⁸ The slow-moving biplanes, with their 25 lb. and 112 lb. bombs, were not designed for the precision bombing of robust steel structures

3   Griffith, P., 'The Extent of Tactical Reform in the British Army', in Griffiths, P. (ed.), *British Fighting Methods in the Great War* (London, Frank Cass, 1996), p.5.
4   Griffith, *Tactical Reform*, p.1.
5   Sheffield and Bourne, *Haig*, p.439.
6   Sheffield and Bourne, *Haig*, p.440.
7   Harris, *Haig*, p.489.
8   Jones, H.A., *The War in The Air, Volume 6* (Milton Keynes, Naval & Military Press, Reprint of 1937 original), p.441.

– but they tried. A total of 205 bombing sorties (including some by light single-seater fighters) were flown on 8 August, dropping 12 tons of bombs. According to the British official history, the German pilots 'fought generally with reckless courage to take toll of the bombers, even though they could not prevent the attacks'.[9] RAF casualties were heavy; 45 aircraft were lost, a further 52 were wrecked or damaged, 57 aircrew were missing, 4 were killed and a further 19 were wounded. The attacks against the bridges continued on the following day, though losses were a little reduced; 36 aircrew killed or captured and 45 aircraft written off. By 14 August, when the offensive had come to a close, 700 sorties had been flown against the bridges and 57 tons of bombs dropped. The RAF was a new service, it had taken over roles previously held by the air arms of the Navy and the Army and both those services wanted to see them repatriated. The RAF, wishing to establish its credentials as a bomber force in its own right, had taken on too difficult a task.

This chapter does not attempt to be a complete account of the last three months of the war (for that readers can turn to the Official Histories or Sheffield's *Forgotten Victory*), nor does it set out to record all the actions that involved battalions of the York and Lancaster Regiment – there were too many to record them all. Selective use has been made of the battalion war diaries to give the reader some appreciation of those fast-moving days. The advance was rapid, leaving little time for the pre-combat planning that was such a feature of the war up to that point. In these last months the pattern was one of a series of 'encounter battles' as the leading battalions came into contact with German forces that had not yet given up the fight.

The month of August saw 2/4 York and Lancaster spending most of its time in training near Henu, 15 km west of Bapaume, the diary entries for that month have no mention of the major assault that had begun at Amiens. On 24 August the battalion was warned that they would soon be moving to the front; 'Orders were received to issue bombs, pack haversacks and greatcoats and for Bn to be prepared to move at short notice early in the morning'.[10] At 05.30, they were on the march. On the following morning, now at Mory (6 km north of Bapaume), they prepared to go into an attack with A company on the right, C company on the left, each with a frontage of 250 yards. This may have been the first month of the 'march to victory', but the Germans were not going to give ground easily. The leading companies managed to advance some 500 yards but in spite of being reinforced, 'were unable to carry forward the line'. During the day, the Germans brought down a continuous barrage 'on the forming up point and the advanced line'. By 4 pm, one of the companies had been forced to pull back 'almost to the forming up point'. Within an hour the Germans were getting ready to retaliate:

9 Jones, *War in The Air*, p.442.
10 WO 95/3090, war diary 2/4 York & Lancs.

The enemy was seen forming up in strength for an attack and at 5 pm he attacked and advanced to within 200x [yards] of our line when the troops with the assistance of the 2/4 KOYLI, who had formed up in rear of our advanced line with a view of going through us to exploit success, charged them with the bayonet, driving them back to 700x from the point of assembly. Here a line was at once consolidated. At night orders were received that as far as possible the 2/4 KOYLI would take over the outpost line, in order that the Bn might reorganise; this was done.[11]

The last months of the war consisted of many actions similar to the one above; all of them relatively small, but each one adding to the overall advance. The 2/4th had taken 63 prisoners, 12 of whom 'were suffering from bayonet wounds'. The fight had also cost the battalion a number of casualties; 8 officers, including 1 killed and 1 who died of his wounds; 214 Other Ranks, including 16 killed, 3 who died of wounds, 166 wounded. After this brief period of action, the battalion was relieved and received 2 officers and 110 men as reinforcements to replace some of the casualties. 2/4 York and Lancaster was now back up to almost full strength with 32 officers and 893 men. The battalion did not have long to lick its wounds and by 2 September (now near Vaulx Vraucourt) the men were preparing to go into action again. Once more, the fight was short and sweet, but with heavy casualties. The battalion lost 2 officers killed, 5 were wounded and a total of 208 men were killed, wounded or missing. In just these two unremarkable incidents, the battalion had lost a total of 439 officers and men from a total strength of approximately 900, almost a 50% turnover in 4 weeks. On the other side of the balance sheet, the Germans were also losing men and materiel. On 2 September the battalion collected 'several trench mortars, over 30 machine guns & three Field Guns' as well as capturing '9 officers (including a Battalion Commander) & 236 other ranks'. The German army may have been in retreat but, like a cornered bear, it was not going to make it easy for the advancing British. Between 24 August and the end of October the battalion had suffered 721 casualties (officers and men), or approximately 75% of the unit. By the time of the Armistice, this had risen to 83%.

The pattern of advance, fight and advance again continued through September and October but we will fast-forward to early November. On the 4th of that month, the battalion was at Orsinval, a little north of the old, fortified town of Le Quesnoy; the defensive walls were a classic example of Vauban's work and were scaled by the New Zealanders when they liberated the inhabitants on 4 November 1918. Over the next five days, 2/4 York and Lancaster advanced some 30-35 km towards the town of Maubeuge on the River Sambre. This put them close to the Franco-Belgian border, and only a few miles south of Mons, where the BEF had begun the war in August 1914. Early on the morning of 4 November, they left Orsinval, crossed the small River Rhonelle – 'no great obstacle' – and joined the attack on the village of Frasnoy. It

11 WO 95/3090.

Memorial to the storming of the walls at Le Quesnoy by the men of New Zealand. (Photo J. Dillon)

may have been only a week before the end of the war, but the German defenders were holding out strongly. The British troops met 'considerable opposition' in Frasnoy and had to resort to street fighting. While other units continued clearing the village, 2/4 York and Lancaster were ordered to march on to the village of Gommegnies, where they were to find billets as shelter from the heavy rain that had set in. The battalion was about to fight its last action of the war.

At 12.00 on 8 November, the battalion was told that they were to be part of an attack the following day 'and preparations were accordingly made'.[12] The following extracts are from the battalion diary:

> 8 November. Bn. moved from MECQUIGNIES at 04.20. The morning was very dark. [...] At 06.30 the attack commenced, the final objective being the village of NEUF MESNIL and the cross roads [map reference given]. Attack was on a two company frontage B & C leading with A as support to C and D to B. The ground advanced over was exceedingly difficult owing to its enclosed

12 WO 95/3090.

nature and the woods and hedges, but direction was well maintained and very little opposition encountered.

The eastern edge of BOIS HOYAUX and the hamlet of LES PETITES MOTTES was reached at 0800. M.G. fire came from [map reference] but the advance was successfully carried on to the final objective. Posts were pushed forward and established on the high ground in [map reference]. At this point intense M.G. fire was experienced from [map reference]. In conjunction with an attack at 15.30 hours by the 5th KOYLI, patrols were pushed forward by B & C Coys to ascertain if the enemy resistance was still maintained. The patrols found MG's still holding out. The position at nightfall consisted of B & C Coys holding the outpost line with A and D Coys in support in houses in NEUF MESNIL.

Since the beginning of the attack, the battalion had advanced a good 7 km, how different from the previous years of the war. By the evening of 8 November, further orders were received for a continuation of the attack, timed for the following morning. The battalion was to 'attack and capture' the town of Sous Le Bois (very close to Maubeuge), then 'establish posts at river crossings'; zero hour was 05.30 on 9 November.

The terrain on which the coming battle was to be fought was urban/industrial:

> The plan of attack was that D Coy should attack due E and capture the ground and factories […] lying between the RIVER SAMBRE and the Rlwy [railway] line. 'A' Coy were to follow through and turning N clear up the village to the street running SW through [map reference]. 'C' Coy attacking NE after mopping up the area were to push through and secure the high ground. 'B' Coy were ordered to mop up the remaining NE corner of the village.

At zero hour the battalion went on the offensive but 'no opposition whatsoever was encountered'. Instead of a street-by-street battle with the Germans, the men marched 'into the town to receive a great welcome at the hands of the inhabitants!' By now, they must have been able to sense that the end of the war could not be too far off. The battalion diary records that 'large quantities of booty of every description was captured'.

Although the men did not yet know it, their last action of the war was now behind them and at 10 a.m. on 10 November, they were relieved and went into billets in Sous Le Bois. The casualty statistics for the month were relatively light; two officers wounded, 13 men killed, 49 wounded and 7 missing. A search of the CWGC web site adds a little more detail to these figures. One officer who died, possibly from wounds, was 2nd Lieutenant W. Campbell, he is buried in Ruesnes Communal Cemetery. The cemetery is located approximately 4 kilometres NW of Le Quesnoy, so Campbell may have been a casualty of the battalion's move out of Orsinval on 4 November; he lies with two other members of the battalion. 2/4 York and Lancaster demonstrates once more the problem of recording casualty statistics. The adjutant believed, immediately after the action had finished, that 13 members of the battalion died in November, in fact there were 18 (including the one officer); 14 of them on 4 November – most of them probably fell in the 'street fighting' around Frasnoy. Private E Goy died the day before the Armistice and is buried in St Sever Cemetery at Rouen. This city was a site for camps and hospitals and Goy probably died there of wounds. Another who is most likely to have succumbed to his wounds was Private W. Cooper who died on 5 November and is buried in Awoingt British Cemetery. The village of Awoingt is situated a little east-south-east of Cambrai and soon after its capture in early October 1918, it became the site of a number of Casualty Clearing Stations; 'the great majority of the burials were made from those hospitals'.[13] Not all injured soldiers died in hospitals near the battle fields. Private H. Hanson died on 2 November and is buried in Sheffield (Burngreave) Cemetery; the city had two large war hospitals, as the region was a large recruiting area for the army. All those members of the battalion who fell in November have 'known graves', all the bodies were located and buried. After the notice of the signing of the armistice, there was one more sad death for the battalion to record. Captain C.B. Dixon had been reported 'wounded' on 10 November but the diary for the 15th stated that he had died of wounds at a Casualty Clearing Station on the previous day. Dixon received a posthumous Military Cross, and is buried at Awoingt Cemetery.

War diaries were for recording facts rather than emotions, which probably accounts for the low-key reporting of the end of the war:

> 11 November; 11.00. Message received that Armistice would come into operation at 1100 hours. Lecture to officers by G.O.C. 62nd Division. General Holiday.

Sadly, for many of the men, this did not mean that they could go home yet. Four days later news arrived that the battalion 'would form part of Army of Occupation and would shortly advance into Germany'. Our account will not follow them there, instead we will pick up an incident that involved the 1/4th and 1/5th battalions in early October. This author's attention was drawn to this through a comment in Richard Holmes' *Tommy* concerning York Cemetery at Haspres on the River Selle. In that narrative style that made his battlefield tours so memorable, Holmes, writes of 'The headstones in the comet's tail of cemeteries that trace the army's path from Santerre across the Belgian border';[14] within that tail is York Cemetery. Among the 137 Commonwealth graves are 'a company's worth of the York and Lancaster regiment, with, up by the back wall, most of the machine-gunners that killed them'. In his inimitable style, Holmes has caught some of the tragedy that accompanied the Advance to Victory; just one of those small vignettes that rarely makes it into the larger histories. The cemetery contains seven named German graves; one of them died on 11 October, one on the 12th and five on the 13th, the day that the men of the York

---

13   CWGC web site; cemetery details for Awoingt British Cemetery.
14   Holmes, *Tommy*, p.72.

and Lancaster were killed. It is fitting that the burial site is named York Cemetery as 103 of the 137 graves belong to men of the 1/4th and 1/5th battalions; all killed on 13 October – just a month before the war ended.

Early on the morning of 13 October, 1/4th York and Lancaster had verbal orders to participate in an attack on the River Selle, zero hour was set for 09.00 on what was, after a wet night, a clear morning; the battalion diary tells us that the men ate a 'good breakfast'. As the battalions advanced, the division on their left (the 51st) could not make the expected progress, with the consequence that the leading troops came under enfilade fire. The German defenders would not be troubled by the British artillery; due to a mix up the previous day, the powers that be believed the Germans were east of the river, not west. Unmolested by the British guns, the Germans poured in 'a tremendous fire from machine guns and rifles, the volume of which was certainly greater than anything the battalion had encountered in trench warfare'.[15] The 1/4th battalion diary states that; 'according to orders we should not have encountered any opposition on west side [of the river]' but the situation was such that 'within a short distance of the river [they] suffered so heavily they could not hold the ground'.[16] By 14.30, 'the remnants of each company dug in, holding the crest of the hill'. The casualties were estimated at 350 men. Additionally, all company and platoon officers were 'hit within an hour of zero'. The attack had removed the majority of the battalion officers so that the only ones remaining unhurt were 'the C.O., the Adjutant and two subalterns, each of whom was put in charge of half the Battalion'.[17] Their sister battalion suffered equally badly with 9 officers and 305 ORs as casualties. One of the dead officers from 1/5th was a Lieutenant attached from 13/York and Lancaster; he had the formidable name of Leon Victor St. Patrick De Landre-Grogan and, with no known grave, he is remembered on the Ploegsteert Memorial. The action that involved the two York and Lancaster battalions on 11 October highlights one of the problems faced by a rapidly advancing army – in contrast to the static trench warfare of the Ypres Salient, the position and strength of the enemy may not be known. At the River Selle on that day in October, the regiment paid a heavy price for being unaware of their opponents positions: to quote from Grant's history of the Hallamshires, 'The British infantryman had once more been ordered to do the impossible'.[18]

This account of the last weeks of the war now turns to two of the three battalions of the regiment in which Private Patrick Dillon served; the 6th (he was with them in Gallipoli) and the 2nd (in which he was captured in March 1918).

When the British offensive opened at Amiens, 6/York and Lancaster were in the Mazingarbe area just a few kilometres from Loos, where the 10th Battalion had had their baptism of fire in September 1915 (see chapter 5). As the battalion's history

15   Grant, *Hallamshires*, p.135.
16   WO 95/2805, war diary, 1/4th York & Lancs.
17   Grant, *Hallamshires*, p.135.
18   Grant, *Hallamshires*, pp.135-6.

tells us, 'It was not until late in September that the 11th Division was required to take its part in any outstanding battle'.[19] It would be wrong to see the Hundred Days as involving all British battalions going forward against the Germans as one wave. After a number of moves during September, the men of the 6th arrived in Baralle (about 8 km NW of Cambrai, on the Cambrai-Arras road) on the 24th. Here 'all preparations were made for the advance fixed for the 27th September';[20] the operation became known as the Battle of the Canal du Nord. The battalion was to be part of a First Army attack 'to capture the Bourlon Wood heights, and then to secure its left flank on the Sensée River'; 11 Division would be operating together with 1st, 3rd and 4th Canadian Divisions. The attack was led off by the 4th and 1st, with 3rd and 11th divisions following. Once the lead divisions had gained their objectives – a line from Fontaine-Notre-Dame, through Bourlon village west to Sains-les-Marquion – the divisions would reorganize and advance on a four-division front. This area of operations lay to the west of Cambrai, and about 500 yards south of the Cambrai-Arras road.

Zero hour for the attack was 05.00 on 27 September with the battalion becoming actively involved a little later:

> The right Coy (B) started to mop up the ground between the railway and Canal [du Nord]. This work was carried on from right to left as the barrage moved northwards. No enemy found on West bank of Canal. Opposition came from pockets of the enemy who were hanging on in woods East of CANAL-DU-NORD and in North portion of SAINS-LES-MARQUION but mopping up parties actively engaged these parties. The right Coy (B) dealt with enemy area [map reference]. Under cover of Lewis Gun & rifle fire sections crossed the bridges [...] and drove the enemy into the woods. Meanwhile our left Coy (C) were engaging the enemy in [map reference]. This party was dealt with in exactly the same way as on the right. Our men pushed over the Canal to the north and rounded up this pocket along with some of those who had been driven into the wood from the right. This operation cleared the EAST bank of the Canal and allowed troops to cross over the bridge at [map reference] without interruption about 11 A.M.[21]

The battalion diary makes the point that the German shelling of the first-line 'was never very heavy' and that it 'practically ceased after the first two hours'. How very different that must have seemed from a year ago. While gaining their objective the battalion had taken 39 prisoners and suffered 89 casualties (of which 10 men were killed); they then went into reserve. However, with the advance continuing all along

---

19   Wylly, *Volume 2*, p.136.
20   Wylly, *Volume 2*, p.136.
21   WO 95/1809, war diary, 6/York & Lancs.

the British front, the battalion was soon called upon to participate in another attack, this time at Epinoy (three km NW of Cambrai).

The Canadian Corps was to attack the enemy on 1 October to secure the crossings of the canal and gain observation over the valley of the River Sensée, 6/York and Lancaster was given the responsibility of safeguarding the left flank of the operation up to the Douai-Cambrai road. The battalion encountered heavy opposition, with many casualties and at the end 'further advance now seeming impossible, the Battalion dug in on a line in front of the wire and held on here till relieved in the afternoon.[22] The action was just one of many in those last weeks of the war, but it stood out from the others because one member of the battalion won the Victoria Cross. Sergeant Frederick Charles Rigg already held the Military Medal when he went into action at Epinoy. Like so many recipients of the highest award for bravery in the face of the enemy, the award was posthumous. The citation in the *London Gazette*, 6 January 1919, read as follows:

> For most conspicuous bravery and self-sacrifice on the morning of the 1st October, 1918, near Epinoy, when, having led his platoon through strong uncut wire under severe fire, he continued straight on, and although losing heavily from flanking fire, succeeded in reaching his objective, when he rushed in and captured a machine-gun. He later handled two captured guns with great effect, and caused the surrender of fifty of the enemy.
>
> Subsequently, when the enemy again advanced in force, Sergeant Riggs cheerfully encouraged his men to resist, and whilst exhorting his men to fight on to the last, this very gallant soldier was killed.[23]

The body of Sergeant Riggs VC, MM, was not found and he is remembered on the Vis-en-Artois Memorial, together with another 127 members of the Regiment. The memorial bears the names of some 9,000 men who fell between 8 August 1918 and the Armistice on 11 November.

On the same day that the battalion learnt of Riggs' award, 2/4 York and Lancaster received notification that Corporal (acting sergeant) John Daykin was also to be decorated with the VC for his actions at Solesmes on 20 October. Commanding the remnants of a platoon, some 12 men, he led them against a strong point where they killed around 25 Germans and took a further 30 of them as prisoners. Not satisfied with that, he then set off alone against another machine gun and returned 'driving 25 of the enemy in front of him and carrying a Machine Gun'.[24] Daykin's medal is displayed in the regimental museum in Rotherham.

---

22 Wylly, *Volume 2*, p.138.
23 Wylly, *Volume 2*, p.140.
24 WO 95/3090/3, war diary, 2/4th York & Lancs.

The battalion continued advancing until 11 November. The battalion diary states that 3 men were killed in November, but the CWGC website shows 9; the difference would be accounted for by some of the 'missing' being later recorded as dead, and some wounded men possibly dying at the Casualty Clearing Stations. The last officer of the battalion to die was Captain S.F. Cartwright, attached from 3/York and Lancaster. The war diary casualty statistics for the month indicate that no officers were killed, but the entry for 5 October (the date of his death) has the comment 'Capt S.F. Cartwright (B Coy.) killed' added after the original entry was made. Cartwright is buried in Sebourg British Cemetery.

There is an interesting entry in the 6th battalion's diary for 9 November, just before hostilities ceased:

> The battn. was provisioned by aeroplanes, bully beef & biscuits being brought by 7 aeroplanes to MICLOT-POLLET [...] at 9 AM. The transport was unable to get up to the battn. owing to all the crossroads being mined, huge craters making roads impossible to wheeled vehicles.[25]

It is quite rare to see this use of aircraft in the war diaries and indicates that the British probably had a large superiority in aircraft numbers, as well as the imagination to utilise them in a transport role. For 6/York and Lancaster, the war was now effectively over. Christmas Day was celebrated, though the diary makes no mention of any New Year festivities. With the conflict behind them, the troops wanted nothing more than to return home. Demobilization was a contentious issue amongst the troops; they believed it to be slow and unfair (for more on this subject, see Dillon, *Allies are a Tiresome Lot*, chapter 9). While the battalion did not have to become part of an Army of Occupation, as had happened to 1/York and Lancaster, they were not all able to return to their families. However, by the end of January, 10 officers and 301 ORs had been 'struck off the strength of the battalion' and returned home. The post-conflict months were a challenge for the regimental officers and their NCOs; how to keep the men occupied, when all they could think of was going home and taking up civilian employment. The war diary shows that they instituted a comprehensive programme of educational courses and talks to try to keep the troops busy and to give them some skills that they might use when they got home. The following list gives an indication of the range of subjects covered: shorthand, book keeping, English, mathematics, physics, arithmetic, writing, reading and general knowledge. Additional evening classes were held in French and economics – the latter for officers only.

Although the vast majority of the soldiers wanted to return to Blighty, some did volunteer (at a higher wage) to remain in the army as is clear from two entries in April.[26]

25 WO 95/1809.
26 WO 95/1809.

6 April; 3 Offs [officers] and 80 ORs (*volunteers* and retainable) [...] to become the 156th POW company.

14 April; 1 Off and 80 ORs (*volunteers* and retainable) [...] to become the 190th POW company. [My italics].

The government had had to increase the soldiers' wages to have any chance of encouraging men to volunteer for service once hostilities ceased. However, the demobilization process did allow for the compulsory retention of some of the men who had been conscripted late in the war. One can only imagine the enthusiasm with which this latter group would have looked forward to staffing a POW camp, while others returned to take up civilian employment.

We turn now to 2/York and Lancaster (part of 16 Brigade, 6 Division, IX Corps), the battalion that Private Patrick Dillon had joined when the 10th battalion was disbanded. Taken prisoner on 21 March, Dillon would play no part in the last Hundred Days. The battalion's part in those last weeks is picked up from mid-September, when 6 Division was sent to relieve the 32nd around Holnon Wood, three and a half miles west of St Quentin. At this point, the Germans were in defensive positions on the high ground between Holnon Wood and St Quentin; the 1st and 6th Divisions were given the job of attacking this line on 18 September.[27] Preparatory attacks (to secure the start line) by 18 Brigade and the French 34th Division, had not been completely successful, but the attack could not be postponed. Practically the whole of 6 Division's front – some 2,500 yards – was taken up by Holnon Wood. The wood not only presented a physical barrier to the attacking troops, it was also 'drenched with gas shells'.[28] To overcome the problem, 16 Brigade had to make its advance around the northern side while the 71st took the southern route. The longer advance and the splitting of the two brigades, 'naturally fatigued the troops and hindered communication and supply'. One consequence of the rapid advance during these late summer days was the lack of time and opportunity for a full reconnaissance; 'Troops had not seen the ground they had to attack over'.

In the centre of the divisional area of attack, on higher ground, was a network of trenches that the British named the Quadrilateral, 'a name of bad omen to the 6th Division'[29] after their time on the Somme. This defensive position was of 'such unusual natural strength that captured German officers admitted that they had fully expected to be able to hold it indefinitely'.[30] It was with the knowledge of that strong point to their front that the troops moved up to their assembly positions on the night of 17 September. At 05.20 the next morning, the battalion went into the attack under a 'splendid creeping barrage';[31] C Company on the right, D on the left, followed by

---

27 Marden, *6th Division*, p.59.
28 Marden, *6th Division*, p.60.
29 Marden, *6th Division*, p.60.
30 Marden, *6th Division*, p.63.
31 Wylly, *Volume 2*, p.382.

A and B in support. Within an hour, the first objective – a line of trenches – had been taken, but the Germans were not going to let the attackers have it all their own way. At 10.00, they launched a 'determined and weighty' counter attack from the village of Fresnoy-le-Petit, to the north-east. Although D company were driven back, the line held. The battalion had advanced 3,000 yards and at one point 'had nearly completed the capture of Fresnoy-le-Petit, but were unable to hold it'.[32] The York and Lancaster men were fortunate in that the Quadrilateral was not directly in their path, the 71st Brigade (on the right of the 16th) drew that straw, but 16 Brigade's advance was slowed by machine gun fire from that strong point. The need to neutralise this position led to the decision to continue the attack on the morning of 19 September. However, that appeared to have been anticipated by the Germans who put down a heavy barrage on the anticipated jumping off points – the advance was postponed. The battalion's action on the 18th had resulted in many of the enemy being killed 'and some 50 prisoners taken, but that was not without cost: 2/York and Lancaster lost 2 officers and 27 ORs killed, 2 officers and 140 ORs wounded and a further 43 men missing, a total of 216 for the day.[33] No doubt, the men would have been grateful that 'for a day or two things remained tolerably quiescent'. Nevertheless, in those last weeks of the war, momentum was everything; the advance (and the attacks that this entailed) would have to be renewed.

With the postponement of the renewed attack until 24 September, the divisional staff could 'devote the interval to a proper artillery preparation'.[34] One of the downsides of a continuous infantry advance is that the artillery does not have sufficient time to move their guns forward, position them and then 'lay' them on their allotted targets. The five-day break gave them the opportunity to re-establish their barrage support for the men of 6 Division. At 05.00, 'under a creeping barrage and assisted by three tanks',[35] the division attacked; 16 Brigade on the left of the front, 18 on the right. In the advance, the 16th fared better than the 18th. Coming down from the north the brigade was able to 'secure the northern face of the Quadrilateral' and 2/York and Lancaster captured the trenches that had been assigned as their objective. The battalion had done well capturing 9 German officers, 300 of their soldiers, two 77mm guns, 1 trench mortar and 22 machine guns. However, the gains did not come without cost; 5 officers were wounded and 140 men were killed, wounded or reported as missing – another 145 casualties. After holding the line until 29 September, the battalion went into brigade reserve at Tertry (about 8km west of St Quentin).

As September morphed into October, the war moved into its last few weeks. While the 6th Division had been resting, the 46th and 32nd had crossed the canal, north of St Quentin, and were involved in heavy fighting around the villages of Ramicourt

32   Wylly, *Volume 2*, p.382.
33   Wylly, *Volume 2*, p.382.
34   Marden, *6th Division*, p.62.
35   Wylly, *Volume 2*, p.383.

and Sequehart – 10 km north of St Quentin. After absorbing new drafts of reinforcements, 6 Division was sent as part of the force to relieve the 46th and 32nd and would join an attack towards Bohain on 8 October. The position to be attacked 'consisted of high rolling downs with deep transverse valleys, giving good cover for supports and forward guns, and on the right a broad longitudinal valley closed by a ridge on which stood the village of Méricourt'.[36] As had become the norm, the division was to attack on a two-brigade front, 16 on the right and 71 to their left; zero hour was 05.10 on 8 October. As they were on the extreme right of the divisional front, 2/York and Lancaster was to cover the right flank of the Fourth Army and connect with the First French Army on their right, 'exploiting any success which might be gained'.[37] We pick up the story from the battalion history:

> The attack went well until we reached the spur running south-west from Beauregard, where we were met by heavy machine and point-blank fire from a 'whizz bang' battery. Owing to the right flank being in the air it was decided to form a defensive flank running along the above spur. In these operations we took four hundred prisoners, two field guns and a large number of machine-guns. The casualties incurred by the Battalion were four officers and one hundred other ranks killed, wounded and missing.[38]

The battalion casualty count since 18 September had now risen to 465 – approximately 50% at a time when the war was nearly over. By nightfall on 8 October, 'Méricourt was taken and the mission of the 6th Division was accomplished'. While that job may have been well done the tired troops were not finished, they were to be back in action on three more occasions before the armistice.

On 10 October, 16 Brigade, with 2/York and Lancaster in the leading wave, was in the assault that resulted in the 'capture of Bohain, of huge stores of war material and the release of some four thousand French civilians'. In these hectic last weeks any period in divisional reserve (at Brancourt-le-Grand) must have been a welcome respite, but on the 17th they moved to the southern edge of the Bois de Busigny to be ready for an attack the following morning:

> At 5.30 the attack commenced, "A" and "B" Companies in the first wave and "C" and "D" in the second; but, the enemy making a comparatively slight resistance, all objectives were in our possession by 7.30. The captures by the Battalion totalled three officers and 211 men, but two officers and 87 other ranks were killed, wounded and missing.[39]

36 Wylly, *Volume 2*, p.383.
37 Wylly, *Volume 2*, p.384.
38 Wylly, *Volume 2*, p.384.
39 Wylly, *Volume 2*, p.385.

In a strange way, the war was about to come full-circle. After the action mentioned above, the battalion spent the next few days on marches to Bazuel, only two kilometres south-east of Le Cateau, scene of General Smith-Dorrien's rear-guard battle during the retreat of the BEF on 26 August 1914. At 07.00 on 24 October the battalion moved out

> To take part in the last action in which during the Great War the 2nd York and Lancaster was to be engaged. [They made] such good progress that by noon The York and Lancaster, the right battalion of the brigade, had completed the capture of the objective laid down for the previous day's attack.

During some seven weeks of fighting 6 Division 'had marched fifty miles' had captured 318 guns and close upon 17,000 prisoners, itself sustaining over 6,000 casualties [more than 550 of those in 2/York and Lancaster]'.[40] The division was relieved on the night of 30/31 October, went into billets at Fresnoy-le-Grand, and then, on 5 November, moved to Bohain where it was accommodated 'in the local schools and other buildings'. Finally, on 11 November, the men had the news they had been waiting for; 'Hostilities ceased at 11.00 hours this morning' – the war was over.

As was the case for so many British soldiers, the signing of the armistice was not followed by an immediate train home:

> The IX Corps was now transferred to the Second Army, under Gen. Sir H. Plumer, to whom was assigned the command of the British Army of Occupation in Germany.[41]

Although many of those who had served since before July 1916 would be demobilized relatively quickly, the remainder would have to spend many months in Europe before they returned to their families and civilian employment. On 14 November, the battalion marched east towards the German frontier, crossing near Malmédy on the 16th 'with drums beating and colours flying'.[42] The modern-day English football fan, aware of the 'success' of the national team against Germany, might draw a wry smile at a comment in Marden's history of the division; 'As *the Germans did not play football* there was a general lack of football grounds'. [My italics.] In the middle of March, the battalion effectively split in two: 13 officers and 276 other ranks[43] (who were not due for early demobilization) entrained for Cologne and were transferred to the 1/4 York and Lancaster. The remainder were the lucky ones who were given their tickets home

---

40 Wylly, *Volume 2*, pp.385-6.
41 Marden, *6th Division*, p.76.
42 Marden, *6th Division*, p.78.
43 Grant, *Hallamshires*, p.144.

and orders were received that 'the 6th Division, as such, would cease to exist in the middle of March 1919'.[44]

The Hundred Days (the Advance to Victory) does not get the same attention from the British public as the monumental battles of 1916 and 1917. By its very nature – a rapid advance in pursuit of a retreating, though not yet defeated enemy – it consisted of a series of encounters, rather than the pre-prepared set-piece battles of the Somme and Third Ypres. A between-the-lines reading of the war diaries of the battalions involved during this period demonstrates that lessons had been learnt and new techniques adopted. However, these successes were not bought cheaply. Those early, iconic battles are rarely named without the attendant casualties quoted parenthetically. During the Hundred Days, the casualties came in a steady stream (as we have seen in the pages above) and were extremely heavy; also, deaths so close to the end of the conflict seem somehow more poignant. It is sad that in the British public's remembrance of the war, the dead of the Somme and Passchendaele are given so much more prominence than those who died securing victory in 1918. It is worth remembering that in those last few months the Allies did drive the Germans out of France and Belgium, and Germany sued for peace. Perhaps because the war poets wrote so little of this phase of the war, the eventual victory is lost in the absorption with the 'futility' of the earlier years. Right to the end, battalions of the York and Lancaster Regiment were at the front of the British line – though the individual soldiers would have been hard-pushed to say how their battalion's effort contributed to the whole.

44   Marden, *6th Division*, p.80.

Appendix I

Finding Private Dillon (apologies to Private Ryan)

In April 2005, my wife and I joined Richard Holmes on his *Kaiserschlacht* battlefield tour. Although the itinerary did not include the front covered by 2/York and Lancaster, I had done some research at Kew into the dispositions of the battalions of 16 Brigade, 6 Division. The copies of the trench maps in the war diaries would prove particularly useful. On the evening of the first day of the tour, I gave Richard copies of all the information I had, particularly the accompanying maps. The following morning, he told me that he felt confident that he could find the area of ground occupied by 2/York and Lancaster on the morning of 21 March 1918, and he intended to change the tour itinerary accordingly.

As good as his word, Richard took us to the village of Noreuil which lay about 1,000 yards behind 16 Brigade's front line when the German's attacked. The area of ground occupied by 2/York and Lancaster and 1/King's Shropshire Light Infantry (KSLI) was directly to the east of the village, see Map 16. Because the battalion diary states that almost all of the men in the front trenches (D company) were wiped out in the initial barrage, it is reasonable to assume that my grandfather was in 'C', 'B' or 'A' company; it would be pure speculation on my part to try to get closer than that. Richard had taken us to within a couple of hundred yards of where my grandfather had been when he was captured (see figure 14), for which I am eternally grateful. I had not had the opportunity to speak to him of his war, but at least I had a definitive picture of where the fighting ended for him.

In a written note in the 18 Brigade diary (they were on the right of 6 Division) Major-General Marden stated that 'it was essentially a soldier's battle in which units under their commanders were set to fight without hope of reinforcements against vastly superior numbers of the enemy supported by an overwhelming artillery' – my grandfather and his mates had little chance. Richard (who had served as a Brigadier in the Territorials and as Colonel of the Princess of Wales Royal Regiment) often stated that you could only truly understand a battle after you had walked the ground: in an email to me after the trip, he wrote that:

Appendix I 263

Professor Richard Holmes on the ground defended by 2/York and Lancaster on 21 March 1918. (Photo J. Dillon)

The big surprise to me was how poor flanking views (and thus flanking communications) were. Any sort of serious penetration on either flank would make that particular position very vulnerable, even in perfect weather.

With the thick mist that covered the trenches on 21 March 1918, the men of 2/York and Lancaster were overwhelmed by the attacking Germans. Sadly, my father died ten years before this visit; it would have meant a lot to him to know more of the circumstances of his father's capture and that I had been able to visit the fields where it happened.

Appendix II

Private Stanley Butwright

Stanley Butwright did not serve with the York and Lancaster Regiment. His story gets a mention as a result of a chance meeting between Andrew Wegg and myself; Stanley was Andrew's great uncle.

Stanley served with the 1/8th Battalion, the Royal Warwickshire Regiment. He was killed on 27 August 1917, just six weeks after arriving in France; he was only 18. Following the losses on the Somme, Stanley was one of those drafted to the battalion as it rebuilt and retrained for further action. By mid-August, the battalion was at Vlamertinghe, west of Ypres, ready to be fed into the battle we know as Third Ypres. On 27 August, Stanley and his new mates were in position for an attack near St Julien, a village familiar to 1/York and Lancaster during Second Ypres.

Zero hour was 1.55 p.m.; a daylight attack against the German lines was unlikely to be cheap in casualties. Andrew has researched the 1/8th war diary and has uploaded an account of the battalion's part in the battle to the internet.[1] One of the battalion's officers, Edwin Vaughan, has included details of the

Private Stanley Butwright, killed in action 27 August 1917. (Photo Andrew Wegg)

---

1 www.hellfirecorner.co.uk/wegg.htm accessed 7 October 2016.

battle in his frequently cited memoir *Some Desperate Glory*.² 'So many of our men had been killed';³ we do not know if Stanley was in Vaughan's company, but he was one of those who died that day. With no known grave, Stanley is remembered on the memorial to the missing who died in the Ypres Salient after 16 August 1917 (almost 35,000 of them), at the beautiful Tyne Cot cemetery, a little south-west of Passchendaele. This is the largest Commonwealth war cemetery in the world, in terms of burials.

Although Stanley's war was over, his battalion – with the rest of 48 Division – was transferred to Italy in late 1917. We met them briefly in Chapter 13.

Apart from his name on the memorial, the family has only a photograph of Stanley in his uniform and one of his identity discs to remember him by. Andrew, like many others, is attempting to understand his great uncle's short war through the brief entries in the battalion diary. In 2017, he plans to visit the area of the salient where the Royal Warwicks fought that August. The majority of those who were killed in that war, and for whom there is no known grave, will not have had visitors searching for their names. By his visit, Andrew will ensure that Stanley is not forgotten.

2   Vaughan, E.C., *Some Desperate Glory. The Diary of a Young Officer, 1917* (London, Papermac, 1994), pp.191-232.
3   Vaughan, *Desperate Glory*, p.224.

Bibliography

UNPUBLISHED SOURCES

Author's Collection
Private Patrick Dillon's diary

The National Archives
TNA WO 71/619 court martial papers of Private Nicholson
TNA WO 95 series of battalion war diaries.
TNA WO 106/308, Lloyd George memo to Committee of Imperial Defence, 1 January 1915.

Imperial War Museum
Carter, C., Private Papers, Doc. 7988.
Cotton, V.E., Private Papers, Doc. 93/25/1.
Hardie, M., Private Papers, Doc. 4041, report for October 1917.
Mortimer, J.G., Private Papers, Doc. 7449.

PRINTED SOURCES

Books
Aspinall-Oglander, C.F., *Military Operations Gallipoli,* Volume 2 (Uckfield, Naval & Military Press, Reprint of 1931 original).
Atkinson, C.T., *The Seventh Division* (Milton Keynes, Naval & Military Press, 2009).
Badsey, S., *The British Army in Battle and its Image 1914-18* (London, Continuum, 2009).
Barrett, D. (ed), *The Reluctant Tommy. Ronald Skirth* (London, Macmillan, 2010).
Baynes, J., *Far From A Donkey. The Life of General Sir Ivor Maxse* (London, Brassey's, 1995).
Blake, R., *The Private Papers of Douglas Haig 1914-1919* (London, Eyre & Spottiswoode, 1952).

Bosworth, R.J.B., *Mussolini's Italy. Life under the Dictatorship* (London, Penguin, 2006).
Brown, M., *The Imperial War Museum book of The Western Front* (London, Pan, 1993).
Buell, T.B., *The Warrior Generals. Combat Leadership in the Civil War* (New York, Three Rivers Press, 1997).
Carrington, C., *Soldier From The Wars Returning* (Barnsley, Pen & Sword, 2006).
Cherry, N., *Most Unfavourable Ground. The Battle of Loos 1915* (Solihull, Helion, 2005).
Clark, A., *The Donkeys* (London, Pimlico, 1991).
Connerty, I., M. Gilbert, P. Hart, L. Macdonald and N.Steel, *At The Going Down Of The Sun. 365 Soldiers From The Great War* (London, Lannoo, 2001).
Crosse, E.C., *The Defeat of Austria As Seen By The 7th Division* (Uckfield, Naval & Military Press, Reprint of 1919 original).
Dillon, J., *'Allies are a Tiresome Lot'. The British Army in Italy in the First World War* (Solihull, Helion, 2015).
Dixon, J., *Magnificent But Not War. The Second Battle of Ypres 1915* (Barnsley, Pen & Sword, 2003).
Dunn, J.C., *The War the Infantry Knew 1914-1919* (London, Abacus, 1994).
Edmonds, J., *Military Operations France and Belgium, 1914, Volume 1* (Nashville, IWM, Reprint of 1933 original).
Edmonds, J., *Military Operations France and Belgium, 1914, Volume 2* (Nashville, IWM, Reprint of 1925 original).
Edmonds, J., *Military Operations France and Belgium, 1915, Volume 1* (Nashville, IWM, Reprint of 1927 original). Referred to in Text as Edmonds, *Vol. 4*. Change
Edmonds, J., *Military Operations France and Belgium, 1915, Volume 2* (Nashville, IWM, Reprint of 1928 original).
Edmonds, J., *Military Operations France and Belgium, 1916, Volume 1* (Uckfield, Naval & Military Press, Reprint of 1931 original).
Edmonds, J., *Military Operations France and Belgium, 1917, Volume 2* (Uckfield, Naval & Military Press, Reprint of 1931 original).
Edmonds, J., *Military Operations France and Belgium, 1918, Volume 1* (Nashville, Naval & Military Press, Reprint of 1935 original).
Edmonds, J., *Military Operations Italy, 1915-1919* (Nashville, The Battery Press, Reprint of 1949 original).
Englander, D., 'Discipline and morale in the British Army, 1917-1918', in Horne, J. (ed), *State, society and mobilization in Europe during the First World War* (Cambridge, 1997).
Erickson, E.J., *Gallipoli. Command Under Fire* (Oxford, Osprey, 2015).
Falls, C., *Military Operations France and Belgium, 1917, Volume 1* (Nashville, Naval & Military Press, Reprint of 1940 original).
Gibson, R., and P. Oldfield, *Sheffield City Battalion. The 12th (Service) Battalion York & Lancaster Regiment* (Barnsley, Pen & Sword, 2010).
Gladden, N., *Across the Piave* (London, HMSO, 1971).
Gladden, N., *Ypres 1917. A Personal Account* (Abindon, Purnell, 1967).

Gooch, J., *The Italian Army and The First World War* (Cambridge, CUP, 2014).
Grant, D. P., *The 1/4th (Hallamshire) Battn., York and Lancaster Regiment, 1914 – 1919* (London, Arden Press). Reprint by The Naval & Military Press.
Graves, R., *Goodbye to All That* (London, Penguin, 1960).
Griffith, P., *Battle Tactics of the Western Front. The British Army's Art of Attack 1916-18* (London, Yale, 1998).
Griffith, P. (ed.), *British Fighting Methods in the Great War* (London, Frank Cass, 1996).
Griffith, P., 'The Extent of Tactical Reform in the British Army', in Griffiths, P. (ed.), *British Fighting Methods in the Great War* (London, Frank Cass, 1996), pp.1-22.
Hamilton, I., *The Tragic Story of The Dardanelles. Hamilton's Final Despatch* (Naval & Military Press, Reprint of 1916 original).
Harris, J. P., *Douglas Haig and the First World War* (Cambridge, CUP, 2008).
Hart, P., *1918. A Very British Victory* (London, Weidenfeld & Nicolson, 2008).
Holmes, R., *The Little Field Marshal. A Life of Sir John French* (London, Weidenfeld & Nicolson, 2004).
Holmes, R., *The Western Front* (London, BBC, 1999).
Holmes, R., *Tommy. The British Soldier on the Western Front 1914-1918* (London, HarperCollins, 2004).
Jones, H. A., *The War in The Air, Volume 6* (Milton Keynes, Naval & Military Press, Reprint of 1937 original).
Keech, G., *Battleground Europe. St Julien* (Barnsley, Pen & Sword, 2001).
Lamin, B., *Letters from the Trenches. A Soldier of the Great War* (London, Michael O'Mara Books, 2009).
Lewis, C., *Sagittarius Rising* (London, Greenhill Books, 1993).
Liddell Hart, B. H., *History of the First World War* (London, Papermac, 1997).
Lloyd, N., *Loos 1915* (Stroud, Tempus, 2006).
Lloyd George, D., *War Memoirs; 6* (London, 1934).
Macdonald, L., *To the Last Man. Spring 1918* (London, Penguin, 1998).
MacGill, P., *Great Push. An Episode of the Great War* (Uckfield, Naval & Military Press, Reprint of 1917 original).
MacKay, F., *Battleground Europe. Asiago, Italy* (Barnsley, Pen & Sword, 2001).
Macmunn, G., and C. Falls, *Military Operations, Egypt & Palestine* (Nashville, IWM, 1928).
Manchester, W., *The Last Lion. Winston Spencer Churchill. Visions of Glory 1874-1932* (Boston, Little Brown, 1983).
Marden, T. O., *A short history of the 6th Division, August 1914 – March 1919* (Uckfield, Naval & Military Press, Reprint of 1920 original).
Middlebrook, M., *The Kaiser's Battle. 21 March 1918: The First Day of the German Spring Offensive* (London, Penguin, 1983).
Miles, W., *Military Operations France and Belgium 1917. The Battle of Cambrai* (Nashville, Naval & Military Press, Reprint of 1948 original).

Mitchell, T.J., *Medical Services. Casualties and Medical Statistics* (Uckfield, Naval & Military Press, Reprint of 1931 original).
Neillands, R., *The Old Contemptibles. The British Expeditionary Force, 1914* (London, John Murray, 2004).
Palmer, A., *The Gardeners of Salonika. The Macedonian Campaign 1915-1918* (London, Faber and Faber, 2009).
Palmer, A., *The Salient. Ypres, 1914-18* (London, Constable & Robinson, 2007).
Passingham, I., *Pillars of Fire. The Battle of Messines Ridge June 1917* (Stroud, 2000, Sutton Publishing).
Pidgeon, T., *The Tanks at Flers Volume 1 & 2* (Cobham, Fairmile Books, 1995).
Powell, G., *Plumer, The Soldiers' General. A Biography of Field-Marshal Viscount Plumer of Messines* (Barnsley, Pen & Sword, 2004).
Priestman, E. Y., *With a B-P Scout in Gallipoli* (Reprint by The Naval & Military Press of 1916 original).
Prior, R., *Gallipoli. The End Of The Myth* (Padstow, Yale, 2009).
Prior, R., and T. Wilson, *Command on the Western Front. The Military Career of Sir Henry Rawlinson 1914-1918* (Barnsley, Pen & Sword, 2004).
Prior, R., and T. Wilson, *The Somme* (London, Yale, 2005).
Rawson, A., *Battleground Europe. Loos – Hill 70* (Barnsley, Pen & Sword, 2002).
Roberts, A., *Elegy. The First Day On The Somme* (London, Head of Zeus, 2015).
Sandilands, H.R., *The 23rd Division 1914-1919* (Uckfield, Naval & Military Press, Reprint of 1925 original).
Senior, M., Haking, *A Dutiful Soldier. Lieutenant General Sir Richard Haking XI Corps Commander 1915-18. A Study in Corps Command* (Barnsley, Pen & Sword, 2012).
Sheffield, G., *The Chief. Douglas Haig and the British Army* (London, Aurum, 2011).
Sheffield, G., *Forgotten Victory. The First World War: Myths and Realities* (London, Headline, 2002).
Sheffield, G., and J. Bourne, *Douglas Haig. War Diaries and Letters 1914-1918* (London, Weidenfeld & Nicolson, 2005).
Simkins, P., 'Co-stars or Supporting Cast? British Division in 'The Hundred Days', 1918', in Griffiths, P. (ed), *British Fighting Methods in the Great War* (London, Frank Cass, 1996), pp.50-69.
Smith-Dorrien, H., *Memories of Forty-Eight Years' Service* (London, John Murray, 1925).
Sparling, R.A., *History of the 12th Service Battalion York & Lancaster Regiment* (Uckfield, Naval & Military Press, Reprint of 1920 original).
Starling, J., and I. Lee, *No Labour, No Battle. Military Labour During The First World War* (Stroud, Spellmount, 2009).
Strachan, H., *The First World War* (London, Pocket Books, 2006).
Strachan, H., *The Oxford Illustrated History of the First World War. New edition* (Oxford, Amazon Kindle, 2014).
Todman, D., *The Great War. Myth and Memory* (London, Hambledon Continuum, 2005).

Townshend, C., *When God Made Hell. The British Invasion of Mesopotamia and the Creation of Iraq, 1914-1921* (London, faber and faber, 2010).
Travers, T., *Gallipoli 1915* (Stroud, Tempus, 2004).
Wakefield, A., and S. Moody, *Under the Devil's Eye. The British Military Experience in Macedonia 1915-18* (Barnsley, Pen & Sword, 2011 Kindle edition).
Wilson, R., and I. Adams, *Special Branch. A History: 1883-2006* (London, Biteback, 2015).
Wilson, T., *The Myriad Faces Of War* (Cambridge, Polity Press, 1986).
Wilson, T., and R. Prior, 'British Decision-making, 1917: Lloyd George, The Generals and Passchendaele', in Cecil, H., and P.H. Liddle (eds), *Facing Armageddon. The First World War Experienced* (Barnsley, Pen & Sword, 1996).
Woodward, D. R., *The Military Correspondence of Field-Marshal Sir William Robertson* (London, Army Records Society, 1989).
Wylly, H.C., *The History of the York and Lancaster Regiment, Volume 1* (London, 1930).
Wylly, H.C., *The History of the York and Lancaster Regiment, Volume 2* (London, 1930).
Wyrall, E., *The Story of the 62nd (West Riding) Division 1914-1919, Volume 1* (Uckfield, Naval & Military Press, Reprint of original).

The Stationery Office
The World War 1 Collection. Gallipoli and the Early Battles, 1914-15. The Dardanelles Commission (London, The Stationery Office, 2001).

Articles
Attar, R., 'Aggrieved PoWs betrayed plans for the Cambrai attack'. *BBC History Magazine*, October (2016), pp.11-12.

Websites
http://www.westernfrontassociation.com/great-war-people/brothers-arms/4239-the-discovery-and-identification-of-the-beaucamps-ligny-fifteen.html#sthash.obl5X3AW.dpbs accessed 2 Nov 2015 – 2/Y&L bodies found at Radinghem

Index

INDEX OF PEOPLE

Allenby, General Sir Edmund 144, 149-150
Asquith, Herbert 223

Byng, General Sir Julian 185-186, 191, 215-216

Cavan, Lieutenant-General Rudolph Lambart, 10th Earl of 133, 169, 231-232, 238, 240, 242-243
Churchill, Winston 58-60, 62, 269

de Lisle, Major-General Sir Henry de Beauvoir 75
Diaz, Lieutenant General Armando 232, 238, 242
Dillon, Private Patrick i, v, viii, x-xi, xiv, 61, 74, 81, 153, 204, 207, 253, 257, 267

FitzClarence, Brigadier-General Charles 25
Foch, Marshal Ferdinand 34, 216, 218
Forestier-Walker, Major-General Sir George Townshend 91, 95, 99
French, Field Marshal Sir John 18, 27, 32, 34, 40, 42, 56, 80, 82-83, 85, 95, 99, 104, 269

Geddes, Colonel A.D. 34-36, 38
Gough, General Sir Hubert 83, 144, 149-150, 167, 169, 173, 195, 198, 204, 215-216

Graves, Captain Robert 39-40, 56, 82, 133, 153, 177, 252-253, 269

Haig, Field Marshal Sir Douglas xi, 41-42, 45-46, 54, 79, 82-83, 85-91, 95-96, 99-101, 103-104, 109, 120, 122, 127, 129, 131, 134, 139, 142, 144, 146-147, 149-151, 155-156, 166-167, 169, 173, 176, 178-179, 185-186, 190-196, 198-200, 209, 215-218, 223, 226, 231-232, 242, 246-247, 267, 269-270
Haking, Lieutenant-General Sir Richard 85, 87, 89-93, 95-96, 270
Haldane, Lieutenant-General Sir Aylmer 141
Hamilton, General Sir Ian 62, 65-66, 68, 70, 75, 269
Horne, General Sir Henry 144, 198, 216, 268
Hunter-Weston, Lieutenant-General Sir Aylmer 120, 122, 127

Jackson, Admiral Sir Henry 60, 62, 124
Joffre, Marshal Joseph Jacques Césaire 81-83, 101, 142

Kitchener, Field Marshal Herbert Horatio 17-18, 32-34, 60, 62, 75, 82-83, 101, 105, 121

Lloyd George, David 42, 58-60, 100-101, 128, 141-142, 166, 196, 220, 232, 267, 269, 271

Lomax, Major-General Samuel 25

Mahon, General Bryan 223
Marden, Major General Sir Thomas Owen 16, 186, 189-190, 204, 257-258, 260-262, 269
Maxse, Lieutenant-General Sir Ivor 215, 267
Monro, General Sir Charles 25, 76

Nivelle, General Robert 142, 146, 155, 166

Plumer, Lieutenant-General Sir Herbert 41, 153-156, 158, 162, 164-165, 167, 169, 173-174, 179, 210, 232, 235, 238, 260, 270

Rawlinson, General Sir Henry 45, 47, 83, 101, 103-104, 109, 111, 116, 119-120, 127, 132-133, 216, 270

Robertson, General Sir William 100, 142, 271

Sandilands, Brigadier-General James Walter 99, 156, 158-162, 164, 184, 237, 240-242, 244, 270
Sarrail, General Maurice-Paul-Emmanuel 223-224, 226
Smith-Dorrien, General Sir Horace 22, 33-34, 40-42, 260, 270
Smuts, General Jan Christian 194, 199
Stopford, Lieutenant-General Sir Frederick 62, 66, 70, 72, 75

Talbot, Lieutenant Gilbert 51, 56
Trenchard, General Hugh 167, 247

Wilson, Field Marshal Sir Henry 133, 166, 231

INDEX OF PLACES

Afghanistan 15, 77
Aisne 18-19, 146
Albert 101, 104, 113, 137
Amiens 210, 216, 219, 246, 248, 253
Ancre 110, 113, 117
Anzac 61-62, 65-66, 156, 173, 179
Arleux 210
Armentières 19, 23, 44-46, 48, 99, 216, 218
Arras vii, ix, 45, 140-144, 146, 148-150, 152-155, 186, 196, 208, 210, 216, 254
Artois 45, 81, 255
Asiago Plateau viii-ix, 236, 238-239, 241-242
Aubers Ridge vii, 43, 45-47, 88, 103-104
Authuille 106, 110, 113, 133
Aveluy 110, 116-117, 132-133

Balkans 15, 221-224, 230
Bank Copse 212
Bapaume 101, 119, 149, 248

Battery Valley 147-148
Beaumont Hamel 120, 141
Bellewaarde 25, 48
Blaga Planina 228-229
Blairville 210
Bohain 259-260
Bois Grenier 21, 46
Bois Hugo 92-93
Bouleaux Wood 136
Boulogne 43, 81
Bourlon Wood 186, 191-192, 254
Boyelles 210
Brancourt-le-Grand 259
Bullecourt 144, 150, 186

Calais 178, 223
Cambrai i, vii, ix, 148-150, 155, 175, 185-189, 191-194, 196, 198, 200, 246, 252, 254-255, 269, 271
Cambrin 85
Canal du Nord 185, 254

Cape Helles 61-62, 64
Chalk Pit Wood 93, 97
Chanak Cheshme Ridge 70
Chantilly 100-101
Chemin des Dames 146, 155, 166
Chocolate Hill 22, 65-66, 68, 70-73
Cité St Auguste 89
Cité St Elie 85, 89
Cuinchy 31

Dernancourt 116
Destremont Farm 137-139
Doiran ix, 223, 225, 227-229
Doulieu 43-44
Drocourt 146, 149
Dumbarton Wood 173
Dunkirk 76, 179, 218

El Firdan 78-79
Étaples 149, 152

Fampoux 148-149
Feuchy Chapel 144, 146, 148-149
Flesquières 190-191, 193, 215-216
Fleurbaix 44, 47-48
Frasnoy 249-250, 252
Franvillers 106
Fresnoy-le-Grand 260
Frévillers 210
Frezenberg 31
Fricourt 101, 103, 110-113, 141
Fromelles 21, 46-47

Gallipoli (Dardanelles) vii, xi-xii, 28, 57-61, 63-66, 68, 70, 71-78, 81-82, 120, 144, 221, 230, 253, 267-269, 270-271
Guémappes 146
Gheluvelt 23, 25, 31, 169-170, 173
Ginchy 132
Givenchy 27
Gomiecourt 212
Gommecourt viii, 101, 111
Grandcourt 116
Granezza viii, 236-237, 241
Guillemont 132-133

Hamelincourt 212
Harp, The 147, 149
Hawthorn Redoubt 120, 122-123
Hawthorne Ridge 120
Helles 61-62, 64-65, 72, 77, 120
Hill 10 70-71, 74-75, 77
Hill 60 154-156, 158, 160, 164
Hill 70 89, 91-92, 270
Hindenburg Line 141, 149, 188
Hirondelle Valley 202, 207
Hohenzollern Redoubt 91, 96
Holnon Wood 257
Honey Trench 151
Hooge vii, ix, 23-25, 31-32, 40, 43, 48-53, 56, 155, 173
Hulluch 85, 89, 91-92, 96

Imbros 64, 68, 72, 74, 76-77
India 15-16, 18, 28, 37, 61, 77, 108
Inverness Copse 173
Ireland 15-16, 100
Isonzo 120, 166, 195, 231-232, 242
Italy vii-viii, xii, 154, 178, 184, 186, 220, 225, 230-233, 235-237, 241-242, 244, 246, 266, 268-269

Kantinje Cabaret 173
Kitchener's Wood 33-34

La Bassée 27, 83, 85, 88, 216
La Boisselle 104, 110, 113
Lagnicourt 202, 204-208
Lala Baba 68-70, 72, 77
Lesboeufs 133
Leipzig Redoubt 110, 113, 116, 119
Lemnos 64, 77
Lens 82-83, 91-92, 94
Le Quesnoy viii, 249-251
Les Boeufs 137
Le Sars 138
Le Touquet 21
Lone Copse Valley 148-149
Loos vii-ix, xiii, 33, 40, 42, 44, 80-87, 91, 93, 95-99, 103-104, 111, 118, 125, 127, 129, 133, 141, 198, 222, 243, 246-247, 253, 268-270

Luke Copse 121

Macedonia ix, 221-222, 225-227, 230, 238, 271
Mametz 51, 101, 110, 112, 120
Maricourt 101, 110
Mark Copse viii, 53, 121, 123, 130
Marne 18, 27, 231
Marseilles 64, 80, 223
Mash Valley 110, 113-114
Marcoing 149
Martinpuich 136
Matthew Copse 121
Maubeuge 249, 251
Mauser Ridge 35-37
Meaulte 137
Menin viii, 23, 25, 31-32, 39-42, 49, 51, 54-56, 170, 173, 175
Menin Road 23, 31-32, 49, 54-55, 170, 173, 175
Messines vii-ix, 153-158, 161-163, 165, 167, 170, 173, 196, 198, 270
Meetcheele 182
Méricourt 259
Meteren 28, 164
Millencourt 104-105
Monchy-le-Preux 144-146, 148-149
Montello 235-237, 242
Morchies 201, 207-209
Morval 133, 136-137
Mory 248
Mount Pleasant Wood 148-149
Mouquet Farm 110, 114, 116
Mouse Trap Farm 33
Moyennville 212-213
Mudros 64

Nab, The 106-108, 113, 115
Neuve Chapelle 44-47, 88, 104, 217-218
Neuve Eglise 217-218
Nonne Bosschen Wood 25
Noreuil 207, 262
North-West Frontier 15
Oosttaverne 156
Orange Hill 148
Orsinval 249, 251

Ovillers 104, 110, 113

Passchendaele i, vii, 58, 103, 155, 165-166, 169, 173, 179, 182, 184-185, 214, 220, 232-233, 238, 247, 261, 266, 271
Piave 232-233, 235-238, 240-243, 245, 268
Ploegsteert Wood 154
Poelcappelle 27, 31-33, 182
Polygon Wood 25, 31
Poperinghe 37, 40, 51, 140, 163-164
Port Said 64, 78
Potijze 31, 39, 180
Pozières 113-114

Quadrilateral Redoubt 111, 120, 126, 133-134, 136, 257-258
Quéant 146, 149-150, 200, 209-210

Radinghem 19, 21, 48, 271
Railway Triangle 149
Railway Wood 49
Ravebeek 182
Rear Zone 198, 215
Ribécourt 190

Salonika vii-ix, 220-230, 245, 270
Salt Lake 66, 68, 70
Sambre 249, 251
Sanctuary Wood 40, 50, 52, 56
Scarpe 144, 146, 148-150
Schwaben Redoubt 103, 110, 116-117
Selle 252-253
Sensée 144, 150, 186, 212, 254-255
Serbia 221-222, 230
Serre 111, 120, 139, 160
Somme i, vii, ix, xii-xiii, 18, 51, 58, 64, 80, 83, 99-103, 109, 111, 119, 124, 127-129, 134, 137, 139-142, 154-156, 169, 190, 198, 215, 220, 241, 244-247, 257, 261, 265, 270
Steenstraat 32
St Eloi 27
St Jean 34-35
St Julien 33, 265, 269

St Leger 210, 212, 214
St Omer 81, 218
St Pierre Divion 110, 117
St Pol 210
St Quentin 257-259
St Quentin Canal 185
Suez 28, 64, 77, 79
Suvla Bay vii-ix, 58, 61-62, 64-70, 72, 222

Thiepval 110, 116-117, 119
Tilloy lès Mofflaines 146
Tower Hamlets 175

Vaulx 201, 207-209, 249
Venegazzu 236
Verdun 101, 142
Vermelles 81, 85, 87, 91, 96
Villers-Bretonneux 218
Vimy Ridge viii, 81, 144-145, 153
Vlamertinghe 29, 140-141, 179, 182, 265

Vraucourt 249

Wancourt 146, 148
Westoutre 31
Wieltje 34-35, 48, 50, 180
Winnizeele 183
Wolf Copse 182
Wonderwerk 110
Wytschaete 27, 153, 156, 161, 163

'Y' Ravine 120
Yilghin Burnu 65, 70-71
Ypres i, vii, ix, xiii, 23, 25, 27-38, 40-42, 44, 46, 50-51, 55-56, 96, 103, 137-138, 140, 153-156, 158-159, 162-169, 171-175, 179-181, 183-186, 190, 196, 210, 218, 232-233, 238, 245-246, 253, 261, 265-266, 268, 270

Zonnebeke 31-32, 38-40

INDEX OF FORMATIONS/UNITS

Armies
British Expeditionary Force (BEF) ix, 18-19, 21, 25-28, 31, 33, 42, 45, 81-83, 96, 99-100, 142, 154, 166, 177, 185, 231, 249, 260, 270
Italian Expeditionary Force (IEF) 18, 133, 232-233, 235, 237-238, 240
New Army 27, 99, 101
First Army 46, 82-83, 85, 87, 89-90, 153, 216, 254
Second Army 33, 40-41, 153-156, 162-165, 179, 210, 232, 260
Third Army 87, 141, 144, 146-147, 150, 153, 185, 190, 198, 204, 210, 214-216
Fourth Army 99, 101, 109-110, 118, 122-123, 129, 131-132, 179, 259
Fifth Army (Reserve Army) 132, 144, 149, 167, 169, 195, 198-199, 204, 209-210, 215

Corps
I Corps 19, 46, 83, 141
II Corps 19, 22, 169
III Corps 19, 110, 112-113, 116, 132, 136, 186, 190
IV Corps 45-46, 83, 185-186, 190, 200
V Corps 34, 215
VI Corps 141, 144-149, 202
VII Corps 144, 148, 215
VIII Corps 109, 111, 119-120, 122, 126
IX Corps 62, 65-66, 72, 156, 257, 260
X Corps 116, 118, 120, 156, 161, 173
XI Corps 85-88, 90, 270
XIII Corps 109-110
XIV Corps 132-134, 169, 232
XV Corps 99, 109, 111-112,
Canadian Corps 144, 255

Divisions
2nd Division 25
4th Division 19, 120, 122, 149-150
6th Division 16, 18-19, 52, 54, 132-133, 136, 186, 189-192, 200-201, 204, 208-210, 257-261, 262, 269

Index 277

7th Division 23, 89, 110-112, 243, 268
8th Division 104, 110, 113-114, 116, 247
9th (Scottish) Division 89, 148
11th (Northern) Division 61, 65-66, 68, 70, 77, 254
14th (Light) Division 52, 223
17th (Northern) Division 62
19th (Western) Division 156
21st Division 81, 85, 91, 93-95, 110-112, 141
23rd Division 97, 99, 132, 158-162, 164, 170-171, 173-174, 184, 232-233, 237-238, 240, 244, 270
28th Division 16, 31-32, 34, 83, 224
29th Division 120, 122
31st Division 111, 120, 122, 126-127, 210
34th Division 110, 112-114, 210
48th (South Midland) Division 176, 182, 232, 238, 240, 242, 266
49th (West Riding) Division 110, 116-118, 179, 182, 217
51st (Highland) Division 190, 192
56th (London) Division 136
62nd (2nd West Riding) Division 186, 189-192, 252
66th (2nd East Lancashire) Division 182
Guards Division 133

Brigades
1st Guards Brigade 25
3rd Canadian Brigade 33
13th Brigade 35, 38
16th Brigade 19, 54, 132-133, 136, 186, 189, 193, 200-202, 207, 214, 257-259, 262
18th Brigade 54, 190, 208, 257, 262
32nd Brigade 62-63, 66, 70, 72, 77
63rd Brigade 81, 90, 92-94, 110-112, 141, 144-145, 148, 150, 153
64th Brigade 93, 111
68th Brigade 171, 174, 243
69th Brigade 174, 242-243
70th Brigade 110, 113, 156, 162, 170-171, 175, 238, 242
71st Brigade 189, 201, 206
83rd Brigade 16, 32, 34, 223

85th Brigade 34, 96
93rd Brigade 210, 212
94th Brigade 111, 120-121, 125-126
108th Brigade 117
112th Brigade 145
146th Brigade 182
148th Brigade 46, 110, 116, 182-183, 217
186th Brigade 191-192
187th Brigade 186, 189, 192-193

Regiments/Battalions
8/Bedfordshire 134, 136
1/Buffs 55, 134, 136-137, 201
2/Duke of Cornwall's Light Infantry 37
2/Duke of Wellington's 37
11/East Lancashire 121, 123
11/Essex 136
5/King's Own 37
2/KOSB 153, 233
4/KOYLI 118, 182
5/ KOYLI 180
8/KOYLI 106
1/KSLI 54-55, 201, 207, 262
8/Lincolnshire 92, 111
4/Middlesex 111, 148, 151
1/Newfoundland Regiment 122
2/Scottish Rifles 104
2/Sherwood Foresters 201, 206
11/Sherwood Foresters 105-106, 115, 138, 162, 171, 238
8/Somerset Light Infantry 81, 92, 111
2/South Wales Borderers 122
12/West Yorkshire 81, 92-94
15/West Yorkshire 212
1/York and Lancaster viii, 18, 28, 31-35, 37-40, 42, 83, 96, 221, 223-226, 228-230, 256, 265
2/York and Lancaster viii-ix, xi, 21-23, 25, 48-50, 52, 55-57, 132-133, 136, 139, 152-153, 186, 189, 191-193, 196, 199-201, 206-210, 214, 257-260, 262-264
2/4 York and Lancaster viii, 170, 186, 190, 255
2/5 York and Lancaster 185, 189, 192
3/York and Lancaster 52, 225, 256

4/York and Lancaster 117-118, 182, 253
5/York and Lancaster 44, 182
6/York and Lancaster 18, 57, 60-62, 64, 68-70, 72, 74, 76-80, 153, 253, 255-256
8/York and Lancaster 104-107, 113-115, 132, 137-138, 140-141, 158, 162-164, 165, 170, 175-177, 232, 238, 244
9/York and Lancaster 104, 107-108, 110, 115, 132, 140, 159-160, 162-163, 170, 174, 232, 235, 237-238, 240, 243-244
10/York and Lancaster 44, 80-82, 85, 87, 90, 93-94, 96-97, 99, 103, 110-112, 132, 145-153
12/York and Lancaster 109
13/York and Lancaster (1st Barnsley Pals) ix, 18, 121, 124-125, 198, 210, 212-214, 253
14/York and Lancaster (2nd Barnsley Pals) 18, 78, 105, 111, 121, 125-126